The War on the
Social Factory

Critical Insurgencies
A Book Series of the Critical Ethnic Studies Association

Series Editors: Jodi A. Byrd and Michelle M. Wright

Critical Insurgencies features activists and scholars, as well as artists and other media makers, who forge new theoretical and political practices that unsettle the nation-state, neoliberalism, carcerality, settler colonialism, Western hegemony, legacies of slavery, colonial racial formations, gender binaries, and ableism, and challenge all forms of oppression and state violence through generative future imaginings.

About CESA The Critical Ethnic Studies Association organizes projects and programs that engage ethnic studies while reimagining its futures. Grounded in multiple activist formations within and outside institutional spaces, CESA aims to develop an approach to intellectual and political projects animated by the spirit of decolonial, antiracist, antisexist, and other global liberationist movements. These movements enabled the creation of ethnic studies and continue to inform its political and intellectual projects.

www.criticalethnicstudies.org

The War on the Social Factory

The Struggle for Community Safety in the Silicon Valley

Annie Paradise

Northwestern University Press
Evanston, Illinois

Northwestern University Press
www.nupress.northwestern.edu

Copyright © 2024 by Northwestern University Press. Published 2024. All rights reserved.

10 9 8 7 6 5 4 3 2 1

Library of Congress Cataloging-in-Publication Data

Names: Paradise, Annie, author.
Title: The war on the social factory : the struggle for community safety in the Silicon Valley / Annie Paradise.
Other titles: Critical insurgencies.
Description: Evanston, Illinois : Northwestern University Press, 2024. | Series: Critical insurgencies | Includes bibliographical references and index.
Identifiers: LCCN 2023048150 | ISBN 9780810146648 (paperback) | ISBN 9780810146655 (cloth) | ISBN 9780810146662 (ebook)
Subjects: LCSH: Community organization—California—Santa Clara Valley (Santa Clara County) | Police brutality—California—Santa Clara Valley (Santa Clara County) | Crime prevention—California—Santa Clara Valley (Santa Clara County)—Citizen participation. | Community–based research—California—Santa Clara Valley (Santa Clara County)
Classification: LCC HM766 .P38 2024 | DDC 361.809794/73—dc23
LC record available at https://lccn.loc.gov/2023048150

*To the families whose loved ones have been taken,
and to my own family, bound through struggle*

CONTENTS

Introduction: War on the Social Factory   1

Part 1

1. Mesha and Idriss: Security, Care, and Insurgent Knowledges   29
2. Oscar and Lovell: The Battle for Fourteenth and Broadway   49

Part 2

3. Derrick Gaines: Community Policing and Counter-Cartographies   77
4. Kayla Moore: Gaia, *Escraches*, and Direct Action   103
5. Alex Nieto: Disinformation and the Domestication of War   125
6. Asa Sullivan: Social Death and the Prose of Counterinsurgency   143

Part 3

7. Justice Campaigns   175
8. Spaces of Encounter   197

A Note on Methodology: Convivial Research, Collective Ethnography, Insurgent Learning   215

Notes   229

Index   287

INTRODUCTION

War on the Social Factory

In early October 2013, the *testimonio* of Yasmin Flores speaking of her son, Daniel Booker, was performed on a street corner in downtown San José by Ana Maria Luera as part of Our Hallowed Ground. This was one of a series of site-specific street performances crafted by Arielle Julia Brown working closely with mothers and families who had lost children and grandchildren to forms of state and state-manufactured violence.[1] Four years earlier in 2009, at twenty-seven years old, Danny Booker was fatally shot in front of five police officers after walking out of a popular nightclub on the corner of 2nd and Santa Clara, where he bled to death on the sidewalk before an ambulance arrived. The story of his life told through the reflections of his mother and performed on a busy San José sidewalk was woven into her own life story and those of a larger community impacted by violence. It was a space delineated by *testimonio*, and was at the same time a heterotopic, heterochronic vigil as family and community members converged on San José from across the greater San Francisco Bay Area, writing the names of their own children and the children of others lost to state and street violence on small stones and arranging them as a border to carve a stage out of the sidewalk.[2] The names on the stones included: *Idriss Stelley and Asa Sullivan, killed by San Francisco police (2001; 2006); Oscar Grant, killed by Bay Area Rapid Transit police (2009); James Rivera Jr., killed by Stockton police and San Joaquin County Sheriff deputy (2010); Alan Blueford and Hernan Jaramillo, killed by Oakland police (2012; 2013); Mario Romero, killed by Vallejo police (2012); Raheim Brown, killed by Oakland Unified School District police (2011); Kayla Moore, killed by Berkeley police (2013)*, and others.

To follow the late afternoon *testimonio*, Universidad de la Tierra Califas (UniTierra Califas), Acción Zapatista (AZ) South Bay, and 50.50 Crew organized a gathering a few blocks away with food to honor Yasmin and the family, the life of Daniel Booker, the many other mothers and families present who had lost loved ones, the actors and those who had imagined and created the site-specific performances, and all those others who had kept up the fight, connecting across families and

1

struggles through rallies and protests and vigils throughout the San Francisco Bay Area.[3] The gathering that followed the performance was a strategic space, imagined as a site of convergence and assembly for a community of struggle to convene and recognize itself in its collective loss and struggle after a shared experience.

In the gathering—an open circle at the San José Peace and Justice Center—a group of close to forty people, mostly women, and almost all women of color, sat in folding chairs, balancing plates of tamales and rice and beans on their laps, some holding children. Several rocked strollers back and forth across the wooden floor and fanned babies in the unusual October heat. There was no agenda, only a desire to come together in a space organized around agreements, based on a shared commitment that these agreements as a facilitation tool ensure a safe space for horizontal learning, care, and listening. This reflects a commitment drawn from "habits of assembly" and facilitation strategies across Mexico and Latin America, a practice considered central to convening space as part of a larger urban Zapatismo, or "a new way of doing politics" organized as a "politics of refusal, space, and listening" where a community gathering to express shared concerns is a form of action that both reconstructs social bonds and marks the beginning of a construction of a new world.[4]

Members of the group agreed to go around the circle and introduce themselves in relation to the struggles and communities each of them claimed. Much of the conversation focused on retelling, with care, stories of children, siblings, grandchildren, parents, and partners whose presence was not possible in the space as a result of various forms of deadly violence and criminalization—their engagement in economies considered illegal by the state, gun violence across communities, punitive school policies that led to juvenile hall, harassment policing that exposed outstanding warrants that funneled people back into carceral institutions, search warrants that revealed more illegal economies, juridical processes that fuel prisons, forms of ongoing surveillance, brutal home raids, K-9 unit dog attacks, police chokeholds and bullets. "They're hunting us down," one woman said. Those present nodded, with low sounds to affirm the statement. "That's why we need to keep coming together like this," another woman responded, "so we can figure out what to do next."

The performance and gathering marked a formative moment in a circulation of struggle across the Bay Area, bringing together families and expanding a collective imagination of community safety. What became visible to those involved was a profusion of sites of struggle generating and co-generating strategic knowledges, or a cartography of interconnected "temporary autonomous zones of knowledge production" (TAZKP) in resistance to an onslaught of violences and criminalization.[5] Situated as a moment of inquiry and reflection in relation to other grassroots investigations, shared documentation efforts, convergences, and direct actions currently underway, the October 2013 assembly coalesced around two critical themes: the need to document violences and connect struggles and families across the state, and the need for consistent spaces where a shared analysis could be generated to confront an ongoing war.

A few years later, following the police killing of her son Colby Friday by Stockton police officer David Wells in Stockton, California, in August 2016, Denise Friday Hall would advance a similar analysis as part of an ongoing collective investigation into the killing of her child: "this is a war against our communities."[6]

This book is a collective ethnography of struggles for community safety in the greater San Francisco Bay Area against what the Zapatistas have named the Fourth World War, a war that the Center for Convivial Research and Autonomy (CCRA) has elaborated as manifest in three central areas: first, as an escalation of policing, an expanding carcerality, and a braiding of counterinsurgency warfare, comprising a form of low-intensity warfare; second, as a war against women, subsistence, and social reproduction; and third, as a war of oblivion.[7]

In this context, this book explores community safety as a struggle for autonomy and as a praxis that challenges the sociological and epistemological foundations on which the policing power rests by making observable the multifaceted resistances to state and para-state practices and Western, neoliberal discursive formations of "security" that support the criminalization, enclosures, dispossession, expropriation, disposabilities, and erasures fundamental to racial patriarchal capitalist accumulation in the current conjuncture.[8] The moments, statements, documents, and other "artifacts" that emerge through this book's collective ethnography make visible sites of ongoing value extraction in an ongoing war that seeks to reorder populations through violence, enclosure, the production of subjectivities, and so on. The book explores how these forces are intertwined and how in turn they entail elements of other forces—for example, criminalization serves to produce targeted sites for state terror; criminalization and terror reflect a process of social control and a strategy of division and dispossession; and together these serve as a justification of securitization, and so on. In the present, as counterinsurgent forces, these practices are employed in the service of a new racial and gender regime and comprise an ongoing, informal war directed against women, the household, and the community, and in particular at the spaces and relations of Black, Brown, and Indigenous life.[9]

Documenting the fight for survival and collective life, and against erasure, this book begins from the observation that knowledge production and especially "insurgent knowledges" have increasingly become central to our struggles against articulations of "security." For Ana Esther Ceceña, relying on the Zapatista struggle as a reference point, "the space of knowledge is a space of struggle; it is forged in resistance and feeds on searching and subversion. It is constructed in the process of resistance against all types of colonization, particularly in the face of those that attempt to alienate the self-generation of other visions of the world."[10] As communities organize themselves through "spaces of encounter" to confront militarized, securitized violence, seek new forms of justice, and regenerate community, these spaces of research and learning function as dense sites of knowledge production, including as counterknowledges.[11]

In making this claim, this book draws on a number of diverse struggles historically and in the present that have recognized the central role that the co-production of knowledge plays, and especially the importance of diverse situated knowledges, ranging from the Combahee River Collective to Colectivo Situaciones in Argentina, to Precarias a la deriva in Madrid to the Zapatistas in Chiapas, in collective moments of resistance and autonomy.[12]

As elaborated more fully in the "Note on Methodology" at the end of this book, collective ethnography emerges out of a recognition that communities of struggle generate their own knowledges as part of moments of opposition and community regeneration. Convivial research as developed by CCRA recognizes insurgent knowledge production as part of the research process, as is further elaborated in the "Note on Methodology."

In particular, this collective ethnography focuses on the struggles of women confronting current conditions of war, and highlights the efforts sustained by mothers and women to respond to tremendous global violence, while simultaneously reflecting a usage that is inflected with Joy James's "captive maternals," those "ungendered protectors and nurturers of besieged communities."[13] As a concept and analysis/praxis, James's captive maternal extends beyond a gesture of inclusion of multiple identity-based differences under the category of woman, and opens possibilities for understanding gender as connected to a set of practices and vernacular expressions, what Ivan Illich explores as the difference between "vernacular gender" and "economic sex," the latter produced under industrial, commodity- and market-driven society.[14] This book recognizes that as a socially produced category, woman/women reflects a set of investments and choices that includes anyone who claims the category woman, or claims a gender-nonconforming or nonbinary identity that also necessarily places them in an antagonistic relation to patriarchy. By "mothers" this work refers to all kinds of mothers, including aunts and sisters and anyone who claims care in relation to community self-defense and children lost to violence. Furthermore, the shortened categories of "woman" and "mother" throughout appear as particular subjects in relation to care work, inscribed by and in resistance to, capitalist formations.[15]

We must also note that the discussion of racial patriarchal capitalism throughout this book is undergirded by Cedric Robinson's excavation of war, violence, and the production of racial differences in the emergence of capitalism, noting in particular his statement that "the tendency of European civilization through capitalism was . . . not to homogenize but to differentiate—to exaggerate regional, subcultural, and dialectical differences into 'racial' ones."[16] This is echoed in Ruth Wilson Gilmore's theorization that "the racial in racial capitalism isn't secondary, nor did it originate in color or intercontinental conflict, but rather always group differentiation to premature death."[17] Both Robinson and Gilmore's emphasis on differentiation offers a way to understand the production of racial regimes within various conjunctures of racial patriarchal capitalism, as well as to read the series of tactics comprising the state's counterinsurgency strategy for managing a new kind of enemy and producing new subjects—the insurgent, the *guerrilla*, the radical militant, the Black thug, the narco-terrorist, the criminal-alien, and so on—but also the heteronormative, stable white family that is cohered through fixed gender positions and relations towards which "security" is directed, as this book explores.

The Fourth World War and "war:police assemblages"

As part of an ongoing Zapatista analysis of violence and relations of antagonism in the context of neoliberal capitalism, Subcomandante

Marcos speaks of the changing nature of war, where we now face a "war from above," one where "it is no longer possible to locate any conflict upon a strictly physical terrain. The terrain of war is more and more complicated (be they large or small wars, regular or irregular, of low, medium, or high intensity, world, regional or local)." It is nothing less than a world war that the Zapatistas call the "Fourth World War"—a war on a global scale that is everywhere and ongoing, a war without borders and without end.

Not content with conquering territory and "demanding tribute" from the defeated forces, in the present era, "the will that capitalism attempts to impose is to destroy/depopulate and reconstruct/reorder the conquered territory." As part of this process, "it becomes necessary to destroy the conquered territory and depopulate it, that is, destroy its social fabric." Marcos emphasizes that this means the "annihilation of everything that gives cohesion to society." In other words, the war from above is no longer only about destruction and depopulation. Through this war the territory itself is reconstructed, at the same time "reordering the social fabric" according to a new "logic, another method, other actors, another objective."[18]

The Fourth World War does not mark a distinction in the current era between war and peace, a distinction that, as Mark Neocleous argues, "has always been questionable."[19] Neocleous's genealogy of the "always already" suture of war power and police power as "processes working in conjunction as state power" describes the police power through the modality of air power, a power from above; the "purpose is to construct a new order."[20] This reordering is ongoing and achieved through tremendous violence. It splinters collective life, and makes life in common increasingly untenable.

Michel Foucault's "politics as war," together with his analysis of power, offer an approach to analyzing a long-standing counterinsurgency (as war and pacification) and expose the presence of an ongoing war as class antagonism, one that a *dispositif* of security and strategies of pacification attempts to conceal. In Foucault's analysis, one form of power does not replace or displace another form; rather, multiple operations of power (sovereign, disciplinary, biopolitical) can occur within a given epoch and function variously through intersecting *dispositifs*.[21] This offers a way to understand the model of war pursued by the state in the current conjuncture as one with antecedents in settler-colonial and other colonial projects, including colonial occupation and the racial control and management of bodies that it requires.[22] Rather than an approach to war as either pitched battles, sieges, and raids within the context of the legitimacy of the nation-state or as advances in technologies responding to evolving enemies; as traditional war between nations; or as asymmetrical war against insurgents, terrorists, narcos, and so on, the approach to war charted here suggests that the word "war," as denoting the wars traditionally undertaken by the nation-state, is now a permanent condition that is inextricable from policing, that is, pacification.[23] Under the rubric of "security" and strategies of pacification in the present, this permanent war continues through a "war:police assemblage" that converges war power with the powers of the police.[24]

Emerging from security studies, the concepts "war:police" and "war:police assemblage" situate policing and the police power in the present as a form of pacification through order-building and order maintenance, and following Foucault's approach to understanding "social relations as a model of war," posit counterinsurgency warfare as a form of biopolitical or necropolitical governance.[25] Such frameworks make it possible to situate policing in the present beyond a repressive and disciplinary power organized around "crime," and instead to understand policing and war as "always already together" as "processes working in conjunction as state power."[26] In this view, the war-police power is a productive power in the service of pacification and primitive accumulation, and one directed at the continual reorganization of life, with its forces aimed most directly at Black, Brown, and Indigenous communities, and at various human manifestations of aberrance, deviance, sickness, transgression, disability, and other "abnormalities."[27]

While concepts like "war:police assemblage" mark transformations in policing and war globally, they also serve to challenge dichotomies historically and in the present that maintain conceptual separations between war and police.[28] The development of counterinsurgency reflects the changing role of the military abroad, a role shaped by a neoliberal emphasis on "security" (and its necessary counterpart, insecurity) that is directed at controlling the population rather than the control of territory, and also by a shift in how policing power in the present organizes a larger war that is global in scope. The term "war:police assemblage" thus highlights both a conceptual blurring and a new articulation of waging war/peace, through a heterogeneous approach that engages civilians through approaches like community policing that incorporate the participation of the target population as well as those adjacent to them, the population who benefit from a security regime in their wish to "fully enjoy the neighborhood as they desire."[29]

This conceptual separation between the two realms (a dissimilitude largely based on abstractions, including the abstraction of nation-state, citizen-civilian, enemy-criminal, criminal-alien, domestic-foreign, and so on) has served a discursive function of masking, historically and in the present, the blurring and overlap that occurs continuously across military and policing functions. Furthermore, the discursive production of separate realms masks both the constant interaction between those realms and their mutually constitutive conditions, including, as Stuart Schrader's work in the specific case of CS tear gas details, how these realms of "at home" and "abroad" were played against each other to "legitimize [the] migration (and adaptation)" of technologies from one realm to the other.[30]

Historically and through a global colonial/security project that continues to evolve, the realms of police and military have been continuously and deliberately mutually contaminated through shared trainings and operations; intelligence-gathering and sharing; theoretical innovations and strategic exchanges; and flows of weapons, hardware, and technologies, as well as the constant circulation of personnel across foreign and domestic spheres.[31] Critical convergences like the counterinsurgency symposium organized by the RAND Corporation in Washington, DC, in 1962 brought together foreign military officers and prominent counterinsurgency theorists to elaborate a theory and practice of population-centric pacification, and were designed to build connections across offices, agencies, forces, and geographies, and coalesce knowledges drawn directly from brutal *guerrilla* wars and anticolonial repression efforts. And while the RAND conference was a key site of exchange that would inform the U.S. counterinsurgency war in Vietnam, the accumulated experiences and strategies from the Vietnam War circulated back into U.S. police departments to inform population-centric policing approaches "at home."[32]

As is more fully elaborated in chapter 3, the most prominent advocate of these kinds of policing approaches, William Bratton, the former Los Angeles police chief and former police commissioner of Boston and New York City, honed strategies learned during his experiences in Vietnam to effect the paramilitarization of the U.S. police and make intelligence-gathering and reporting central to community policing approaches through programs like Compstat.[33] Similarly, Daryl K. Gates, the former chief of the Los Angeles Police Department who made intelligence-gathering and home raids central to an approach that used extreme brutality against Black, Brown, and Indigenous communities in Los Angeles and who openly stated, "we're in a war," organized a policing approach based on the experience of counterinsurgency in Vietnam even though he did not directly serve there.[34] Techniques of torture from "abroad" were imported back into a range of police departments as in the case Jon Burge, a former commander in the Chicago Police Department who had previously been a soldier in Vietnam and was notorious for incorporating widespread and long-standing torture into his policing approach against Black community members. This was also true of the U.S. government's Office of Public Safety and former police officers affiliated with that office, including Dan Mitrione, who developed techniques of torture through his work with the CIA in Latin America that were later imported back into a range of U.S. federal agencies and trainings.[35]

Community members, grassroots groups, and scholars have continued to document how, operating within local agencies and as international security advisors, police chiefs, commanders, and former soldiers turned police officers have applied counterinsurgency tactics and theorizations to reorganize police departments into paramilitary formations, impose torture techniques, centralize intelligence-gathering, connect intelligence-gathering to criminalization, and use a range of other strategies previously honed and practiced as a result of both direct participation and mutual contamination with counterinsurgency operations abroad. In turn, recent developments in military, including naval, strategy explicitly draw on policing practices exported from local police departments, for example, Los Angeles policing models under William Bratton that manage populations through the control of space, relying heavily on air surveillance.[36]

As I explore more fully in chapter 2, "The Battle for Fourteenth and Broadway," the "war:police assemblage" has become increasingly visible in moments of spectacular policing in response to protests in recent years, as in the WTO protests in Seattle in 1999; the repression of the Oscar Grant rebellions in Oakland in 2009–10 and Occupy Oakland in 2011–12; the Ferguson insurgency of 2014 following the police shooting of Michael Brown; the Baltimore insurgency of 2015 following the police killing of Freddie Gray; the Dakota Access Pipeline protests at Standing Rock in 2016–17; the actions on the U.S.–Mexico border against migrants in 2018–19; and the tremendous and widespread insurgency beginning in the late spring of 2020 following the police killings of Breonna Taylor in Louisville and George Floyd in Minneapolis. Militarized equipment and technology—from tear gas and riot gear-clad forces to sonic weapons and armored crowd control vehicles resembling tanks—were on full display to manage these insurgencies. These tools were deployed alongside other modalities of policing that grassroots researchers and journalists recognized and surfaced, exposing forms of surveillance and intelligence-gathering as well as violent tactical teams organized in paramilitary formations operating to control various protests.

Such alarming scenes have provoked public scrutiny into the flow of technologies between military arenas and local law enforcement agencies (including federal agencies focused on domestic arenas). This has exposed direct transfers through programs like the federal 1033 Program, which recycles vehicles, equipment, and other material supports from the U.S. armed forces back into local police departments largely through Department of Justice grants as well as non-state transfers—including through donations to police departments from the private sphere, further blurring divisions and establishing security as a mode of para-state violence.[37]

These and similar spectacular manifestations of domestic policing are critical to a state of ongoing low-intensity war, and the insurgencies have increasingly exposed the police forces waging this war—both those belonging to the spectacle, and also those outside the spectacle in the day-to-day policing and in the manufacturing of criminalization and violence. These insurgent moments have also further exposed a strategy of differential policing: while the militarized formations and operations that have appeared in the nightly news documenting recent protests come as a shock to many Americans, they reflect what many Black, Brown, and Indigenous communities across the United States have witnessed and experienced for decades: a level of policing that has always more closely resembled a foreign theater of war.

State-Manufactured Violences

Aimed at the management of the population, these new forms of warfare not only target the population with direct forms of violence authored through the state's agents and agencies, practices and actions, strategies and tactics, and so on. This warfare simultaneously organizes and produces multiple forms of indirect violence as state-manufactured violence. Like the "informalization" of war theorized by Rita Segato, state-manufactured violence is immediate and everywhere; it is also residual, generational, and everyday: a violence from outside that continues to ricochet within families and communities long after the state agents have focused their attacks elsewhere. In broad strokes, state-manufactured violence can be classified in three central areas, where the state (1) participates in those activities it also polices; (2) orchestrates forms of violence where the community attacks itself; and (3) undermines safety and community cohesion, perpetuating violence and social decomposition. In a landscape of escalating para-state violence and the informalization of war as part of the Fourth World War, an analysis of the connections across forms of manufactured, authorized, and complicit violences between state and non-state actors, merging state and private interests and funding, becomes more urgent if we are to untangle and lay bare these connections as part of our struggles around community safety.[38]

To further elaborate a taxonomy of state-manufactured violence, participation in illicit or illegal actions can include the ongoing and sustained corruption and brutality in a police department or segment of a department that perpetuates and/or exacerbates illegal economies or economic rivalries, or which contributes directly to conditions of violence in the community. While often understood or discursively produced as "corruption," this in fact can be seen as a form of "authorized crime" that contributes to the unsafety of the community, such as when police officers steal drugs or guns from community members or from evidence rooms/drug lockers and resell the drugs or guns back into the community; when officers plant "drop guns" or drugs on community members and then supply corroborating testimony in court to convict community members; or when off-duty officers work as "private security" against the same community members that are the targets of policing.[39] This can also include accepted but highly questionable and often "grey" policing tactics and policies; for example, undercover agents setting up community members for a sting or encouraging, aiding, and abetting a snitch culture, both of which can result in death or injury; and other forms of more or less legal entrapment.[40]

These practices proliferate across police departments and agencies in the present, and it is often the community that organizes itself to map and make the abuse visible. In California in the 1990s, scandals involving beatings, kidnapping, and planting evidence were exposed in two of the state's most prominent police departments, first in wanton violent acts of the elite anti-gang CRASH unit of the Los Angeles Police Department's Ramparts Division (and at least partially brought to light through the Ramparts scandal), and, in similar patterns of abuse exposed by its victims, in the Oakland Police Department in what became known as the Oakland Riders scandal.[41]

In the second category of state-manufactured violence, agents or agencies of the state directly orchestrate and foment forms of violence where the community attacks or surveils itself. This can include releasing someone into a hostile situation, as when gang members are picked up by police and dropped off in rival territory; or when prison officials move prisoners into the general prison population after debriefing them. Another type of state-manufactured violence is when police officers name specific community members as responsible for acts of violence against other community members during interrogations or police stops, and then pass along that information/disinformation—for example, fabricated accounts and the home addresses and names of the alleged perpetrators—while often at the same time returning weapons and releasing detainees back into the community armed with details or mis/disinformation about a prior act of community violence (for example, when police pass along the name of a community member as responsible for the death of someone's brother or sister). And finally, there is the type when agents publicly round up youth and bring them into the station for questioning, and then launch a targeted attack so that gang members strike back at the youths' perceived collusion with the police.

This second category can also include various Neighborhood Watch programs and different forms of community partnerships, notably where nonprofits or other groups work closely with police or other law enforcement agencies in programs that highlight youth outreach and communication between police and community. Some of these situations can result in direct violence towards youth who are participating in programming that they may not know involves the police; for example, if members of street organizations believe the youth have shared compromising information with police, whether the youth are aware of the situation or not.[42] And while some instances of state-manufactured violence can be more directly tied to the state than others, many community members point to a violence that arrives from outside even while its origins are unknown. In the words of community activist Anita Wills whose son Kerry Baxter, Sr. and whose grandson Kerry Baxter, Jr. were both lost to gun violence (the former currently incarcerated on a disputed homicide charge involving a gun and the latter shot in an unresolved homicide, both in Oakland): "someone is bringing guns into this community."⁴³ The guns are not manufactured in the communities themselves but arrive there through a web of forces in an informalized war.

The third category of state-manufactured violence involves those strategies, tactics, practices, and agents advanced by and through the state that exacerbate unsafety in communities by undermining relationships and community cohesion, and perpetuating violence and social decomposition. Policing and the prison industrial complex as a whole produce this, organized as an "industrial tool" of criminal justice or through discourses of "law and order."⁴⁴

More specifically, this category includes those strategies, tactics, practices, and agents that sever, disrupt, and reconfigure the bonds and relations of family and community and increase vulnerability to state-sanctioned social death; reorganize or discipline the community into formations that are more conducive to securing a capital relation for the purposes of exploitation or accumulation, maintaining social control, or articulating racialized and gendered hierarchies that render particular community members more susceptible or vulnerable to violence; and removing, dispossessing, evicting, or de-territorializing communities and individual members in ways that produce, perpetuate, or exacerbate violence, creating conditions that increase someone's vulnerability to violence, injury, or death.⁴⁵ These are active and ongoing processes. The third category can also include a range of more expansive projects of community unsafety that perpetuate social decomposition, such as redlining practices, redistricting policies, development and redevelopment projects, various forms of legal eviction, and gerrymandered allocations of low-income housing vouchers—all of which exclude, homogenize, or reorganize particular communities in space and territory.

Christopher Lowen Agee's work on policing in San Francisco from the 1950s through the early 1970s documents "a broader postwar policing strategy that sought to hide and constrain, but not eradicate, San Francisco's gay and lesbian population."⁴⁶ In this sense, warfare directed at a queer and pathologized community through a war on "immorality" was waged by the police and served as a site of expropriation and extraction through graft.⁴⁷ While this certainly reflects what is generally understood as "corruption," it simultaneously produces a population in relation to a boundary that allows police to "protect" and maintain heteronormative propertied families by maintaining sites of deviance that also establish policing as a mechanism of extraction.

Similarly, Agee documents policing practices in San Francisco's Hunters Point neighborhood following its reorganization as a low-income "ghetto" after the Second World War (and the subsequent de-industrialization that occurred as military contracts previously focused on battleship production were refocused elsewhere, outside the former naval shipyard). Classifying "two styles of discretionary policing in low-income neighborhoods of color," Agee argues that local police subjected that community to a spectrum of harassment policing (arrests for minor infractions), forms of humiliation, curfew restrictions, and excessive force. And yet, parallel to this, for example, following a shooting in the community, these same police extricated "themselves from the neighborhood and establish[ed] a perimeter designed to contain but not extinguish the violence."[48]

These practices carve out sites of value production. They are extractive first and foremost in the sense articulated by Verónica Gago and Sandro Mezzadra, given that the binary of heteronormativity/deviance operates in relation to expulsion and inclusion such that value can be extracted against the threat that this boundary constantly reproduces.[49] In such a policing approach to low-income neighborhoods, in a context where community self-defense, including community cohesion as a form of community safety, has been forcefully deactivated by the state, cordoning off violence and abandoning a community to state-produced ravages is not only a form of state-manufactured violence, it increases the demand for state-determined security. A deliberately sustained chaos requires strategies of surveillance, containment, and intervention. This then is transformed into demands for more, better trained and equipped police and thus more funding, more training, more equipment, more saturation patrols, more intelligence-gathering, and so on—or, in the doctrine of counterinsurgency: command, control, communication, and intelligence.[50]

The circulation of crack cocaine into Black and Brown communities across U.S. cities as part of the federal government's Iran-Contra deal in the 1980s, reflects a federal policy of state-manufactured violence organized as value extraction that altered the U.S. landscape, functioning to reorganize, de-territorialize, and decimate targeted communities already disenfranchised and excluded from many sectors of the state's legitimate economy. The U.S. government's manufactured War on Drugs criminalized targeted populations, stimulating an illegal economy through the sale and circulation of drugs, accompanied by vast surplus values along a chain of multiple players as drugs, guns, and large sums of money were exchanged across streets and through homes (and also across oceans, mountains, skies, borders). Through this war, the state was able to advance disproportionate sentencing laws by designating crack cocaine differently than "powder cocaine," thus profiting from the very populations where a particularly addictive form of the drug circulated with government complicity, undergirding incarceration at an unprecedented scale and creating conditions of possibility for the current carceral regime.[51]

The alternative or "illegal" street economies spawned through this policy were at the root of the "gang" wars that rose to new heights in the 1980s and 1990s.[52] And the conditions of violence in the wake of the War on Drugs provided a context where communities in many cases supported an increased police presence, embracing militarized securitization as a way to address the escalating violence made more possible as community structures were decimated by addiction, incarceration, violence, and loss at the very moment the social wage was being rescinded.[53]

The policy also provided a justification for increased border security, particularly along the U.S.–Mexico border (but also along the U.S.–Canada border), and brought those borders deeper into the nation-state itself. Thus, another war was produced—deployed as the War on the Border as new, reimagined, and amplified collaborative initiatives took shape between local and federal agencies, often in the form of task forces which helped facilitate the transfer of technologies and training between federal and local agencies working together on specific operations.[54] Communities were subjected to conditions of permanent war, inescapably linked to accumulation, that is, the Fourth World War.

The Los Angeles Rebellion following the police beating of Rodney King and the verdict of 1992 in many ways can be understood as a community response to the state's perpetuation of permanent war across Los Angeles. Emerging as part of a community-wide effort to call attention to the state's deliberate obstruction of gang truces initiated from within communities by the gangs themselves, the insurgency marked a community's struggle to expose the state's investment in destabilizing communities and deploying violence as part of its larger project of "security."[55]

And these manufactured violences converged and multiplied, producing shifts in policing and especially making possible an increase in street-level policing, further justifying policies like stop and frisk. They also brought law enforcement into regular, direct contact with the population and into the relations of social reproduction and community life. They eased interventions in people's homes, as reflected in expedited processes for police to obtain search warrants; the legalization of "no knock raids" that minimized the role of judges; and a drastic rise in SWAT deployment.[56] In short, the mere speculation (or fabrication) on the part of the police of the presence of drugs or drug-related activity, together with the production of criminal subjects, including "gang" members and "illegals," provided greater justification for any kind of intrusion, on the streets and in people's homes. In tandem, the sprawling advance of convictions primarily among targeted populations gave rise to a web of parole and probation restrictions, many of which proved impossible for people to manage vis-à-vis the state. Felonies and fines proliferated.[57]

All of this provided a justification for increased state intervention in the everyday spaces of community life. Thus, one war set another war in motion or advanced its terms and scope; in this context, "home invasions" can be understood as a strategy of control and also accumulation, including the production of information and the simultaneous production of abjection directed at targeted subjects and populations. Such raids reflect continual attempts at intrusion in the intimate relations and functioning of families, households, neighborhoods, and communities.

As Pamela Thompson notes in "Growing Up in Compton," written from inside the Central California Women's Facility in 2016, during the 1980s and 1990s in Compton and South Central Los Angeles, when police raided homes in Black and Brown neighborhoods, community members recall police expropriating family photo albums, an act that allows police to identify, classify, archive, map, and know the individuals, relations, and connections across the communities that the state polices.[58]

A New Intensity of Policing

Critical writing on policing continues to shift thinking on the function and role of law enforcement in a settler-colonial society organized from its inception around Indigenous genocide and chattel slavery, exposing multiple genealogies of racial patriarchal capitalism and its dependence on violence.[59] This book draws from the work of numerous scholars and research efforts to advance the premise that we have entered into a new phase of racial patriarchal capitalism that is directing policing at communities with an intensity that we have not previously encountered. The book creates a contextual argument where "defund the police" is a call for the emergence of an entirely new world, revealing that it is no longer strategic to imagine that demilitarization can simply involve scaling back the armaments and military-grade equipment that have found their way from operational theaters of "foreign" wars into domestic police departments, or reallocating resources to other agencies. Police shootings will not end, nor will racial and gendered state violence attenuate as a result of more training of any kind for law enforcement, or more monitoring of policing agencies, or "closer ties between police and the community," or greater diversification of police officers, or more capable command leaders or department chiefs—in other words, it is not a matter of policing "catching up" to a neoliberal multicultural America where biases can be overcome or sensitivities developed.

Rather, approaching policing as pacification and counterinsurgency warfare reveals that everyday policing and acts of police terror are fundamental strategies of reorganization that are critical to the maintenance of racial patriarchal capitalism, with its deep roots in histories of accumulation, dispossession, and the manufacturing of disposability. From the Indigenous Americas to the Middle Passage; from reservations to plantations to factories; from colonial institutions to urban ghettos; and across prisons and domestic borders, these racialized geographies and their attendant *dispositifs* cordon off territories, arrange bodies, and control populations in space. From here, this book asks, how do we think about this new moment of racial patriarchal capitalism, marked by privatization, global militarization, war:police assemblages, expanding carceral regimes, increased visibility of force, and new strategies of social and political control?

Throughout this book, an insistence on bringing into focus critical moments that narrate resistance as criminal and linking these to overlapping processes of capitalist expropriation and extraction allows for a research approach that takes seriously the community and the activities of women and families targeted by violence as a key site of struggle, while providing a tool for understanding discursive violence and forms of criminalization as central to masking conditions of permanent war.[60] Relying on what Ranajit Guha calls the "prose of counterinsurgency," this exposes the production and circulation of "criminal" and "insurgent" populations as a divisive strategy in a long, complex, low-intensity war. This book is therefore a necessary interrogation into the epistemology of "crime."[61]

Community Safety

Against the onslaught of the Fourth World War, an autonomous struggle for community safety is unfolding across the greater San Francisco Bay Area in parks, plazas, and streets; living rooms and courtrooms; on the steps and chambers of city halls and the sidewalks in front of police stations; in community rooms, school auditoriums, theaters, and churches; in funeral homes and prisons; on fields and hillsides; and in kitchens, *taquerias*, and bars. These are common spaces, occupied spaces, contested spaces, lived spaces, and at times "spaces of encounter"—spaces where information, memories, stories, *testimonios*, and questions are circulated, exchanged, and collectively reformulated, where relations are forged and sustained, renegotiated and strengthened, and where the collective work of regenerating community is continuously taking shape. As "temporary autonomous zones of knowledge production," these "everyday spaces of prefigurative, networked, and convivial pedagogies [that] refuse to impose a preordained or established structure for learning" serve to highlight the importance of reclaiming processes of knowledge production and insurgent learning in communities' struggles for autonomy.[62]

All struggles contain strands of struggles for autonomy. These struggles are neither homogenous or monolithic, nor is it possible to narrate them in a unified or complete way; but together these struggles reflect a desire to live dignified lives without violence and to retain control of the conditions of our existence. This includes the capacity to protect and care for each other and our collective future in contexts of mutual aid, through relations of "bad debt" in the "fugitive public"[63] Thus, the struggle for community safety in the Bay Area is comprised of and intersects with many vibrant struggles, connecting a range of creative rebellions and refusals articulated in a vast imagination in movement.

Community safety is a conceptualization of an autonomous response to the violent imposition of racial patriarchal capitalism. It has emerged over time from the work of a number of projects, organizations, collectives, and collaborations through a profusion of encounters among diverse groups in the Bay Area and beyond as a category of struggle that also marks a specific moment of autonomy. A critical moment in a collective articulation of community safety emerged in February 2013 when members of the Fray Bartolomé de Las Casas (Frayba) Center for Human Rights in Chiapas, an organization mobilized to confront multiple forms of state violence, including attacks against the Zapatista and

Indigenous communities in southern Mexico, traveled through California on a tour in collaboration with the Mexico Solidarity Network and converged with the Center for Convivial Research and Autonomy (CCRA) and UniTierra Califas, which collectively were able to host and attend several gatherings across the Bay Area during the tour. FrayBa shared their "social defense process," a working strategy to confront a range of violences and support dignified and self-determined local struggles. Organized to ensure that the struggles of families remained at the center of a collective effort, the social defense process articulated by FrayBa is a process of accompanying a community in their struggle for a self-determined justice, organizing a defense network and forming councils across different communities. Their process also establishes a collective, horizontal documentation strategy as part of a community-based legal defense approach. The FrayBa tour catalyzed local struggle at a critical time during Bay Area resistance to excessive policing. Veteran Bay Area Zapatista activists, comrades, and collaborators from across various communities of struggle, and folks recently thrown into direct confrontation with the state in response to police repression at protests in the area and the increased visibility of police killings locally and nationally, began to articulate an emergent praxis of community safety.[64]

While no one "invented" community safety, CCRA has advanced community safety as a convivial tool, convening a range of diverse gathering spaces, together with families and other grassroots projects to collectively elaborate a situated process and praxis of autonomy rooted in convivial research and insurgent learning. Drawing on the articulation of FrayBa as a process that insists that the struggles of families remain at the center, CCRA has elaborated a strategy for community safety that includes several key components—documentation/collective knowledge production, community defense, self-determined justice, and fierce care—all rooted in ongoing processes of assembly. Each of these components serves a specific purpose in contributing to a community's autonomy, that is, its ability to organize, govern, and regenerate itself. As a strategic concept, community safety is theorized as a category of analysis that brings into focus a moment of disruption, a new space of opportunity as a result of resistance: it is an emergent praxis within that new space; a site of new knowledge, as well as the recovery of knowledges as part of a praxis; a site of knowledge production; and an objective for achieving greater autonomy.[65] Thus, community safety functions to make visible the chasm between state-organized "security" and a community organized around its own resilience and survival. It is fundamentally a convivial tool, one co-generated to advance the dignity and autonomy of a community.

The FrayBa tour was one of many threads connecting Mexico and Latin America with Bay Area struggles. With the emergence of the Ejército Zapatista Liberación Nacional (EZLN) on the world stage in 1994 following the passage of NAFTA, and as the Indigenous National Congress (CNI) has grown more powerful in recent years alongside the Zapatistas, Zapatismo and Indigenous autonomy have emerged as key points of reference and connection in examining intersecting forms of state and state-manufactured violence and conditions of extractive, racial patriarchal capitalism, with groups from across the greater Bay Area regularly participating in a number of *conversatorios*, *seminarios*, *talleres*, and *encuentros* across southern Mexico, including those convened in the Zapatista *caracoles* across EZLN territory in Chiapas. This book charts this influence through two intertwined projects nurtured by Zapatismo and Indigenous autonomy: the Universidad de la Tierra Califas (or UniTierra Califas), a space of autonomous learning situated within a larger network that includes long-standing UniTierra projects in the Mexican states of Oaxaca and Chiapas; and the Center for Convivial Research and Autonomy, a transterritorial research collective organized with a focus on convivial tools as critical to anti-racial patriarchal capitalist community regeneration.[66]

There is an active rhizomatic structure unfolding that traces these threads. Following the Zapatista Women's Encuentro in March 2018, in July 2019 mothers from Black Lives Matter 2.0 Stockton traveled together with members of CCRA and UniTierra Oaxaca and a group of women and girls from a Mixe community in Oaxaca to the CNI's Women's Encuentro in Veracruz. There they connected with other mothers and families who had lost their children to feminicide, and mothers and families of the disappeared, as well as families from Central America whose children had been killed or gone missing while migrating across Mexico.[67] Through these encounters, a new politics of knowledge production and shared learning is taking shape.

The struggle for autonomy marks the emergence, in the words of Colectivo Situaciones, of a "new social paradigm," one no longer organized around the class concepts and agents of the old Left, one no longer invested in seizing state power or reinhabiting the old institutions where power seemingly lurked. Rather, this new social paradigm, imagined and brought into being in connection with emergent global struggles, marks a struggle against a market- and commodity-driven society, and instead seeks a life in common as new subjects no longer bound by the relations of capital and the infinite repetition and reproduction of new labor, racial, and gender regimes. This emergent social paradigm reflects a new understanding of power and social organization, advancing horizontal politics and new ways of knowing: collective ways of being.

Ana Esther Ceceña explores the "complex relation between knowledges and emancipation," and notes that the present we occupy is "a moment of cultural upsurge that exceeds the limits imposed by capitalism," one that demands new theories, including those around the role of knowledge production itself.[68] For Ceceña, this analysis must place at its center the role of subjects and the production of subjectivities within, against, and beyond capital.[69] Subjectivation and the process of knowledge production are intertwined with the undoing and reweaving of social relations: "struggle, everyday life, survival, and all the different forms and spaces where social relations are expressed provide opportunities for learning and for the construction or destruction of knowledge from multiple sources."[70] It is through these relations that collective ways of being are nurtured, reinvented, and made to endure against the war from above, a war in part organized as "security" and an accelerating management of all forms of social life.

In this reading, community safety as a praxis and a convivial tool is elaborated through a diffuse vernacular practice and grassroots knowledge production that refuse criminalization, along with an epistemology of security and modes of securitization. Community safety manifests in a reclaiming of territory through occupations and counter-cartographies that function simultaneously as oppositional mapping and collective practice. It advances a commitment to document, archive, and circulate knowledge of those violences that have been experienced and marked at various local levels; it is a resistance that insists on communicating, *this is what is happening to us here*. Community safety reflects a larger project and process underway of autonomous justice, and the commitments of an insurgent community that refuses to abandon a practice of justice to a state-sanctioned process, including the time/space of state institutions. It insists on open spaces of gathering in order to weave and reweave relations. It also refuses the imposition of silence, orienting instead around questions and listening and asking as an act of fierce care, as in the question that emerged in the autonomous learning spaces of UniTierra Califas, *what did you hear in silence?*[71]

The Social Factory

Originally coined by Mario Tronti, the term "social factory" emerged out of Italian autonomous workers' struggles in the 1960s and was elaborated over subsequent decades through the Movimento di Lotta Femminile (Women's Struggle Movement) and later the Lotta Femminista (Feminist Struggle), and proliferated in the "wages for housework" and "wages against housework" efforts internationally.[72] The "social factory" was claimed as a site of struggle to make the labor done in the home visible as a site of value production, and at the same time to expose the wage as an instrument of capital that both masked and devalued domestic labor, simultaneously denigrating those (primarily women) who performed labor done in the home. Organized across a multi-sited movement, the feminists emerging out of *operaismo* developed a gendered reading of capital relations that exposed the privatization and invisibilization of violence and the production of gender regimes as fundamental to capital.[73]

This book's collective ethnography relies on feminists' work to develop the social factory as a strategic concept to examine the current crisis of social reproduction and care and to simultaneously highlight the social factory as an antagonistic space: one where multiple resistances take place and knowledge is constantly being produced and engaged. This allows for a reading where the social factory is the site of reproduction of the community, while at the same time it is an extension of capitalism and the state into people's everyday lives, as sites of and producers of value through consumption, labor, social reproduction, and so on.[74] Here, the social factory is explored as a site, space, and set of relations of nurture and care, but also as a site of discipline, exploitation, invisibilization, and violence, where capital displaces its own costs of reproduction onto women, the family, and the community.[75] The social factory is the streets, sidewalks, schoolyards, homes, and myriad other spaces where capital attempts to manage conditions for the production and accumulation of value and for its own preservation. In the present the social factory is a site of extraction: value is produced and extracted in the tension of stability/instability, inclusion/abandonment, and fear/desire.[76] Value is produced through criminalization and pathologization, that is, an array of violences. In one instance, for example, the insurgencies in Ferguson revealed how that city's government was targeting the Black community in order to generate revenues.[77]

In their analysis of social reproduction, *operaista* feminists examined the ways that the forces of state and capital combine to interrupt already existing bonds among workers (both waged and unwaged) and thwart emergent relations among the working class that would potentially threaten capital's attempts at discipline, command, and control.[78] Relying on pacification and consent as a strategy of class composition from above, the forces of state and capital that cohere through the social factory can be understood through what W. E. B. Du Bois called "democratic despotism," where whiteness emerges through the cooperation of the principal sectors that enjoy, for example, the "wages of whiteness."[79] Violence directed elsewhere is tolerated and justified through forms of criminalization in exchange for illusions of security and access to commodities "at home."[80] Beyond consumption, criminalization and pathologization offer a way to manufacture fear which produces value.

The emphasis here is to read the social factory through the category of war. Directed at the population, this warfare aims to reorganize the social and spatial relations of family, home, and community. As a category, the social factory exposes how capital seeks to stabilize (and alienate) particular communities or groups (and in so doing, stabilize production, reproduction, and consumption) while destabilizing others. In the context of South African apartheid, Angela Davis argues that the "consolidation of African families in the industrialised cities is perceived as a menace because domestic life might become a base for a heightened level of resistance to apartheid." Davis excavates the fear of government officials that the presence of women in urban centers would "lead to the establishment of a stable black population," and writes that "apartheid is eroding—with the apparent goal of destroying—the very fabric of Black domestic life."[81]

In terms of the Fourth World War, differential destabilization functions as dispossession, a strategy aimed at reorganizing populations and remapping territories according to a new social order. The counterinsurgent command to "clear, hold, build" or "destroy, build, secure" occurs at the level of the household, the heteropatriarchal family, the neighborhood, and the social relations that define and cohere at these levels.[82] The social factory also makes observable a range of normative impositions including, following the work of Fred Moten, forms of "uplift" directed at Black social life to encourage privatized domesticity, where homogenizing, assimilative forces gain traction, and where rebellion and criminality become co-indexed as failure. As Moten notes, "normative uplift can never be fully separated from the white supremacism it is supposed to combat."[83] Thus, the social factory in this analysis functions as a critical site of "differential inclusion" and "differential stability" in the formation of racial and gender regimes historically and in the emergence of new racial and gender regimes in the present. Critical moments in the emergence of these new regimes can be marked by Hurricane Katrina, and the 2007–08 subprime financial crisis, a moment Denise Ferreira da Silva posits as the "most important racial event of this century."[84]

Against this, spaces of family, home, and community stand as potent sites of autonomy, as ongoing sites of refusal forged through a nexus of relations, sustained care, collective memory, and shared histories and cultural practices. These spaces endure as bulwark and refuge, sites of fugitivity and escape, where collective ways of being historically and in the present are reproduced continuously against the forces of capital and state that seek to divide, fracture, and impose new relations conducive to forms of governance and accumulation. Beneath and beyond these forces, and despite tremendous violence, communities assert a relentless claim to, and defense of, a life in common.[85]

Among the struggles that emerge from the social factory in response to multiple intersecting violences is the struggle over care. We theorize a "fierce care" that draws on current feminist formulations around precarity and care work (including those emerging out of the Italian feminisms from the *operaismo* era), and the long-standing work of Black feminists to claim and theorize care and define reproductive justice as a collective right to safe and healthy conditions for social reproduction, and more recently through spaces convened as part of UniTierra Califas. This "fierce care" resists the onslaught of capital's efforts to exploit and subsume care work and other intimacies and forms of social reproduction, while also remaining committed to a care that is collective, an effort in common against dispossession and disposability—in short, "fierce care" seeks to unravel the rope of capitalist imperative and settler-colonial logic.[86] "Fierce care" marks a refusal to let others be isolated by forms of violence authored by the state or through state-manufactured violence. It is a mode of organizing and maintaining relations and networks against what Rita Laura Segato calls the pedagogies of impunity and cruelty in the current "apocalyptic phase of capital."[87]

Fierce care is integral to community safety: both function as convivial tools for what they make observable and for the praxis invented and reinvented continuously as an assertion of autonomy.[88] In exploring a proliferation of resistances, new strategies of justice and care emerge that are prefigurative; they expose and disrupt the sociological and epistemological underpinnings that lie at the foundation of premature death and the state-sanctioned violence of emergent racial regimes; and at the same time, they nourish collective survival—bringing something into being under the conditions of the present that has not existed before, and continuously remaking interpersonal and community relations.

In this sense, through a convivial research and insurgent learning approach that stresses the collective forging of new tools of community regeneration, this book offers an analysis and hope for a way out of the current escalation of violence by elaborating and advancing a locally rooted, co-generative investigative approach where collective knowledge production and learning serve as a key practice of decolonization, making way for life-affirming conditions in the present.

Chapter Outlines

This book is divided into three parts. The first chapter introduces Mesha Monge-Irizary and her son, Idriss Stelley, at the intersection of an escalating militarization and a crisis of care, and examines Mesha's sustained efforts to document and investigate police violence following the San Francisco police shooting of Idriss in 2001. It situates Mesha's ongoing efforts to produce and circulate counter-narratives as vernacular, insurgent knowledges, and to weave together families at the roots of struggles against police violence in the present. The second chapter examines a critical rupture made possible by the confluence of two prominent struggles in Oakland: the prolonged insurgency emanating from Oakland after the police shootings of Oscar Grant and Lovelle Mixon in 2009, and the Occupy movement of 2011. The remaining chapters of the book unfold in the breach that widened in this wake.

The second part of this book is organized around specific justice struggles that expose counterinsurgency strategies in the present, and the tools that families and communities develop and hone to confront this violence. The police killings of Derrick Gaines in South San Francisco and Kayla Moore in Berkeley are explored as complex moments in the emergence of a new era of Bratton-style policing and in the formation of racial and gender regimes enforced through state violence. With the *escraches* of Argentina borrowed and reworked as a key point of reference, these chapters examine autonomous, creative forms of struggle, including counter-cartographies that families and communities invent against the complexity of this violence. The third chapter in this section focuses on the struggle for justice following the San Francisco police killing of Alex Nieto, highlighting the control of information as a key strategy of counterinsurgency and elaborating a critical moment in unmasking the conditions of permanent war directed at particular communities. The final chapter in this section examines the trial in the San Francisco police killing of Asa Sullivan and the attempted criminalization and imposition of "social death" through the judicial apparatus and through the neoliberal "prose of counterinsurgency" working in tandem with acts of state terror.

The final part of this book focuses on the interconnected justice campaigns of families and networked spaces of encounter in confrontation with counterinsurgent warfare as moments of autonomy organized to reclaim social reproduction, a politics of care, and vernacular lifeworlds outside of capital.

Lastly, the book includes a "Note on Methodology," elaborating a convivial research approach as a collective praxis at the center of struggles for community safety.

Part 1

CHAPTER 1

Mesha and Idriss
Security, Care, and Insurgent Knowledges

When San Francisco police murdered her son Idriss Stelley in the Metreon movie-theater complex in downtown San Francisco on June 13, 2001, Mesha Monge-Irizarry engaged. Although for Mesha, the struggle following the loss of Idriss would prove brutal, and nearly deadly, as she struggled with grief and loss, within a day of the killing of Idriss she recognized that she was in a collective struggle for her child and for the children of others.[1]

In the wake of the killing of Idriss, Mesha charted a path of "fierce care" marked by a refusal to accept the silence that the state and its proliferation of agents seeks to impose, and a refusal to participate in the isolation that families can experience following an attack by the state. She began the patient and harrowing act of weaving together hundreds of families who had lost children and loved ones to state violence and connecting people through unfathomable losses. In the midst of her own loss, she accumulated stories, terrible details that she collected and held.

Over many years, Mesha has formed a salient node, coordinating and networking and regularly co-convening and participating in community gatherings, co-organizing direct action spaces, and conducting numerous independent investigations into police killings. This work has formed the basis for a profound documentation strategy that is central to a community's capacity to organize collectively around its own safety.

The San Francisco Police Department's (SFPD's) killing of Idriss Stelley in 2001 would shift the terrain of community mobilizations across San Francisco. Mesha's efforts form the basis of a struggle with families at the center extending across the Bay Area and beyond that continues into the present, more than two decades later. It would emerge as a struggle increasingly aware of its confrontation with the neoliberal security state and counterinsurgency warfare.

Escalation and Violence

Idriss Stelley was young and Black. He was a student, activist, artist, and community member who tutored youth and spoke multiple languages. In the days leading up to the incident that would claim his life, Idriss was struggling with episodes of mental and emotional disorientation. On the evening of June 13, Idriss became distressed while watching a film in a movie theater with his longtime girlfriend, Summer Galbreath. Galbreath placed a 911 call explaining the situation and asking for mental crisis support. When questioned if Idriss had a gun by the dispatcher on the phone, she insisted that he did not. Later reports from the police made much of a knife with a three-inch-long blade attached to a thirteen-inch chain that Idriss supposedly swung threateningly around; by all accounts of those who knew Idriss, this was a small pocketknife with a short chain that attached to his belt, like a wallet chain. Galbreath conveyed clearly that Idriss was in crisis but not violent. She then called Mesha.[2]

Yet, instead of medical or crisis assistance, the San Francisco Police Department arrived and evacuated the theater, clearing and securing the area and isolating Idriss inside. Nine officers confronted Idriss alone between the empty rows of seats inside the Metreon theater. At least four officers opened fire. Among those who fired were Arshad Razzak, Joseph Garbayo, Georgia Sawyer, and Thomas Walsh, who was struck by the bullets of another officer during the shooting. Idriss's girlfriend stood at the edge of the theater entrance on the phone with Mesha as the incident unfolded. On the other end of the phone, Mesha heard the forty-eight shots that took her son's life.[3]

Almost immediately Mesha fought back. She initiated an investigation independent of the state's process and in connection with the *San Francisco Bay View* newspaper, a Black abolitionist newspaper in San Francisco's Bayview-Hunters Point district, the neighborhood where Mesha lived and raised Idriss. With the support of the editors, longtime Bayview-Hunters Point community members Willie and Mary Ratcliff, Mesha began the first of what would be many subsequent investigations into police killings, questioning from the beginning the decision to use deadly force and carving an enduring rage against the police: "They butchered my child."[4]

Coinciding with the grassroots investigation underway, Mesha and the community around her organized protests and rallies across the city—on city hall steps, in parks, in the street. Among the first tactical moves of the grassroots investigation was to address the callous and salacious retelling and framing of the violent incident in the press, with Mesha speaking out from the context of her community of support.[5] Additionally, as part of the collective investigation underway, the Bay Area Police Watch noted that despite numerous requests from Mesha, significant information continued to be withheld by the state, including the names of five witnesses to the Metreon shooting, essentially making it impossible to verify the state's version of the story independently, or contest its numerous discrepancies.[6] Three months after her loss, Mesha filed a civil claim, *Idriss Stelley v. City & County and SFPD*. The press conference announcing the filing became a site where the community, with Mesha at the center, was able to emphasize how much remained absent from the account given by the state in its story of the killing of Idriss.

To prevent the case from going to court, the city and county of San Francisco proposed a settlement of $500,000 to account for "damages," but the terms of the settlement stipulated that the police refused to accept any level of culpability for the killing of Idriss. Calling the settlement "blood money," Mesha used what remained after the legal team took its portion to set up a small collective project she called the Idriss Stelley Foundation. She set up a free hotline for community members, including witnesses who might have information about a case, and began redistributing funds to support other families targeted by the state and with the goal of bringing communities together in shared spaces.[7]

"State of Insecurity": Reverberations across the Care Crisis

As early as the mid-1990s, community members had begun responding with collective alarm to San Francisco police killings of people experiencing mental crisis.[8] Neoliberal securitization, austerity and privatization, and the rollback of the welfare state left a frayed social safety net and a skeleton of institutions to respond to mental crisis issues.[9] Social services were transformed into a site of "militarization of care" as the neoliberal security state set out to normalize SWAT teams as an effective response to people in crisis, often claiming lives in moments of spectacular violence.[10] For while the welfare state reflected hard-won victories, mostly waged by Black women, including for the social wage, it also marked a moment of enclosure; as care and forms of social reproduction were shifted onto the state, vernacular competencies and infrastructures gave way to a dependence on industrial tools, a process that interrupts and impedes community autonomy and sustainability.[11] The destruction of the social welfare state underway for decades has coincided with an expanding "externalization of the home" where the work of caring for others that was previously managed in the home, from food preparation to caring for children and elders, was increasingly displaced outside of the home, and privatized. Caring was not only made vulnerable to market forces, but practices of vernacular care were relocated outside the relations and rhythms of everyday life.[12] Mesha laid bare this crisis, asking, "Do you know how much I wish that the police was not called on my child when he had a psychotic decomposition? They shot him forty-eight times. Nine officers."[13]

From within this crisis, communities were caught between resisting this new site of militarization while simultaneously pressuring for more officer training as officers were increasingly being dispatched to respond to people in crisis.[14] The killing of Idriss in 2001 prompted two different kinds of trainings for the SFPD following intense community pressure spearheaded by Mesha. In the first instance, and in a familiar community appeasement gesture following an incident of violence that could not be easily justified by the state, the lawsuit required all SFPD officers to complete ninety hours of crisis training each year. The training was designed to prepare officers to recognize someone experiencing a mental crisis and to develop de-escalation strategies. The training was rescinded several years after its mandatory implementation.

According to one community member who watched a video of the SFPD's killing of a man experiencing a mental crisis after the trainings and policy had been eliminated, "the officers were in command-and-control mode . . . and if you're dealing with a person who is experiencing hallucinations in their head, they're not going to respond to commands. They're going to become afraid, and they're going to try and defend themselves."[15] Such assessments reflect an increasing disillusionment and alarm at the prospect of police responding at all to people in crisis, whether trained or not, since many community members argue against the practice of police becoming first responders when care is needed. Meanwhile, police violence against people with mental disabilities or experiencing mental crisis has continued to rise as the care crisis deepens.[16]

The second SFPD "training" linked to the killing of Idriss occurred a decade later, in 2011, when police reconstructed the 2001 scene in the Metreon theater where Idriss was shot repeatedly in a use-of-force simulation, an exercise for teaching and assessing policing tactics and responses. As part of this reconstruction, the SFPD invited local KRON and CBS news reporters to participate in a mock re-killing of Idriss in the theater. They then featured the reenactment of the killing on the evening news and posted it across social media where it is still readily accessible.[17]

The reenactment features suspenseful and dramatic music while an aggressive subject lunges toward reporters with a knife, and is followed by a debrief segment with then SFPD Sergeant Mike Nevin, who repeatedly frames the situation in terms of the threat that it poses to the officers. The segment both opens and closes with laughter at the mock killing, including from reporters and officers gathered as part of the training. For many who recognized the reenactment as one based on the killing of Idriss ten years earlier, they contested the details, arguing that under the guise of a hypothetical, anonymous reenactment, the replayed scene was in fact recognizable to many people across the Bay Area, given the spectacular violence and media attention that had accompanied the first killing a decade earlier. To those critically watching shifts in policing and repression, they argued that the reenactment served to justify a violent response through its altered presentation of detail.[18] It also imprinted the violence into the collective memory of Bay Area residents again, an act that attempted to reaffirm, and normalize, the role of police in the present.

Rita Laura Segato theorizes the present as a conjuncture of "apocalyptic capitalism" framed by two intertwined pedagogies: the pedagogy of impunity and the pedagogy of cruelty, where new modern subjects take shape in relation to forces that seek to acquire through discipline an indifference to violence and a lack of empathy, where there is no accountability for harm caused, no censure of violence.[19] In this sense, the reenactment video can indeed be seen as a training—one that normalizes violence, flaunts impunity, and attempts to teach a careless disregard for human life. The training video, and its enduring afterlife on YouTube, affirms what is possible: that a community member can be rapidly isolated and then executed in a public space under the full legitimacy of the state.[20]

As a critical element of counterinsurgency warfare, state violence functions as a site of discipline across multiple fields as increasingly brash displays of violence occur in spaces of shared community life, propagating fear. It is a violence that produces and reproduces the biopolitical/necropolitical racial regime; each killing reinscribes a hierarchy of vulnerabilities to myriad forms of violence. As a strategy of repression, such actions not only evoke fear, they stimulate a biopolitical fear/desire, which occurs in the context of capital relations, *to remain among the living*.

Investigations from within a Crisis of Care

In her inquiry into the current conditions of capital and the state as "government of the precarious," Isabell Lorey reminds us that precarity cannot only be understood as threat and insecurity, but rather argues that precarity is a "process of normalization," or "the regulation of modes of precaritization." As such, precaritization functions as a "neoliberal instrument of steering and a technique of governing."[21] Under neoliberalism, precarity as a form of vulnerability is imposed through a reorganization of the labor relation towards heightened instability (a crisis reflected in inconsistent work, lower salaries, fewer protections, and so on).[22] Segato expands this beyond the labor relation to assert that "precariousness does not refer necessarily to poverty or lack, but points at the precariousness of relational life, after the destruction of the solidity and stability of the relationships that root, localize, and sediment affects and everyday life."[23]

In their collective research inquiry through "the circuits of feminized precarious work," the Madrid-based feminist collective Precarias a la deriva elaborates a precariousness that is "not limited to the world of work"; rather, they argue that precariousness is best understood "as a juncture of material and symbolic conditions which determine an uncertainty with respect to the sustained access to the resources essential to the full development of one's life." Drawing on the Italian workers' movement of the 1970s in seeking "to break through the isolation and individualization of post-Fordist living and working conditions," Precarias refashions a tool borrowed from the Situationists to investigate the conditions and situations of its members' own lives.[24] Encountering a general strike in Spain in June of 2002 that neither accounted for or reflected their informal, invisible work or their position as precarious workers, a group of women already organized through a social center in Madrid to collectively manage precarious living, activated a *derive* or "drift" as a collective research approach. Wandering the space of the strike, they engaged those present in the streets through a range of situated questions, a strategy of "interviews in movement" that later developed into a more cohesive and sustained research project. Through "the drift" as a tool of moving inquiry, Precarias engages the crisis of care and social reproduction, and the experiences and knowledge production emanating from these spaces and relations, in order to "enact new, lived spaces of everyday life and create new practices and networks of resistance."[25]

Through the drift, Precarias has animated a tool to reflect and respond to the crisis of care; it is a tool that can be shared—brought to bear in different geographies and to illuminate a range of struggles. It can also illuminate other resistances organized around inquiry into collective conditions of existence. Thus, the drift can make visible and communicable that these practices of feminist inquiry organized around care are happening in multiple spaces as collective investigations from within the crisis of care. In this sense, the drift is a convivial tool; a practice against isolation and individualization, the drift braids together a life in common, and strengthens a community's ability to reproduce itself in meaningful ways.[26]

Similar to the work of Precarias a la deriva of Madrid, and Oficina de Derechos Sociales (or Center for Social Rights) in Seville and their engagement in "co-research about the circuits of precarity," the collective inquiries pursued by Mesha and a network of families emerged out of a context of neoliberal securitization and the conditions of the present organized around instability and vulnerability.[27] These are inquiries into the violences that shape lives and communities as they resist and respond in a collective refusal to be erased. Their research forms an archive of counter-narratives of police shootings, in-custody deaths, and state-manufactured killings across the greater Bay Area, marking a sustained and collective inquiry into premature death. These inquiries offer a reading of the *dispositif*, and expose the production and organization of subjects in the fabrication of biopolitical order. They lay bare the strategies and the epistemologies of the forces deployed to enforce this order—one that relies on what Ruth Wilson Gilmore calls "a death-dealing displacement of difference into hierarchies that organize relations."[28]

And, like the drifts of Precarias, communities responding to police violence have forged a number of convivial tools that are critical to their collective investigation and community regeneration. One such tool has been the space and practice of vigil in response to police killings, as a way of carving out space for a community to gather, grieve, and share what it knows. A space of situated vigil often marks the first stage in a community's own investigation into an incident of violence, often organized quickly—a car, broken glass, blood, or other remaining wreckage may still be on the scene at the time the community gathers. As a practice, vigil offers a critical opportunity "to reconnect with people around the scene."[29] The vigil is also a safe space, surrounded by others who often witnessed the same incident unfold, and who compare notes and share stories. Often, they report various forms of intimidation in the immediate aftermath of a police killing: police directing them back into their houses while a body lies motionless in the street, and instructing them to close their blinds. Or the police may ask for valid identification from any witnesses and then run their names, possibly arresting them on the scene for old warrants, or their citizen status is questioned or disclosed. These names can then be shared with federal agencies, including Immigration and Customs Enforcement Agency (ICE). Police often confiscate cell phones that may include civilian footage of an incident or its immediate aftermath, seizing independent evidence and simultaneously exposing webs of relations and vulnerabilities. Often, however, the vigil occurs before people have been intimidated by the police with more official warnings: that an investigation has been opened and they are not allowed to speak to anyone about the incident, under penalty. These restrictions imposed by the police attempt to ensure that the only story that can emerge is the one conducted by and sanctioned by the state.

As community spaces that unfold adjacent to the spaces determined and contained by the state, vigils provide a critical site of counter-epistemology that establishes a base for confronting the machine which families are about to face. In addition to witnesses, families are able to connect immediately to other community members and access a mobilized community that learns of the vigil and seeks it out. From there, Mesha and others often assist with locating and attending meetings organized by the police, including town halls called by police immediately following a killing, where critical information, even if untruthful, is dispensed that families can use as their fight unfolds. Without being connected to a larger support network, a family might only hear about the police meetings through the news after the meeting has already been held.

Police killings demand that families confront the state for information while also engaging "justice" processes. Families are subjected to the state's logic and discipline; it is a space of enclosure. These first meetings are critical spaces to access information about the ways the state begins to frame an incident early on. They thus provide opportunities to reflect collectively across an organized community in order to better confront strategies of misinformation and disinformation. To make use of this as a site of confrontation and knowledge production involves organizing the community and family to attend the regularly scheduled Police Review Commission meetings, so that families and supporters might join in the public comment section and lodge their demands and questions. Critically, these are also spaces where the community can mobilize to speak in contestation of an organized pro-police presence that takes on the public comment section to support law enforcement actions, as well as their discursive claims.

These public meetings, together with vigils and other spaces, serve as sites of collective archiving. They bring together names and faces that reflect a multiplicity of violences and are entwined with other archiving sites and practices, including e-mail group conversations and chat spaces that function as a kind of underground network where new names and families are continuously added over the years. The living archives created through these struggles are a collective process in reclaiming the life taken.

Various forms of grassroots investigations take place at the sites where community members monitor, document, and archive the violence that continuously restructures the lives of entire communities, and they do so both prior to, at the moment of, and beyond the violence as event. Rather than relying on officers who narrate their own actions in the service of preserving law and order (narratives supported by departments and by police union representatives from the Police Officers Association), these grassroots investigations emphasize and validate local knowledge. Such moments of investigative "drift" might involve traveling to neighborhoods following a killing to speak to witnesses, an action that makes possible the construction of an alternative narrative, one that reflects what the people who lived in the community and witnessed the incident saw, experienced, and know about the way a community is being policed.

Often, these are spaces of ongoing "relational *testimonio*" where lives lived in deep bonds with others and with larger communities are shared through and in the context of the experience of collective violence, where the reflections are co-generated and emerge from a space of shared dialogue.[30] These circulate as "community knowledge" through vital systems of information that are central to a family and even to a neighborhood's survival strategy. Stories reveal patterns of predatory behaviors: police stalking individuals or focusing inordinately on particular homes or street corners for hours or sometimes days prior to a violent event—or in at least one instance, where a father and son from the same police department stalked members of the same family across generations. Or children are stalked as they move through city streets and public areas by the same officers that killed their siblings.[31]

These shared stories often expose threats and intimidation directed at family, friends, and community members in the aftermath of an incident: families return home after a loved one has been killed to find police cars parked in front of their homes flashing their lights on and off throughout the night. Or when court jurisdictions require families to travel to other less familiar cities, some families report local police following them into public venues, harassing them with traffic and parking tickets, and tailing them out of town. Neighbors tell of a child who witnessed from a second-story window the police shoot a man who had his hands up in the air and how later the police, under the guise of social workers, visited the child at his school and questioned him without his parents present, a strategy that simultaneously re-narrated for the child what he saw through the lens of law-and-order maintenance.[32] Or, in other stories, police pick up children from school unannounced and drop them home following an incident, demonstrating to the family and community that they know where the child and the family live.[33] Or witnesses and friends of the victim suddenly leave town, or turn up dead, including in drive-by shootings that remain unsolved.[34]

The sites of grassroots investigation are simultaneously coordinated with a number of research and direct action spaces: for example, vigils or rallies are organized on the street to connect families and develop analyses; cop-watching or Know Your Rights trainings are convened in the area where the killing occurred in order to alert the community and archive the violence; and workshops or skill shares are organized across groups to co-construct open systems of information and to collaboratively produce counter-narratives. These spaces serve to weave in a larger community and create networks around a particular act of violence. They are critical to proceeding through the various stages of a people's investigation: gathering witness statements as well as relevant documents (police reports, dispatch transcripts, and so on); submitting requests for information to produce this information; reviewing related literature; creating taxonomies and maps of the state's responses following a killing, as well as taxonomies of the laws, department protocols, policies, departmental units, and practices related to the incident; establishing strategies for a careful counter-reading of state documents, and convening adjacent autonomous learning spaces to sift through details and documents collectively. The counter-narratives are then circulated through press releases, strategic op-eds, community reports, and social media. In the rare event that a police killing makes it to trial, a number of spaces, including the space of the trial itself, are organized as direct action spaces of research and insurgent learning. In more or less formalized processes, these investigations proliferate as groups link research with "direct action casework," including collaborative community efforts organized around refusal, accountability, and autonomy.[35] Working together with other autonomous sites of information exchange, including independent newspapers, grassroots counter-narratives have been critical in forcing the state to fabricate new explanations that expose its own "prose of counterinsurgency" as well as revealing other counterinsurgent strategies.

These efforts interrupt those representations advanced by the state almost immediately after the community's confrontation with law enforcement, and are a response to the state's attempts to cast those killed by the police as criminal, violent, intoxicated or high, threatening, or somehow "deserving" of violent state intervention and outside of a community of care. These "people's investigations" contradict what the state attempts to impose as truth and expose processes of criminalization that the state deploys to justify its own violence, masking a form of domesticated warfare. Thus, community investigations establish sites for collaboratively producing, archiving, and circulating knowledge that at the same time is critical to a community's dignity, process of healing, and struggles for justice outside the state.[36]

As communities arrange what they know and form hypotheses that are tested against collective experiences, they also develop strategic knowledges. Not limited to the realm of "truth," these knowledges can reveal the state's attempts to mask its own violence and the community's efforts to reclaim its own safety. In this context, then, community investigations are a struggle for marginal discourses to claim a truth as a means of advancing a community's own autonomy against a low-intensity conflict and the related biopolitical regimes of governance.

Theorizing Foucault's "subjugated knowledges," Avery F. Gordon notes that "these fugitive, outlaw, insurrectionary knowledges are not hidden in the institutions of official knowledge but are their disqualified secrets."[37] One critical aspect of thinking through struggle involves collectively formulating questions that begin from this moment of disqualification. Knowledges that are "subjugated" and "disqualified" are at the same time "insurrectionary knowledges," comprised of details and experiences that have been displaced by dominant narratives, exiled through discursive statements and mechanisms, forgotten, or dismissed as local and relegated to the realm of the provincial, ignorant, or unsophisticated. Foucault categorizes these knowledges as "disqualified knowledges" or "buried knowledges."[38] Critically, the silences that attempt to overwrite these knowledges are not removed from power, as Foucault's genealogical approach uncovers through a search for ruptures and displacements, absence and quiet.[39] For Foucault, subjugated knowledges mark those knowledges that institutions like the state have attempted to bury, while those that are "disqualified" are seen as too "local" to have much merit in the context of a universalizing Western episteme.[40] Similarly, Sara C. Motta draws on Maria Lugones to assert that a "coloniality of knowing-subjectivity" is productive of gendered practices, gendered ways of knowing and social relations, and that through this coloniality, "emotional, embodied, oral, popular and spiritual knowledges are delegitimized, invisibilized, and denied."[41] As mothers and others engage in struggles for justice for their children, they take on a larger collective struggle against erasures and the attempted imposition of oblivion; they widen the rupture in the Western episteme, generating and expanding space for new knowledges and new ways of knowing to emerge.

The Body as a Site of Knowledge Production and Value Production

Family members are relentless in their efforts to see, touch, and comprehend what happened to their loved ones following acts of state violence. Thus, there is always an independent investigation unfolding as families filter through countless details over many years—tire marks on a road, bullet holes or bullets lodged in a building or sidewalk or doorframe (often in houses families cannot afford to move out of), clothing dried with blood, forms and statements, witness accounts, news stories, lab reports, video clips from body cameras or mounted security cameras, dispatch reports, 911 transcripts, photographs, drawings from the coroner—an endless array of artifacts and documents, many partial or redacted or illegible, horrific shards for a family to sort through. And the details that are surfaced often regularly contradict the narrative (and documentation) they receive from the police.

It is the Chief Medical Examiner's (CME) Office that provides the official autopsy report on the body, which includes information on exit and entry wounds, gunpowder residue tests to determine if a person fired a weapon before being killed, toxicology reports that attest to even trace amounts of substances (including substances that "masquerade" as other substances, such as when a child has been prescribed Adderall in response to a diagnosis of ADHD, and the toxicology report concludes that amphetamine is in the child's system). These reports are often a powerful component of criminalization, and provide valuable information for the state to build its narrative and justify violence. Yet they also contain openings that the community can use to learn and know where to respond.

The body itself is a site of knowledge production; it exposes contradictions and reveals state strategies. In the case of police shootings where a family has visited a victim's body and counted the bullet holes in their loved one's body, the number counted by the family is often not the same number produced by the mainstream media and police reports. In some cases, these are drastically different numbers, an accusation framed by the Idriss Stelley Foundation as "minimization by the corporate press on the number of bullets pumped into [people]."[42] The actual number of holes may in some cases indicate a higher number of officers present on the scene than reported by the state. The direction and angle of punctures in a body may contradict narratives that seek to establish that an officer felt threatened—wounds may confirm if someone was lying on the ground with an officer standing over them when they were shot, or they may show that a person may have been trying to run away. The holes can reveal the use of a type of firearm or a level of force that was incommensurate with the threat posed by the subject and when read against witnesses' accounts.

In responding to conditions of state violence, communities must innovate critical methodologies organized with knowledge production at the center. For example, in response to extrajudicial killings and enforced disappearances of Sikhs by the Punjab police, primarily between 1984 and 1994, researchers working across families and communities formulated a ghastly but effective equation that indexed the purchases of firewood by various police departments with the amount of wood required to burn a body in order to estimate and prove the extent of the "disappearances" as a counterinsurgency strategy of forced disappearance advanced by the police.[43] Such "observables" form a powerful investigative tactic for confronting the state's lack of disclosure surrounding its own violence. Across the Bay Area, family members have pointed to an "observable" that forms an important yet gruesome research methodology: the hours represented in the final bill charged by the funeral home provides a critical site of knowledge production in cases where the body has to be significantly reconstructed in preparation for an open casket funeral. It is not uncommon for a loved one's face to be unrecognizable, in skin tone and structure, following a police killing. Funeral directors will share information confidentially with family members which contradicts official reports, including about the level and sequence of violence (yet it is difficult to determine how ready morticians and funeral home directors are to make public information that contradicts state reports).

Families have also been able to document damage to a loved one's body by taking photos with cell phones at the morgue and thus are able to provide critical counter-information to state narratives. Further complicating this issue, while funeral homes are privately owned, in some counties in California, the CME or Coroner's Office is under the Sheriff's Department. While this is not the case for San Francisco County, it is the case for Alameda County (which includes Oakland and Berkeley). In most counties, regardless of the agency structure, CME offices and law enforcement agencies work closely together.

The intimate relation between police and coroner came to light in one instance in November 2017 in San Joaquin County in the Greater Bay Area, when the forensic pathologist Dr. Susan Parker resigned after less than a year of employment in protest at the agency's close and dishonest connection with local law enforcement. Parker asserted that the sheriff "attempted to control and influence death investigations performed by the Coroner's Office," revealing "that he 'forcefully' tried to take over physician scheduling," and accusing him of attempting to impact the "professional judgment and conclusions" of the staff.[44] The accused, Sheriff Steve Moore, took office in January 2007 and remained in that position through 2018. In one city in San Joaquin County alone, Stockton, CCRA, in conjunction with local families and groups, counted fifty-three law enforcement-related fatalities that would have passed through the CME's office under the supervision of Sheriff Moore through the end of 2018.[45] That number does not include deaths in the community as a result of state-manufactured violence, for which those who stand accused are readily handed sentences as long or longer than their lives.

Some families have revealed disturbing details from autopsy reports, including cases where the fingernails of a loved one had been removed during the autopsy, or in some cases patterns existed of removing victims' hands. The speculation from the family was that there might have been evidence under the victims' fingernails that would have disproved the police version of events. For example, if traces of flesh that could identify an officer were found under the fingernails, it might prove that there had been a close altercation rather than a "gunfight" that justified an officer-involved shooting, or it might indicate that the person had engaged an officer in an act of self-defense. There are stories of organs being removed or surgical cuts made to the body that the family doesn't understand and no one will explain—an array of gruesome details that provoke terror across communities and of which families try to make sense.

Such details and stories circulate as critical moments of *chisme* (translated loosely from the Spanish as "rumor" or "gossip"); *chisme* often serves a strategic function in circulating disqualified knowledges. Rather than the quiet, intimate, private space of mourning among family that often surrounds a loved one's body and the accompanying autopsy report, families have connected to make these details public, even enlarging and publicly displaying photographs of loved ones on the coroner's slab. Mesha has not shied away from these difficult details in the circulation of stories, and other mothers have advanced a similar set of commitments, in some case explicitly referencing each other's courageous acts, like those of the mother of Emmett Till in her refusal of a closed casket at her child's funeral. In a similar vein, Dionne Smith-Downs of Stockton, the mother of James Rivera Jr., has traveled nationally, including to support families in Ferguson following the killing of Mike Brown, with blown-up images of the severely mutilated body of her son, James, taken at the Coroner's Office.

As families share their stories, this circulation provokes other information shared from autopsies to surface—a collective process of sifting through what stories the ghastly details held or implied, listening for resonances, aligning the narrative produced by a dead body against the narrative of the state, attuned to the contradictions. These acts emerge from a careful collective process and reflect a community's collective rage, pain, and commitment to resist, and are powerful violations of the public/private divide that both make visible the attack on the social factory and respond to the violence directed at intimate spaces of Black and Brown social life.

Often, families are prohibited from any access to a body for as long as a week or more on the basis that the case is under investigation. The costs associated with storing a body for additional time are exacerbated by the conditions of the death itself, for example, how violent the death was on the body. In many cases, families are also under pressure to cremate a loved one quickly because the per diem morgue rates can be as high as $80–$100 per day and cremations are less expensive than burials, which the family often cannot afford.

In this regard, a critical element in a community's autonomy would be its access to an independent autopsy, which at the present time the state has made prohibitively expensive. Families face incoherently difficult decisions while still collectively traumatized and reeling about what to do with a loved one's body: should they choose cremation which is nearly half the cost, or burial in case any evidence might be preserved for the future? They may themselves have faced grueling interrogations in spaces manipulated by the state directly following the killing and may not have yet been allowed access to the body which is still in the morgue; they are thus unable to pose questions and see the contradictions as the people who knew that body and its rhythms and patterns best. In addition to reasons of faith and a loved one's wishes, families struggle to find money for a burial because they are hesitant to destroy evidence that may be preserved to tell the story of what happened. For many families across the Bay Area who have lost loved ones, they keep score of which bodies are buried and which were cremated, and which ones could be exhumed at a later date if needed. They lament compromises and decisions constricted by money that may have erased part of the story that needs to be told.

A Living Hammock

For many families, the struggle for justice for a loved one occurs in a context of tremendous financial hardship, and the killing exacerbates that struggle. This necessarily becomes part of how they organize collectively, activating and constructing extended networks of support across multiple homes and cities to manage the impact of the crisis and to achieve some level of normalcy and stability. Some families who have organized themselves around one vehicle may lose or be forced to change jobs for lack of transportation while the car in which their child was shot remains in police evidence lots for months or years; new circuits of transportation across the city and regions must be established, often through collective processes. Some families are forced to reorganize their domestic space; children may be shifted to a home where the trauma can be better contained or managed following the killing of a parent or sibling. This may include a new school system and new schedules as family members coordinate to redistribute their incomes, so as to immediately compensate for the absence of some form of support or income for which the victim held responsibility.

In some cases, the violence of losing a loved one disrupts a family so completely that the family is paralyzed and cannot move forward, or the continued struggle to confront the violence and the state itself comes at costs that prove too high to bear for an enduring period, particularly given that often those families targeted have been marginalized and dispossessed across multiple registers and have often faced a series of other attacks by the state that position them as always responding to crisis. Sometimes settlements are offered that can alleviate a state-produced problem elsewhere in their lives, and so families accept settlements rather than push forward to the courts in what is often a complex strategy of collective survival—the family may need to procure legal representation or make bail for other loved ones caught up in the carceral state; to retrieve vehicles from lots that have been impounded because of an officer-involved shooting, and the family is nonetheless charged by the day for lot fees. They may need to pay medical bills, sometimes ones related to the incident itself, even if their loved one did not survive. They may need to pay funeral and burial costs and fines that have accumulated at the morgue; or to pay off debts that in many cases accumulated while the family was traumatized by the violence and sometimes lost their jobs or used up all their vacation time and sick leave, when they were still grieving and searching for answers. Often other family members are targeted by police violence or arrests as families attempt to keep organizing; it is not uncommon for other violences to follow in the wake of these killings, tearing at the social fabric of family and community.

In managing the crisis, families extend to survive, reaching out to church groups or various neighborhood institutions. The first task is often to raise funds for funerals. Families organize bake sales on front lawns, in some cases with police bullets freshly lodged in the door frames of their own houses where their child was killed days before. They coordinate fundraiser barbecues and car washes in corner store parking lots where a local storeowner donates the cost of the water. Local bars and clubs are mobilized to hold a raffle or dance party and circulate the earnings back to the family. And while organized around financial necessity, families also convert these into powerful spaces of dissent and direct action, searching for answers, seeking out support networks, and learning from other families. Families who are able to remain in the struggle, often those in communities where support networks are able to remain intact, will learn of the new violences and come through to pay their respects and connect, sharing food and memories and the latest details emerging from the incident, with everyone finally sitting down when the queue of cars dwindles and dries up, and it gets too dark to continue washing them. Counter-narratives emerge to percolate and reverberate across communities.

For Silvia Federici, the production and circulation of knowledge is critical to how we "communalize the reproduction of everyday life," where knowledge production, including the "reclaiming of collective memory," is a critical terrain of struggle in the battlegrounds of the present.[46] Mesha's work has been a powerful force in the production and circulation of knowledge critical to a community's capacity to organize itself around its own safety and resist a range of capitalist and state enclosures. Her work refuses the narrative and discourse of the state at all levels (including at the level of epistemology) and refuses to accept that state violence is logical or necessary; it refuses to forget those lives taken and refuses to accept the erasure of life or community; it refuses to let one killing or act of violence exist in isolation, and each act of counterknowledge that she puts forward weaves together multiple targeted victims and myriad acts of state violence; it combines counterknowledge with direct action and spaces of community assembly; and it recognizes and insists that the families and the knowledge that they produce as counterknowledge remain at the center of the struggle.[47]

Knowledge production is central to a community's efforts towards regeneration and self-determination as stories map the existence and generation of insurrectionary knowledges and counter-discourses.[48] This shared recognition confirms a different truth than the one advanced by the state as "security"—namely, these knowledges, and their circulation confirm that war exists as "a permanent social relationship, the ineradicable basis of all relations and institutions of power."[49] The circulation of disqualified knowledges in these spaces produces a "living theory" that takes shape through everyday practices and experiences of violence, it exposes the condition of multiple intersecting violences as it "emerges from situated struggles and refuses to impose an already determined or imagined future."[50] Making space collectively to "listen" to disqualified, subjugated, insurgent knowledges and taking seriously living theory as a space of knowledge production offers a site of vernacular valorization.[51] It opens a space for the knowledge and theory produced by Black and Brown mothers and families and the communities organized around them to reorient a critical insurrectionary praxis outside the state, outside the valorization of the "Left," outside the counterinsurgent tyranny of the nonprofit industrial complex with its imperatives to represent, empower, and make choices about where to "build leadership" and "uplift the voiceless"—in short, a commitment to living theory resists competing extractions. For the Center for Convivial Research and Autonomy, "living theory privileges collective ways of knowing and struggling, underscoring that any given struggle necessarily produces theory."[52] Notably, for CCRA, living theory also refuses to impose a future—we must arrive where we are going through walking together.

With each new act of violence, a prehistory of militancy and care is activated and an already organized community extends like a net to catch and cradle the new loss and try to support the family however they can manage together. The spaces and moments where communities gather outside the state form what Gustavo Esteva of UniTierra Oaxaca describes as a "living hammock," a network of different moments that is expandable as a support system but does not rely on the permanence and dependability created by institutions.[53] Mesha's constant presence provides a continuity, a warp and weft that has proved invaluable in the collective memory of the struggle and its strength. She helps surface and connect resistances and "care communities" from other parts of the state, including groups and families from northern California, that will end up traveling to the Bay Area for the federal district court if the cases make it to trial.[54] This is also true for those families who have continued to fight, whose sustained presence ensures that the memory of multiple losses, violences, and resistances extends back through the community, recalling years of losses. The enduring presence of these families contests police violence as a mere "aberration" and points instead to a new level of systematic, systemic, everyday violence unfolding. These antagonisms are struggles for dignity and mark a critical moment of disavowal in a community reorganizing itself according to its own self-defense and autonomous justice. They reflect a collective commitment and engagement with complex forms of accompanying, or "walking with," that are the basis of community safety, rooted in fierce care and an urban Zapatismo that engages struggles "beyond solidarity."

CHAPTER 2

Oscar and Lovell
The Battle for Fourteenth and Broadway

As a Space

The intersection of Fourteenth and Broadway is a space of dissent and possibility. A space of convergence. A contested space. A tactical space. A space of research, movement, and circulation. It is the main intersection in downtown Oakland, a heterotopic, atavistic space. Its corners and perimeters are flanked on one side by office buildings of Beaux Arts classical architecture, with white granite and white terracotta cladding. On the other side are large banks, monoliths of concrete and urban industrial steel with blue-tinted glass windows. The intersection is a locus for circuits of commerce and capital, movement and transportation, working and living. Bus stops crowd each corner, and BART entrances open and descend below the street. To the northwest of the intersection, beyond a grassy plaza and an oak tree, is Oakland City Hall; a small, gently sloping amphitheater lies in front of its main doors.

Fourteenth and Broadway and its proximate civic space in front of city hall is a critical space of protest and convergence in the Bay Area, reflecting a territory that is physical and symbolic. It is a space of both negative resistance (in Negri's sense of those forms of resistance which directly engage and challenge the imposition of capital—for example, the wage strike—or that engage the state but do not yet exist outside it); and a space of positive, prefigurative politics (or those processes that advance autonomous, self-organized activity). It marks an intersection of refusals where the working class resists capital's attempts at domination and asserts commitments to build and claim new practices and relations as part of a larger class struggle. It represents a battle zone and a recurrent site of knowledge production.[1]

49

Here a range of forces meet, engage, contest, and coalesce, and emerge as something different. Struggle takes its shape through an inheritance of resistance, and the space forms a living archive where legacies are recalled to invigorate and understand the present—from dock strikes to department store strikes that morphed into the General Strike of 1946, to the insurgent claims staked by Black, Brown, Red, and Yellow Power movements, including the Black Panther Party and the Chicano Movement and Third World Resistance; from queer liberation struggles to the women's movement to student movements to antiwar and anti-imperialism rallies; speak-outs against policing and prisons; labor and union and anti-fascist battles; anti-apartheid and anti-occupation solidarity struggles from South Africa to Palestine; struggles against waves of displacements and gentrifying forces; Indigenous land struggles to Earth Day gatherings to climate justice actions; from the resistances of Redwood Summer down through to Chiapas— myriad marches and actions traverse, surround, and hold the space. It is a space of encounter and rebellion across the Bay Area and beyond.[2]

In times of rebellion, the spatial nexus of Fourteenth and Broadway often shares a dynamic relation with the Port of Oakland; refusal connects them. Relying on the port to activate blockade as a strategy of obstruction in the circulation of capital, flows of products, and workers, the movement and logic of these rebellions link the docks to the city center, often with masses of people moving between the two sites.[3] The port itself has a militant history; over the last century it has been activated repeatedly as a strategic node of blockage against a range of war:police assemblages at home and abroad.[4] The workers that control the docks, specifically the International Longshore and Warehouse Union (ILWU), in collaboration and mutual rebellion across ports and diverse struggles, can activate a shutdown over 2,000 miles of coastline and delta, from Bellingham, Washington, to Stockton to Oakland to San Diego and all ports in between, notably including the port complex of Long Beach and Los Angeles, the largest port in North America and the busiest port in the western hemisphere.[5]

In moments of dissent, streets flowing into the intersection transform into arteries of insurgency. In response, these same streets can be instantly converted into militarized traps as police declare unlawful assembly and issue orders to disperse over loudspeakers. Signaling the onset of an escalating strategy of policing that sets in with sundown, these dispersal orders reverberate across the space; we've all heard the air crackle at Fourteenth and Broadway.

Fourteenth and Broadway can be mapped as a "temporary autonomous zone of knowledge production" serving as a node in a larger network that relies on Oakland as a point of critical articulation in a cross-region resistance. As a TAZKP, the intersection offers a space for new questions to be posed collectively and negotiated in relation to other struggles and networked spaces of encounter.[6]

It is through such circulation that an anti-security politics in the present takes shape as a diverse autonomous initiative organized through the components of justice, defense, fierce care, and assembly; these four elements comprise an emergent community safety, and therefore what we can rely on when we observe it. As various forces converge on the intersection to contest the institutions of the state, justice as a category is questioned and renegotiated. Practices of community self-defense and fierce care are explored and proliferate here, on the territory of Fourteenth and Broadway and its adjacent plaza. Both spaces function as sites of assembly, or multiple assemblies, as sites of a praxis that exceeds all containment. Here, community safety becomes a counter-project to "security" through a number of forces that resist and confront counterinsurgency and the state and also reflect a lived prefigurative politics.

As a critical zone in the reclaiming of the commons and the institutions of the commons, and as a space of encounter that is always a space of co-learning, communities of struggle rely on this battleground space to actively reconfigure the geography of the Bay, to find each other in a remade geography.[7]

As Rupture, Phase One: Oscar Grant and Lovelle Mixon

Fourteenth and Broadway also marks a recent space of rupture, one amplified by a convergence of events and forces. An incident took place in the early morning hours of January 1, 2009, at Fruitvale Station that is now well known, when a minor police detention turned into an execution. As BART (Bay Area Rapid Transit) police pulled a group of Black and Brown young men off a train, BART officer Johannes Mehserle, flanked by fellow BART officers Tony Pirone and Marisol Domenici, shot one of the youths, 22-year-old Oscar Grant, in the back in front of his friends while Grant was lying detained face down on the platform. Onlookers suddenly transformed into witnesses, as revelers returning home from New Year's Eve parties watched from subway cars stopped on the tracks and began recording with cell phones, including many who recorded the scene and then concealed and refused to give up their phones or their footage despite police attempts to confiscate both. Within a few days, images of the killing started to surface, and circulated around the world.[8]

What followed was rage at the killing and at the absence of any sanction of Mehserle. On January 7, the first wave of what became known as the "January rebellions" moved through Oakland, with demonstrators smashing windows and taking over streets as fires consumed garbage cans, dumpsters, and cars. Nonprofit leaders close to the municipal administration attempted to channel the force into pacification and were quickly overrun; the rebellious presence in the streets refused to acknowledge any leadership that sought to contain or measure or convert it into calm and "acceptable" forms.[9] The police arrested hundreds but the rebellion continued and escalated, refusing to cede the streets. The actions forced the Alameda County district attorney at the time, Tom Orloff, to arrest and file charges against Mehserle, marking the first time in California's history that a police officer was charged in a fatal shooting while on duty.[10]

For many across Black and Brown communities in Oakland and beyond, the violent detention of Grant and his friends by police and the immediate escalation to fatal violence that was made visible in the killing of Grant was a reflection of violence that was not unfamiliar to their everyday experiences with police in their neighborhoods. For other communities across different geographies and racial demographics who did not share an experience of heightened over-policing, the execution of Grant brought police violence and questions of race into full, stark view. Grant came to symbolize for the West Coast the deadly attacks by police on youth of color and specifically Black men. Even further, through the publicly visible presence of his young daughter and her mother, as well as Grant's mother Wanda Johnson and his uncle, Cephus Johnson ("Uncle Bobby"), Oscar Grant in many ways also came to represent the state's violent destruction of Black families targeted by the state. As recordings of the killing continued to circulate across the globe, all eyes were on Oakland.

And despite a concerted effort on the part of the police, the dominant media, and nonprofit industrial complex (NPIC) leaders to gain control of the narrative and the response to the killing, it proved difficult to justify the police actions. Attempts to criminalize Grant had gained little traction, in part because the family and the larger organized community were strategic in communicating the loss to the community by circulating images of Grant smiling and holding his young daughter. In fact, the circumstances of the shooting itself made it largely impossible to understand Grant as a threat, and what became striking about the killing of Grant was not only the blatant deadly violence exacted against him in response to a minor incident, but the corollary that emerged that highlighted his innocence. For many, even among those who voiced criticism of the protestors' tactics during the January rebellions—condemning property destruction and extolling peaceful resistance—not only did the police shooting seem unjustified, but the outrage that followed the shooting appeared largely appropriate and warranted. With the shooting of Oscar Grant, the larger public had begun questioning whether in some instances police were responding to youth from particular communities with too much violence.

While it was BART police who had killed Grant, the January rebellions brought the Oakland Police Department (OPD) out into the streets in an attempt to contain the community's rage with mass arrests. In the streets, the rage at the killing of Grant had turned against the OPD as much as the BART police, and against policing more broadly. This was compounded across Oakland by an extensive pattern of humiliating and brutal policing throughout the late 1990s led by a group of Oakland police officers known as the Oakland Riders that many in the community had experienced or learned about from others. The violence meted out nightly by the Riders in Oakland's Black and Brown communities that had surfaced in 2001 forced the Oakland police to enter into a mandatory Negotiated Settlement Agreement in order to avoid federal oversight; this included an oversight body charged with monitoring and bringing the department into compliance with a series of recognized standards.[11] At the time of the murder of Grant (and as late as 2022), the terms of the Negotiated Settlement had not been reached, meaning the department was not in compliance for over nineteen years. Oakland has a particular history of racist policing, including deliberate departmental recruitment policies from areas and organizations in the South known for their own history of racist attitudes, beliefs, and practices. This, together with the Riders scandal and the subsequent failures to extract the department from the Settlement Agreement, formed a backdrop to the policing of Oakland.[12]

As the rebellions continued, city hall and its supporters, the business class and merchants, much of white Oakland, and even a handful of leftist groups, in an attempt to carve out their own programs and supporters, condemned the property damage as "violence" and leaned on this assessment to advance a critique against anarchists and "ultra-leftists." This supported the divisive strategy set into motion through the corporate media—that the rebellions were the result of "outsiders" (read: white and anarchist) descending like hoodlums to attack the local small businesses (and by extension families) of downtown Oakland, and did not reflect the desires or the mobilized force of Oakland's Black and Brown communities.

The dense nonprofit industrial complex that proliferates across the East Bay and largely profits off the problems of Black and Brown Oakland worked to contain the rebellions as well.[13] As was well documented, debated, and challenged at the time across groups, many of the large, youth-oriented nonprofits faced direct pressure from the city of Oakland and the threat of lost funding if they did not find ways to keep youth off the street and diverted to nonviolent activities during some of the peak events following Grant's murder. For nonprofits whose programming was oriented around Black and Brown youth, the rebellions made observable their role in the privatization of struggle, a politics made visible to the movement in a series of blatant capitulations to city hall in an attempt to invisibilize community outrage and clear the streets.[14]

The January rebellions bore witness to the multiple tactics used by the state to dissipate the struggle through division. The broken windows of the businesses in downtown Oakland that accompanied the flow of outrage in the streets became an oversignified terrain across which to distribute the actions of the "right way" to protest versus the "wrong way" to protest, and "good protestors" versus "bad protestors." In the words of Sylvia Wynter, the "revolts were, at one and the same time, a form of praxis and an abstract theoretical activity."[15]

In the breach, new questions could be formulated and negotiated to expose the state's pacification efforts in place, to unmask the war; this emerged as one of the most salient aspects that both made possible and defined the rupture. Militant research, or thinking and acting from within the heat of the moment of the rebellions in the street, was critical to widening the rupture, as the rebellions fomented a proliferation of conversations and new relations. Independent journalists circulated debates and identified divisive strategies, narrating what was at stake. There were zines, blog posts, pamphlets, radio shows, and direct actions; workshops and panels; and events and workshops from clubs and bars to coffee shops to campuses to community centers.

Connections and coalitions and various solidarities and affinities were activated and discovered across groups in the wake of the rebellion, and over the next year and a half in anticipation of the trial of Mehserle. Oscar Grant's image, in various artistic representations, sprang up everywhere—in newspapers and on flyers; on T-shirts and jewelry; on placards in storefront windows and wheat paste posters across the city walls of downtown Oakland. When windows were boarded up by local businesses in anticipation of a new rebellion or in the destruction left in one's wake, more posters appeared of Oscar Grant on the new boards themselves. The resistance was so intense in the months and year following the killing of Grant, that the decision was made to move the trial to Los Angeles.

The rebellions had cleaved a new opening of struggle that would continue to widen over the months and years to come, flowing into the larger Occupy movement and beyond to lay the ground for the emergence nationally in 2014 of Black Lives Matter and the Movement for Black Lives.[16] As "Black rage" was felt and seized by many others across the Bay Area under the phrase, *I am Oscar Grant*, this extended moment brought to the forefront questions of resistance that exceed the state.[17]

In the assessment of one collective, "the Oscar Grant movement prefigured much of the contemporary activity that has put Oakland at the forefront of social struggle in this country."[18] In what George Ciccariello-Mayer would call the "long arc of struggle from Oscar Grant to Occupy," the rebellions formed a crucial layer of the terrain on which the Occupy movement would take hold in the Bay Area, with Oakland at its center. This long arc of struggle unfolded from within a crisis of capitalism, including, in the analysis of Jason E. Smith, "massive capital flight, the soaring unemployment, the erosion of the State's role in social reproduction, and the resurgence . . . of strains of fascism."[19] This was the terrain of the extended insurgency manifested at Fourteenth and Broadway.

But before Occupy emerged as a nationwide response to the 2009 financial crisis and its imposed conditions of austerity and precarity manifest through debt and dispossession, another violent incident occurred in Oakland less than three months after the execution of Grant that left an indelible mark in the rupture. On March 21, 2009, when another young Black man, Lovelle Mixon, was stopped by Oakland police during a "routine police stop" on the 7400 block of MacArthur Boulevard in East Oakland, he opened fire, killing two officers in the street.[20] Mixon escaped the scene and fled to his sister's apartment, where he was tracked by a SWAT team that unleashed a barrage of chemical gas, bullets, and fire in the apartment. From the closet where he had retreated, Mixon killed two more officers before being fatally shot by OPD Officer Patrick Gonzalez.

If the January rebellions and extended actions across Oakland following the execution of Grant had activated a new space of struggle, Mixon's actions fully surfaced the war. The upheaval that Mixon introduced into the rupture immediately reorganized the already disrupted stasis. The killing of Grant and what happened in its wake—the widely circulated footage and international solidarities; the continuous mass demonstrations in the streets; the response it forced on the district attorney; the ongoing destruction of downtown Oakland; and the pending trial of Mehserle—had placed the police in a precarious position vis-à-vis the population they were tasked to serve and protect. In the immediate aftermath of Mixon, the OPD acted swiftly to bring together police from across the Bay Area, California, and the United States, organizing a massive and elaborate spectacle of a funeral for the slain officers in the Oakland Coliseum. As the life and family of Lovelle Mixon was immediately criminalized in the media, the state closed ranks in a stadium filled with mourning officers.

For the police, then, Mixon's act offered an opportunity to reclaim lost territory. Supported by the press, the police immediately began layering a criminal history onto Mixon, who was labeled a "cop killer" at the same time that he was aligned with a series of heinous crimes, including allegations of a double rape (a charge which remains unproven.) Simultaneously, the department and its supporters were able to activate a narrative about the dangers for police in Oakland (and beyond) while asserting the presence of a violent element in the population. In this context, not only were police necessary to protect the population from dangerous criminals, but decisions made in split seconds with sometimes deadly consequences were a necessary part of the job and a reasonable response to an ever-present threat posed by Black and Brown criminals, read youth.[21]

This reframing was critical to ensure the legitimacy of the department to continue to kill. It was also critical for repositioning and gaining advantage in a number of other cases of police violence active at the time and heading for trial that had generated outrage and where there hadn't been a clear threat. Among these, on the other side of the Bay, were the prominent killings of Cammerin Boyd (2004) and Asa Sullivan (2006), both fatally shot by the San Francisco Police Department, and both of which were being manufactured as "suicide by cop" cases to undergird the dangers of policing young Black men.

Thus, with the events of March 21 and the OPD killing of Lovelle Mixon, the momentum gained in the January rebellions was besieged by a number of contradictory currents. While for the state, Mixon became synonymous with the deadliest day in California law enforcement history and was crafted prominently into a symbol of criminality and violence, for others this symbol was contested and was also a site of silence. Across much of the liberal Left, it was easier to quietly ignore Mixon's act or issue a broader condemnation of violence that reestablished the role of the police in general while producing an innocent Grant as the exception.[22]

Others, including community members and organized collectives in Oakland and across the Bay, refused to abandon Mixon or acquiesce to his erasure, or allow him to be put in service of security or pacification. Groups including the Black Uhuru Movement in Oakland held vigils, claimed Mixon with signs at protests and rallies, and confronted the criminalization of him directly. Community members in East Oakland responded specifically to the charges of "double rape" (which the police surfaced days after the shooting) to expose the state's strategy in narrating the violation of women so as to criminalize Black men.[23]

Other community groups also reached out to weave Mixon's family into a larger struggle and reclaim Mixon, with the argument that to erase Mixon was to deny the war. For many across East Oakland and beyond, Mixon emerged as an example of dignified resistance to unabating harassment, brutality, and inescapable cycles of incarceration constructed by the state. In the eyes of some, Mixon was a hero, the "rabbit with the gun" who fired back, and served as evidence of the police occupation of Oakland and its enduring anticolonial struggle.[24] The independent media circulated counter-narratives and an analysis from below, relying on Mixon to reassert the presence of the Oakland police as that of an occupying army, policing colonial subjects who could never be full citizens.[25]

Combined, Grant and Mixon functioned as a kind of good subject/bad subject dichotomy, and even those who might have been sympathetic to an analysis of structural racism that produces an "oppositional" subject found it easier when Mixon's legacy was not fully embodied or present in the surge to define justice for Oscar Grant. The questions around justified state violence and more "deserving victims" unquestionably emerged from many spaces simultaneously, and later surfaced prominently in the late summer of 2014 to provoke a sharper analysis to frame a number of incidents of violence. The sustained Ferguson uprising following the shooting of Mike Brown on August 9, 2014, occurred in close proximity to two other police killings of Black men that rose to national visibility—the choking of Eric Garner in Staten Island on July 7, 2014, and the shooting of John Crawford in Ohio on August 5, 2014—though there were others, often uncounted in state archives, killed by police during this period too. With Eric Garner, who was accused of selling cigarettes illegally (a detail that was later disproven), the questions were posed around "legal" versus "illegal" activity and a justified killing. With John Crawford, and later Tamir Rice, both from Ohio and both of whom had toy guns at the time they were killed, the questions revolved around toy guns / functioning manufactured weapons, which had also been central to the 2014 killing of Andy Lopez in Santa Rosa, California; this reflected back on earlier debates around armed/unarmed as a condition of justification or condemnation. In the case of Brown, debates arose around the question of college-bound/not college-bound, which reflected other debates around employed/unemployed as communities sifted through the discursive traps laid by the state to mask violence, justify the threat posed, and engage both the white community and communities of color in the politics of "the life worth living."

In Oakland, despite the prominence of Oscar Grant, Lovelle Mixon would also not go away, and as Sam Stoker's short documentary *The Ghosts of March 21st* recognized, nor would the many ghosts that came before and that gave shape to Mixon's life. In Stoker's film, the landscape of East Oakland where Mixon lived and died is presented through a cartography of police killings, police dog attacks, home raids, and other instances of state violence that targeted the area in the years leading up to the killing of Mixon.[26]

Any refusal to abandon or erase Mixon opened space for holding contradictions: one did not have to condone violence to listen to what Mixon and his actions were saying about the conditions of policing in Oakland; those struggles that refused to discard or condemn Mixon further activated the rupture. They relied on the narratives of Mixon's mother and family who shared that Mixon was frustrated with probation officers who often missed or rescheduled mandatory probation visits, and that Mixon was unwilling to go back to prison. His family reconstructed the world that Mixon navigated, as one where he could not fully access a future that was livable.[27] Through his family, the struggles then were able to draw on the life of Mixon to expose not only the violent over-policing of Black and Brown communities but the daily harassments and humiliations he had faced, the forced reorganization of the home and time through the arbitrary and punitive imposition of probation, a future dispossessed, the horrors of prison.

Foucault reminds us that "penal law was not created by the common people, nor by the peasantry, nor by the proletariat, but entirely by the bourgeoisie as an important tactical weapon in this system of divisions which they wished to introduce."[28] In the attempted criminalization of Grant and the more sustained criminalization of Mixon, policing takes on the legacies of "othering" central to the colonial project and the separating and isolating of the "militant" that are central to counterinsurgency warfare. Alongside the violence, penal law and its targeted application reflect Du Bois's "white man's bargain" which ensures the maintenance of racial hierarchies, including the reproduction of whiteness.

Beginning in the spring of 2009, Grant and Mixon became points of reference in a collective and sustained interrogation among communities of struggle in their efforts to confront myriad forms of racial violence. Grant's "innocence" and Mixon's "insurgency" were often counterpoised as the larger movement struggled to justify differentiating between the "good victim" and the "bad victim" of police violence, and a space was simultaneously opened to interrogate the politics of organizing around explicitly authored state violence and forms of state-manufactured violence reflected in police and carceral violence, as well as homicide rates. Families who had lost children at the hands of other families' children or in inconclusive attacks struggled collectively to expand the discourse on racialized violence beyond police killings. This interrogation fed an analysis that was critical to the process of unraveling the complex interplay of "security" masking low-intensity conflict, and critical to building community safety as an autonomous initiative outside the state and police. More critically, it surfaced the production and classification of "good" versus "bad" victims as a strategy to divide the community.

While some attempted to explain Mixon and make him intelligible and sympathetic through an analysis of structural violence, the larger questions that Mixon posed through his actions transformed into debates around a community's right to self-defense. These questions have always been at the forefront of Black, Brown, and Indigenous struggles in their efforts to make visible conditions of war, including occupation, and often form the basis for self-determination struggles.[29]

The killing of Oscar Grant had forced a collective confrontation with state impunity in instances of violence exacted on youth of color. Mixon brought questions of community self-defense to the forefront, laying the terrain, with Grant, and with the rebellious energy that rose up to claim them both in the wake of the violence, for an emergent collective analysis of policing in the current conjuncture. This ran parallel with a battle initiated in 2010 against gang injunctions in Oakland, mobilized under the Stop the Injunctions Coalition, in which Critical Resistance played a notable part.[30] Beyond forms of structural racism and repression, there existed an urgency for something that could not only explain violence through the actions of racist police (though this remained a problem with a particular history in Oakland), but that could also account for a series of policing strategies aimed directly at community networks and family structures, and orchestrated across specific delineations of territory. The Stop the Injunctions Coalition made manifest and invited an analysis of different policing strategies aimed at different geographies, as well as drawing attention to targeted behaviors and activities deemed "illegal" versus "legal," a designation that does not correlate with conviction levels or policing strategies, but rather makes "crime" visible as an epistemological obstacle.

The ongoing rebellions amplified an interrogation of "crime" in relation to property and belonging against this organized pushback. Discursively, this was a battle over a dominant frame that responded to the rebellions by insisting on "property destruction" and "outsiders" and "looters." Each of these proved instrumental in advancing a collective analysis. In the first instance, it was not only a question of whose property was protected by the police (downtown business owners), or how we can reconcile the destruction of property with the taking of a life (there is no reconciliation), but what is revealed about the forces of social antagonism in this emphasis on property damage.[31] Questions of property destruction in relation to a larger discussion of justice brought into focus what Lisa Marie Cacho theorizes as "white injury," where damage to white property takes priority over violence against particular communities.[32] For many, among them anarchists and other militants who refused to cede the streets, these were also questions of violence, revolution, and war, and evidenced the front line of a larger developing strategy to directly confront the state and fight back.

Yet, beyond this, each instance of property damage that arose from the rebellions was critical to advancing a collective analysis and, in turn, the beginnings of an emergent collective subject, however temporary—one that began to think more thoroughly about questions of enclosure, extractivism, and the commons. The question of property destruction was closely aligned with a discourse of "authentic belonging," asking, who really could claim Oakland? Who had the "right" to destroy it? Those protesting and resisting in a myriad of ways from a myriad of places fought hard to claim each other against this onslaught. A pamphlet was widely circulated at the time that addressed the media spin of outsiders, "Who Is Oakland?" During this period throughout the Bay Area, from readings at the Modern Times Bookstore and radical spaces like 518 Valencia shared by Freedom Archives and AROC (Arab Resource Organizing Center) in San Francisco; to public conversations like that between Angela Davis and Grace Lee Boggs at UC Berkeley; to the EastSide Arts Alliance and The Holdout/Qilombo in Oakland; and in other smaller gatherings across numerous organizations—these ideas were constantly being sorted out in open spaces of exchange. Questions of violence, belonging, and the production of racial regimes generated further questions about community, conditions of precarity, gentrification, dispossession, and migration, both individual and collective.

Maria Mies and Veronika Benholdt-Thomsen highlight Garret Hardin's justification for the need for enclosure, or the necessary privatization of the commons and the individualized governance over limited resources that draw upon a rational model of crime control; "when men mutually agreed to pass laws against robbing, mankind became more free, not less so."[33] Theorizations arose from within an emergent Bay Area community safety struggle to challenge this reactive logic of property and property damage through diverse practices as people strive "to recover, establish, or enhance their ability to determine the conditions of their own existence, while allowing and encouraging others to do the same."[34] On the eve of Occupy, these were questions around privatization, enclosure, and the commons. Was not the physical assertion of presence and protest, after all, that Fourteenth and Broadway belonged to the people?

Meanwhile, the question of "looters" surfaced a continuity with the LA rebellions and the aftermath of Hurricane Katrina in New Orleans, exposing an ongoing process of criminalization, which in turn exposed subjects who were only legible as criminal.[35] This was a powerful moment of collective recognition against the backdrop of a trial that had been moved to Los Angeles, and where each member of the jury had a relative who was employed by law enforcement.[36] How could there be any justice for Grant in the courts?

A related collective question that reached articulation in the rupture confronted a central slogan that emerged, with Mehserle at the center, to "Jail All Killer Cops." The slogan had an uneasy circulation in the context of extreme rates of incarceration in California and a powerful abolitionist movement. Where did this demand fit in the context of a larger anti-carceral, abolitionist struggle? A punitive demand that not only advocated prison but reaffirmed the courts as a site of justice raised questions among many groups who were otherwise clearly fighting against the carceral state and at the same time fighting to reclaim justice from the state. This reflected a confrontation with liberalism: if the modern bourgeois state was established by placing the state at the center of all arbitrations, thus removing justice from the traditions, vernacular practices, and autonomy of the community, such a strategy was worthy of interrogation.[37] What appeared initially from this confluence of vectors was a questioning of the strategic engagement with the state as a site of justice and a belief that no matter how many times Oakland changed its mayors to reflect a more progressive party or brought in a new police chief to "clean up the force," there was little justice to be achieved through city hall or the Oakland or Alameda courts.[38]

The marches sparked again through the summer of 2010, reaching a crescendo in July in parallel with the court process, a commitment to keep pressure on the trial and the promise to hold space in its aftermath. In the days awaiting the outcome of the trial which would immediately signal a convergence at Fourteenth and Broadway, many traveled to work carrying plastic bags with lemons or cloth soaked in vinegar that could later be tied over the nose and mouth to mitigate the effects of tear gas. With Oakland at the center, the Bay Area was in rebellion amidst tear gas, flash-bang grenades, and mass arrests, including "kettling maneuvers" that trapped protesting crowds at the intersection itself, or funneled them into neighborhood rotaries and then closed in from all sides.[39]

The actions that exploded across Oakland night after night in 2009 and 2010, far from being failures, were spaces where knowledge was continuously produced and circulated as part of a growing effort to share and comprehend state strategies, including across families and justice struggles from the outlying areas that came with their crews and connected and reconnected with the struggles of the East, South, and North Bay. These were critical spaces of encounter and convergence—not just of people who joined together from points all across the Bay, but where different vectors of struggle converged as well, sifting through questions of violence, impunity, state-organized justice, and community self-defense. On the day of the verdict in Mehserle's trial in July 2010, a huge painted banner was unfurled from the traffic light post at Fourteenth and Broadway, "Oakland Says Guilty." The action signaled both a claim to autonomy and a refusal of state-organized justice and state-sanctioned violence.

Following the verdict, the pressure regularly returned to the streets to ensure that Mehserle would be sentenced at his upcoming hearing scheduled for November. In the days leading up to the hearing, the entire West Coast port system was shut down for a day, an action made possible through a series of affinities and a coalition that had at its center the longshoremen's union, ILWU Local 10, which served the dockworkers at the Port of Oakland and represented many African American workers. This was the ground in Oakland where the first tents of the local Occupy movement were set up.

As Rupture, Phase Two: Occupy

When Occupy first emerged on the East Coast in the fall of 2011, and then a short time later, on October 1, when the plaza in front of city hall in Oakland was overtaken by the first tents, the desire for a more complex theorization of capital was already alive. Nationally, the Occupy movement challenged the corporatization of government at the same time that it struggled to articulate new possibilities through prefigurative practices that attempted to break from the ossification of the old Left. The movement emerged from what was for some a heuristic realization and for others an anticipation of horizons proscribed by student loan and other forms of debt and increasingly precarious working conditions, combined with a lack of health care and an unpredictably violent housing market. It was a rejection of a world with "no future."[40]

Occupy Oakland drew some of its momentum and experience from the alter-globalization movement spaces of the 1990s, which had included a series of powerful strikes along the Oakland docks. Like the larger Occupy movement, it took its shape from the surge of rebellions and new political imaginaries emerging from the Global South—Spain, Argentina, Brazil, and in Mexico, the states of Chiapas and Oaxaca.[41] It also grew out of and alongside a series of student strikes and occupations at the University of California (UC), Berkeley, and UC Santa Cruz. Occupy Oakland was also significant for the way it was drawn into dynamic relations with already strong existing movements to confront California's growing transformation into a carceral state, including abolition movements against the police and the prisons. During the Occupy movement's marches and protests, including the general strike and port shutdown, and many spaces of convergence such as the mock trial held by Occupy the Justice Department on April 24, 2012, and the rally and speak-out of Occupy 4 Prisoners outside the gates of San Quentin on February 20, 2012, it was common to see a speaking platform comprised of insurgents of the 1960s, '70s, and '80s who were still actively fighting from within local and national struggles. The first Occupy encampment at Oscar Grant Plaza lasted from October 10 to 25 in 2011, and the second lasted from October 26 to November 14 of that year. Occupy Oakland encampments were also established at Snow Park near Lake Merritt and Veterans Camp during this time. While all the camps were eventually dismantled by a constant onslaught of law enforcement, including early morning raids and violent attacks by various agencies, the camps were also vigorously defended by a broad range of groups from the Left and members of diverse communities across the Bay Area. While the focus and the most visible Occupy energy was centered in Oakland, there were also powerful Occupy actions and an encampment and assembly in San Francisco, and also an assembly in San José. People and actions circulated between and across the various spaces of Occupy.[42]

The sharpening of struggle and collective energy of the recent Oscar Grant rebellions was reflected in one of the first gestures of the Oakland General Assembly, convened in the open-air tiered semicircle of the amphitheater in front of city hall, where the decision was made to rename the nearby civic space of Fourteenth and Broadway from the municipally named Frank Ogawa Plaza to Oscar Grant Plaza. Occupy reflected a convergence of forces of desire and struggle in the creation of diffuse networks and multiple strategies.[43]

The Occupy movement's presence nationally and in its manifestation as the Oakland Commune was significant as assembly and encampment.[44] Drawing from the prolific assemblies across South America, Mexico, Spain, and elsewhere, the Occupy movement's emphasis on the assembly as a key tool in organizing offered opportunities for reflecting on the vanguardist and party representation politics and their residual strategies of mass organizing and conscientization that dominated large sections of Bay Area political life. It also emerged as a critique and offered an alternative to the representational democracy that was the ideal to which modern electoral politics aspired and attempted to organize people towards. Thus, the Occupy movement's emphasis on "horizontalism" marked a rejection of both hierarchy and representational politics, as well as a rejection of the crisis brought on by corporate government as a whole.[45] "Horizontalism" served as an invitation to take systems of information and multiple ways of knowing and being seriously.[46] Simultaneously, the assembly functioned as a site of radical democracy that made visible the despotism inherent in the liberal representative system. It made prominent a form of coming together that encouraged the possibility of placing an interrogation of knowledge production and epistemology at the center of organizational strategies.

As an encampment, Occupy Oakland had to reckon with a historical legacy of settler colonialism, occupation, and dispossession. Indigenous activists, scholars, and community members engaged the energy of Occupy and worked to carve space for reflection and action as part of a deliberate and focused effort to decolonize.[47] These forces deepened the theoretical analysis as part of the space of rupture opened by Occupy by insisting that foreclosures and dispossession in the present resulting from the housing crisis had to be understood in a longer context of the dispossession of Indigenous land, sustainability, and autonomy.[48]

Alongside a sustained effort to engage questions of territory and re-territorialization made prominent through the strategy of the occupation, Occupy Oakland's encampment and its many tents simultaneously opened a new space of politics that placed care and autonomy at the center of its practice. This "politics of care" was made visible and emerged through health clinics, child care collectives, art spaces, and free schools and libraries, and emerged as a critical prefigurative space within a more widespread political practice.[49] These prefigurative encampments provided a space of elaboration for these extended struggles against the invisibility of forms of care work; the social factory as a set of relations organized around care merged with the street to reveal the entwined attacks of capital and the state aimed at the site where the community reproduces itself.

Alongside a series of brilliant protests, shutdowns of banks, marches, "tours" of financial and corporate headquarters, and teach-ins, Occupy Oakland offered spectacular moments like the general strike and port shutdowns that brought tens of thousands out into the streets together—workers, students, anarchists, environmentalists, union members, queer forces, teachers, undocumented people, people of all ages and backgrounds and experiences in struggle.[50]

Critically, Occupy Oakland unfolded against moments of spectacular policing and violent repression as law enforcement from multiple agencies across California converged to attack tents and protests. Emily Brissette's analysis of Occupy Oakland engages similar questions and issues concerning violence that surfaced during the Oscar Grant rebellions, examining forms of violence at protests, including moments of spectacular policing, as well as forms of structural and epistemic violence that "often give rise to the protest in the first place."[51] In a continuation of the violent repression in the Oscar Grant rebellions, and escalating with new strategies and technologies, tear gas, armored vehicles, "flash bang" grenades, rubber bullets, beanbag rounds, sound machines, and lines and lines of riot police appeared regularly in downtown Oakland. Mass and brutal arrests targeted protestors through tactics that included kettling, flying wedges, and snatch squads. As part of this violent patrol and repression strategy, the Oakland Police Department assembled a "Tango Team" comprised of officers with histories of violence, many of whom had been involved in more than one deadly force incident, among them Sergeant Patrick Gonzales, Officer Eriberto Perez-Angeles, Officer Victor Garcia, and Captain Ersie Joyner III. Here, journalists, cop-watchers, and militant researchers from within the protests provided critical research about police and various repression and surveillance strategies and tactics, with journalist Ali Winston counting that at the time of Occupy Oakland, "between them, [Tango Team officers] Garcia and Joyner have been involved in at least seven police shootings."[52] The exposure of policing strategies like Tango Team that were then circulated across the movement not only rendered legible the state's investment in violent repression of protest, it surfaced the scope of violence directed at particular communities in the absence of a visible insurgency.

Beyond the assemblies, the encampments, and the direct action and mass presence in the streets, Occupy Oakland was also significant for the way it migrated away from the city center to take over parks and construct deliberate spaces of community across neighborhoods, including through a series of barbecues, skill shares, and speak-outs. By the time the Occupy movement was largely crushed in its most visible manifestations at the center of cities across the United States, it had produced a number of convivial tools that were picked up and morphed across struggles, and were adjusted for local contexts in order to confront various violences and dispossessions and to strengthen and network community resiliencies.

Against Hired Guns

In the wake of Occupy Oakland and its large general assemblies in Oscar Grant Plaza, several spaces of reflection and action were convened to open the possibilities for oppositional knowledges and new collective strategies to emerge. In early March 2012, a temporary convergence of organizers under the name Against Hired Guns invited community members to gather in the basement of a fading department store in downtown Oakland, a few strides from Fourteenth and Broadway.

Against Hired Guns had formed in part as a response to a series of Oakland police killings and in particular as a way to circulate information and documents that were emerging following the killing of Raheim Brown in Oakland on January 22, 2011, by Oakland Unified School District Officer Barhin Bhatt, who had been hired by the school district after being fired from the OPD for brutality. Members of this loosely identified configuration had also begun distributing leaflets across neighborhoods in Oakland immediately following police killings with a sketch of a figure wearing a T-shirt with the words, "I am Oscar Grant," and a short analysis of the role of police in society.

The goal of the tactic was to respond quickly to incidents of state violence by alerting the community that the violence had occurred, not to offer a substantial counter-narrative of the event. Rather, the leaflets could be seen as part of a larger strategy against the invisibilization of those targeted and violently removed from the community and as a provocative tactic in instigating grassroots inquiries that could then develop into more sustained people's investigations. In many cases across the Bay Area, even community members who know or have heard that a police attack took place in their midst are unable to track down information regarding the name or any history of the person. In this sense, the Against Hired Guns leaflets simultaneously served as markers against erasure, listing street intersections and the time of the incident that could be traced later and read against reports that the police posted annually under mandatory transparency legislation. In some instances, community members would not learn the name of the person who had been killed until the police departments published these annual records, often many months after the incident when the loss to the community was no longer so immediate and raw. Like the re-territorialization and renaming of Oscar Grant Plaza in October 2011, Occupy had also initiated the Raheim Brown Free School and Library, which formed a critical part of the landscape of self-organized community spaces during the Occupy movement and was named after the life of someone taken by violence.⁵³

As one of the first large gatherings following the waning of Occupy and the repeated and spectacular engagements with police across downtown Oakland, the Against Hired Guns gathering in spring 2012 in the department store basement was constructed as a space to reflect together across the Bay about our collective responses to police killings, see ourselves as a community of families and networked members, and reflect on questions and strategies from different corners of struggle. Here, communities spoke together to question the effectiveness of organizing themselves according to punitive forms of justice adjudicated through liberal institutions, as well as the importance of assessing response strategies vis-à-vis the state as a movement. There was a shared affirmation of the need to respond to each police murder in the community as a community. The question was also raised as part of generating a collective analysis, "how do we move beyond responding to one death at a time?"⁵⁴ The reasoning, hard-won through collective experience over time, was that the state anticipates this, counting on our collective exhaustion and eventual fragmentation. The power of the gathering in downtown Oakland was that it converged points of struggle and various groups after the massive repression of the Occupy movement; it marked a commitment to continue meeting together and building a collective analysis.

From Palestine to Ferguson to the Bay Area

Writing from within struggles against neoliberalism in Argentina, Colectivo Situaciones marks a collective learning that is underway as struggles in the present make a definitive shift to engage autonomy: "At long last we have learned that power—the state—understood as a privileged locus on change—is not the site, par excellence, of the political . . . Struggles for dignity and justice continue: the world in its entirety is being questioned and reinvented again."⁵⁵ Beyond the old Internationals and the alliances of nation-states organized into "worlds" (First, Second, and Third), struggles in the present connect, network, and learn along new vectors, exploring new concepts and questions.

The moments of rebellion in places like Oakland served as a collective laboratory where questions and convergences percolated, signaling a desire to merge sometimes disparate struggles in efforts to understand racial patriarchal capital and the state, and functioning as critical spaces of rebellion, contestation, and knowledge production. When in the summer of 2014 Palestine was exposed to weeks of violent attacks by Israel, solidarities already in place and recently activated in response to the paramilitary killing of Comrade Galeano in Chiapas earlier in May were quickly activated again. Enduring for weeks across San Francisco and Oakland, the protests against Israel's attacks resulted in a historic port blockade for several days. This noteworthy mobilization left an Israeli ZIM ship unable to unload on the Oakland docks. Palestine solidarity actions—full of rage, grief, and resistance—were already in the streets by the time the first chants hit the West Coast, "I can't breathe" echoing the resistances to the killing of Eric Garner in Staten Island and the call that heralded the insurgency in response to the killing of Mike Brown in Ferguson in August of that year, "Hands up, don't shoot."

All summer the streets were alive across the Bay: traffic that had been blocked going one way on Market Street in San Francisco the previous week for Palestine was stopped going both ways at Van Ness and Market as the Justice for Alex Nieto march held the intersection for an extended period; everyone was chanting with hands raised in the air in connection with the insurgency in Ferguson. For weeks, families with posters of their children killed by the state walked side by side with others who for days had very little sleep as part of the rotating ZIM ship blockade at the dock. The same was happening in Oakland, as marches wove their way from three different directions to meet up at Fourteenth and Broadway, surrounded by large deployments of riot gear cops blocking streets and attempting to force marchers to disperse in other directions. As John D. Márquez and Junaid Rana's excavation of late summer 2014 points out, "the fires of Ferguson were connected to a broader matrix of insurgent acts against racial capitalism the world over, mobilizations and clashes in Paris, Baltimore, London, Chicago, Gaza, Oaxaca, Baton Rouge, Rio de Janeiro, and Unis'tot'en territory." These authors argued that a "decolonial approach is made possible by insurgent acts."[56]

This remained true when by the end of September, news began circulating of the forty-three students gone missing from Ayotzinapa in Guerrero, Mexico, revealing not only the collusion but also the undifferentiated functioning between narco traffickers and the Mexican state. This activation can be traced to multiple strands of the struggle—from those strands that wove Palestinian solidarities together with prison hunger strikes and prison and jail abolitionist movements, to Black and Brown power movements and long-standing anticolonial struggles, including those for Puerto Rican liberation, and highlighting the continued incarceration of political prisoners from Leonard Peltier to Oscar Rivera Lopez (since released), to those members of the Black Power movement still locked up. The immediate resonance with Ayotzinapa was due in large part to the enduring presence of autonomous collectives and spaces like Acción Zapatista, Radio Autonomía, Chiapas Solidarity Network, UniTierra Califas, and the Qilombo social center, as well as a growing resonance between anarchist, autonomous, and Zapatista struggles, including many people from the Bay Area who had traveled to the Zapatista Escuelita ("Little School") in August 2013. They also reflected networks of families and communities activated and held through "societies in movement" and generational connections across the border among a range of Chicanx, Latinx, and migrant communities.[57] As mobilizations against state violence circulated across borders and solidarities were rewoven, multiple (and multiplying) efforts to demilitarize became more visible, more legible to each other.

The enduring insurgency and collective learning underway in the "long arc" between Oscar Grant and Occupy reflected a moment of fruition in an emergent collective analysis that had been building and percolating across many spaces in the United States, where a confrontation against police brutality was made central to a project of destabilizing and deconstructing "security." Its manifestation served to advance efforts of community safety as a series of self-organized spaces within, against, and beyond the state.[58] Central to this community safety project was a reorganization of the ways that knowledge was produced through struggle.

It also grew out of rebellions and occupations across the United States with the collective realization that we were all watching the same armored vehicle approaching us together in the streets from occupied Gaza to Oakland. This process was not only about building a new collective analysis; autonomous and prefigurative elements began to take shape in a much more cohesive and deliberate way.

Throughout the extended rebellions and mobilizations, these moments of "thinking across the Bay" from a number of perspectives have continued to shape both tactics and theory into the present. In "Spatial Equivalents in the World System," Fredric Jameson reflects on whether space can be political, considering Gehry's architecture in the context of residual and emergent architectural forms. For Jameson, in relation to space, the building "thinks a material thought."[59] The spatial parameters of Fourteenth and Broadway, as a "space of encounter," give shape to territory where the struggle can be understood as trying to think itself in relation to space and the "materiality" of an emergent collective subject.

What began to emerge from the convergence of forces embodied and reflected through the territorial intersection of Fourteenth and Broadway manifests a larger shift in organizing strategies in struggles across the Bay and globally to recognize a different kind of movement-building, one which insists on articulating the terms of its struggle outside the framework of liberal politics, or what Richard J. F. Day calls "the politics of representation, recognition, and inclusion."[60] Fully aware that such logic belies an investment in the state as a site for meaningful social change, justice, and equal protections, the deliberate commitment in struggles across the Bay and globally to recognize a different kind of effort organized around skill shares, investigations, assemblies, and new ways of being together, offering ways to engage, to borrow a phrase from the Zapatistas, "a new kind of politics."[61]

This effort can be read as a moment that both makes state violence visible and takes seriously the regeneration made possible through community-based, self-valorizing activities.[62] Critical to this effort is a reorientation of power relations and struggle; it involves locating sites of struggle outside of the traditional sites of politics and the institutions of the state, including "'reading' political activity and assessing realms often overlooked as sites of struggle."[63]

The emphatic and strategic Black Lives Matter movement that emerged to confront police killings across the United States and which took hold in the wave after the Occupy campaigns, can be (and was) picked up in many ways to assert many forms of resistance and refusal; it can also be read as an assertion of self-valorization, outside of the state. Decentralized across local contexts, communities of struggle engage Black Lives Matter in diverse ways.[64] Black Lives Matter can be read through three strands of engagement, which while not mutually exclusive also reflect vastly different political commitments: as a social movement organized toward inclusion, as direct action, and as a "space of encounter."[65] These strands reflect the questions emerging around a "new way of doing politics" that sprang from the ruptures in spaces like Fourteenth and Broadway to confront the violences of the current conjuncture.

Sharing Convivial Tools

A powerful legacy of the battle for Fourteenth and Broadway is reflected in the many collective analyses emerging from the street as the convergent and overlapping forces and energy from the Oscar Grant rebellions to Occupy and beyond into Black Lives Matter struggled together to understand the rupture. The attempt was not only to understand it but to widen it; to fracture a continuum completely. Pamphlets were written and circulated "in the heat of the moment." Several of these attempted to locate missed or lost opportunities, various failures, and raised questions of lost momentum.[66] Others reflected on the rupture through the lens of militant research, recounting lessons learned through mass struggle gleaned in the streets, relationships built, debates undertaken, intersubjective lessons internalized.[67]

Most agree that the rupture immediately produced a number of tools for analysis and struggle, as a range of local efforts seized, shared, circulated, and repurposed these tools as convivial tools—modified to regenerate community and advance possibilities for autonomy. Space was deliberately constructed as a site of knowledge production through the creation of "stationary drifts" and moving occupations, as grassroots tours of downtown San Francisco's centers of financial violence echoed across the Bay and its peripheries in community "walks" that traced policing, stalking, and shootings, exposing landscapes of state violence. Learning from the reclaiming of public space that was central to the rupture, organizers, including families targeted by violence who had joined the space of Fourteenth and Broadway, adapted blockade, occupation, encampment, and assembly as intertwined strategies for obstructing state functioning and capital flows and bringing diverse groups together from across regions. While in many instances, including in analyses of Occupy and spaces across the Left, assembly becomes overdetermined by decision-making, its real power is as a site of convergence and shared knowledge production. In Stockton, San Francisco, and San José, families and organizers recognized this and imported occupation and assembly into local parks and other public spaces but primarily highlighted the practice of convening, creating talking circles, and sharing, activating spaces where knowledges could be shared and new relations fostered and woven together. Across the Bay, a proliferation of re-territorializations was put into effect, often immediately on-site following police shootings, that served as spaces where details of violent attacks gave way to exchanges of knowledge about policing strategies directed at homes and neighborhoods. An entire range of documentation and monitoring of state violence came into being, learned through the collective experience at Fourteenth and Broadway. These documentation and sharing projects formed critical foundations for organizing around community safety and defense. Skill shares were arranged as the street medics of Occupy trained local groups, including People's Community Medics, to respond to not only tear gas but gunshot wounds, seizures, and heart attacks and to engage the community around health and safety concerns. These efforts refused to be contained or dismissed according to questions of scale, but rather intervened as kernels of possibility, a site for the circulation of subversive systems of information, disqualified secrets, and insurgent knowledges.

The encampments and the attention they refocused on social reproduction and care were critically refashioned into a series of convivial tools. In this context, strategic concepts were collectively developed as sites of knowledge production and praxis, among them "fierce care" as a site of community regeneration.[68] Theorized across numerous Uni-Tierra Califas spaces, fierce care offers a way for us to recognize and orient forms of militancy and resistance across the social factory, opening a way of seeing and engaging that extends beyond the "street" as the privileged, or most legible, site of rebellion and outrage. Beyond mutual aid and care work, fierce care orients both the struggles and the collective subject that emerges through shared acts with the claim that these are not distinct spheres. Rather, moments of resistances, or a prolonged insurgency organized as "fierce care," work alongside and in intimate learning with the struggles in the street. Fierce care advances a refusal to allow others to be abandoned or isolated when targeted by the state. It is a claim to a commitment to collective ways of being and a refutation of the imposition of the individual and the production of the individuated, individualized subject. It is a commitment to a "we."[69] This is the possibility that emerged, and continues to take shape, in the rupture made possible through the battle for Fourteenth and Broadway.

Part 2

CHAPTER 3

Derrick Gaines

Community Policing and Counter-Cartographies

On June 5, 2013, the one-year anniversary of the South San Francisco Police Department (SSFPD) shooting that took Derrick Gaines's life, his family returned to the Arco gas station parking lot where he had been shot the previous year to hold a space of vigil. This was part of a series of public vigils that the family and community organized in the months following the shooting of the fifteen-year-old South City youth.[1] Claiming the Arco parking lot, they grieved and marked their loss while remembering Gaines's life collectively in an open, public space. In response, the South San Francisco police deployed a SWAT team to surround the vigil's perimeter.

One year earlier, at 8:30 P.M. on the evening of June 5, 2012, Gaines had been hanging out with friends when they were approached and questioned by a police officer in the gas station parking lot. Gaines reportedly had difficulty maintaining sustained eye contact with the officer, and when questioned, he had backed away and turned to run, with some difficulty as he had a physical disability which impacted his movement. As Gaines turned, SSFPD Officer Joshua Cabillo hit him over the head with his service revolver, knocking him to the ground, and a brief scuffle ensued between the youth and the officer. A gun—antique and broken—fell out of Gaines's pants while he was sprawled on the ground. According to witnesses, while the gun was quite a distance from Gaines and not within "threatening" reach, Cabillo stood over Gaines, aimed his service weapon, and shot the fifteen-year-old point blank in the throat.

A paramedic qualified in CPR who witnessed the incident attempted to approach Gaines and offer critical life-saving support. Officer Cabillo refused to let the civilian near Gaines's body. After some time, Cabillo attempted to do the CPR himself. Gaines died shortly after arriving at the hospital.

According to Dolores Piper, Gaines's great-aunt and a critical person in his family support network, the gun that went skittering across the pavement was an "old, collector-type gun" that fifteen-year-old Gaines had likely been using as a prop for a rap video he had been making with his friends earlier that evening. Gaines and the friends he was with when the police officer approached them in the evening parking lot were all youth of color. They had reportedly been spending more time hanging out in the Arco parking lot because a city park nearby was closed.[2] In response to this closure, the youths had repurposed urban commercial space as a kind of commons, an act that exposed them to police intervention, justified on the grounds that their behavior looked suspicious.[3]

Immediately following the killing of Derrick Gaines, the SSFPD seized Gaines's cell phone. They raided Gaines's family's home and searched his room without a warrant, removing several items. Gaines's mother, Rachel Guido-Red, testified to the police actions following the killing: "They searched Derrick's room, and they searched the garage. They didn't find anything, but they didn't really say what they were looking for."[4] Police also interrogated several of Gaines's friends. In the weeks and months that followed, police monitored community gatherings and refused to make public their own investigative reports from the evening of the incident or share them with the family.

At a rally a few months after the killing of Gaines, one mother whose daughters had been friends with Gaines narrated her own community experiences with the SSFPD, including an incident where Officer Cabillo had entered her home and "had his gun held to [her] daughter's head for no reason," and another incident where SSFPD officers "entered her home with guns drawn," noting that as a result her daughters are now "scared of the police."[5] In the open space of a community gathering, an incident of violence when narrated and shared unearths other violences against the community.

In the police reports from the Arco incident, Gaines pulled a gun and aimed it at the officer. Both the police and the media framed Gaines as a "gang banger."[6] According to Dolores Piper, officers communicated to the family that "they are very involved with the kids in the local schools" and they know the kids that are "struggling."[7] The SSFP's gang response strategy focuses on youth, explicitly prioritizes public schools as sites of direct intervention, and assigns specific task forces to identify "gang members" and gather intelligence on neighborhood youth.

The police presence in public schools and in public spaces frequented by youth in relation and proximity to schools proliferates moments of contact between police and youth and increases the likelihood of criminal offenses by young people. Damien Sojoyner's work on the complex relation between prisons and schools situates these sites and practices as part of a longer continuum, with colonial roots in demarcating space where Black life is under constant supervision.[8] The SSFP officers conveyed that they knew Gaines and knew about "his problems," and were attempting to cast him in their discursive logic of an ever-present threat, narrating him through a "prose of counterinsurgency fully and decidedly constructed by the state."[9]

Witnesses on the scene at the Arco gas station and community members who knew Gaines classify the constructions by the police as untruthful. Contradicting police reports, those who witnessed the shooting deny that Gaines ever pulled a gun on the officer or that any gun was ever accessible to Gaines during the scuffle. Piper rejected the state's classification and refutes the notion that Gaines was struggling or "at risk." Against their narrative, she instead asserts that he was a sociable, smart young man who was invested in his studies, his friends and community, and passionate about his music and social justice—an assessment supported by Gaines's teachers and other community members.[10]

When the family and community resist these frames that the police and media attempt to impose, and if enough convincing or malleable fragments cannot be retrieved by police from a cell phone or a bedroom or a garage, or from the details solicited in invasive and traumatizing interrogations of family and friends to be spliced together into a compelling statement of criminality, the deadly misrecognition by the police must then be made plausible (and thus acceptable) by establishing the perceived threat posed by the youth, or by Black and Brown youth as an abstraction, a signifier for collective fear. The epistemological framework of security anchors the officer's act of violence as legitimate; the entirety of Black and Brown youth are potential gang-bangers, and the threat is everywhere. In this war zone, violent effects of misrecognition on the part of the state are preemptively legitimized through concepts and acronyms like "threat perception failure," which are meant to convey the sense of fear and urgency that produced the decisive act of violence by the police, however flawed. It is a concept deployed to protect the police.[11] In this frame, police violence is dislocated from the position of an act of violence; instead, it is a response, already justified, to a perceived threat. The focus shifts to the "threat" (ensconced in abstractions and fear) and the "perception," thus displacing the violent act from the center of the analysis of what happened.

The overall discursive framework anchored by the *dispositif*, security, and gang-banger nexus—organized through legislation, specialized police programs, federal gang-focused grants to local police departments, policy papers, media framing, racial discourse, sentencing enhancements for convictions, injunctions, and curfews, as well as by more generalized abstractions of fear, "threat," criminality, and so on—is in fact so effective that while accidents of misidentification and the subsequent deadly response provoke public outrage, they often fail to go much further than to elicit calls from the public for more training or specialized training, or policy changes; or else the incident, through a logic that protects the institution of the police, is ascribed to a "bad apple cop" who is prone to violence—regrettable but acceptable as collateral damage in a war against gangs and street violence.[12]

By August, less than three months after the killing of Gaines by Cabillo, San Mateo County District Attorney Steve Wagstaff condoned the department's use of lethal force as "tragic" but justified.[13] But through a deliberate and repeated act of vigil, the family and community initiated an ongoing space of encounter, carving an opening for the reiteration of witness statements and the production of community knowledge of Gaines as well as the officer who shot him and then refused to administer life-saving care—thus making visible that the violence took place in the absence of a threat. The violence exacted at the Arco station lays bare that beyond the spectacular policing on display at protests, forms of violent policing occur within the everyday and are integral to a larger policing project.

In convening repeatedly over time, the family and community graphed the space and act of vigil onto the parking lot, advancing a methodology for collective investigation and counter-mapping, and thus putting in motion a collective process that situates the officer's act as an exercise in terror directed at a community, a public execution, that took place in front of witnesses and community members and which was followed by an authoritative refusal to permit life-saving aid to a dying child. Such an act not only challenges the state's commitments to pacification through violence, it exposes the state's investment in controlling space and movement.[14] In the community's redrawn map, the shooting death of Derrick Gaines emerges as a critical exercise in counterinsurgency, namely, an act of sheer force and raw brutality exacted alongside saturation patrols and in the context of an ongoing accumulation of information across a community.[15] Through the process, a moment of extreme violence takes its position within a larger strategy of pacification discursively framed and imposed as security, as keeping the community safe.[16] A security landscape comes into focus where "community policing" stands in for counterinsurgency, explaining how the arrant violence and justified execution of a youth of color in the early June days of summer vacation becomes commonplace.

After years of supporting other families across the Bay Area and state and participating in shared spaces and hearing stories of other youth, largely from Black and Brown communities, who had been killed by police, Dolores Piper, who is white, would reflect at a gathering: "Before this occurred, I had no idea of the forces out there that Derrick was up against."[17]

Yet in confrontation with this violence, Dolores engaged—organizing with her family the space of vigil, connecting with other families, speaking with others in the community, narrating her own family's experience, and setting into motion a collective counter-mapping project from a position in South San Francisco, creating spaces of co-research and participating in a range of spaces across the Bay to understand the forces that stole Derrick's life.

Advancing an analysis is a political act. Raquel Gutiérrez Aguilar states that it is her goal "to identify and trace the components of a matrix to make it possible for us to analyze—desire and produce—social emancipation."[18] To analyze is to participate in a project of desiring and producing social emancipation; analysis is never an academic or isolated process of "knowing," but rather the practice of a collective subject imagining and generating its own emancipation and autonomy.

"War:police": The Emergence of Community Policing as a War on Youth and the Social Factory

The killing of Derrick Gaines exists in the context of a new era of warfare. Beginning in the early 1990s with his appointment as commissioner of the New York City Police Department by Mayor Rudolph Giuliani, William Bratton arose as emblematic of a new form of policing euphemized as "community policing," an approach that Alex Vitale and Brian Jordan Jefferson refer to as "command and control" policing based on its "intensive and invasive practices."[19] Rachel Herzing of Critical Resistance in Oakland situates "Bratton-style policing" as an approach "aimed at restoring public order by aggressively enforcing, through sweeps, ticketing, and arrest, minor quality of life infractions such as public drunkenness, littering, or begging."[20] Often referred to as "harassment policing," Christian Parenti narrates the shooting death of Abner Louima by New York police in Brooklyn in 1997 in order to expose brutality as an extension of Bratton's harassment policing.[21]

Building on President Lyndon Johnson's "war on crime" program and the establishment of the Law Enforcement Assistance Administration (LEAA) and its role in the rise of SWAT, as well as the rise of other paramilitary police formations in response primarily to domestic insurgency in the 1960s and '70s, in the early 1970s, Bratton began introducing paramilitary strategies and formations into community policing models, including the deployment of heavily armed teams to patrol specific neighborhoods.[22] Beginning with the Boston Transit Police, a critical aspect of Bratton's policing overhaul involved ramping up armaments and establishing a force that resembled and functioned in closer alignment with military operations.[23] This project continued over decades and became more expansive at critical moments, including Nixon's "war on drugs" campaign, declared in 1973.

"Bratton-style policing" targets specific activities and behaviors for intervention in the name of maintaining order, advancing a long-standing U.S. commitment to punitive population management.[24] Drawing on counterinsurgency tactics honed in reciprocal dynamism domestically and abroad, the community policing ushered in under Bratton is counterinsurgency woven together through a range of local, state, and federal agencies, both national and international, including through targeted trainings and consultancies.[25] Brutal and intrusive, decentralized and aggressive; proactive and punitive; rooted in "broken windows" theory and organized as "zero tolerance" and "quality of life," this emergent urban policing reflects a culmination of strategies that brings together harassment (including practices like "stop and frisk"), intelligence-gathering and the accumulation of information (including programs like Compstat, gang databases, and fusion centers), and increased community engagement (including foot patrols and specialized teams) to shape a neoliberal securitization directed at pacification.[26] Bratton's emergent policing strategy deliberately coupled street suppression with intelligence-gathering.[27]

Counterinsurgency scholar Laleh Khalili not only highlights the importance of information-gathering and cartography in the counterinsurgent project (noting that "in addition to mapping people, spaces are also mapped in counterinsurgencies"), but simultaneously draws attention to the imbricated imperative for the counterinsurgent to know the dynamic *relations* between people and space.²⁸

The central role of information-gathering, knowledge production, and cartography has deep roots in the colonial project across empires.²⁹ Across recurrent modalities of settler-colonial and colonial occupation, pacification strategies took the form of curfews and combined rules of association and rules of assembly, thus attempting to designate and control access to territory, and simultaneously attempting to police relations and restrict gatherings. Often discoursed as public safety or emergency measures, these restrictions were clearly aimed at incapacitating insurgency and were often accompanied by "shoot to kill" policies.³⁰ The restrictions and rules of assembly were woven into colonial policies to respond to slave rebellions while simultaneously criminalizing Black social life through, for example, colonial "anti-tumult ordinances" such as the one passed in Philadelphia in 1700 that restricted gatherings of four or more slaves unless they could prove "they were on their master's business."³¹

For Joseph Gallieni, a French military commander in France's African colonies in the late nineteenth century, "an officer who has successfully drawn an exact ethno-graphic map of the territory he commands . . . is close to achieving pacification, soon to be followed by the form of organization he judges most appropriate."³² Gallieni's legacy and counterinsurgency's lineage of colonial military knowledge and information-gathering imperatives was likewise manifested in the infamous Bureaux Arabes in French-occupied Algeria, an institution that can be assessed as an accumulating archive of colonial knowledge, a process of harassment and control, and a machine in the production of colonial subjectivities and desire.³³

Reflecting a similar investment in the study, surveillance, and accumulation of details on the relations, social life, and "culture" of the population as a critical targeted site of counterinsurgency, this mandate is likewise expressed through long-standing federal and cross-agency programs like COINTELPRO in the United States, as well as more recent approaches such as "social network analysis" or "human terrain systems," developed by the U.S. Army in 2005–06.³⁴ Jacob Kipp describes the focus of this program as analyzing "the social, ethnographic, cultural, economic, and political elements of the people among whom a force is operating . . . defined and characterized by sociocultural, anthropologic, and ethnographic data."[35]

For Subcomandante Marcos, "war imposes a new geography."[36] Concomitantly, Bratton-style policing is an approach that evolves with investments in mapping and databases, one grafted onto forms of domestic law-and-order policing already in use across departments, including a range of data-gathering, statistical crime mapping, and location-based approaches.[37] Pacification relies on this "precise ethnographic map."[38] With community policing models, policing increasingly becomes a dense site of knowledge production; as a police presence increases in particular neighborhoods and areas, officers are deliberately put into more direct and intimate contact with the rhythms and relations of everyday life, ensuring that everyday life itself is increasingly documented and monitored, that is, policed.

Under Bratton, intelligence-gathering rose to a new level and shaped the conditions of possibility for policing strategies aimed at the future. Coordinated through Compstat, intelligence gathering as deployed in Bratton-era policing reflects a means of both engaging with and mapping the community with an end goal of community policing. In its most immediate sense, Compstat is a statistical approach for reporting on "crime." As part of this project, officers monitor, document, classify, categorize, archive, and share information about the community being policed. Intelligence-gathering and documentation depend on and thus produce an increase in police contact. Situated within a larger framework of law-and-order policing, intelligence-gathering also generates "crime," since its mandate demands detailed documentation and results for a department's statistical analysis, purpose, and funding. While these results could be documented through arrests, they were also documented through killings.

Compstat not only organized (and created) "data" relative to people and populations, but when combined with "broken windows" policing and specialized patrol teams that target youth and gangs, it simultaneously manufactured criminal subjects, making it a primary crime-fighting technology in Bratton's arsenal. The power of Compstat's data-gathering and statistical technologies lies in the archive that it creates as well as the process it establishes. Bratton acknowledges that the primary effectiveness of Compstat is not achieved through the information that is gathered, organized, and stored (the monitoring of populations), but in the relations within the department that the routinized practice of gathering and reporting produces and proliferates. This includes the competitive but shared investment—across officers, teams, departments, and agencies at all levels—in helping to create a world where "crime" is stopped before it occurs. What Bratton was able to achieve with Compstat was a perpetually expanding policing logic, and a disciplinary space that would continue to produce officers who are trained to apply a police power addressed at a population even before crime happens.

With related programs like Neighborhood Watch that encouraged civilians to observe and report on each other in the name of "collective security," this monitoring spread beyond department meetings to shape and contaminate community relations, making the role of the police central to how a community reimagines its own safety in terms of an abstraction of security, and reorganizes itself in alignment with the social order of the police. In an era of cognitive capital, Compstat operates as a critical technology in the production and reproduction of policing (and capital) as a relation between the community and law enforcement agents and among members of the department and larger agencies. The result was that of "a vague and everywhere threat."[39] An undefined insurgency framed as "gang violence" and a larger landscape of unknown threats goad predictive policing models.[40]

Mapping populations is contingent on understanding the relations between people, families, groups, and communities in an attempt to make visible and "knowable" the web of relations that make survival, autonomy, care, resistance, and resilience possible. A complex operation of biopower aims at managing not only individuals as metonymic of larger populations, but more specifically, as a power aimed at managing the relations between and among populations. Critical to this functioning of power is the disruption of the relations (community bonds, networks of support, family relations, and other collective experiences) that resist a particular management operating in the service of the state and capital.

Police patrols and stops, together with investigations and various juridical spaces related to the courts, produce a context for the state to create its own maps of relationships, networks, and connections across a community or a neighborhood and across generations. In the state interrogations that transpire across the *dispositif* of "security," as in juridical spaces following arrests, for example, communities are archived in their relations to each other, the state, and to particular geographies. Each incident that the state frames as a crime produces witness statements, police reports, depositions, court testimonies, citations, and so on. Law enforcement repeatedly interrogates community members about how long they have known people, and in what capacity, often asking them to categorize and qualify the relationship for state records. They probe who travels and associates with whom. The work of police and lawyers links people with particular neighborhoods, intersections, and streets in the archives of the state.

The archives produced bear witness to tactics aimed at knowing and controlling populations through a combination of administrative processes and force or the threat of force. Technologies for the control and management of populations work in conjunction with large databases and are synchronized, including across prison walls, to classify "gang members," "special threat groups," and so on, cataloging information that can determine convictions and sentencing on the outside (including through "gang enhancement sentencing"). Inside of prisons, these technologies can determine who is forced into solitary confinement, administrative segregation, and enhanced sentencing. From these different points, the knowledge produced is easily activated to divide, isolate, and manage populations. The interrogations also provide traction and a mass of "data" that allows departments to further solidify compelling arguments for the presence of gangs and justify an arsenal of methods to fight these threats. The information gathered through these endless interrogations of the state against the community can be organized as data to provoke the "need" for new technologies to survey, classify, and accumulate information about populations. This in turn fuels Silicon Valley's digital tech development of surveillance and the need for organizational strategies, for example gang databases, and accumulation and sharing strategies, as evidenced through the rise in federal fusion centers.[41]

In addressing the binary inherent in an approach that is "premised on society being divided into two groups, the 'orderly' upstanding, law-abiding citizen and the 'disorderly' criminal-in-the-making," INCITE! Women of Color Against Violence also point to the role of the policing power in producing subjects and populations.[42] Once in existence, the binary construct is used to justify policies that treat the disorderly person as one who "needs to be policed, surveyed, watched, relocated, controlled."[43] "Bratton-style policing" produces subjects and populations through policing and acts of violence as an intimate violation aimed at "sites" of intervention.

For the execution of Derrick Gaines to be acceptable for the majority of residents in South City, its target had to be established for the greater public as the dangerous gang member that the police, through its specialized units, seeks to identify, reprimand, and remove from the neighborhood as part of its regular duties. Criminalization and racialization intersect in a policing apparatus/strategy designed to produce new subjectivities targeted by policies and discourses of "security."

Buttressed by President Clinton's Violent Crime Control and Law Enforcement Act in 1994, which funneled billions in federal funds toward policing and prisons, including funding to Community Oriented Policing Services (COPS) to hire and deploy an additional 100,000 officers on the streets, Bratton-style policing spread across departments and agencies through trainings, transfers of officers, and consultancies, and was adapted and innovated at the local level both nationally and globally. In the new conjuncture of neoliberal securitization shaped by "Bratton-style policing," the intensification of "cops on the street" materialized not only in the heightened presence of officers in certain neighborhoods, but in the creation of new units organized into specialized teams structured as paramilitary units. Beginning in the 1980s and escalating through the 1990s, Alex Vitale notes that "by 2003, there were estimated to be 360 such units, the vast majority of which had been in place for less than ten years."[44] Federal task forces aimed at gangs and "safe streets" paralleled and accompanied the creation of these teams across local police departments.[45] Teams were then deployed according to particular areas based on patterns of crime and predictions of future crimes, ensuring that Black and Brown neighborhoods that were already heavily policed and monitored were subject to "saturation patrols" especially directed at spaces of community life and circulation. In short, intelligence-gathering merged with "placed-based" policing and an increased police presence on the street, often advanced by paramilitary-style units or "teams" designated to patrol specific neighborhoods. Violence followed in the wake of the patrols.

Notoriously, under quality of life and community policing approaches, crime rates dropped while brutality escalated. In the case of Oakland, for example, the passage of Measure Y in 2004, also known as the Violence Prevention and Public Safety Act, directed funding generated from property and parking taxes to increased police resources and community-based violence prevention programs. The advance of Measure Y-funded programs paralleled a rise in officer-involved shootings. Within a year of the passage of Measure Y, the Oakland Police Department (OPD) deployed "crime reduction teams" (CRTs) as part of a strategy for policing Oakland, which also included "hot spot policing" targeting particular areas for denser patrols and arrests. In Oakland, as across other departments, the CRTs were organized as aggressive units. Supervisors in charge of the units were known for their violence and brutality in the community and continued killing as part of the CRTs.[46] Similar units were developed as part of the operations divisions of most police departments across the state and nation. In other cities, SWAT teams had already been converted into aggressive, brutal crime-fighting units, as with Fresno's Violent Crime Suppression Unit in 1994.[47] The rise of these aggressive units and multi-agency paramilitary units ran parallel with a rise in SWAT paramilitary raids.[48]

Dolores Piper made a note of the SSFPD policing formation and their practices within the community. In her observations and analysis, "Officer Cabillo was part of a special Neighborhood Response Team (a police unit aimed at combating gang violence in the neighborhood), which swings into high gear when school is out."[49]

Part of the SSFPD's Operations Division, the Neighborhood Response Team (NRT) is the department's gang unit.[50] The SSFPD frames the NRT as "a unique unit . . . created to build and maintain effective communication between the Police Department and members of the community," with the goal of increasing safety in the community through an emphasis on "diligent gang suppression and proactive law enforcement activities." Central to this mission are "community outreach and a 'zero tolerance' policy toward gang activity." According to the SSFPD, NRT officers "strive to create positive relationships with members of the community by conducting foot patrols in the residential areas, contacting business owners and employees, facilitating community meetings, and initiating positive interactions with the children in our neighborhoods."[51]

The NRT in South City is the product of an investment in community policing in the new era of warfare ushered in by Bratton: it exists as a zero-tolerance approach to gang suppression and is a key component of the city's community policing strategy. The NRT explicitly operates for the purpose of gathering information on suspected gang activity, and identifying gang members and at-risk youth. Working within public schools and in conjunction with the larger county-level Gang Intelligence Unit, officers on the NRT make contact with juveniles "either on the street or in the schools."[52] The department also holds community meetings to assess and share with the public the threat of gang activity and to solicit complicity for its street suppression initiative. Community meetings play a critical role in community policing approaches; in appearance, these community meetings seem to be a space for dialogue and exchange between police and community, seeking collaborative solutions to issues of shared concern. These spaces are not that. The appearance of updating and listening on the part of the police is a site of placation and pacification, surveillance and scrutiny, and is simultaneously an avenue for communicating threat and fear in order to justify further funding and ongoing intervention.[53]

Within a little over a year of its inception in South San Francisco, the Neighborhood Response Team had made roughly 300 arrests.[54] The NRT began in early 2011 with two years of seed money funding. That funding was set to run out by the end of 2012, the year Gaines was killed. In the logic of seed-funded initiatives, such a project that materialized through securities investment must find funding elsewhere to continue past its initial funding period. Based on this logic, seed-funded projects often must justify their impact and demonstrate consumer support to qualify for and receive extended funding. Thus, they are also generally positioned in competition with other projects for funding. In the case of the NRT, a few months before the killing of Derrick Gaines, a public poll was circulated in a local paper to draw attention (and elicit support), asking the community to decide whether the NRT served a more important function than other community-based programs offered through the police department, including the Gang Resistance Education and Training Program. In its opening argument, the poll offered the statement that violent crime and vandalism had decreased significantly in the time frame since the SSFPD instituted the NRT.[55]

On May 4, 2012, one month prior to the killing of Gaines, the NRT conducted a massive "gang sweep," making nineteen arrests. In addition to large-scale gang suppression operations, the four-person NRT, led by Sergeant Danny Gill, "cruised" neighborhoods, stopping and questioning young people that they didn't "recognize," taking notes and photographing them.[56] A few months prior during a "ride along" with ABC news staff, Sgt. Gill offered an interpretation of gunshots that had echoed through the night as they rode through "gang turf": "It could have been the gangsters letting us know they know we're here or a warning, 'this is our turf, not yours,'" Gill said.[57] Through practices like "ride alongs" with police units, the mainstream media affirms the ongoing scale of the "gang problem," rehearsing the conditions of continuous violence. Police narratives of battles to reclaim territories captured by gangs circulate across the evening news.

Population and Territory: Spaces of Life

Beginning in the 1980s, an intricate combination of legislation unfolded in California at the intersection of population and territory in coincidence with new policing approaches and carceral strategies and began to form a dense web of entanglements. Laws like the Street Terrorism Enforcement and Prevention Act (STEP Act) of 1988 laid the groundwork for gang criminalization and sentencing enhancements related to "gang activity." California's Proposition 184 (1994), the notorious "Three Strikes" law, ensured draconian sentencing and fueled carceral expansion as part of President Clinton's Violent Crime Control bill, while Proposition 21 (2000) carved out provisions for increased sentencing and penalties for youth, including enhanced sentences for gang-related activities, as well as the death penalty for "gang-related" murders, and also initiated life without parole (LWOP) sentencing. These propositions emerged alongside initiatives aimed at undocumented populations, for example Proposition 187, and as legislative acts occurring in the wake of the 1992 LA rebellion.

In conjunction with this legislation, the Violence Prevention and Public Safety Act (Measure Y; 2004) emphasized securing "crime-ridden" neighborhoods by increasing the number of "cops on the street" in tandem with developing more violence prevention programs. Like the STEP Act and Propositions 184 and 21, Measure Y was aimed primarily at Black and Brown youth. But while the previous legislation primarily addressed sentencing enhancements, Measure Y marked another decisive gesture to increase the presence of police in the community. Each of these legislative acts can be understood in what Laleh Khalili terms "liberal counterinsurgency"—in this case, where the legislative, juridical, and carceral institutions are graphed onto streets and the flows of the inhabitants, making justifiable any violence that the police exert there. The public is complicit in this; they have authorized this violence through the democratic system.

For legislation like the STEP Act, Propositions 184 and 21, and Measure Y to pass, the public has to believe that the streets are dangerous and that violent criminals roam unchecked. The deployment of police patrols, sweeps, and a range of operations is escalated in Black and Brown neighborhoods as these patrols and stops extend into other coded urban spaces in order to maintain restrictions on space. These deployments operate against a circulating discursive backdrop of "gang-bangers" and "superpredator" youth (and other "illegalities" of being); the presence of the police themselves communicates that there is a constant threat, and simultaneously that the police are there to protect the public. Buttressing the increased police presence on the street, court hearings and trials provide opportunities to secure convictions, affirming the need for an expansive prison system while offering opportunities for the dominant media to further construct dangerous criminal subjects, thus justifying the need for more law enforcement. The escalating arrests that result from harassment policing and a stated commitment to "safe streets," together with the network of anti-gang laws and enhancements, direct more punitive measures at a community and further fuel an expansive carceral regime that dominates the present.

This strategy of expulsion to remove threats from the street repeatedly interrupts a community's efforts to reproduce itself. Proliferating from these arrests, if a key wage earner is incarcerated or killed, their family can quickly lose a home, rental unit, and transportation, as well as access to that person's wages. As a strategy of crime control, this form of policing destabilizes families and communities and disrupts social reproduction networks and diffuse relations of care. The accompanying legislation frames the attack on the social factory.

Undergirding the logic and strategy of community policing in a neoliberal context, place-based policing coincides with securitization, privatization, and strategies of enclosure and is critical to reproducing racial regimes that are conducive to capital and its "order of accumulation."[58] Like *"quadrillage* and *ratissage"* (literally, a strategy of "divide and rake" developed as part of the French occupation of Algeria) and other colonial pacification strategies aimed at the management of populations in relation to territory, "Bratton-style policing" involves methods that "under the guise of community policing . . . break up neighborhoods into militarized police zones, often alienating and angering community members rather than engendering hope or safety."[59] This has become a hallmark of the neoliberal security state: space is organized geographically through a series of borders and demarcations manufactured and maintained through forms of differential policing.[60]

The new war "from above" is one that "imposes a new geography"; it is an "attacking force [that] destroys and depopulates its own territory . . . and reconstructs and reorders it according to its plan for conquest or reconquest."[61] The violence at the Arco gas station that took Derrick Gaines's life, and the SWAT perimeter a year later that attempted to contain a community organized to remember and refuse, occurred at the intersection of four central vectors that reflect this "war from above": (1) placed-based strategies of exclusion/expulsion and quarantine that both discipline and produce subjects and discursively frame subjects and territory in co-constitutive relation, for example, "gangs" and "turf"; (2) harassment policing accompanied by brutal and punitive violence exercised through paramilitary display and spectacle; (3) intelligence-gathering and mapping organized around the production of knowledge/epistemologies of security and shaping new forms of policing (and governance), including "predictive policing"; and (4) counterinsurgency approaches as "community policing" where police actively engage the community through pacification-as-war.

Such approaches in the present occur within a logic of "border regimes," in the words of Maribel Casas-Cortes, that "attempt to distinguish and separate populations according to mobility rights," and identify those that need to be contained or trapped in space.[62] Such approaches do not only restrict; they impose biopolitical hierarchies (as necropolitical racial regimes) that are communicated and circulated across communities. They form dense nodes of power/knowledge for the proliferation of state and policy praxis.[63] This is also a moment where biopolitical power operates concurrently with sovereign power, or the right to kill. In the relation between territory and populations in systems of control, security strategies are advanced to separate the wealthy from the disenfranchised, the white from the not-white, the propertied from the precariat, and so on. Gated communities, guarded neighborhoods and properties, and the less visible restrictions around "public" spaces like upscale shopping districts and "community gardens" are marked biopolitically.[64]

An analysis of these areas of urban space contrasted with areas that are heavily surveilled, cordoned off, and otherwise "enclosed" offers a map of the neoliberal security state and territories organized as enclave economies. This map is shaped by intersecting strategies of policing that are designed to respond to and produce uneven development, violence, and populations marked as disposable.[65] Often, specialized territories like those carved out for gang injunctions are established to manage adjacent areas and territorial proximities in an effort to establish racial boundaries to contain Black and Brown communities.[66] Or, the gang injunction can expose a city's longer development trajectory, manufacturing or exacerbating instability in particular neighborhoods as a strategy of dispossession and reorganization—one conducive to manipulating property values and real estate financialization along the ever-shifting borders of the enclave. These spaces simultaneously reveal and enforce what Sandro Mezzadra and Brett Neilson call "differential citizenship" where some bodies move with ease, while others are marked for interruption, arrest, containment, and expulsion.[67] In the words of the Zapatistas, *Now is the time in which, when the one from below asks why he is being attacked, the answer from the one above is: "for being who you are."*[68]

Space is produced as a site of quarantine and restriction at the same time that subjects, including "gangs," are produced in relation to space through policing. These are sites of value production and extraction that perpetuate a demand for greater securitization, and more police and policing.[69] But within this, sites emerge that can be seized in the service of a new counter-cartography, one that rebukes the security regime and reflects a community's active engagement in the production of urban space.

Operative Maps and Counter-Cartography: Remapping as a Convivial Tool

The vigil organized to remember Derrick Gaines was not a one-time event. It was, for example, as much protest as vigil, a critical gesture of reconnaissance. And even as an "event" it occurred as a repetition, a sequence reestablished yearly as an anniversary, a celebration of life, a condemnation, and together with a number of rallies and speak-outs, as a site of justice imagined and enacted by the community. It serves as a space for family and community to refuse a number of impositions—the narrative frames advanced by the police, the media, the District Attorney's Office with its reports justifying each shooting, and the entire apparatus and discursive regime of criminality aimed not only at Derrick but at the larger community. The vigil opens space for an alternate sequence of events, connections, and meanings to take shape, challenging the rubric of securitization that attempts to organize life. The inquiry "from below" returns to the "scene of the crime" and maps the possibility of something else unfolding. Refutation and inquiry surface as the first acts in the emergence of an autonomous justice.

These refusals reverberate out from the act of vigil itself; the vigil reflects a multiplicity of statements, acts, questions. The vigil manifests as a response to rage and grief. It is a deliberate and collective assertion against erasure: first as "cover-up" through the frame advanced by the state, and in a larger sense against oblivion—of an individual life and also of a community's shared and multiple experience of securitization and violence. The vigil as a site of knowledge production disrupts the knowledge production of the state.

Susanna Draper draws on the Combahee River Collective to analyze the International Women's Strike on March 8, 2017, as "opening up multiple forms of memory from which to narrate and reflect on an action-process."[70] In the work of Draper and others theorizing the feminist strike, the strike as action-process makes possible a collective and local mapping of precaritization and neoliberalism. Here, the vigil is read alongside recent work emerging from feminist struggles, particularly across Latin America, to situate "the feminist strike" not as a single event, but as ongoing and situated within a process. Liz Mason-Deese notes that the feminist strike and other recent innovations in the feminist movement "point to a feminist methodology that starts from mapping specific experiences of violence and exploitation and connecting them through practices of situated assemblies and coordinating networks."[71] Drawing on these analyses, the vigil is a form of struggle that makes possible a similar mapping of neoliberalism and its apportionment of vulnerability and violence. The vigil brings into focus the precaritization of life and a securitization organized through criminalization, a graph of the necropolitical racial regime.

The vigil is at the same time a deliberate act and an open question; it is the action-process that opens a space and makes the counter-cartography possible. It carves out the space for a community to speak of and assess the ways that they have been targeted and is a critical, material space of investigation in the search for answers following a deadly act of violence. In this way, the vigil can also be understood as an act of "fierce care" and as a convivial tool.[72] As a deliberate strategy of reclaiming space and resisting erasure, the community initiates and advances a collective process of investigation and inquiry, graphing memory onto space. This shared process of mourning and knowledge production stimulates the emergence of a collective subject. It marks the practice of a community organized around its own investigation and knowledge production, its own assertion of a justice claimed by the community in refusal of the state's terms. Such counter-mapping reclaims the territory, refuses erasure and oblivion, and is critical to a community's efforts to repulse securitization, and reclaim safety on its own terms. This reclaiming does not share tendencies or modalities of reconquering, but instead serves to pose a question, to stake a claim against the state; it is an active act in the reproduction of space that is critical to how a community experiences and remembers space. For Katherine McKittrick and Clyde Woods, this is the work of Black geographies: "Black geographies disclose how the racialized production of space is made possible in the explicit demarcations of the spaces of *les damnés* as invisible/forgettable at the same time as the invisible/forgettable is producing space—always, and in all sorts of ways."[73]

As a key space in a community's grassroots investigations, the vigil surfaces and exposes further details about officers and policing strategies, making observable particular tactics and strategies of the state as well as discourses that articulate media, policy, and other mainstream institutions. In the case of Derrick Gaines, the family and organized community leveraged the space of vigil to draw attention to and make intelligible a nexus of operations in order to highlight a department's priorities, including police efforts to secure additional funding and make contact with youth. The families' questions about why and when and how violence was directed at their family member invite a broader view of the timing, locations, and occurrence of police operations in their communities. In this way, the vigil can be situated alongside the *escrache* as a collective praxis of knowledge production, autonomous justice, space of encounter, strategy of assembly, direct action, and ritual/celebration.[74] In fact, the anniversary vigil for Derrick Gaines clearly forced the state to respond to the community's assertion and claim to memory and justice, drawing out a SWAT operation in an attempt to contain and reclaim the space.

Nicholas Mirzoeff theorizes a recent shift in counterinsurgency warfare where information-gathering becomes central to the production of new forms of visuality, where militarization involves total surveillance and air strikes from above, but more importantly where the battlefield and modes of war are organized through "the commander's view" and the counterinsurgent's ability to "enter the map" of the targeted territory based on a full knowledge of the visual graph. This echoes Mark Neocleous's theory of air power as policing power that describes the operations of the police, similar to Subcomandante Marcos, as "a war from above."[75] For Rita Segato, the current moment reflects a change in the territorial paradigm, as new wars seek to control and impose a specific experience of territory, emerging as war on women and feminized bodies.[76] In a U.S. context, this war from above is dependent on information-gathering to produce securitized landscapes; it manages populations through acts of violence and also through forms of displacement, ongoing and new dispossessions, and the constant reorganization of populations and their relations to territory. To effect this ongoing reorganization, it is critical to know and to disrupt a community's habits and rhythms of everyday life.

For Javier Toret and Nicolás Sguiglia in "Cartography and War Machines," "cartography [is] understood as an abstract prototype for the analysis of a problem in map form," where "making a cartography of an Other-territory"—a border zone of high strategic importance co-inhabited by social processes of great intensity and violence—"become[s] a necessary tool to orient ourselves and practices/praxis."[77] Cartography is a tool that provides a way "to identify the hot spots of contemporary conflict, its dynamics and actors, its movement and those trajectories that go from temporary uneasiness to the desire of building an alternative to one's own situation."[78] Similarly, Marta Molina describes research projects pursued in neighborhoods and "operative maps" in her discussion of worker's inquiry and co-research as a critical component of resistance and struggle.[79]

Against a moment of incredible violence against a youth of color exploding in a banal commercial space, the family and community of Derrick Gaines with Dolores Piper at the center return to seize space as a "space of study" and to construct, in Molina's terms, an "operative map" or temporary autonomous zone of knowledge production.[80] Critically, their process of collective cartography makes visible a geography organized through a "militarization of space," drawing attention to the rhythms of policing that ramp up at the close of the school year and target youth, exposing the mundane spaces where "the war has entered the city."[81] Their map traces the function and mission of the Neighborhood Response Team as a specialized unit rooted in a "zero tolerance" policy towards "gang activity" that applies a persistent surveillance across targeted neighborhoods, endlessly augmenting its databases as it cruises, questions, documents, and catalogues the lives, movements, and relations that exist there. Their map exposed NRT Officer Cabillo, who racially profiled Gaines through both "stop and frisk" and "hot spot" approaches and then took his life. The operative map marks the attacks on the family that took place in public, it marks the raid on the family home following the shooting, and the invasion of other homes across the community by the SSFPD over time. It records both the suppression of information related to the incident and the circulation of disinformation and misinformation about Derrick and the incident after the shooting. It becomes a map for understanding and conveying the manufacturing of criminality. It also is a map of state responses: the

SWAT unit that surrounded the community and space of vigil a year later, as well as the civil suit that exonerated the police department.

Through their actions and with Dolores Piper at the center, the family and community forge a convivial tool for collectively bearing witness; opening space for other community members to place on a shared plane similar stories of invasion and violent officers; archiving community-based knowledges; and analyzing policing so as to help a community advance its own safety by naming what threatens it.[82] As a convivial tool, their operative map is a temporary autonomous zone of knowledge production, a form of inquiry as re-territorialization, or a re-signifying of territory that makes possible a repository as "an inventory of knowledges" through a cartographic representation of the violence that besieges a community even as that violence is labeled something else by the state. The map reflects a critical praxis of counter-cartography advanced as communities reclaim and redefine their living landscape, and is a critical tool in an emergent claim to community safety. It is at the same time an act of re-subjectivation, both of the community's dead and through the collective commitment and practice of those involved.[83] However temporary the vigil's occupation of the Arco parking lot may be, it carves an opening for an imagination of another politics. As action-process, the vigil disrupts commercial flows at the same time that it reignites collective memory, opening a front in the war against oblivion, a war that relies on deracination, the making and remaking of territories and the reorganization of populations. Each cartographic act resists this; it is also a moment of sinew, an intersubjective practice against forgetting.

With each act, however ephemeral, including the act of collectively reclaiming the Arco parking lot, a counter-cartography is mobilized against the territorial assertion advanced by the state as violence and then securitization.

Remapping and the Social Factory

The history and present of racial patriarchal capitalism can be read through the violence that demarcates and violates the public and private spheres. For Rita Laura Segato, "the history and constitution of the public sphere participates in and is intertwined with the history of patriarchy and its structural mutation beginning with the modern colonial capture of the village world. Thus understood, the history of the public sphere or state sphere is nothing less than the history of gender."[84] Maria Serrano and Silvia López write: "the space we live in is something intimate which constitutes our subjectivities at the same time that urban space—the streets, the squares—are 'the public' par excellence, precisely that which is recognized as political."[85]

Alongside Segato's discussion of patriarchy and public space, Saidiya Hartman situates the racialization and criminalization of private space through a discussion of Black homes through the assessment of the state: "For state authorities, black homes were disorderly houses as they were marked by the taint of promiscuity, pathology, and illegality, sheltering nameless children and strangers, nurturing intimacy outside the bounds of the law, not organized by the sexual dyad, and not ruled by the father; and producing criminals, not citizens." Hartman concludes: "The domestic was the locus of danger; it threatened social reproduction rather than ensured it."[86]

The police shooting of Derrick Gaines was also an attack on the home. Critically, without a direct experience of the ongoing harassment policing and directed state violence over time that Black, Brown, and Indigenous communities face on a regular basis, Piper brought this violence into full public view and refused to see it as an aberration or an instance of mistaken identity. By organizing the family's rage and grief into an interrogation of violence, she made visible a continuity of policing from home to street in the South City enclave—a policing that is at once everywhere, and one that, directed at Black and Brown lives, homes, schools, and communities, nullifies the perceived boundary between private and public.

Returning to the theorization and practice of the International Women's Strike that emerged across the Global South to confront a myriad of capitalist violences, the strike opened and reflected a process that makes visible forms of violence and struggles around social reproduction, organized through both direct forms of state violence and informalized war. For Draper, "[the strike] . . . uncovers a multiplicity of processes that are connected to the everyday economy, forms of violence, and the struggles that condense the factory of social reproduction itself."[87] Reading the vigil following an act of state violence alongside the strike as forms of struggle and as action-processes, the deadly attack aimed at Derrick Gaines exposes connections between counterinsurgency and social reproduction, or the war on the social factory.

Following the police killing of Derrick Gaines and the community's act of vigil, a space of inquiry was opened where stories could be shared and woven to produce a new meaning and reflect the community's struggles back to itself in a collective process. The operative map they were able to produce with the Arco parking lot at its center revealed forms of policing, including information-gathering and police investigation strategies, that connect streets to spaces of the daily reproduction of life. Their map makes visible that school routes and adjacent spaces utilized by youth, as well as youth relations among themselves and the community, are connected to "at-risk" homes. Information-gathering as central to community policing fabricates and "predicts" young "criminals" and, with the same brush, fabricates the degenerate home, a projection and prediction that produces the home as the site where young people's "struggles" and "troubles" and the concomitant risks that the youth pose are fostered and fomented.

The vigil following the killing of Derrick opened a space that exposed how community policing approaches crossed over into the home as an invasion/interrogation following the killing. It also revealed that the policing that occurs on the street directed at particular communities is already conceived as intimate, personal, transgressive of boundaries; it makes continuous the experience of policing across the private and public spheres. Dolores Piper has repeatedly and widely acknowledged that her experience with police is different based on the position she occupies as someone who is a white woman with a certain level of social and economic stability and access in South City. However, the violence that targeted Derrick targeted him as Black, even though the home where Derrick resided with his great-aunt and to which the police returned as a site of invasion is not located within a circulation of Black or Brown community life regularly targeted by state violence. Piper speaks to an experience that reflects her knowledge of homes marked by whiteness, citizenship, and property ownership where policing as power and praxis affirms the boundaries of the front doorstep, the threshold, the family, the car. In so doing, she also affirms strategies of differential policing, acknowledging the experiences of other communities as often hidden or masked among some spaces across the enclave.[88] Through the re-territorialization of the vigil, the family and community were further able to produce and expose the second or follow-up suppression/pacification strategy—the deployment of the SWAT team to secure the perimeter of a community gathered to mourn in public, to interrupt and contain the intimate, collective act of mourning.

Mark Neocleous reminds us that police power is "creative and productive."[89] A focus on information-gathering that drives harassment policing not only polices "existent" subjects, it seeks to continuously reproduce new, mostly criminalized and pathologized subjects through its engagement with the population at a multiplicity of points.[90] As a critical aspect of this imperative, securitization organizes and reorganizes the necropolitical racial regime to carve out populations, or sections of a population, as targeted for intervention and discipline. For these populations—Black, Brown, and Indigenous communities in the United States in this case—policing abrogates the boundary between public and private, between street and home. While on the other side, in white communities, policing materializes through its protection of that same boundary that it nullified elsewhere.

In short, some homes are raided while others are guarded. In the differential policing approach that is community policing, some homes exist as a target of invasion that includes everything from the sidewalk to the living room, while for others the boundary that marks out the private realm is respected (and reproduced) as part of the reproduction of a stable, productive family unit organized as the domestic/private. Policing and the social factory reproduce a democratic despotism that is necessary for capital accumulation.[91]

Here the social factory, as a site of reproduction and as a site of the production of value, is critical to understanding policing in the present as war. The execution that took the life of Derrick Gaines simultaneously was the act that rendered his home violable for invasion, in the form of an investigation, one where "the police searched everywhere but found nothing" and at the same time "didn't say what they were looking for." Community policing, as order-based policing, manifests as an attack on the social factory in that it continuously makes permeable the line that is crossed by invasion, repeatedly voiding the line between public and private that organizes civil society (a society that is white and organized around private property, including the "property" of whiteness) through the constant threat of invasion.

Yet these invasions of Black, Brown, and Indigenous spaces are unremarkable in the eyes of the state and its rightful citizens. They are not only normalized as a logical strategy and outcome of policing, but are continuously manufactured as necessary. In the securitized logic of the state, spaces of Black and Brown life, home, and community are open to scrutiny and invasion because they are always identified as open to intervention and constant surveillance.[92] In this policing approach, spaces of social reproduction, from the home to the sidewalk to the parking lot repurposed as an after-school hang out, are rendered constantly violable, open to interruption.

Fred Moten situates "broken windows policing" within a genealogy of racial violence as an "extension of lynch law."[93] Relying on the theory of "broken windows," policing strategies attempt to circumnavigate questions of racialized harassment and targeted racial violence by seemingly directing policing practices at property. At the same time, policing power articulates access to space and circumnavigates due process. Black, Brown, and Indigenous life, and death, are offered up for public consumption. Policing practices that target Black and Brown communities attempt to impose an order where life, and its unfolding across a myriad of spaces, is produced and maintained as a site for humiliation, discipline, and terror. Policing constantly reproduces and maintains a racial regime.

For Saidiya Hartman, "intimate life unfolds on the street"—the street, the alley, the tenement hallway are all spaces where Black social life transpires through a number of occupations, as spaces of assembly.[94] With a strategy of policing that is directed at spaces where intimate "private" life has entered the public, Black and Brown social life—in this case, a cluster of young boys of color hanging out in June after shooting a music video—is policed in a way that is intimate and deployed as a form of interruption. As a form of warfare, this kind of policing—physically proximate and exercised as violation, engaging and humiliating—is continuous across the boundaries of "public" and "private." The Black home as a site of social reproduction and community is simultaneously a site of biopolitical surveillance and is targeted for constant reorganization.[95]

Community policing and an investment in gang suppression provide a prominent strategy for policing the social factory. They are a way to interrupt life on the street through interrogation and detention and a way to enter the home and disrupt its relations and rhythms, while at the same time they construct a space of everyday life open to policing as continuous from home to the streets, and expanding into racialized geographies outside the home. Community policing did not only establish an approach to invade the home (Black and Brown homes) in the name of "community"; it pursued the inverse: it further externalized social reproduction by targeting the relations and networks of shared survival and care that exist outside the home, as part of home, extracting value across a continuum.

In seeking to establish the home and family unit as a critical component in the construction of a racial regime, policing aimed its strategies at all spaces of collective life. It extended its attack on the social factory to the networks and relations that make subsistence possible, seeking to reorganize those relations into its own order. Working in conjunction with relations of capital, property, and enclave, policing organized as counterinsurgent warfare forces a policing of Black and Brown social life into the streets in order to police the intimacy of this social life publicly. It invades the private sphere to demonstrate that there is no escape from this total war; the war is everywhere, and it is a war against social reproduction. This is also the inquiry and the struggle that mothers, grandmothers, great-aunts, and other family members are engaging in the streets and when they strategically reclaim public space as a collective response to violence. As "open spaces of encounter," these spaces can be seen as both an effect and strategy of multiple players to negotiate this externalization at the intersection of capital's crisis and the policing of youth of color and space.

Every year since the killing of Derrick Gaines, the family returns to mourn and remember; in the space of the Arco gas station on a June evening, the community makes explicit the violence that targets it unevenly and publicly, and stands in resistance against this. They claim and catalyze a new geography.

CHAPTER 4

Kayla Moore
Gaia, *Escraches*, and Direct Action

On April 17, 2013, on a bright afternoon, a colorful gathering commenced outside the entrance of the Gaia Building in Berkeley. It spilled over the sidewalk as residents left the building and joined or passed through the crowd. A large purple cloth lettered, "Happy Birthday Kayla" was stretched above a portable speaker where family and friends stood up to read poems and share remembered moments. In between, some Lady Gaga and Michael Jackson music set the beat as large chocolate cupcakes with multicolored sprinkles were passed through the crowd. On another hand-painted cloth, "Justice for Kayla Moore" reminded those gathered of the ongoing struggle of people refusing to forget. Mounted on an easel draped in flowers and a sparkling cloth was a blown-up glossy photo where a beaming, light-skinned Black woman held a baby and a cell phone, cradling both and smiling at the camera.

Around the perimeter of the gathering that had spread to take up the entire street at the side entrance to Jupiter's Bar in Berkeley—a birthday party which kept growing—people handed out leaflets as the crowd grew. Within this space, the questions emerged and circulated: "Where's the police report?" "Where's the coroner's report?" "What happened to Kayla Moore?"

Kayla Moore was a transgender woman of color living with a dual diagnosis of schizophrenia and a series of practices involving prescription and non-prescription drugs through which she managed this orientation to the world, together with the steadfast care of her family and friends.[1] On the evening of February 12, 2013, she'd had an argument with her girlfriend Angel, was talking a lot about dinosaurs, and was sitting in her Berkeley apartment with two other familiar people present with her, her friend and a state-approved caretaker who was making her food and fixing her hair as she began to calm down. This mid-February evening, Kayla was approaching her forty-second birthday, and was in a state of confusion which those around her, both family and friends who loved her and the state agencies who knew her, were familiar. She was wearing, as she usually did, a bright flowing muumuu that covered her 300-pound frame.

What happened next and how it unfolded deserves attention. In response to a crisis call placed by her caretaker, six Berkeley Police Department (BPD) officers arrived at Kayla's residence and knocked at the door. Police knew they were responding to a "possible 5150": this was police code for an involuntary psychiatric hold, and indicated that the subject of the call might be experiencing some of form of mental instability that the police might regard as grounds for that person's being committed on psychiatric grounds to a local facility. Police had been to Kayla's home on similar mental health calls in the past. Had it been within normal working hours, a Mobile Crisis Unit would have also been deployed, but the hours of operation for the Berkeley Mobile Crisis Team on that day were 11:30 A.M. to 10:00 P.M., and the crisis call came in outside of these hours at approximately 11:48 P.M., thus ensuring that the first responders who arrived were police.[2] The caretaker came out and gave the police the key. Kayla was not violent, disturbing the peace in any way, or even interacting with anyone outside of her Gaia apartment.

From there, six officers under the command of Officer Gwendolyn Brown entered Kayla's home, ordered her caretaker back out, and removed and then arrested the other friend present after running a check and finding that he allegedly had an outstanding warrant. Without the authority of a warrant and under no threat, BPD Officer Brown made the decision, despite Kayla's clearly agitated state, to arrest Kayla and forcefully remove her from her home. That process did not proceed without resistance from Kayla.

Within a few minutes of the decision to arrest her, Kayla Moore had already stopped breathing. She had been forced onto her stomach and under the weight of six police officers, handcuffed. Her feet were tied at the ankles as she lay face down on a futon on the floor, half stripped of her clothes, her bare torso exposed. From the police's own reports it is clear that while they called for a spit hood to be brought up from the fire truck on the street below to be put over her head, no attempts to supply artificial breathing were made. Throughout the incident, Kayla is referred to as "it." She was pronounced dead at Alta Bates hospital at 1:34 A.M. on February 13.[3]

Kayla's body as a target of state violence first surfaced in a Berkeley newspaper the morning after she was killed. The *Daily Californian* reported that a 41-year-old man with "possible mental health issues" had died in police custody on the 2000 block of Allston Way.[4] Her race was not noted. The newspaper quotes a press statement released by the BPD that continued to refer to Kayla as a man. According to the police statement, quoted in the *Daily Californian*, "(he) became increasingly agitated and uncooperative to the officer's verbal commands and began to scream and violently resist," and "after struggling with officers, they were able to gain control of the subject and place him [sic] in restraints."[5] The statement noted that after the officers had placed the person in restraints and on a gurney, at some point they realized that he (misidentified) was no longer breathing; they attempted to perform CPR, but the person was later pronounced dead. Thus, on the day following the incident the state, supported by the media, launched its first erasure of the incident as well as the first erasure of Kayla. According to their narrative, a person misidentified as male with possible mental illness had simply expired while resisting police care.

This fact of an in-custody death following an "involuntary psychiatric hold" at the hands of the police provoked the first interrogation from the community, which marked the start of the autonomous justice project known as the "People's Investigation." Within the next few days, members of Berkeley Copwatch followed the address listed in the paper to the Gaia Building, a new Mediterranean-style apartment complex towering over downtown Berkeley, and began interviewing residents as they came out of the building, all of whom referenced a woman who had been killed.

Witnesses described hearing screams, and seeing officers outside the apartment that they described variously as "sweaty," "limping," and including one with a torn shirt. They described Kayla as not white, large-proportioned, and friendly. Several noted that she had only recently moved into the building, and that she had sometimes approached people about buying and selling drugs, and that they knew of several people in the building who had bought drugs from her, though they were vague about the type of drugs circulating through the building.

The first phases of the investigative effort involved tracking down further details about what happened on the night that Kayla was killed and connecting with her family. Initiated by Berkeley Copwatch and organized with the family at the center of the investigative efforts, the People's Investigation over time grew to include the participation of many groups, including the Center for Convivial Research and Autonomy (CCRA), Critical Resistance, Peers Envisioning and Engaging Recovery Services, the Coalition for a Safe Berkeley, and others. Many groups continued to show up to speak and share information from across struggles at rallies, city council meetings, vigils, and other direct action spaces, including supporters from the Idriss Stelley Foundation, Justice for Alan Bluford, Communities United Against Violence, the Tsega Center in Oakland, the 50.50 Crew in San José, the NAACP, Radio Autonomía, and other groups.

Within the first few weeks, a series of Public Records Act requests were submitted to the Berkeley Police Department requesting state-produced information from the evening when Kayla was killed. Grassroots investigators also called the coroner's office and learned that a hold had been placed by the Berkeley Police Department, barring any information from being released. This hold extended to Kayla's immediate family, who were likewise unable to access any information regarding Kayla's body and her in-custody death.

In addition to critically reading state documents, the People's Investigation created a number of tools, including a taxonomy of officer involvement that made observable the way the violence unfolded, relying on both militant research and convivial research approaches to theorize and act both against and outside the state.[6] These tools emerged from a shared commitment to understand what happened the night of Kayla's death, including both analyzing and naming the moment when police became first responders and how they escalated a situation to a point of extreme violence.

Why Did They Die?

Following a series of savage murders of Black women in Boston beginning in January 1979, the Combahee River Collective issued a pamphlet, "6 Black Women: Why Did They Die?" The document circulated widely as an interrogation into the conditions of invisibilization and impunity of racialized, gendered violence in their community, as the numbers of deaths mounted and eventually rose to twelve Black women who were brutally killed over the course of the investigation.[7] Enraged by city officials' indifference to these murders—or even an acknowledgment that the violence was occurring—the Combahee River Collective responded in a number of critical ways. Recognizing that these murders collectively unfolded at the intersection of race and gender, they collectively advanced an analysis of the violence facing Black women as a form of vulnerability to death (to borrow from Gilmore) inherent in white supremacist patriarchal capital relations. They mobilized to raise awareness in the broader community that would situate the problem without further criminalizing those targeted by the violence; they charted possibilities for self-defense at both the individual and community level that refused to force women into a reclusive position out of the streets (i.e., in the home or under the "protection" of men); and they explicitly engaged the issue as a collective, community safety issue.

The Combahee effort offers one critical genealogy of people's investigations as powerful moments of convivial research and prefigurative politics, and as institutions of the commons, organized around safety and fierce care. The first gesture, as we listen to their efforts and reappropriate their tool in the present, is the formation of a collective question towards community self-organization, *why did they die?*

In a struggle to understand how a community member becomes a target for annihilation by agents of the state, and an effort to read community resilience and autonomy against this violence, in the days and weeks following the death at Gaia, the People's Investigation raised the critical question: Why were the police there in the first place? Why did Kayla die?

In this most immediate sense, the death of Kayla Moore in police custody occurred in the context of a crisis of care, one where those services previously provided by the state or as "care work" provided within families and communities, have been increasingly eroded, displaced, or made impossible. Following the dismantling of the welfare state and in conditions of neoliberal precarity, the privatization of social services, and thus the availability and access to critical resources, are delimited by the wage and one's access to it.[8] Services are neither guaranteed nor consistent for all, including, critically, in Kayla's case, access to the Berkeley Mobile Crisis Team.

Intertwined with neoliberal "security," the crisis of care, with our bodies and relations to each other at the center, reflects an escalating privatization and militarization in the current conjuncture as the state administers a version of securitized "care" that has displaced the rhythms of family and community life. Beyond the police responding to crisis calls, Manuel Callahan theorizes the militarization of care as "a strategy of occupation that allows and normalizes home invasion and internal, sporadic checkpoints in the home."[9] And as the People's Investigation launched to respond to the killing of Kayla Moore notes, "our lives are being militarized on a daily basis."[10]

The unfolding sequence as care becomes militarized can be traced through forces of state and capital that are dependent on and continuously reorganize race and gender as categories and relations. In order to forge categories and relations that are profitable, stable, and in other ways beneficial, the forces of state and capital must disrupt and break those relations which obstruct or challenge them, and continuously reestablish forms of composition which are favorable to them, relying on strategies of decomposition that often include violence but can also include concessions, which also, in turn, function as sites for reorganizing race and gender. In the biopolitical technology articulated by Foucault as "some must live, but others may die," the "may die" is far less benign, and far more violent, than its laissez-faire tone implies.

Through the collective space of learning that was the People's Investigation, the "militarization of care" emerged as an analytical category exposing the intersection between an increasingly militarized police force and a politics of care.[11] But it is also critical to examine where this violence is directed—whose homes are invaded as part of the occupation?

Before the incident that took Kayla's life occurred, if an architect had rolled out a map showing all the units in the Gaia Building at 2116 Allston Way, and in consulting this map a building manager filled in details of the renters who had signed leases for each of those units, it would likely have been possible, with near certainty, to determine who would be removed from that building on a stretcher, no longer breathing, after a routine police call. How is such speculation possible? *Why did they die?*

The Gaia Building is structured around a large atrium. It sits on the edge of the UC Berkeley campus and is home to students who have moved out of the dorms to live in an independent but safe complex. Like much of the architecture of the new development projects in Berkeley, it is in the "Mediterranean style," boasts a panoramic study room, a rooftop garden, parking garage, and close proximity to restaurants, cafés, and nightlife. The building is located within a block of the Downtown Berkeley BART station. Inside are 24-hour surveillance cameras and a chess set that rests on a table among many plants in the expansive foyer. According to students posting on Yelp! the building is "a pinnacle of luxury," and the roof is great for parties. The reviewers note that while the units are overpriced they are convenient and modern, and also warn potential renters to exercise caution in dealing with a landlord who extracts a fourteen-month lease in the fine print of the agreement. From the sidewalk, the structure towers over downtown Berkeley, with large glass windows and a heavy locked glass door that is accessible by code.[12]

Kayla's unit was classified as Section 8, or affordable city housing. In many cases across the Bay Area, such units are made available through agreements between the municipality and developers in line with legislated housing allotments in new buildings. This usually involves a series of incentives for the developers, who may not otherwise be able to build in particular areas based on tenancy rights and low-income protections earned through earlier hard-won struggles for survival and against forces of dispossession and accumulation.[13]

Prior to moving to the new Gaia Building, Kayla had found housing in the Tenderloin district of San Francisco, where she had lived in a series of "SROs," or "single room occupancies," over the years. These were often in run-down hotels with shared bathrooms, where living was possible through a combination of state and federal aid, often also made through agreements that included incentives for landlords, for example tax breaks.

Where state and federal aid did not cover Kayla's living expenses, a complex system of support was in place. Her family continued to support her by delivering groceries to her on a near daily basis, working night jobs, taking out credit card loans, and becoming certified as caretakers so that the money for caring for Kayla could be funneled back into the support structure already in place. In addition, Kayla worked where she could, including as a phone sex operator, one of the few jobs available to her, given the discrimination against transgender people and her restricted employment possibilities as someone diagnosed as schizophrenic at a young age, leaving her with scant employment history to draw on to leverage more consistent employment.[14]

The killing of Kayla ranks among the staggering number of Black, Brown, and Indigenous people, some of whom are women, killed by police on a daily basis across the United States. Her killing belonged to the profound forms of state and state-manufactured violence, including fatal attacks by police, directed at transgender people. It also registered with the increasing number of people suffering from mental illness or other disabilities who are killed as a result of encounters with police.[15]

Kayla was, in the words of her sister, Maria Moore, at a press conference organized by the People's Investigation, a perfect trifecta—Black, transgender, and schizophrenic.[16] While Kayla posed no visible threat to the state or capital at the time she was killed, each of these assignments marks a particular vulnerability to premature, state-sanctioned death and has a traceable genealogy.[17] This condition does not belong to Kayla, but to a web of forces working in collusion to create a vulnerability to state violence.

In an ongoing settler-colonial logic of "disposability," Blackness becomes a site of biopolitical abandonment and the ongoing production of anti-Black racism.[18] A diagnosis of schizophrenia, which is rendered a particular intelligibility in both the logic of capital and the logic of biopower, as well as capital's dependence on the violent imposition of gender hierarchies (organized through binaries), fuse to allocate a high probability for premature death.[19] As a trans woman, Kayla defied recognition within fixed gender binaries. Precarias a la deriva observes: "one thing is certain: capitalism has also learned to tolerate and to take advantage of other sexualities, but always when it can limit them and assure their intelligibility in some fashion." Trans subjects pose an incessant problem of intelligibility for the state's administrative categories.[20] As queer scholarship and grassroots praxis have continued to expose, this inability to "fix" certain subjects poses a threat to the social order, particularly in relation to gender and sexuality.[21]

In police and media statements, there were also multiple references to Kayla's size and weight, in an attempt to make her responsible for her own death.[22] It is not a contradiction of the violences exacted in this new moment of capitalism that someone can be both "left to die" through technologies of disposability and at the same time violently eliminated, in this case by transphobic police. Kayla was simultaneously made vulnerable by a system that strategically abandoned her at the same time as she was targeted for elimination by trained agents of the state. Value can be extracted from both conditions.

To illuminate capital's biopolitical mechanisms at play in determining which lives are "livable," H.L.T. Quan uses the term "savage developmentalism," pointing to what remains "ungovernable" or "uncontrollable" under the current order of development (often named "progress").[23] Savage development carves a "border" between "developed areas" and "underdeveloped areas." In the case of the Gaia Building on the night of Kayla's death, this border became observable from one housing unit to the next, with Kayla's unit being classified as "Section 8." An apartment designated Section 8 situated within a modern apartment complex in the urban Global North can exist, in Raul Zibechi's terms, as a "zone of non-being." It becomes an assailable space, vulnerable to invasion. Yet as Zibechi also explores, these zones of non-being simultaneously claim practices of regeneration outside the logics of capital and the state.[24]

Analyzing a series of subject-producing *dispositifs* that articulate relations in capital's current conjuncture, autonomist theorists have struggled to both identify and claim "the ungovernable." Both Silvia Federici and Gustavo Esteva theorize the emergence of a new subject in the current regime through the production of the "urban marginal," a subject who poses a threat not for who they are in terms that inscribe an essentialized identity, but for their refusal to submit to enclosure and capitalist subsumption—their ungovernability.[25] These subjects and their doppelgangers—those positions they refuse to fully inhabit as recognizable subject positions, including migrants as well as gender queer subjects and particularly those disenfranchised by capital—surface as targets in the Fourth World War.[26]

Harry Cleaver elaborates the problem that an autonomous subject can pose: what capital "cannot digest it must purge or be poisoned by." Historically, he points to a number of categories gleaned from "mainstream bourgeois social theory" for organizing "unintegrated, unmanageable working-class autonomy," including "the deviant, delinquent, deficient, uneducated, primitive, backward, underdeveloped, criminal, subversive, schizophrenic, infantile, paranoid, sick, and so on." These terms justify repression and violence; in our struggles against this repression, Cleaver propounds, "we must investigate the nature of such autonomy and its relationship to capital's own valorization *with great care*."[27]

Convivial Tools and New Imaginaries of Justice

As a community-based justice project organized around research, direct action, and community speak-outs convened together with people from across the Bay Area—Berkeley, Oakland, San Francisco, San José—the People's Investigation was first and foremost a refusal to allow the state to erase a life from the community. As a process of grassroots justice, it unfolded through a series of ongoing "spaces of encounter" in a larger community safety initiative. The People's Investigation generated tools and can itself can be understood as a convivial tool—it opened a critical space of engagement where a community could come together outside of state-sanctioned justice and regenerate itself in its collective response to violence as it imagined and enacted alternatives.

The birthday party was one such critical moment in the People's Investigation, providing an opportunity to challenge the state and make its violence, and Kayla as the target of that violence, visible. It served as the site to demand that the Berkeley Police Department release the official police investigation's findings into the death in custody that had occurred at the Gaia Building two months before, while at the same time providing a vehicle for a community to reclaim space without police censure and to obstruct a street without having to petition in advance for permission to march.

While the demand for information was addressed to the Berkeley Police Department, this demand was contextualized within the framework of an autonomously organized, open process called the People's Investigation. As a temporary autonomous zone of knowledge production (TAZKP), it served as a space of community research where knowledge was generated collectively about the incident that had occurred, the context in which it had occurred, and the investigative process taking shape. The "space of encounter" carved out through the birthday party and direct action functioned in this instance as a site of "living theory," or as "an effort to document and examine the forces arrayed against us as a proposition to change the condition we find ourselves without imposing a fixed, already determined future."[28]

Kayla Moore's birthday party marked a moment where stories, witness accounts, and perspectives were shared across various connections and conversations throughout the gathering as residents left the building and inquired about the party; family members and friends offered a history that spoke to the life lived over time and the community's loss; and community organizers and others loosely identified as the investigation collective circulated with flyers and questions. The sidewalk became a space for sharing information or collective research about what happened and why it happened the way it did. Through the birthday party encounter, stories were shared of police abuse, targeted attacks against people with disabilities or experiencing mental crisis, of experiences with police as racist and transphobic, together with conversations on community-focused care, and what it means to be a community experiencing violence at the hands of state agents while working to understand justice and community safety on their own terms.

In the festivities of a warm April afternoon, it was possible to disseminate large amounts of information, including hundreds of flyers that were critical of the police response and what we named through collective discussions "the militarization of care." As an event, the birthday party was situated within a longer struggle stretching over months that was the People's Investigation. In the *ateneo* spaces of UniTierra Califas over the first year of the People's Investigation, the birthday party was theorized in relation to the many spaces that unfolded as part of the investigation. As part of a commitment to learning across struggles, and drawing directly from the work of the HIJOS human-rights group in Argentina, the space of the party was theorized as a site of direct action and as an *escrache*, where "the *escrache* is a call to struggle"; it opened a political space to confront the architects and authors of the state violence.[29]

In the case of HIJOS, the *escrache* was a colorful demonstration that opened a necessary space for confronting, many years later, the architects of the forced disappearances by the military junta of over 30,000 young people that formed a critical strategy of state-sponsored terror during Argentina's Dirty War from 1973 to 1984. A struggle first taken up during the height of the junta's rule by the Mothers of the Plaza de Mayo as an unwavering demand to return their children alive, the Mothers' actions transformed into a sustained public occupation of space that refuted not only the state's terrorizing violence but its discursive framing of their children as violent militants. Out of this legacy and an ongoing context of impunity, HIJOS emerged to confront those responsible for the murders of their parents; many of these junta leaders were still living lives of wealth and comfort despite authorizing and exacting, over more than a decade, atrocities on a horrific scale. Through a collective effort to expose, boycott, and eventually drive into exile those responsible for the murders, HIJOS organized neighborhood by neighborhood, building a strategy of protest over a sustained period and typically by parading near their home or workplace, finally culminating in a massive street demonstration, or *escrache*, that surrounded the individual homes of junta leaders, who had in many cases, with the support of the Argentinian state, kept their past violences hidden from neighbors and community members until the arrival of the *escrache*.

In this context, for HIJOS the *escrache* is a process that recognizes that the demands for justice have not, and cannot, be met by the state, and it refutes the possibility of a state-organized justice. In their theorization, "the *escrache* only exists as a response to the demand for justice." It emerges in the absence of justice while simultaneously recognizing that "the struggle expressed by the *escrache* goes beyond the

State of Rights and can't be absorbed by it."[30] While the *escrache* functions to expose and reveal, the "essence of the *escrache* is lost if trapped within the logic of negotiation."[31] Instead, the articulation of demands circulates as a system of information in the community, and the space of the *escrache* is a space of TAZKP.

In assessing HIJOS's intervention in the absence of justice in Argentina, while some theorists have focused primarily on the shame and the "outing" made possible by the *escrache*, this was only one tactic of the *escrache*; it was not the *escrache*'s totality. Other elements of the *escrache* included community-organized boycotts that could function to exile the perpetrator of state violence from the neighborhood where they resided and had lived in relative obscurity despite their violent history. The *escrache* was also marked by a vibrant street party, often the culmination of many months of organizing. In the words of HIJOS, "*escraches* are situations of resistance and of new forms of existence: situations where autonomous forms of existence (which are different than those of Power) are produced and then spread to every area of life."[32] Thus, the *escrache* serves as a site of living theory for understanding actions within, against, and beyond the state.[33] In responding to brutal violence authored by the state and which the state has refused to acknowledge as a site of injustice, the *escrache* remains in militant confrontation with the state's violence and violent history.

Yet, at the same time, the "*escrache* is not inscribed in a frustrated desire for inclusion but in its opposite: a desire for justice that persists in spite of this frustration."[34] It is a direct action "space of encounter." In their work on "economies of dispossession" as an ongoing process of settler-colonial racial patriarchal capitalism, Jodi A. Byrd, Alyosha Goldstein, Jodi Melamed, and Chandan Reddy draw attention to abstractions (for example, liberal frameworks that articulate the "human") that organize equality and commensurability, where freedom (or in this case, the equally lofty concept of justice) is framed as "inclusivity into the very categories from which some subjects, rendered other, objects, or dead, have always already been denied, foreclosed, and precluded."[35] Disability and queer/crip activists and scholars continue to mark sites of inclusion/exclusion manufactured by the state, capital, and a range of biopolitical technologies in what David T. Mitchell names "ablenationalism," where what is human is measured in terms of a global system of value.[36] Each of these represents sites of knowledge production that point to an outside that is beyond inclusion/exclusion, where new subjectivities, for example queer/crip subjectivities, emerge in defiance of systems of commensurability. The *escrache* reflects this desire for justice that lives beyond and outside the state.

State violence brings the state into people's lives; it produces reactivity as it requires a targeted community to respond. Through the terms of its own engagement, it can manufacture exclusion at the same time that it proliferates disempowerment—withholding information or even a loved one's body, delaying investigations, forcing families to engage processes of "justice" that the state can then manipulate through delays, bureaucracy, obfuscation, and even the spatial configuration of the institutions that families must try to access and understand, which reinscribe the authority of the state at every turn. This is critical to our collective understanding of the struggles confronting police violence as community responses that are necessarily imbricated with the state.

Yet trans lives continuously expose the fact that in their existence as subjects under the law, they are "ungovernable"—the entire legal apparatus is based on a subject recognition that does not include what it refuses to find legible.[37] Furthermore, inclusion for some means exclusion for others. Or the exclusion of some establishes inclusion for others. This fundamental contradiction shaped the interrogation of justice unfolding. The theorization of the *escrache* was a tool borrowed from HIJOS and also from Colectivo Situaciones, and refashioned to try to advance our own autonomy in this context.

Like the *escraches* following state violence in Argentina, the birthday party for Kayla Moore marked both a refusal and a relocation. While the community collectively demanded the official documentation of the events leading up to the fatal outcome and the state's own summary of how Kayla died, in the act of convening a People's Investigation conceived as a site of community knowledge production organized through an ongoing series of open gatherings, it was a refusal to concede responsibility or articulate justice through the terms and institutions of the state.[38]

The space of the party was on one level a site of open mourning in the neighborhood, but at the same time it was celebratory, strategic, and intimate. Working together with Kayla's family and friends throughout the investigation was instrumental in generating a relocation of both the site of struggle and the possibilities for a shared justice into the neighborhood through the shared "space of encounter." The birthday party was not merely a tactic. It was above all else a moment when a community could gather to remember a community loss, outside of the production of Kayla's death by the state, which had in many ways governed the community response since her death in February. It was, in its immediate sense, convened outside the state.[39]

At the same time, the birthday party functioned as a direct-action moment to advance a militant research strategy, given that part of the effort for justice was centered on a desire to know what happened the night of Kayla's death, information which the state refused to disclose.[40] Thus, the high visibility of the party provided an opportunity to exercise a civic demand through a request under the Public Records Act (PRA), a legislative act compelling disclosure in response to public demands for transparency and information. This opened space for conditions of accountability across a series of institutions and also made visible a number of emerging issues of concern that coalesced in the moment Kayla died in custody. The police report containing the primary testimony by police as part of the internal investigation (in other words, as interviewed by other police) immediately following Kayla's death would provide a reading of the state's efforts to contain and justify her death.

As a finale to the party, a PRA Request was drawn up on a sheet of extra-large poster board, and the group traveled en masse to the Berkeley Police Department, where the theatrically sized request was taped to the front door of the headquarters by Kayla's family. The birthday party and its PRA Request in the absence of any official inquiry simultaneously exposed that there was no independent inquiry initiated through the municipal, county, or state offices following a death at the hands of the police.

This prompted a larger critique of the role of the Berkeley civilian review board. While civilian review boards and other institutions designed to monitor the police, which emerged in many cities out of struggles of the early 1970s and in response to the sudden escalation of a militarized police force, continue to be touted as independent, these claims are contested within municipal structures and are considered by most to be largely ineffectual, outside of their existence as a liberal "safety valve" in moments of community outrage. Despite these failures, the boards are repeatedly invoked across a range of political spaces seeking responses to police violence. The *escrache* and grassroots investigation exposed the logic of liberal counterinsurgency that is operating behind these ineffectual civic institutions.[41]

The demands of the birthday party were restated at the Berkeley City Council meeting on April 30, 2013. Within days, the Berkeley police released to the public a trove of documents, including the coroner's report and the police report through which the strategies of state attempts at containment could be read.⁴²

The birthday party was one of several networked spaces of reflection and direct action as part of the People's Investigation. These also included a community speak-out organized together with anti-police groups, mental health providers, and community organizers that drew attention to the issue of police responding to people in crisis in the community. Working together across groups, the People's Investigation was able to learn and imagine collectively autonomous possibilities for community care and safety that did not rely on the police or the state.⁴³ These included various "safe house" models available for people experiencing crisis, organized as non-punitive spaces where people could retain autonomy over their decision processes. A community-wide conversation was also generated through the People's Investigation about ways community members could be trained to respond to people in mental crisis in a safe and adept way, including a number of safe alternatives for calming people down, using strategies like "emotional CPR" or eCPR.⁴⁴

Throughout, there was an effort to shift these gatherings to function more fully as spaces of assembly, as community members shared their own and their families' struggles with mental illness, and together discussed a number of programs and practices that offered ways to support each other without relying on the police. The investigation as a process advanced boisterous rallies at City Hall and heated City Council meetings as well as press conferences, and it shared spaces with other families from across the Bay Area who had lost loved ones to forms of state violence.

Refusing the State

In the six months after the birthday party, two gatherings were organized. In October 2013, the results of the People's Investigation in the form of a final report were delivered to the Berkeley Police Review Commission (PRC), an independent police oversight board which had not advanced its own investigation in any serious capacity. The report was delivered to the commission at a public meeting, and was accompanied by a large gathering of people who had participated in the struggle for justice for Kayla over the course of the past eight months since the police killing. At the opening of the PRC meeting, the commission attempted to manage the space in order that the report be delivered to them as if presenting evidence. This resulted in an awkward scuffle as both groups tried to reposition the tables at the front of the room. Members of the People's Investigation refused the attempted reorganization of the space, and turned to face away from the commission and the police. Facing the community who had participated in the many gatherings, conversations, and actions, members of the People's Investigation, as a collective subject, shared the report of their findings with the crowd in a room filled with posters and slogans taped to the walls remembering Kayla.

The result was a refusal to acknowledge the authority of the impotent and co-opted review board, flanked on one side by a table of uniformed police officers, and instead manifested a commitment to listen to each other's experiences at the intersection of care and policing. The commission was forced to concede the entire agenda to the People's Investigation, as community members spoke to each other about their experiences with police violence, truncated services for those in mental crises, and increasing cuts to disability services. Motley and powerful, the statements from the community to the community lasted over three hours. As a backdrop, the police and the commission attempted to maintain an absurd pose of authority in order to communicate an intact jurisprudence.

Six months later, to mark the anniversary of Kayla's death and coinciding with another PRC meeting on February 12, 2014, the People's Investigation held a candlelight vigil outside the Gaia Building. Over a hundred community members together with the family gathered for a sidewalk vigil and then embarked on a procession with LED-powered tea light candles and banners down Shattuck Avenue, a main street in downtown Berkeley. This time, when community members who had marched from the vigil to the PRC entered the meeting room, they did so to shouts of "fuck the pigs!" hoisting massive painted "Justice for Kayla" banners on poles that were stomped noisily against the ground. The PRC, and the attendant row of uniformed police officers, including the Berkeley chief of police at the time, Michael Meehan, were unable to speak or commence the meeting amidst the noise and sharp comments aimed at the commissioners and the police.

It had been a year since the murder of Kayla by the BPD and four months since the release of the sixty-page People's Investigation report, and the independent civilian review board still had not released any information about the investigation into Kayla's death they had announced a year earlier. There was a strong intergenerational presence in the civic space of the PRC of diverse people in defiance of gender norms and across a range of dis/abilities: some wore the balaclavas of the Black Bloc, and many stared in anger or sneered at the array of officials at the front of the room. People clustered around the edges of the room, badgering the commission about the results of their investigation, demanding the civilian review board's report, and inquiring about the status of one PRC member in particular, John Cardoza—an appointed member of the independent commission who was also the father of Berkeley Police Sergeant Benjamin Cardoza, who had been present on the scene the night that Kayla's life was taken. Those in the room denounced the conflict of interest, speculating loudly whether this might explain the absence of an independent report issued by the commission in the year since the killing.

Kayla's sister, Maria Moore, convened the room with grace and the full backing of the rebellious crowd, and posed the same critical questions while opening the floor. Where was their investigation? Why was Cardoza still on the commission? During the lulls when questions were directed at the commission before the cacophony resumed, those gathered pushed for details about the work of the commission. The commissioners were livid, and tried to call out people they recognized from the community in an attempt to elicit unilateral negotiations and through this tactic to control the crowd. The inadequacy of the commission, and its role in protecting the police by serving as a buffer between the community and the department, was revealed completely.

After close to two hours of confrontation, jeers, and enraged and informed questions from the floor, a group of Kayla supporters clustered by the exit door and shut down the lights in the meeting hall, leaving everyone in total darkness, with the police asking that the lights please be turned back on, to roars of laughter echoing through the dark. Finally, one officer walked through the dark room to turn the switch back on and then returned to his seat flanked by the rest of the department, only to have the lights go out again, amidst peals of laughter. This time, the police had to station an officer by the light switch. The meeting was effectively over, and the community procession filed back out into the streets, sharing insights and reflections before dispersing across different points into the night—on bikes, in wheelchairs, in cars, on foot, and on BART, back to homes in Berkeley, Oakland, San Francisco, and beyond.

These spaces of direct action and full-fledged insubordination were formative moments in an (always) emergent collective subject organized around fierce care for a community member that had been violently taken, and in contumacious disregard of the state that was trying to minimize and justify its own violence. Yet, despite these moments in an emergent community safety effort, the grassroots response through the People's Investigation did not necessarily reflect a unified strategy; it proceeded in multiple directions at once.

For some, the investigation served as a call for police reform in the form of gender sensitivity trainings or use of force policy (both of which, abolitionists argue, serve to expand the policing function by funneling additional funds to departments). For others, the struggle in the wake of violence served as a point of leverage to push for a stronger or more effective Police Review Commission, although many questioned the independence and composition of such a commission, arguing that it retains the problems of municipally appointed "representatives" who do not represent those most impacted by police violence but instead are mired in both a politics of representation and in administrative city politics as a whole. For others, meanwhile, the PRC was just another institution of pacification that serves to mask and justify the role and presence of police in maintaining a bourgeois social order and repressing social antagonisms.[45]

The People's Investigation process was seen by some as a strategy of demilitarization, a vehicle for replacing police officers with professionalized certified mental health workers; while to others, these strategies seemed, in the articulation of HIJOS, "trapped in the logic of negotiation" or still complicit in fortifying a state responsibility for care—a process of manufactured dependency that could be dismantled at any time and which still in no way guaranteed access to those occupying positions of "ungovernability"—or a professionalization of care. Many were wary of the connections between professionalization and privatization, and were also wary of processes that designated specialized experts who would be deployed beyond community processes. For some, this also seemed another mechanism in what Precarias a la deriva theorizes as an "externalization" of the home and by extension, care—in short, following a logic of capital that further removed social reproduction from a community's own vernacular processes.[46]

Some advanced the People's Investigation through a different set of investments, reflecting an exploration of the relation between "fierce care" and ungovernability. This offered a site for exploring how an anticapitalist politics that takes ungovernability seriously might respond to the state violence that targeted Kayla. In the struggle for justice for

Kayla, we explored how our actions might refuse the laws of a state that denies life to those subjects it can't "fix" with its language, taxonomies, categories, forms, bathrooms, identification cards, prisons and modes of confinement, and health care policies—in short the "administrative violence" and the entire carceral, biopolitical regime that annihilates, through ongoing (re)production, those who are ungovernable.[47]

Thus for some, the spaces opened by the People's Investigations—from the first inquiries following the killing (as an act of fierce care) to the ongoing investigation and the report itself (as an act of dissent and refusal), to the various riotous spaces concatenated across time and space in response to the violence (as an act of delegitimizing the state and as a "call to struggle")—were spaces where insurgent knowledges could circulate against categories that apportion violence and death; where a new imagination of justice tethered to the vernacular rather than to the state and its violent abstractions could breathe, where "alternative socialities" could be forged.

Veracini notes the advance in the present of a settler-colonial logic of extermination and erasure expanding to envelop increasing numbers of people under the rubric of disposability.[48] In their collective analysis of the violence of Indigenous dispossession, Byrd et al. argue that "capitalism is not only constitutively racial capitalism but also, likewise, a way of hierarchically organizing and disposing social life predicated on and operationalized through empire and colonialism as a counterformation to Indigenous peoples and the recalcitrance of racialized lives that refuse and exceed its totalizing aspiration."[49] In the space opened by the Combahee River Collective's insistent question, "why did they die?" it becomes less possible to imagine state or professionalized certified answers or solutions. Kayla died because she embodied a refusal and an excess that defied the totalizing aspiration of the forces of racial patriarchal capitalism. These forces organized a world where she was among the "some may die" because there was no way for her to be "counted among the living."

In a similar analysis of Indigenous dispossession, Indigenous scholar Joanne Barker reflects on the Occupy movement in Oakland and nationally and its relation to debt and the subprime lending crisis. Barker constructs a conceptual tool, using Indigenous "territory as an analytic" to situate the 2008 financial crisis in a broader historical context of debt and dispossession of Indigenous people and communities that has continued into the present.[50] Barker argues that "Indigenous territory refutes the viability of inclusionist methodologies and their promises of social justice and equity—as if inclusion can resolve the problem of erasure," and she refuses dichotomous solutions structured around omission/inclusion or absence/presence.[51] If we acknowledge the historical and ongoing dispossession that lie at the base of the U.S. imperialist nation-state, there is no relation to law, or debt, or property, or rights for Indigenous people or others who can exist outside this contradiction and this site of erasure. Barker asks, how might we use (and share as a tool) "territory as an analytic" for understanding other struggles, asking of other territories, "do the Indigenous peoples of that territory have the recognized status and rights necessary to legally contest their dispossession?"[52]

It is not just that there was no way for Kayla to be "law-abiding"; there was no way for Kayla to exist in relation to the law.[53] A recognition of this dispossession is a call to struggle beyond inclusion, beyond negotiation, beyond the state. If territory, in Barker's terms, offers a location to position ourselves to contest a claim, how might we take up Barker's invitation, itself woven into the struggles to decolonize Oakland, and rely on "territory as an analytic" that refuses to accommodate erasure; that unmasks the bureaucracy to reveal the violence it manages; that repudiates rights in favor of mutual obligations and new relations? How might we organize ourselves outside the state through a responsibility and commitment to a fierce care between us, rather than demanding that a city provide sensitivity training (or any kind of training) for its war for police to manage what the state already won't let live? This reorientation offers ways to move beyond the demand that a city dispatch certified professionals in the place of police, and instead offers possibilities for reclaiming our own networks of care.

Fierce care, then, can also weave new social relations, mark a site to connect across dispossession and learn together, imagine new ways to reproduce ourselves as a community and struggle together for, in the words of Naisargi N. Dave, a queerness "that doesn't need to reproduce itself in recognizable forms."[54]

Part of the fight for justice for Kayla Moore will always be a fight to remember and refute the abstractions and subsequent taxonomies of violence that organize subjects and that determine all of our lives in the present. Sidewalk birthday parties, city hall police commission meetings organized through a defiant blockade—these insubordinate celebrations of a community's power refuse not only authority/expertise and the vertical hierarchies that it continues to manufacture, but open new spaces. We can find ways to take care of each other.

Struggles Connect

After a series of marches and rallies in advance of the court dates for the civil suit filed by Kayla's family, Judge Charles Breyer of the U.S. District Court for the Northern District of California first threw out claims against the Berkeley Police Department of excessive force and wrongful arrest in October 2017, and in March 2018 dismissed the remaining Americans with Disabilities Act claim, thus effectively dismissing the case entirely. As of 2019, the case is on appeal. The struggle for justice for Kayla Moore continues, with Maria Moore at the center, weaving across struggles.

In July 2016, this included a town hall organized by the California Coalition for Women Prisoners in response to an ongoing suicide crisis at the California Institute for Women (CIW) in Corona, outside of Los Angeles. In 2016, the CIW was functioning at 130 percent capacity and had a suicide rate that was eight times higher than the national average for people in women's prisons. The town hall established critical links between the violence and abuse occurring inside the prison walls and the violence outside. The statement announcing the gathering read: "At CIW, people are dying as a result of direct neglect by cops, and from medical and mental health neglect. Outside, women are being killed by police."[55]

The event brought together the sisters and mothers of Kayla Moore, Erika Rocha, Shaylene Graves, and Jessica Nelson—all women of color who had lost their lives in contexts of state violence. Erika Rocha and Shaylene Graves had both died inside the CIW in circumstances of abuse and neglect in the months prior to the town hall; and Jessica Nelson was shot and killed by San Francisco police in the city's Bayview district on May 19, 2016. The gathering also brought together family members of Stacey Rojas, Yvett Ayestes, and Sarah Lara, a group of trans and queer prisoners at the Central California Women's Facility in Chowchilla who were attacked (and survived) on November 11, 2015, by California Department of Correction and Rehabilitation personnel for documenting and mapping guard abuse and guard violence directed at trans and queer prisoners.[56]

These spaces reflect an increasing effort to make visible forms of violence targeting Black, Brown, and Indigenous women, and trans and queer people, as well as people with disabilities. They also reflect an effort from struggles on the ground to learn from other targeted families and build connections—both advancing the visibility and reach of their own justice struggles and expanding a collective understanding of state violence, state-manufactured violence, and their realms of operation.[57]

Rather than competing for visibility with the more visible forms of police violence against young men of color, the connections forged by mothers and families functions as a moment of fierce care marked by an effort to connect across incidents and violations and thus understand the scope and reach of the violence. These struggles are connecting a greater number of families over time. As the carceral regime continues to reach across generations and geographies, and into the same families and communities saturated by an ongoing low-intensity war, these struggles draw on networks of resilience and care that families and communities have forged over time in their ongoing efforts to survive an onslaught of capitalist violences—enclosure, dispossession, forms of erasure. They continue to create new paths and spaces of encounter, circulating counterknowledges and reweaving the relations necessary for autonomous survival.

The EZLN warns that "truth and justice will never come from above," and says: "We see and hear that all of these people receive only lies and mockery from those who proclaim to administer justice and who in reality only administer impunity and encourage crime . . . Truth and justice will never, ever come from above." They continue: "We will have to construct them from below . . . And on the Roman scale of our sorrows, we will weigh what they owe us. And we will send the bill . . . and we will collect it. We will then indeed have truth and justice. Not as a handout from above, but rather as a conquest from below."[58]

CHAPTER 5

Alex Nieto

Disinformation and the Domestication of War

"We want names!" This call issued in front of the San Francisco Federal Building was for Alex Nieto, a life taken on March 21, 2014. It was December 3, 2014; the first court date of the civil suit *Refugio & Elvira Nieto v. City and County of San Francisco*. Under the name "Justice for Alex Nieto" (J4AN), a collective of community members and friends of Nieto with the Nieto family at the center had been organizing since the San Francisco Police Department (SFPD) shooting in Bernal Heights Park that took Nieto's life. Through marches, rallies, speak-outs, ceremonial gatherings, and other direct action spaces, including "burritos on Bernal," a monthly evening vigil walk up the hill where Nieto had been killed, the family and community had continued to come together to remember, grieve collectively, and seek justice.

Their mobilizations pressured the city to disclose more details about the circumstances of the killing. On this December day eight months since the killing, the family and community gathered in the plaza with their demands and offered coffee and flyers to people crossing the plaza and entering the building, informing them of the status of the case. Department of Homeland Security agents watched the plaza action from inside the building's securitized lobby. Among the groups gathered was an anarchist collective based at Station 40, a social center in the Mission District, a historically Chicanx/Latinx district of San Francisco which, beginning in the 1960s and '70s and escalating with the waves of the dot-com era, had witnessed increasing displacement as more white and middle-class and wealthy young people moved in. The Mission District was the area that the Nieto family called home, and the area that mobilized most visibly in the wake of the SFPD's killing of Nieto.

On the morning of the rally, the Station 40 crew handed out free hot coffee with anti-cop phrases marked on the cups to those gathered and those passing through, an effort connected to their monthly "Coffee Not Cops" action that met at the entry to the 24th Street Mission (BART) Station in the city. In an area notorious for a saturated police presence, both visible and undercover, the group met regularly to share coffee while cop-watching and encouraging others to cop-watch. On this day they set up in San Francisco's Civic Center as court support.

At the center of the rally, the parents of Alex Nieto, Refugio and Elvira Nieto, stood under black umbrellas sheltering them from a cold rain. They addressed those gathered in Spanish and a few words in English. Between them they held a banner with the words, *Justice and Love for Alex Nieto*.

A little over eight months prior, on March 21, 2014, Alex Nieto had been shot at least fifteen times by San Francisco police while sitting on a hill overlooking the city at sunset. He had been eating dinner before going to his evening job as a security guard at the El Toro nightclub in the Mission District. Police arrived in response to a 911 call placed by a man walking his dog who indicated that Nieto looked suspicious while eating his burrito. Nieto, the caller had noted, had a Taser holstered on his hip. Within minutes of their arrival the police shot Nieto dead. At the time of the shooting, Alex Nieto was twenty-eight years old. The Taser he wore on his hip was legal in California and was a required weapon for his job as a security guard.

Alex Nieto was the first person killed by San Francisco police in 2014, the eleventh killed since Greg Suhr became chief of the SFPD in April 2011, and the eighty-third person killed by law enforcement in San Francisco in twenty-five years.

In the town hall meeting organized by the SFPD five days after the shooting, SFPD Chief Greg Suhr announced that four officers fired the shots that killed Nieto, but he refused to disclose the officers' names. Eight months later, the officers' names still had not been released. Speaking to this delay and lack of disclosure, Deputy Chief Attorney Margaret Baumgartner asserted that the city was unable to release the officers' names on the grounds that a threat had been made against the department as a result of the deadly incident. After eight months of community pressure and under order of the magistrate judge, the deputy chief attorney was forced to reveal more information about the police presence at the time of the incident. While she claimed to not have an exact count of all those involved in the incident, in addition to the 4 officers who fired the deadly shots, there were approximately 8 to 10 other officers present at the time Nieto was killed. Beyond this, there were approximately 20 more officers who arrived to secure the homicide scene after the shooting.

George Ciccariello-Maher argues that "a key pillar of police power is their demand for privacy, enshrined nationwide to the detriment of the public and of the victims of their violence, with several cities and states making it difficult to make public the names of those who kill in the name of the state." With the California Supreme Court decision in *Copley Press v. the City of San Diego* in 2006, together with California's Police Officers' Bill of Rights in 1977, the records of police actions have been essentially sealed from public view, a policy in place at the time that Nieto was killed. According to the American Civil Liberties Union, the *Copley Press* ruling "held that records of an administrative appeal of sustained misconduct charges are confidential and may not be disclosed to the public. The decision prevents the public from learning the extent to which police officers have been disciplined as a result of misconduct." Ciccariello-Maher further explains that it is the Police Bill of Rights that ensures that California is essentially "at the vanguard" of a trend towards police privacy, arguing that it is this piece of legislation that "effectively shields public servants with guns from even the most basic level of public oversight."[1]

On January 1, 2019, new police transparency requirements went into effect as a result of public pressure that led to the passage of SB 1421, Peace Officers: Release of Records. The new legislation requires police departments to publicly disclose details about the internal investigations and other records following a police shooting, use of force, and sexual assaults committed while officers are on duty as well as other forms of misconduct. Leading up to the law going in effect, law enforcement unions sought to prevent the implementation of the legislation at the level of California's Supreme Court. The Police Officers' Association attempted to block the law entirely; several agencies, including the San Bernardino County Sheriff's Employees' Benefit Association, challenged the law's retroactive mandate, arguing that it should only apply to incidents and investigations that took place after the legislation went into effect. With California's Supreme Court denying numerous attempts by police unions to undermine the legislation, reports surfaced across the state of agencies "scrubbing" their history and dumping thousands of pages of documents on the eve of the new transparency rules.[2]

For those challenging police violence, obstacles to transparency are at the base of an ongoing impunity, as the state refuses to release information about its own acts of violence. However, what "transparency" means or how it relates to prominent calls for accountability remains murky. As a demand, SB 1421 affirms the need for transparency while simultaneously exposing the extent of the state's attempts to obfuscate its brutality. Just the threat of the legislation's pending enactment served to expose a myriad of interconnected practices—for example, the role of unions in protecting police actions and the scramble to shred police documents on the eve of the law's coming into effect. While opponents of SB 1421 fought against transparency on the grounds of officer safety and the danger such transparency would pose to ongoing investigations and operations within departments, what is in fact exposed is the imperative that the use of force remain beyond censure. Undergirding the frantic attempts by the police unions is the belief that police methods and practices should not be open to scrutiny; the resistance from police unions and departments confirms the importance of secrecy and obfuscation in the functioning of police power in the present.

Counterinsurgency warfare considers the control of information as a critical aspect of its strategy. John A. Nagle, a retired U.S. Army lieutenant colonel and counterinsurgency strategist and expert, states explicitly, "the control of information is strategically decisive in counterinsurgency."[3] While counterinsurgency doctrine maintains the need to balance brutality with legality, its chief architects simultaneously emphasize the importance of establishing an arena where police and armed forces can act without fear of censure or oversight. To this end, the counterinsurgency theorist David Galula advocated reinforcing the local police and armed forces, while simultaneously stripping the judiciary and strengthening the bureaucracy.[4]

Arguably (and struggles on the ground in fact do make this argument), the moment deadly force is used by police, the judiciary has been stripped and the police become judge, jury, and executioner. In a broader sense, counterinsurgency warfare depends on the strategic circulation of misinformation and the organization of disinformation. This includes the management of strategic silences and omissions. A bureaucracy can function on multiple levels as part of a successful counterinsurgency strategy; this can include an obstruction of transparency in the name of protecting both the safety of its officers and the secrecy of its investigations. The moments of secrecy, silence, obstruction, delay, and enclosure are key instruments in both the perpetuation and domestication of war.[5]

Beyond calls for transparency, this information can also be (and is) deployed strategically to traumatize a family and community and decompose or exhaust a struggle; for example, in cases where the police announce the release of critical body camera footage from a killing months or years after the incident. In some cases, the media is told but not the family, and the family has to learn about the release of the information on the evening news. In other instances, footage is released after an enduring period and after significant community pressure, and the footage may show nothing about the incident itself—a few frames of a fence or a car, for example, that tell a family nothing. In others, the footage is released in segments over time, and the family is called in repeatedly and is given a very narrow window, for example, a day or two, to determine if they want to see the footage, or can make it within the time frame. For example, sometimes their loved ones were killed in a different city, and they must leave work on short notice to travel within the narrow time frame provided by the state. They must decide, after months or years, if they are prepared to see the killing of their loved one. And then they may decide and accept the state-orchestrated viewing, and the footage may not even contain a frame of their loved one but instead a sidewalk or a patch of lawn. Or, in other instances, the execution in its entirety may be played for them to bear witness.

The series of rallies that culminated in the December 2014 rally in front of the Federal Building drew attention to the absence of police department transparency following the killing of Nieto. Exposed was a department, backed by the city, relying on a distant threat against officer safety to justify shielding its officers in the aftermath of a killing. (Informed community knowledge circulated at the rallies, and other gatherers shared that the threat had been placed by a person in another country via an online post in the comment section of Facebook.) Furthermore, the rally made clear how the protection of the officers simultaneously interfered with the legal process. How could the lawyers bringing the civil suit against the city on behalf of the Nieto family begin their depositions when no information had been released about whom from the department to depose?

In the case of an officer-involved shooting (OIS), the police department initiates a series of investigations. According to the SFPD's General Orders, these include interviewing and submitting police reports immediately following the incident from all those present, as well as commencing an investigation with the internal affairs unit. The department is also required to issue eleven separate notifications of the incident across offices and departments. Yet the department is not required to disclose any information generated throughout this process.[6]

The long delay meant that the department itself, together with the district attorney, managed all details, records, interviews, and statements over the course of the weeks and months following Nieto's death. Any statements from the officers and witnesses who had been at the scene of the SFPD killing in response to the questions by the plaintiff's legal team would be uttered at a considerable distance from the unfolding of the incident itself—at the moment of the December rally, eight months had gone by without a formal recorded statement on the violence to anyone outside the official structure of the state.

In this way, the city effectively filtered from the immediate moment of the incident all of the statements of those present on the scene. At the same time, the city's maneuvers to conceal information ensured that if the case made it to court, the trial would likely occur years distant from the moment of the killing. Like many justice struggles surrounding incidents of state violence, these obstacles ensured that the Nieto family's struggle would be a protracted one.

Furthermore, in all OIS cases, the District Attorney's Office also begins its own investigation of the incident. This investigation occurs within an intricate web of relations and shared histories across the offices of the state. At the time that Nieto was killed, the San Francisco district attorney was George Gascon, who had served as chief of the San Francisco Police Department from 2009 to 2011. Gascon replaced Kamala Harris as San Francisco district attorney when she became attorney general of California. When Gascon accepted the position of district attorney in 2011, he was replaced as SFPD chief by Greg Suhr, who was chief of police at the time that Nieto was murdered. Thus, while there are multiple investigations that are initiated, these investigations are not without ties and relations over many years between high officials in the police department and those in the DA's office; as the investigative structure in place at the time that Nieto was killed demonstrates, the city's district attorney emerged from a career of policing and direct ties to the SFPD.

In another example, within a few years following her departure in 2009 as SFPD chief, Heather Fong was hired by the federal Department of Homeland Security as an assistant secretary in the Office for State and Local Law Enforcement to serve as a liaison between law enforcement agencies across the state—local, state, tribal, and territorial. In short, in addition to contracted mutual aid agreements, coordinated trainings, and other interagency cooperation, there is a significant level of coordination across agencies that draws on histories, relations, and an accumulation of intelligence gathered from local populations and situations, and that circulates through departments and agencies at all levels as people circulate through these same stations and offices. While the public often pushes for additional investigations by bodies outside the department, claims to independent investigations, both at the level of the District Attorney's Office and through departments like the Department of Justice, should be understood in this context.

The pressure following the SFPD shooting marked a strategic effort on the part of the community to surface details critical to their own grassroots investigation and the family's struggle for truth. Already, these efforts had forced the city to reveal that there had been an estimated thirty-four officers present to manage the incident. From there, the community mobilized to learn which officers were on the scene the day of the killing and what role they had played. As the Nieto family testified at the rally, spoken mostly in Spanish: they were still waiting to learn what happened to their son.

Relying on details as they became available, a community comprised of Nieto's family and friends, lawyers, and concerned civilians embarked on the process of assembling and archiving the state's actions and statements as a way to advance the investigation of the incident, mapping the strategies in place that led to the killing and cataloging the steps the state took to construct Nieto as a threat. The family made public that following the shooting, the police had come into their home without a warrant and searched Nieto's room, without sharing with the family that Nieto was already dead. Through direct actions supported by a community-organized web presence and social media strategy, the family also shared the autopsy report, which contradicted the original narrative released by police to the public.[7]

While in some case the state autopsy report can expose inconsistencies in the police narratives, increasingly, families and community members are calling for independent autopsies to be conducted following a police killing, since the Chief Medical Examiner's (CME) Office is seen as often supporting state narratives and ritually justifying police violence through physical, scientific evidence. In the case of San Francisco, the CME Office is situated within the Forensic Pathology Department of the city and works closely with the police department following a killing. It is not uncommon for the police to restrict the release of an autopsy report for many months and in some cases even years on the basis that the case remains under open investigation.

There is a long history for the role of San Francisco's CME Office in both justifying violence and interfering with accurate record-keeping regarding incidents of state violence. One prominent case involved the killing of Aaron Williams by the SFPD in June 1996. Williams, a Black man, was attacked by twelve police officers who repeatedly kicked him, "hog-tied" him (a position where a person's wrists and ankles are bound together behind their back), and pepper-sprayed him repeatedly in the face, eventually covering his face and mouth with a mask. Williams died after being left for an extended period in the back of a police van in high temperatures. The twelve-officer team that attacked Williams was led by SFPD Officer Marc Andaya, who under his previous tenure with the Oakland Police Department, had "37 prior complaints of police brutality, five lawsuits alleging racism and abuse, and one other death of an unarmed man of color" prior to being hired by the SFPD.[8]

The death of Williams following beating and abandonment was attributed by San Francisco CME Boyd Stephens to "excited delirium," also known as "acute excited delirium" or "sudden in-custody death syndrome" and other similar names. This "syndrome" that emerged in the mid-1990s frames the person killed by police as responsible for their own death following an encounter, and is attributed to such factors—usually following a beating or other incident of excessive force—as the person's weight, breathing capacity, heart functioning, or supposed drug or alcohol use. Cast as an emergent "syndrome," it served to weave the Medical Examiner's Office into the justification of police murders.[9] Alongside the security *dispositif* that serves to manage war, the control of information can include information that is strategically released, withheld, denied, delayed, reframed, twisted, justified by incongruous or selective or partial or backwards science, and so on.

The community response following the SFPD killing of Alex Nieto reflects an ongoing commitment to convene spaces where knowledge can be shared and accumulated across years of state violence. The community's efforts to learn details about the violence that has targeted it and to share experiences surrounding this violence works in service of their own and larger struggles for justice. The concrete details edge the family and community closer to an understanding of the incident that took a life—an act which in all cases severs the relationships and bonds that form a community and hold it together across space and time.

These details are also critical in challenging the state's attempts to devalue the life that was taken, and by extension, the attempt by the state to devalue families and communities through multiple forms of criminalization following an incident of state violence. Criminalization becomes a key instrument at the intersection of the state and capital for managing social antagonisms and masking a war directed at specific populations and the relations that bind them; it functions to produce subjects as dangerous, threatening, and to place the rest of the population "at risk."[10] While revealing this was a key achievement of the struggle for J4AN, perhaps its most salient effect was that it exposed the efforts of a department to obfuscate information and to produce silence.

Moments of resistance like the Nieto rally in December often have as their most prominent and legible strategy the call for specific information to be disclosed or documents to be released. Yet even when these actions are aimed at the institutions of the state, the resistances are never encompassed entirely by the demands they call out. On one level, the demands function as a tool and site of engagement with the state.[11] They contribute to a moment of collective affirmation that such knowledge exists and that the state is actively protecting this information from disclosure. However, neither the demands nor the spaces constructed to voice them are focused exclusively on the state, as the series of other actions in the J4AN make evident: as direct action spaces they exceed the liberal frames of "accountability" and "transparency." These spaces are constructed from within a diffuse relation of power, and the demand that the state relinquish its secrets is a challenge.

Such spaces and the demands put forward through them expose a "security" apparatus that protects police who kill. Organized from within the community, these spaces reveal the functioning of the police department, and by extension the state, as they manage their own violence against the community in the name of security.

Jorge González's methodology of constructing observables offers an approach for delineating "security" versus "community safety," reflecting two contradictory epistemological positions and accompanying practices. This analysis of the neoliberal security state provides an opportunity to map strategies of differential policing that occur, in this case, within the economic contours of the Bay Area as an enclave economy. Yet, the emergence of new forms of capitalist organization of accumulation and imposition do not displace the old forms, and numerous layers of these processes can exist simultaneously, targeting different populations, territories, types of work, socialization processes, and so on.[12]

Beyond this, these community-organized spaces are spaces of research and interrogation where knowledges are exposed and generated that are critical to a community's resilience and survival against the onslaught of counterinsurgency. These knowledges hold the capacity to shape collective refusals and acknowledgments. As such, they are sites of self-valorization—as a collective practice outside the valorizing apparatus of the state—and key sites in a community's struggles for autonomy.[13]

From Ferguson to the Bay Area

A few weeks prior to the Nieto rally, on the other side of the Bay at Humanist Hall in downtown Oakland, the Inter Council for Mothers of Murdered Children (ICMMC) hosted a gathering that brought together families targeted by state violence from the North Bay, East Bay, Peninsula, and Central Valley.[14] Following the prominent police killings earlier in the summer of 2014 of Eric Garner in Staten Island (July) and Michael Brown in Ferguson (August), ICMMC founders Anita Wills and Dionne Smith-Downs had traveled to Ferguson and joined in the rebellion, sharing stories with community members there of the intersecting violences targeting their families and communities, and sharing from struggles unfolding in the Bay Area.

The November gathering was framed as "Fighting Jim Crow from Ferguson to the Bay Area," and marked an effort to more fully connect enduring racial violences as well as local struggles and the late summer insurrection in Ferguson. A woman from each of seven families across the Bay Area retold an incident that had brutally ended or imprisoned the life of a loved one. Joined together on a raised stage at the front of the hall to tell their stories were Cadine Evans, sister of O'Shaine Evans of Oakland, killed by undercover plainclothes San Francisco police officer David Goff while sitting in his car on October 7, 2014; Mesha Monge-Irizarry, mother of Idriss Stelley, killed by a tactical team of San Francisco police officers that included Arshad Razzak, Joseph Garbayo, Georgia Sawyer, and Thomas Walsh and others while standing alone in a movie theater on June 12, 2001; Dolores Piper, great-aunt of Derrick Gaines, shot in the neck while lying on his back in a gas station parking lot by the South San Francisco police officer Joshua Cabillo on June 5,

2012; Cynthia Mitchell, sister of Mario Romero, killed by the Vallejo police officer Dustin B. Joseph while sitting in his car talking with a friend outside his home on September 2, 2012; Dionne Smith-Downs, mother of James Earl Rivera Jr., killed while pinned in a crashed van by Stockton police officers Gregory Dunn and Eriz Azavard and San Joaquin sheriff's deputy John Nesbitt, on July 22, 2010; Anita Wills, mother of Kerry Baxter Sr., imprisoned on a 66-year sentence under questionable policing practices and court procedures in September 2003; and the grandmother of Kerry Baxter, Jr., killed on the streets of Oakland in an unresolved homicide on January 16, 2011. Kathleen Espinosa, who had since moved from San Francisco to Spokane, Washington, remained present in the Bay Area struggle by sharing a statement that was presented to those gathered about her son, Asa Sullivan, killed while cornered in an attic crawl space by the San Francisco police officers John Keesor and Michelle Alvis on June 6, 2006. All were young men—Black, Brown, Indigenous, mixed race.

Even before the highly visible killings in Ferguson and Staten Island over the summer of 2014, and later in Baltimore in the spring of 2015 with the killing of Freddie Gray and again with the killing of Breonna Taylor in Louisville and George Floyd in Minneapolis in the spring of 2020, the rallies, marches and vigils across the greater Bay Area in response to police killings had been growing in frequency and intensity over the course of recent years—from the murders of Oscar Grant (January 1, 2009) shot by BART police officer Johannes Mehserle while face down on a subway platform and left to bleed out; to Kenneth Harding, Jr. (July 16, 2011), whose last dying moments on a Bayview public plaza were cordoned and isolated from all contact by a police perimeter maintained by SFPD officers Richard Hastings and Matt Lopez; to Raheim Brown (January 22, 2011), shot by Oakland Unified School District (OUSD) police officer Barhin Bhatt while sitting in a car outside a school dance (OUSD officer John Bellusa was also on the scene and later deposed against Officer Bhatt); to Alan Blueford (May 6, 2012), shot in a driveway by Oakland police officer Miguel Masso; to Kayla Moore (February 13, 2013), crushed under the weight of at least five Berkeley police officers in her own apartment (BPD officers on the scene included Gwendolyn Brown, Kenneth Tu, Brandon Smith, Brian Mathias, Tim Gardner, Nikos Kastmiler, and Sergeant Benjamin Cardoza); to Anthony Lopez (October 22, 2013), shot by Sonoma County sheriff's deputy Erick Gelhaus while walking down a street in the afternoon.[15]

Against this onslaught of police violence, families and community members continued to respond by holding vigils and making banners and flyers naming the family member killed. They connected with other families to speak about their losses in common spaces and at rallies. They led marches that filled streets and sidewalks across the Bay. They took over freeways and congregated in front of city halls, court buildings, police stations, campuses, churches, and in local parks.

The November event at Humanist Hall reflected this sustained moment, marking one of the larger self-organized convergences of families coming together in a shared community space to speak about the violence that had targeted their family and the ensuing struggle for safer communities and for justice—the meaning of which, as several families spoke about, became central to the struggle itself. As families came together from across regions—urban and periphery—their stories overlapped in the space, weaving together disparate geographies and experiences of racial violence reflected across many years. In speaking, women remembered through relational *testimonio* the life lived and the dreams of the person taken, and the others left behind. Almost all recalled the precise details of the violence—including the number of bullets that had destroyed that life.[16] They spoke of the aftermath of violence as well, and the struggle to hold a family together while grappling with loss and at the same time embarking on justice struggles organized around what had been taken.

Each woman's story unfolded with a violent death and a gaping hole at the center of a web of policing practices and strategies surrounding the moment of violence. They spoke to the state's efforts to devalue the life of the person taken. Speaking directly to the circulation of disinformation and misinformation, families retold the damaging impact of police departments working in tandem with a dominant media to criminalize those killed after the shooting. One of the women recalled the death of her brother, "It's like they killed him twice—once with bullets and again in the news." Other families nodded to affirm this.[17]

The assertion, "they killed him twice" exposes the state's attempt to erase its own acts of violence by constructing a narrative that catalyzes what Lisa Marie Cacho has elaborated more fully as "social death" for the individual target of violence, as well as for the larger community. This moment of discursive criminalization is one that recurs throughout family narratives as a state strategy they face, often one that isolates them from the community following a killing. Yet, as the *testimonios* and actions from the community make visible, this attempted allocation of social death is always an incomplete, frayed strategy which communities resist and confront across multiple sites and at multiple levels. This statement by the sister of Mario Romero following the killing in Vallejo marks the unequivocal refusal of the state's imposition of a social death by his family and larger community, and a moment of naming the state's strategy across a larger architecture of security that includes the mainstream media.

As families come together to share stories across geographic spaces, their mobilizations make observable racial violences as well as resistances that can be understood in relation to regions and spatial zones shaped by capital. Racialized geographies can include, for example, access to private property and the management of property values buttressed by state policies; as well as property inscribed by racialized understandings of "crime" and proscribed by policing strategies such as gang injunctions; forces of displacement and dispossession that shift the demographics of urban and rural areas; a "proliferation" of borders, to borrow from Mezzadra and Neilson, that ensure that checkpoints of various forms are managed in the interior space of the state; and so on.[18]

The stories of the families gathered at Humanist Hall revealed resonances across racialized geographies. Families testified to homes being searched by police immediately following a killing. In most cases, the search occurred before the family learned that a loved one had been killed. In many cases, details that were offered by the state at the time of the search were deliberately misleading regarding the incident of violence that provoked the search, often functioning to draw the family in to the state's process of criminalization following a killing. *Did he ever speak of depression or taking his own life? Did he have a history of trouble, or friends that were troublemakers? Did he carry a gun often?* And so on. There were multiple stories of family members being detained by police and interrogated for hours after a killing without being told of the fate of a loved one. Through the stories shared, families exposed multiple forms of criminalization, counterinsurgency, and state scrutiny targeting their communities, families, and homes.

While the J4AN December direct action at the Federal Building's courthouse exposed the state in critical ways by making use of what the state sought to keep as its secret, the families gathered at Humanist Hall constructed a space for community *testimonio*, sharing what Donna Haraway theorizes as "situated knowledges" that have been overwritten, silenced, or in some cases rendered nearly inaccessible to logic.¹⁹ Here, in a community gathering among families, *testimonios* gave rise to questions, formulated in an open space. Why would officers from six different agencies stalk a sixteen-year-old boy at midday, fire 48 shots at him, and then refuse to let his mother near his dying body? Why would the state circulate incomplete information about the number of agencies involved in his murder? Why would a task force empty a movie theater and fire 48 bullets into a young man standing alone at its center? Why would police enter a home on a "well-being check," chase someone who they were not looking for and who had not threatened anyone in any way into an attic in his own home, and then shoot him 17 times as he crouched at the far end? Why would police approach a parked car where two young men sat talking in front of their home and begin firing into the car, and then jump on the hood of the car to fire additional shots, 40 in total, through the windshield and into the men sitting inside? How can a community reclaim justice and manage its own safety in this context?

As with both the December J4AN rally in San Francisco and the ICMMC gathering in Oakland, these gatherings can be understood as systems of information that expose and contest the state—its policies and practices, its narratives, and its violence. In revealing the state's tactics and strategies, they narrate a low-intensity war targeting the spaces where a community reproduces itself, where it lives, plays, and thrives. But they do not only expose violences. These are "insurrectionary knowledges" that emerge collectively to testify to the struggles being waged from within communities.²⁰ When families come together through shared experiences of loss, they refuse those "political operations of power" that individualize them, and instead advance their struggle as a collective refusal.²¹ In gathering to share *testimonio*, communities expose the multiple violences directed at them—lived, survived, systemic, everyday, structural, material, symbolic, and epistemic. They form vital sites of self-valorization and regeneration against and beyond the state.²²

Knowledges and Community Safety

The spaces of the Nieto rally and the ICMMC gathering reflect the multiple ways that communities access, share, and generate knowledges through which to challenge state violence and also state-organized justice, while at the same time rebuilding and protecting their communities. In the search for answers to what happened to Nieto, the community struggle was instrumental in surfacing subjugated knowledges. Armed with fragments of what the state did to Nieto, those in the justice struggle simultaneously engaged these spaces as sites of speculation and circulation. Drawing on collective experiences of previous police trials, community members reflected on the impact of the police refusal to release the names of the officers on the scene that day. They speculated that in the event the Nieto case made it to trial, the gap of months between when the incident occurred and when those present were interviewed outside the protective shield of the state might later be synchronized with certain lacunae in memory that might emerge across retelling. The lacunae itself could serve to justify inconsistencies in officers' accounts; or, what was present as historical knowledge could be easily dismissed by the time the case made it to trial—the facts eroded by time.[23]

Like many cases, the speculation rested on other information already gathered as a community built its own case against "official violence." This included the autopsy report cataloging at least fifteen bullets fired into Nieto, demonstrating that Nieto had been shot several times in the back, with several shots fired from an angle below him—as if he had been moving away from the attack up the hill. Community members also speculated as to one reason for the state's refusal to release names: the department needed time to manufacture a viable narrative about *how* the incident transpired to support its narrative about *why* it transpired. As the J4AN collective noted, the presence of many officers on the scene presented particular challenges if the story was being manufactured: it made it difficult to establish consistency among all the officers in the official state narrative. This lack of consistency posed problems for the specific officers named in the civil suit as well as the police department whose practices and policies, and contradictions and fabrications, were made visible. It also put the state itself at risk by provoking questions about its functions in the name of security.

Across mobilized and interconnected families, the December rally at the federal courthouse, like the ICMMC gathering, was a moment where shared struggles intersected. The Nieto family was joined by the family of Yanira Serrano-Garcia from Half Moon Bay on the six-month anniversary of her life being taken by law enforcement. On June 3, 2014, while experiencing an acute mental crisis, eighteen-year-old Yanira Serrano-Garcia was killed by Deputy Mehn Trieu of the San Mateo County Sheriff's Department in response to a phone call placed to the fire department by a family member seeking support for the family and Yanira. Deputy Trieu arrived on the scene and within minutes shot and killed Yanira.[24] Yanira's brother, Anton Garcia, traveled to support the Nieto family and share the *testimonio* of his family with others gathered there. Garcia had mobilized across the Bay Area following the state killing of Yanira, connecting with families who had had loved ones violently killed by law enforcement in similar circumstances, specifically, following a call for assistance in dealing with a family member in crisis that ended with a police killing.

In addition to supporting families at court dates and other interactions with the state, Anton Garcia organized actions in Half Moon Bay, including a birthday party direct action. Organizing in Half Moon Bay holds a particular set of challenges given its demographics as a quaint, small beach town for tourists, many of whom escape for a few days from urban San Francisco and other parts of the Bay. For others, the seaside town is not a retreat but a site of precarious survival, as they work service-industry and related jobs of capital "logistics." Many of those from the ethnic Mexican community to which Yanira and her family belong are undocumented, and their participation in each mobilization ran the risk of engagement with the police and other law enforcement. In this context, it becomes critical for families to network with other struggles for support and safety. These are always moments of "fierce care," as families and communities stand together in the wake of individualized attacks by the state.

The network in place among families and the capacity for this structure to absorb new families was evident as other family members with a shared experience of violent loss arrived without having met the Nieto family, themselves newly propelled into the struggle through a shared experience of violence and loss. As Mesha Monge-Irizarry has noted, "sometimes the only thing these struggling families have in common is the murder at the center of their lives."[25] As comrades in Oaxaca remind us of mothers connected in struggle through the disappearances and feminicides of their children, what holds these families together is "fierce care," a collective push forward that refuses to leave any one family behind.

As families come together with this as the primary point of intersection, rather than a shared political goal or position, and often without a shared neighborhood or even a shared language, there is a particular need to theorize the struggle from the point of situated knowledges and through the relations of care that are crafted to weave and sustain these struggles. Although in many cases families do not have a history of struggle readily recognizable by many on the Left, they are, from the moment of violence, engaged in a struggle for justice and truth, actively contesting and questioning the state as they are forced to engage it through a series of institutions and services—the police, the chief medical examiner, the funeral home, the lawyer's office, town hall and city council meetings, and the courts. Furthermore, each act of violence occurs in the context of an already mobilized community that families can access and become involved in, learning and building new theories and strategies together; they are engaged in a sustained and collective research and learning process to collaboratively produce knowledge.

As the Nieto family prepared to enter the courthouse in the Federal Building, one side of the plaza was flanked by family members holding a large banner printed with a black-and-white drawing of Alex. Even for those who had not known Alex, his face was widely recognized across San Francisco based on a series of wheat paste posters with his likeness plastered throughout the Mission District following his killing in March.[26]

From the far end of the plaza, the family of O'Shaine Evans arrived with their justice banner billowing in the cold rain and wind, painted with a Jamaican flag and massive colored letters, *Justice for O'Shaine*. It had been less than two months since O'Shaine Evans had been killed by the SFPD. As they arrived, O'Shaine's sister Cadine Williams and mother Angela recalled chants from other spaces connecting moments of state violence across local, regional, and international struggles. The chants linked the heightened attacks on Palestine from earlier in the summer of 2014 with the police violence in Ferguson, naming parallel processes of racialized targeting by the state, "From Ferguson to Palestine, being Black is not a crime." In other chants, those gathered called out the names of those killed by law enforcement locally and beyond.

Then the militant chants that the mother and sister of O'Shaine had started when they arrived with their banner died down, and crossing the circle of twenty to thirty people in the space of the plaza, Cadine approached Alex Nieto's mother and father and said directly, "What happened to your child? What is his story?"[27]

Two weeks later, for the December solstice, the longest night of the year, the Nieto family and their supporters held a *posada* (a traditional celebration across parts of Mexico commemorating the biblical journey of Mary and Joseph looking for a room in an inn to spend the night). The Nietos were joined by families who had been present at the

ICMMC gathering in Oakland in November and others that had been at the courthouse in early December. Also present to speak were the families of Errol Chang, killed by Pacifica police just a few days before Nieto on March 18, 2014. Like Yanira Serrano-Garcia, Errol Chang was among the rising number of people killed by police while experiencing an acute mental crisis. A Daly City SWAT team surrounded his family home in a six-hour standoff, throwing several "distraction devices" (smoke bombs) through the windows, and finally storming the residence and shooting Chang, despite clear and documented attempts by Chang to surrender.[28] Also present at the *posada* was Laurie Valdez, whose partner and father of her child, Antonio Lopez Guzman, was tased and then fatally shot in the back by two San José State University police officers on February 21, 2014. The two officers involved in the killing were Sergeant Mike Santos and Officer Frits van der Hoek.[29]

Children whose families had been murdered were present too, with small tea candles in plastic cups. The Peninsula families, South Bay families, East Bay families and North Bay families were joined by a crowd of several hundred people at the entrance to the 24th and Mission Street BART station. There were *mexica* dancers with tall feathers swaying amidst the smoke of copal, one dancing with an infant strapped to her chest. As the sun dropped and the Mission District took on an evening chill, the dancers and families led a procession, winding through the lower Mission streets on the long march up to Bernal Heights Park. The banners announcing the justice campaigns were wide enough to shut down streets, while two vertical banner flags, one scripted with Alex Nieto's name and the other simply scripted with "Justice," flapped high above the march, at the tops of the trees and ducking under wires as the *posada* procession wove up the hill, leaving behind it in the opposite direction city hall, the federal courthouse, the precincts, and those institutions that had been its targets at other moments of action. Near the head of the march, a long black banner read, "Safety for who? Rest in power Alex Nieto. Never forgive, never forget."

CHAPTER 6

Asa Sullivan
Social Death and the Prose of Counterinsurgency

On the three-year anniversary of the day that Asa Sullivan's life was taken by San Francisco police, an exchange circulated between Asa's mother, Kathleen (Kat) Espinosa, and Asa's older brother, Kahlil Sullivan, in San Francisco's Black radical newspaper, the *San Francisco Bay View*. In their exchange, Kahlil wrote, "This is the third year without any answers to explain what happened during interactions between the SFPD on 6/6/06 and my younger brother, Asa."[1] Through their printed correspondence, a family's own militant grassroots investigation emerged from a place that refused to let Asa be claimed by the state.

Asa Sullivan's life was taken on June 6, 2006, when San Francisco police entered his Parkmerced home, and tracked him into an attic crawl space where officers Michelle Alvis and John Keesor shot him sixteen times. Asa was Black with clear green eyes, and that June he had long, thick hair plaited neatly against his scalp in fine braids that reached well past his shoulders. He was twenty-five years old and the father of a young child at the time his life was taken. The only witnesses to the killing were the police who killed him. Asa's story will always contain this silence.

This silence is at the base of the family's investigation. It is held as a space of collective disavowal from which questions are generated to understand an act of violence that targeted their family. In the printed correspondence on the anniversary of their loss of Asa, Kahlil marks the intense situatedness of his own research strategy in the collective investigation the family initiated immediately when they learned something had happened to Asa. Kahlil's strategy is corporal, embodied. He writes:

> I went into that attic myself, just as he had that night, and climbed to the area where he was last alive. I saw my brother's blood covering the floor and walls. There were holes from bullets everywhere, in the rafters and the walls. From where he would be positioned, it looked like bullets sprayed up from the bathroom below through the ceiling into the attic. A big hole was in the attic floor over the bedroom, where they must have pulled him down. I couldn't help but cry while I was in that place, trying to put myself in his place to find out what happened.[2]

In the same space of reflection, Kahlil recalls the initial framing by the state:

> The first report was my brother had a gun, and my brother shot at them. When he shot at them, they saw a flash from his alleged gun, barely missing one of their heads, so then they returned fire and killed him, fearing they were trapped. Then the chief of police made a statement to the news that my brother took a shooting standing position with outstretched arms in a two-foot attic and the officers did what their training told them to protect them from danger.[3]

He proceeds to carefully document the different stories advanced by the state at different stages:

> Then the chief herself changed the report twice and said the facts were not clear, they were just preliminary reports and he was holding a cylindrical object in his hands that the officers thought was a gun. Then the report was changed again, stating he held an eyeglass case. After 14 hours of their crime scene team investigation there with my brother's body, they found no weapon. The chief portrayed my brother like he wanted to get shot and the officers reacted appropriately.[4]

Kat responds to Kahlil in the printed exchange:

> You were brave to go up into the very attic where Asa was killed . . . The horror of Asa being shot in various parts of his body and face 16 times, with more bullets bouncing off in that

> tiny attic space sickens me. Kahlil, you know first hand Asa could not even stand all the way up in that small attic space. I could only look up in the huge hole cut into the ceiling where I was told Asa's body had to be taken out. I listened to your descriptions of what you saw. I thank you for investigating and putting yourself in the last place Asa was alive.[5]

In her response, Kat also affirms the commitment to this shared research as part of their struggle for justice. She writes, "We speak for Asa now. Asa cannot tell us in his words anymore. Your words, Kahlil, are a comfort to me."[6]

The exchange between Kat and Kahlil stands as testimony to the powerful collective investigations of the family to reclaim Asa at all costs from what Cyndi Mitchell, in the wake of the Vallejo police shooting of her brother, Mario Romero, in 2012, calls the "second death," where the first death is the police killing, and the second death is the murder in the mainstream media. The exchange between Kat and Kahlil marks an enduring rejection of this "second death" the state seeks to impose through the narrative constructed following the killing. There is an inquiry here, in Kat and Kahlil's exchange, a research approach based on a refutation, a geometry of space and bullet holes, an insistence against lies and forgetting that forces the state into a new narrative. Both Kat and Kahlil speak to a moment of militant research and reflection as they force themselves to return to the site of violence and contemplate the hole they were offered as part of an explanation by the state. From here, they affirm that they will fight on for Asa together.

Shortly after the killing of Asa, Kat made a statement in the newspaper coinciding with the filing of the civil suit: "It's not about the money, it's about the truth."[7] What followed over the next eight years and beyond was a sustained effort on the part of Asa's family to learn the truth and to try to tell Asa's story, in his absence. From June 2006 to October 2014, Asa's family fought a relentless battle to bring a civil suit to the federal courts to ensure that the officers who killed Asa and the department that protected them would have to answer for their actions against the family and community. The officers present, involved, and responsible for the incident that resulted in the violent death of Asa Sullivan included Michelle Alvis, John Keesor, Paulo Morgado, Yukio "Chris" Oshita, Tracy McCray, Darren Choy, Eric Leung, and others.

Asa's family was well aware that the courts could not deliver justice or a compensation that corresponded in any way to the loss or the trauma that has continued to reverberate.⁸ The struggle for truth was from the outset inextricable from the question of what happened and why. It marked a struggle against, in Ranajit Guha's phrase, "the prose of counterinsurgency," a prose "fully and decidedly constructed by the state."⁹ Theirs was a collective refusal by the family to accept the "facts" the police tried to make reality fit into, and a refusal to accept the social death of criminalization that was being apportioned to all of them as a family by the state via Asa. In an argument that the state would build and supplement over time, Asa, the state argued, no longer wanted his life when the police found him in the attic. In the prose of the state, Asa had chosen "suicide by cop," both desiring and orchestrating his own violent death at the hands of the police. To assemble this grammar, the state had not only to prove this desire and the effective strategy, but to prove that Asa's life was one that was not worth living.

The collective efforts over time of the family to expose and contest this thus laid bare something larger and far more powerful than a "truth" of what happened: they exposed the substratum and the aftermath of a police killing, including the space of the trial itself, as potent interconnected sites of counterinsurgency warfare aimed not just at Asa but at the population as a whole—to eliminate the criminal/insurgent and gain the support and trust of the population: violence, pacification, security.

2 Garces

On June 6, 2006, the night that Asa Sullivan's life was taken, San Francisco police officers entered the residence at 2 Garces where Asa was staying on a Code 910, a "well-being check," in response to a call from a neighbor who suspected the apartment unit in the Parkmerced housing complex was a "drug house."¹⁰ According to the neighbor's testimony, there were cars and people coming and going late into the evening, there was noise spilling out from cars in the driveway and from inside the house, and it was unclear at times who was living in the residence.¹¹

When officers arrived and pushed open the door and made their way through the residence, they would later report that they were doing so out of "care" to make sure there was no one in the unit that needed their assistance.¹² At the time, there were two people staying at the Parkmerced unit, Asa and a friend. On hearing the police enter, Asa fled to a small attic crawl space but was quickly detected. Below, officers also located, and handcuffed Asa's friend, and asked him who was in the attic. His friend explained that Asa was not armed, and there was no other way out of the house aside from the front door.

Officers Alvis and Keesor followed Asa up into the crawl space, while a third officer, Paulo Morgado, stationed himself on the pull-down ladder with his torso in the crawl space. They were joined by Officer Yukio "Chris" Oshita. With Asa backed into the furthest end of the dark attic crawl space and attempting to hide under insulation between the joists, four officers trained their guns on him, shouting or cajoling at various times, while from downstairs, more officers made their way into and through the house, shouting commands to each other, while still other department voices came through radio transmissions. Police stationed below repeatedly banged against the ceiling directly beneath the spot where Asa had retreated.

Asa eventually was coaxed into a seated position at the far end of the attic. Officers reported shining flashlights in his eyes. A call was placed for the canine unit and Asa was informed that "the dogs were coming."[13] At least one officer reminded Asa that the date was June 6, 2006, or "666," and warned Asa that any actions that occurred might send Asa "straight to hell" or "to a very dark place."[14]

There was no way out of the attic and the officers had established this. With their guns trained on him, Asa began striking his heel through the plaster ceiling into the bathroom below. Officers who were stationed downstairs during the brief standoff would later offer their assessment at the trial—it seemed as if Asa was trying to kick his way out from where he was trapped.[15]

At some point, though on what basis is unclear, in the police's efforts to secure the situation, Asa ceased to be someone who was potentially in need of care from the police in their response to a "well-being call," and instead became someone who posed an unknown but potentially severe threat to them. Within a matter of minutes, in the police assessment of the situation (reflected in their interpretation communicated in the radio transmissions), Asa quickly transitioned from "subject" to "suspect" despite the fact that no incident had called the police to the house and he was unarmed and had committed no crime—nothing had occurred that would merit or solicit the response he was suddenly faced with in his residence.

According to the SFPD's CAD log, at some point during the interaction while he was cornered in the attic, police classified the situation as an "802" over the radio; in translation, this meant he was assigned a category of threat that would determine—and in fact eclipse—his likelihood of surviving the incident. In police code, an 802 refers to the California Penal Code and is the designation for "suicide by cop."[16]

Whether the officers commanded Asa to put his hands up and he began to raise them and then they fired; or he didn't put his hands up and they fired; or whether, as the claim was made in the summaries produced through the state investigation later and then in court, he wielded an eyeglass case towards them in a threatening way that resembled a gun, it is difficult to definitively know, as many of the statements in the trial as well as the statements in the investigative reports either contradicted each other or were based on questionable practices. Furthermore, the only witnesses to live through what happened in the attic were the police who killed him. What is certain is that Officers Alvis and Keesor opened fire, shooting Asa sixteen times.

A friend of Asa, Bernadette Harakati, would later leave a message on an online memorial site for Asa: "Hey Ace, Remember when we was standing on the balcony on the 10th floor of the Holiday Inn about 5 am and the smog was down over the city lol and you were singing Air Force One by Nelly whilst we both wrote our names in the condensation on the windows, I often wonder if our names are still there."[17]

Community Policing in San Francisco

Asa's killing was part of a new conjuncture of pacification aimed to manage social antagonism through neoliberal securitization. It unfolded within a complex web of forces in the economic enclave: whiteness and property, racial boundaries and intrusion; access to waged labor/racialized wage hierarchies and enclosure; and criminalization and exclusion. It reflected a low-intensity war organized as counterinsurgency warfare in the present—community policing approaches that include a neighborhood watch system that was put into place as a key strategy of the SFPD's community policing initiative and then activated by a neighbor; the unprovoked entry and ensuing raid on the house; the tactical progression of the police through the house and their role in escalating violence to deadly force; and the attempt to contain and narrate the violence through a number of obfuscations and deceptive policing practices that began with the internal investigation as the initial stages in building the strategy for the trial. It was the sustained efforts of Asa's family that exposed the workings of this war in the present.

Between 1990 and the time that Asa was killed in 2006, law enforcement had shot and killed at least 49 people in San Francisco and had been responsible for another 10 deaths, including in-custody deaths or other forms of violent abuse or deadly negligence, bringing the total to 59 deaths in the fifteen and a half years prior to Asa being killed.[18] A few months prior to the killing of Asa, Karen Ecklund, a white woman, had been fatally shot in San Francisco following a pursuit by the California Highway Patrol (CHP) that ended with her trapped in a dead-end alley and a CHP officer firing at her repeatedly as she was immobilized.[19] Two years earlier, on May 5, 2004, the SFPD had shot and killed Cammerin Boyd, a Black disabled man who numerous witnesses testify had his hands in the air when he was shot.[20] At the time of the killing of Asa, the SFPD was under intense community pressure to explain why they had first claimed Boyd was shooting at them despite witness accounts to the contrary; and when they later admitted he had no gun, to explain why they had killed an unarmed man with his hands in the air.[21] The case being built against Boyd at the time that Asa was shot was part of an emergent strategy developing in conjunction with the courts: the two SFPD officers who killed Boyd "claimed they acted in self-defense when fatally shooting a man who sought 'suicide by cop.'" The San Francisco district attorney at the time, Kamala Harris, refused to file criminal charges, and the officers were eventually exonerated.[22] San Francisco police would fatally shoot an additional four people in 2006: Oliver "Big O" Lefiti, Charles Breed, Michael Harrington, and Marlon Ruff.

The killing of Asa occurred in the context of a shift toward community policing that began in the early 1990s—taking shape under the "broken windows" theorizations of George L. Kelling and the proactive, punitive, and "zero tolerance" practical application spearheaded by Bratton.[23] In their scholarship on community policing, Victor Kappeler and Larry Gaines highlight the importance of "active police involvement with people through a wide range of programs designed to reduce fear. Police must get people out of their homes and get actively involved in their communities." For Kappeler and Gaines, "this means police must become directly involved in community activities and become organizers of community."[24]

This approach brought police into more direct contact with the community; officers were assigned to particular neighborhoods, promoting and ensuring greater proximity to and knowledge of the relations, habits, and rhythms of a community; and specific programs and strategies were implemented to encourage a community to monitor and report on neighbors in the name of "safety." The approach was aggressive, intimately connected to the community, and in certain neighborhoods, it prioritized arrests where previously warnings would have been issued. The result was "soaring criminalization, largely of people of color, and increased police brutality."[25]

In San Francisco, a Bratton-style community policing approach appeared at roughly the same time that it was emerging in New York City.[26] In the SFPD's Community Policing assessment published in November 2006, a few months after the killing of Asa, the department's investment in both a proactive approach to policing and policing based on community engagement was evident, including through programs like Safety Awareness for Everyone (SAFE) and Neighborhood Watch programs. The priorities of the Taraval Station in place at the time of the killing, where Officers Keesor and Alvis were stationed, reflected a growing commitment to Neighborhood Watch as part of a series of community programs that integrated the police and the diffuse shared practice of policing into the community by encouraging closer relations between police and community, and also promoted reporting by neighbors on other neighbors to the police.[27] An SFPD report on current efforts issued by the SFPD and the San Francisco Mayor's Office a few months after the killing of Asa, claimed: "Taraval officers have assisted in educating residents in the procedures to report incidents and crimes."[28]

Counterinsurgency theorist David Galula reflected in *Pacification in Algeria*: "it was therefore imperative that we isolate the rebels from the population and that we gain the support of the population.[29] As a strategy of counterinsurgency, these priorities and the moments and relations that they provoke break down the social fabric of a community—where the neighborhood watch is supported by armed force. Colleen Vignati, the neighbor who called the SFPD to report what she thought was a "drug house" (despite later confirming she had never seen anyone doing drugs), reported in her deposition statements that she had been encouraged by police to call them if she saw anything out of place. Her call reflected the department-wide SFPD initiative underway at the time. Likewise, according to her statement, she was encouraged by the police to call them if she saw the front door to the unit swing open. According to her own testimony, when Vignati placed the call on the night of June 6, 2006, she had been encouraged repeatedly by the police to do so. It was her call that affirmed and reiterated the criminalization advanced by the department through its new policies and priorities, and that would justify intervention and any subsequent violence. When Vignati alerted the police that she had seen the door swing open at 2 Garces, she brought the police to the house and under the rubric of community policing, authorized their entry.

Beginning in the 1990s and reaching an escalated pitch in the year Asa was killed, police and federal agencies across the United States were pushing the boundaries of aggressive police raids, including through the use of SWAT teams and "no knock" raids.[30] In alignment with this national policing practice, the SFPD has a history of questionable entry practices that reflect an aggressive, proactive invasion approach coupled with brutality, and a disregard for privacy and property in the residences of racialized, disenfranchised, and criminalized communities. On October 30, 1998, as part of a multi-jurisdictional effort involving the district attorney's office, the FBI, DEA, ATF, and an SFPD SWAT team under the command of Kitt Crenshaw, ninety officers raided the Western Addition apartment complex in San Francisco, brutalizing and terrifying its mostly Black community. In a similar aggressive approach on September 15, 1999, over sixty officers, including the SFPD and federal agents, again conducted a raid on the Western Addition. Named Operation SafeHome IV, the raid was part of a crackdown aimed at an alleged "drug turf war."[31] These shockingly brutal raids paralleled similar aggressive entry practices targeting Black and Brown communities across San Francisco at this time and further normalized police violations and invasions of Black and Brown communities and homes.

Multi-agency raids, SWAT raids, and increasingly brutal and invasive home raids advanced alongside other questionable and illegal entries primarily aimed at low-income homes and housing units, including single-residency occupancies. A lawsuit filed in 2012 against several SFPD officers who illegally entered residences and stole from residents, and subsequent investigations exposed sprawling corruption associated with the long-term practices of police entries in the SFPD.[32]

Under the rubric of a national "war on drugs" and "war on gangs," the proactive, aggressive strategies combined with "quality of life" tactics that are at the base of community policing increasingly brought police directly into the homes of particular communities. These invasions occurred within the context of a series of policies, strategies, and decisions that were already in place based on knowledge gathered before an event or incident, including demographic information organized as biopolitical regimes. The interventions raise questions not only about policing practices and training; they simultaneously articulate an understanding of "home" and "safety" across the enclave, and who can claim these. Thus, in the prose of counterinsurgency, not only are the police actions and the justifications for killing "fully and decidedly authored by the state" in Manuel Callahan's terms, but this prose is constructed—and its construction is made possible—against a backdrop fully mapped and framed by counterinsurgency practices, including the production of strategic knowledges about the population, aimed at reorganization, control, and pacification.[33]

Parkmerced and the Shifting Enclave

In June 2006, Asa was staying at Parkmerced with friends and helping to fix up the interior of the 2 Garces unit to ensure that those living there would receive their full security deposit when they moved out. However, the conditions of possibility for state invasion and violence had been set in place long before that June.

Located close to San Francisco State University, the Parkmerced complex was designed in the years after World War II as "garden living" for middle-income families who could not afford the high rates of more central San Francisco properties.[34] Beginning in the 1980s, following its purchase by Leona Helmsley, the complex steadily deteriorated. While at one time Parcmerced had been one of the largest rent-controlled properties in the Bay Area, providing many Section 8 subsidized housing units, under a "revolving door of property owners" the property was subdivided and sections were sold off, including to San Francisco State University.[35]

In 2005, a year before Asa was killed, Parkmerced had been purchased through a "predatory equity" scheme, meaning that the current rent income for the properties was not high enough to repay the mortgage debt. Real estate speculators engage in predatory equity deals when the real estate market is strong, with the plan to replace low, rent-controlled rates with new, higher-paying leases. Thus, it requires that rent protections be gutted, establishing the groundwork for evictions.[36] Alongside this, Parkmerced landlords had established a practice of suddenly raising the rents as high as 28 percent between at least 2004 and 2007, and likely before.[37] When the idea to demolish large sections of the property was put before a planning commission in early 2011, the move exposed development plans that had been in the works for years for developers to construct over 7,000 new units, including high-rise condos that they hoped to sell for $800,000 per unit.[38] None of the new units would face the same rent control restrictions, and Section 8 housing was not part of the newly redrawn development plan.[39]

The San Francisco district attorney at the time, Dennis Herrera, was "dead set . . . to fast track the massive project" in a move that would instigate the eviction of at least 1,500 families.[40] At the time that the SFPD entered the apartment complex at 2 Garces and tracked Asa Sullivan into an attic crawl space in 2006, the foundations for demolition and reorganization had been laid—deteriorating living conditions, shifting property ownership, subdivisions, and the disruption/decomposition of what had been a working-class family community.[41]

Redevelopment is situated within longer histories and "economies of dispossession" and is closely aligned with forms of criminalization. Amidst the intersecting machinations of developers, real estate speculators, investors, politicians, and others, District Attorney Herrera was in the process of naming "criminal gangs" and implementing gang injunctions across the city.[42] Herrera first targeted the Bayview neighborhood through the Oakdale Mob in 2006. By June 2007, Herrera had expanded to file two lawsuits across other historically Black and Brown communities in San Francisco, targeting first the Mission District through the Norteños, and then the Western Addition on the edge of the Fillmore District, against the Chopper City, Eddy Rock, and Knock Out Posse gangs. Later, injunctions targeted Visitacion Valley, attempting to establish a buffer or contained space between the Parkmerced complex and Bayview-Hunters Point.[43] Visitacion Valley, like Bayview-Hunters Point, had become home to Black and Brown communities in connection with the shipbuilding industries of World War II. These communities had been pushed out of the Fillmore and Western Addition neighborhoods in the 1960s and 1970s through demolitions, evictions, and a corrupt system of "certificates of preference" issued through urban renewal programs of the Redevelopment Agency.[44]

Rents in San Francisco consistently rank among the nation's highest. Background checks, credit reports, proof of income, and substantial move-in rates that often include first and last month's rent create additional obstacles. In some instances, a co-signer who is often a parent with property, savings, and provable income is required if younger people do not meet the standards of what is considered a reliable renter. Section 8 housing, or low-income housing, is notoriously difficult to find in the city, with years-long waiting lists.

Across the city, it is common for residents to live in apartments on a lease where none of the original signers still live in the apartment, in order to maintain the housing at a rent-controlled rate. Precarious income and other obstacles have necessitated such negotiations in order to live in a city growing amidst the vast wealth of Silicon Valley; San Francisco is constantly displacing and dispossessing renters and homeowners alike. This displacement and dispossession is itself a technology of disposability, as people without property or the right to privacy are far less likely to remain "among the living" in a biopolitical regime.

At the intersection of various forces of criminalization, speculation, and finance, the Parkmerced complex in 2006 represented a site in relation to other sites of differential property values, including its proximity to spaces of containment and racial quarantine established as buffer zones between the poor and the rich.[45] It functioned as a critical node through which the reorganization of populations takes effect.

For neighborhoods/populations also targeted by criminalization, the negotiations to find housing require further contortions. Asa had a prior conviction. He and his friend had been staying on air mattresses while working on the drywall, at the invitation of a friend whose name was on the original lease. Asa's mother, Kat, would later narrate these negotiations within a context of family networks of support at the trial. Asa had spent much of that year living with Kat in Santa Clara and commuting to appointments related to parole in the city. Kat recalls driving him to the CalTrain station early in the mornings so he could catch the train to attend the variety of appointments in the city on which his successful parole completion was contingent. At the trial, Kat recalled a large whiteboard in the kitchen of their home in Santa Clara, with the schedule for the upcoming week and month charted out between his work hours and appointments, so she knew when she needed to take him to the train for San Francisco. Once there, Asa spent some of that time with his young son, a toddler at the time, at the home of the child's mother. Depending on the train, the trip from San José to San Francisco is between an hour and ninety minutes each way, meaning Asa would need to spend up to three hours for round-trip travel several days a week to meet the appointments on which the terms of his probation rested, while at the same time managing employment demands. Some evenings he slept in a car with his younger brother, Sangh.

Across the economic enclave that is the Bay Area, these commutes become necessary as people are forced to live in less expensive zones surrounding urban centers while the employment, services, and resources required for survival and citizenship remain in those same centers from which poorer people have been displaced. Additionally, criminal charges, convictions, and incarceration disrupt people's employment and possibilities for employment, as well as their ability to sign leases and access housing. Many young people targeted through criminalization move in with extended family members during periods of transition as they seek to transcend the restrictions imposed through carceral regimes. Often, those family members have also been priced out of urban centers, thus requiring a reorganization of family life just to meet the transportation requirements for one member to adhere to the probation restrictions imposed by the state.

The Immediate Aftermath of a Killing

In the aftermath of a police killing, families are subjected to an illogical maze while the state advances and tests the first tentative syntactical blocks of an always volatile and emergent prose of counterinsurgency. When they learned something had happened involving Asa, Asa's family immediately engaged. Sangh went looking for answers and Asa at the police station the day after Asa was killed, unaware of what had transpired or even that they had lost Asa.[46] Once there, Sangh was interrogated by police for six hours and was not able to learn anything about the fate of his brother—to be clear, he was interrogated by the police without being told his brother had been killed by the police. As part of this interrogation, and later forming the testimony that would be read aloud at the trial, Sangh narrated the close relationship with his older brother Asa, "I saw him every day. We slept in cars together. He told me, take care of yourself if something happens to me."[47]

Kahlil documented this process as, following the killing of Asa, the department homed their interrogation in on the family:

> We did not get his remains until a week later, so the city's medical examiner could check for gunpowder residue and do an autopsy. We were not even allowed to identify his body. The first one of my family who tried to find him at the coroner's office was my youngest brother. He was taken to a room and interrogated about Asa for six hours, like he too committed a crime. It was not until a week and a half later we finally saw Asa at Duggan's mortuary; we all finally saw Asa's dead body.[48]

Through Sangh's actions and Kahlil's documentation, together they expose a site of entrapment and brutal psychological torture. Sangh's insistence on locating and determining what happened to Asa produces a critical and profound moment of knowledge production; it exposes the barbarous and cruel machinations of counterinsurgency aimed at families and communities to legitimize the presence and actions of the police and the state.

SFPD Officer Thomas Cleary was the homicide investigator who interrogated Sangh the day after Asa was killed.[49] Years later at the trial when questioned by the family's lawyer about the six-hour interrogation and standard procedures in dealing with family members following an incident, Officer Cleary stated that "conversations with the family are generally not recorded because they are usually basic information."[50] Yet the police relied on the misleading interrogation to criminalize Asa first in the papers and later in the trial in such a way as to sanction the state's violence, claiming it was Sangh who confirmed their narrative of "suicide by cop." The media reports attest to the family's ongoing refusals and struggle, citing, "in the suit, the family said police had falsely reported that Sullivan had been armed and shot first, then 'seemingly manipulated and obtained statements from a (Sullivan family member) to the effect that Mr. Sullivan was suicidal.'"[51]

As a term, "suicide by cop" first emerged in the early 1980s, ostensibly to describe actions where a person challenges the police to shoot them, usually by threatening police with a weapon with the supposed goal of provoking a fatal response. Coined by a former police officer and instantiated by psychologists to condone and obfuscate police violence, the term "suicide by cop" is frequently employed to justify acts of deadly force by police against people experiencing mental crisis, or killings that occur in the absence of a weapon or recognizable threat.[52] "Suicide by cop" inverts the attribution of violence and shields officers from their responsibility in a killing; it reverses the responsibility for a murder while conveying a sense of "inevitability."[53]

The designation "suicide by cop" requires a series of statements and actions for it to be affixed to a subject. The state needs to establish that a subject is suicidal, or in other words, has nothing to live for and seeks a violent death through confrontation with the police. To this end, from the beginning of the response to the violence at 2 Garces, the state had to produce a particular subject. The population that the police seek to protect and pacify, first as the public and much later through the concentrated, synecdochal jury on behalf of the public, had to understand the police engaging a person with no reason to live.

Ariela J. Gross's work is valuable in this context as she examines the juridical space/process of the trial historically as a site of racial (and gender) contestation and production in relation to questions of citizenship. Her analysis situates these juridical processes as productive of race and gender beyond the time/space of the courtroom to shape larger understandings and relations of citizenship and belonging.[54]

At the trial, the police asserted that they did not record the conversation, yet they gave evidence that Sangh told them Asa had said to him, "If I die, it will be my own fault."[55] It is unclear to which question during the six-hour interrogation this was given as a response, if at all. According to police statements, at some point Sangh also told police that his brother "did not want to go back to jail."[56] The trial revealed that many of the seemingly unrelated questions that were asked—during a period of intense duress, and not knowing what had happened to Asa—were taken out of context and amplified to criminalize Asa in the papers and justify the killing. It is important to recall as well the intense community pressure at the time to explain the killing of an unarmed Cammerin Boyd.

It is also critical to note the clarity of Sangh in assessing the actions of police—it was through not only his first action in search of Asa, but his second action, that the strategies of the state became manifest in all their devious cruelty. Once Sangh learned that Asa had been killed by police, he understood clearly the process that he had been subjected to during the interrogation. This is evident in his second action: he returned to the police station to ensure that his statements reflected an accurate representation of Asa, now from the retroactive position of knowing that it was the police who had killed Asa, rather than, as had been implied in the first interrogation, Asa who had been involved in a crime or who had somehow been hurt.

The project of criminalizing Asa and building the case that would justify the state's violence began in these moments. Based on the narrative put forward at the trial, it is possible to extrapolate that these questions involved an interrogation of Asa's mental state, his moods, his work, personal details, and any history of violence. These details would emerge, edited and remixed, years later in the trial—relying on Sangh's responses under duress to put forward to the jury the argument that Asa had reached a point where he did not want his life any longer. When questioned at the trial about why information had been withheld from Sangh, Officer Cleary responded on behalf of the police, "we are not authorized to tell him anything. It is the medical examiner's duty to inform the family, not the police."[57]

Yet, it is the police who determine when the Chief Medical Examiner's Office can release any information about the body or the case, or whether the investigation is still "in progress," in which case a police hold can restrict the release of any information. While most police departments are bound by policies stating that the department's hold on the release of information not exceed a certain time frame, it is often longer than this stipulated time before information is released, with no explanation given by the police.

In a manifestation of collective refusal and fierce care, Kahlil and Sangh collaboratively exposed the initial strategy of the state through their own investigations. The family's response also involved repeated attempts to navigate a media that had simultaneously dealt in fabricated evidences and appeared to have access to select details that the family did not. This included the delay of a week and a half after Asa was killed before they could finally see his body at the funeral home, after the CME completed his autopsy and tests were done to try to determine gunpowder residue by the evidence teams, even though no gun had been found at the scene. The family's interrogation required navigating various institutions across the state apparatus. The state, in turn, attempted to contain and also slow down the family's efforts. Deliberate delays were accompanied by other strategies to disrupt family bonds and antagonize relations among those who loved Asa the most, at a time when all were grappling with an unfathomable loss. ·

The story of the police shooting of Asa began to circulate in the mainstream media, and the justification for the shooting began to take shape as the first stages of what would become the defense. But in fact, the story of what happened to Asa was one that the state immediately stepped in to author. The incident that transpired initiated a series of internal investigations. According to department protocol, the first phase of the internal investigation begins immediately following an officer-involved shooting (OIS), as written testimony is taken from all officers involved in the incident and present on the scene when they return to the precinct. While some witness statements were taken immediately after the incident, others were inexplicably delayed by up to a month.[58]

Several witness statements were, based on the department's own regulations, contaminated, as was the case when the two officers who had fired their weapons, Officers Alvis and Keesor, were allowed to ride back to the station together in the same patrol car, against department policy.[59] The Police Officer Standards and Training manual outlines the conditions under which these investigations take place. Standard operating procedure designates specifically that officers involved in a shooting be separated from each other following an incident as a measure to ensure the integrity of the evidence-gathering procedures and the documentation of testimony that is immediately taken as part of the internal investigation, including statements from those present as actors and witnesses. Ostensibly, this practice is in place so that officers involved in a shooting do not compare stories and wittingly or unwittingly synchronize the details of their accounts before their statements are taken in the first, immediate investigation.

In the case of Asa, the state initiated another investigation that produced another series of testimonies several weeks later. Several months later, a third series of testimonies were taken from the officers involved. In addition to the internal testimonies of officers being interviewed by other officers, there were several other investigations. As is standard, the internal affairs unit began conducting its own investigation of the department immediately following the shooting. The city District Attorney's Office also opened an investigation, as in all instances of officer-involved shootings. Additionally, the homicide unit began its investigation into the incident itself. Months or years later, in cases where a department is being called into court, as in the case of Asa, the lawyers working to bring the case to trial bring the officers in again for depositions. It is not clear how or when these investigations are coordinated or which one takes precedence, much less what evidence is gathered or when it is used to make the state's case absolving itself from any wrongdoing.

In the days and weeks that followed, Asa's family connected with other families through Mesha Monge-Irizarry, providing a point of contact to immediately construct critical systems of information across a larger mobilized community and circulate the family's knowledge of the incident and deductions based on its own situatedness and proximity to a loved one and their familiarity with state violence. This provided the first step in circulating upcoming actions and spaces as families reacted immediately to the killing in search of answers and support. A candlelight vigil was held outside the Parkmerced residence where Asa was killed, followed by protests, a series of marches, picnics, and other gatherings.

Asa's family joined in a number of spaces over the next eight years, and with Mesha, continued to document their process—contributing greatly to the collective understanding and memory of the community, and advancing the shared analysis of a community of struggle. With Asa's family, this meant that in the days and weeks following their loss, they merged with other families—including families who were also just being thrust into the same space, all encountering each other.[60]

The protracted struggle that accompanied the push to the courts opened on many fronts across the Bay Area—confronting the state, challenging dominant media representations, provoking new questions and formulations of justice, and weaving acts of care within a community organized against multiple, interlocking forms of "security." In part, the struggle was waged to ensure that the incident in which Asa's life was taken could not be erased or rewritten by the state. As such, it could never be contained by the courts. Nor could it be reduced to a simple process of rebuking the narrative advanced by the only witnesses on the scene, the police themselves. It was also a process of refusing the state—rejecting not only its legitimacy, but the very criminal subjects that it attempted to produce in its efforts to secure governance across a broader population.

In her analysis of "social death," Lisa Marie Cacho examines how "the criminal, the illegal alien, and the terrorist suspect are treated as obvious, self-inflicted and necessary outcomes of law-breaking rather than as effects of the law or as produced by the law."[61] Over the course of the long battle to the courts, Asa's family had been exposed to a series of lies and retractions on the part of the police department. They experienced not only the loss of Asa, but a criminalization that engulfed the entire family; beginning immediately after the shooting, it was Asa and his family who were under scrutiny by the state for the violence that the state itself had produced. To justify its own act of violence, the state directed its attack at the site where Asa had been cared for and nurtured in an effort to eventually establish for the jury and the public that Asa's life, even to him, was one that was not worth living.

For Ranajit Guha, writing about the context of colonial India, the state relies on a prose of counterinsurgency as a form of colonialist knowledge; the prose of counterinsurgency deployed in colonial India was not only a strategy of colonial control (disciplinary, repressive, based on territorial sovereignty, and so on); it marked a project of disqualification where the insurgency of the peasant was narrated by the state (and conversely, then "authored" by the Left to serve its own revolutionary praxis).[62] It follows that if war is a social relation, social death is one aspect of a prose of counterinsurgency. Further elaborating this prose, Manuel Callahan's analysis of earlier frontier defense on the U.S.–Mexico border focuses on state investigations following violence as a site in manufacturing a prose of counterinsurgency, noting that "in every way the investigative apparatus developed by the U.S. supported the ideological work required of settler colonialism, producing specific statements regarding territorial expansion and control, and making frontier defense a critical racial project." For Callahan, the confrontations between Anglo settlers, backed by the state, and Mexicano and Indigenous peoples were struggles that were "expressed in opposition to larger processes of social and material enclosure and articulated through race."[63]

The state's investigations are in service of the prose of counterinsurgency; they are integral to the manufacturing of criminal subjects and obfuscating social antagonisms and resistances. From the moment of the state's killing of Asa, the state's investigative approach "support[ed] the ideological work required" to produce Asa as a criminal, to "appropriate" defense and establish the necessity of law enforcement, and displace both in the larger landscape of social antagonism in which this specific counterinsurgency strategy was at play. From the outset, the investigations denied Asa a subjectivity as anything other than a threat and a criminal.

This unfolded against another obfuscation. Shortly after Asa was shot, Kahlil had filed a complaint with the Office of Citizen Complaints (OCC) of the city and county of San Francisco for a wrongful death case. Kahlil documented the response from the OCC: "I got a letter in the mail with two check-marked boxes with words beside them stating my brother's wrongful death was due to policy and training errors."[64]

Liberal Counterinsurgencies and the Trial for Asa

In liberal counterinsurgency, the juridical process itself is a site of counterinsurgency. For Laleh Khalili, this is a potent space for the "invocation of law and legality" and serves to convey a state functioning in accordance with agreed-upon norms of justice and citizenship, advancing lofty ideals of equality and fairness. Khalili writes: "What distinguishes warfare by powers that claim adherence to liberal principles is the invocation of law and legality as structuring the conduct of war, an absolute dependence on a set of clearly defined procedures and administrative processes as a means of ensuring regulatory and ethical compliance, and finally a discourse of humanitarian intent."[65] Similarly, Bernard Harcourt argues, "Our government does everything possible to legalize its counterinsurgency measures and to place them solidly within the rule of law—through endless consultations with government lawyers, hypertechnical legal arguments, and lengthy legal memos."[66] The courts are not only sites of "unjustice"; they legitimize the terms of the relation of war, they mask the relation of war.

Yet police trials also reveal this façade because they expose how the police investigate themselves. The courtroom became a site of knowledge production, undergirded by the collective militant research investigation pursued by Asa's family. The trial made visible, for example, the internal functioning of the department following a killing, including the department's reliance on the Management Control Division (MCD), a subdivision under the office of Risk Management responsible for internal investigations and the maintenance of officers' personnel files related to discipline and use of force in managing risk after an officer-involved shooting.[67] According to the SFPD, the MCD "conducts internal investigations and maintains officers' personnel files in relation to discipline and use of force issues."[68] Through this, the trial also exposed breakdowns in police protocols. At least one officer present on the scene that night, Sergeant Tracy McCray, was not interviewed by anyone in any officially recorded capacity immediately following the incident, and was never interviewed by homicide investigators, only by the Management Control Division, or only by the office assigned to manage risk.[69] In violation of SFPD general orders requiring that the testimony of all officers on the scene be taken immediately following an incident of violence, Officer McCray's statement was not taken until a month after Asa was killed.[70] Despite this, Sergeant McCray's testimony featured prominently in the trial. Approaching the space of the trial as a space of knowledge production and of direct action takes seriously these strategies of the state.[71]

During the trial many details of Asa's life emerged in fragments, almost always meant to convey a particular view about the way Asa lived his life, the things he grappled with and the choices he made. Asa and Sangh had lived out of cars. Asa was staying at 2 Garces in the hopes of having a $1,000 security deposit returned to renters whose names were on the lease but Asa's name was not on the lease; it was not his home, he had no home. Or, even earlier, Asa's childhood was presented as a site of repeated intervention and knowledge production, his family continuously monitored by the state—Child Protective Services, juvenile hall, jail, probation, jail.

In many ways, the trial and the juridical processes that surround it function as a *dispositif* in the production of both racial subjects and social death, where "rather than simply a neutral space of rational arbitration between street-level policing on one hand and punitive institutions on the other, in many cases, the state-organized justice process itself targets family and community bonds in destructive ways."[72] From the Black Power movement to recent struggles including Occupy, while solidarities and court support have remained strong, conversations also continue regarding strategies that repeatedly have sent the struggle into the courts, a process that drains resources and can fatigue resistance efforts over time. Largely due to an inability to see criminalized populations as resistant populations, less emphasis has been placed by critical criminology scholars on analyzing the juridical process as a site of counterinsurgency. Instead, the emphasis generally focuses on questions of court bias or structural racism, rather than seeing the courts as a node in an architecture of social control that depends on racial hierarchies and criminal and illegal subjects.[73]

Relying again on Cacho, this notion of "social death" explores how the value of human life becomes legible through violence—racialized, sexualized, spatialized, and state-sanctioned. For Cacho, this scale of value cannot be understood only in racial terms, but rather, "social value is also contested and condoned through legally inflected notions of morality."[74] Cacho writes: "because the law is presumed to be both ethical and irreproachable, the act of law-breaking reflects poorly on a person's moral character."[75] Given this, she argues, for people relegated to a particular category of "social value," there is little that they can do to represent themselves as "moral and deserving"—not only of rights, but of life.[76]

Read against his race, the state attempted to narrate Asa's life in a way that justified its killing of him. As soon as police entered the apartment, in the retrospective gaze of the state that structured the space of the trial, it was confirmed that Asa was "criminal by being, unlawful by presence, and illegal by status."[77] He did not have the option to be law-abiding. This explains the shift that occurs discursively from a subject in need of state care administered by the police to a suspect that posed a deadly threat and, as a consequence, is now an enemy of a caring state.

The Coterie of Experts in Defense of the Police

In the trial for Asa, the City Attorney's Office assembled a number of expert witnesses for the city and county of San Francisco to defend the police: among them, a police training expert, a crime scene analyst and forensic and blood spatter expert, a psychologist and a psychiatrist, former police officers, and a criminal defense attorney.

Don Stewart Cameron was hired to testify based on his long history of training local and federal law enforcement agents. In his testimony, Cameron elaborated on police training, naming strategies that both the military and police use for clearing a building, including "third eye clear" and "slicing the pie." Cameron testified that the role of the police at 2 Garces that evening was one of "community caretakers," a role which granted them, first, the authority to enter the building and second, to proceed with strategies for clearing the building. His assessment supported the testimony of Officer Oshita who was at 2 Garces, and also justified the actions of the officers on scene that evening. Oshita spoke of the need "to locate potential victims or possible suspects," and substantiated that the team's actions were in alignment with SFPD policy: "When clearing an attic or a room you want to do it as quickly as possible. The attic needed to be cleared. That's what we're trained to do."[78] Together, as expert and authority, Cameron and Oshita legitimized the entry, escalation, and response that resulted in the killing.

Senior Crime Scene Analyst Alexander Jason, a specialist in shooting incidents and an expert on how bullets "perform" in the body, along with a blood pattern analysis expert, "read" the crime scene. Jason confirmed that he had been paid over $100,000 in this particular case by the defense to provide research and expertise. He also testified, under repeated questioning by the family's attorney, Ben Nisenbaum, that in his many years of work as an expert witness in the San Francisco Bay Area, he "had never offered an opinion against the city of San Francisco."[79] Put more clearly, he has in all instances been paid to legitimize the actions of the police.

Jason's initial visit to the attic crawl space to assess the blood spatter was over a year and a half after Asa had been killed. Nisenbaum's cross-examination exposed that according to the police's own records regarding SFPD evidence room access, the only time that Jason had reviewed the evidence related to the incident in which Asa was killed was one day before he submitted his final 26-page report clearing the police of all responsibility. Put more clearly, the assessment of the evidence from the crime scene presented to the court was either analyzed and then written in its entirely in less than a day, or it was written without examining the critical evidence on which Jason's testimony was based.

Two paid witnesses offered psychological expertise. Crisis management expert Dr. Kris Mohandie was paid as a clinical police and forensic psychology expert witness to testify in support of the police actions in managing the crisis situation that they had created and escalated over the twelve minutes that Asa was trapped in the attic crawl space. Mohandie commended the officers' decision to announce the threat of dogs as well as the threat of hell. In his assessment, these reflected "excellent" strategies in negotiating with a subject in crisis.[80] Psychiatrist Dr. Emily A. Keram, who had never met Asa or his family, submitted a lengthy assessment of Asa's family and childhood, and confirmed that Asa desired to die by "suicide by cop."[81]

The U.S. Army's *Counterinsurgency Field Manual*, published the same year Asa was killed by police, lays out how in contexts of counterinsurgency, civilian organizations "bring expertise and capabilities that complement those of military forces engaged in COIN operations." It notes that "at the same time, civilian capabilities cannot be brought to bear without the security provided by military forces. The interdependent relationship of all these groups must be understood and orchestrated to achieve harmony of action and coherent results."[82] In Bernard Harcourt's analysis of counterinsurgency, "legality serves to distance the commander in chief from the killing."[83] This recalls Ivan Illich's discussion of the role of the expert as "self-justifying" and as a critical support for maintaining the "industrial tools" of modern society, including the court system, the education system, the medical/health system, and so on, all of which degenerate society, producing both alienation and dependency.[84]

While positioning itself as a mediator and its "witnesses" as disinterested experts, the court itself is actually an integral component in these interdependent relationships. Working in unison to ensure that no money would be awarded in damages to the family for the loss of Asa that might concede or imply any level of accountability for the violence on the part of the police, the expert witnesses attempted to prove through their expertise that Asa had made no meaningful bonds with other people throughout his entire life, nor would any meaningful bonds be made in the future. Therefore, they argued, no damages were due to his son. One expert witness testified that because Asa had missed his Sheriff's Work Alternative Program (SWAP) work detail and as a result had an outstanding warrant, he would have been facing up to thirty-two months in jail. The argument was that this was another reason for the violence that Asa allegedly brought upon himself.

At the trial, the defense team for the police and the city constructed timelines on large poster board evidence sheets to demonstrate to the jury all the ways that Asa's life was not worth living. Various details were stitched together from the manipulated interrogation of Sangh to corroborate claims made through the timelines. One chart was a timeline titled, "Mr. Sullivan's Criminal History and Suicide Attempts," that was used to show that Asa had spent time in jail and to confirm the state's conclusion that Asa "was not turning his life around. His life was in a free fall."[85] The second chart titled, "Mr. Sullivan's History the Month before the Incident," included documentation produced by the defense lawyers demonstrating that Asa's former employers, Goodwill Industries, had "let him go" when he didn't come in for a shift after several warnings over the course of several months.[86]

These "events" were used together with statements taken out of context to conclude of the shooting that "it was what Mr. Sullivan wanted them to do. He forced the officers' hand. They did whatever they had to do. This isn't what they wanted to do."[87] The killing was, the state argued, what Asa wanted.

Asa's mother, Kat, and the home she kept together with her family as they grew was also drawn into the criminalizing narratives of the chart—as documents were shown and graphed for the jury of all the moments where Asa's young life had intersected with state institutions to convey a history of failed parenting. No matter that the chart could just as easily be read as the intrusions of a disciplinary and punitive state in the discursive production of an "unruly" child. His mother was made to testify that yes, he had been taken by Child Protective Services, even though she had fought hard and won to get Asa back. The charts became a visual mechanism through which the family was criminalized to win the case.

Asa's fate in the court, much like in the attic, was foreclosed by displacements that occurred prior to such moments. For most jurors raised on courtroom dramas and American morality tales, the moments when the psychiatrist assessed a person incapable of human bonds, or when the blood spatter expert conclusively read the pattern of Asa's breathing upon impact by the bullets to determine if he lunged at the police, served to promote the façade of justice. For the jury, including the U.S. public following the trial in the papers and on the news, instead of a barbarous and brutal militarized killing exacted on a life that could claim no protection before the law, the case represented a mystery ready for unraveling. As a *dispositif*, the court produced juridical subjects eager to uphold a line between right and wrong. They were produced through the process, and at Asa's expense, as moral citizens adjudicating on behalf of a national community. As an assemblage, the trial represented something beyond its courtroom confines: a coherent juridical process that undergirded, in Khalili's terms, liberal counterinsurgency. It was a critical process in legitimizing and remaking a liberal regime that regulated warfare.[88]

Each day of the month-long trial, the family members were shown enlarged glossy photographs of the patterns of Asa's blood to corroborate the analysis of the paid blood spatter expert. Similarly, the contents of Asa's pockets from the evening as he sat crouched in the attic were also produced as evidence. These included his keys and a series of blood-soaked business cards—including one with the name and number of his probation officer. The trial marked the first time they were seeing the contents of Asa's pockets from the night he was killed, including items familiar to them—the everydayness of Asa's life.[89]

Much of the trial and the instructions given to the jury focused on the purpose of the officers' entry into 2 Garces and whether Asa and the other resident had the right to a reasonable expectation of privacy. To establish this, a substantial amount of documentation was procured and debated, along with witness testimony, in order to put forward convincing arguments as to whether Asa had a legitimate right to be at the residence. Thus, in addition to having to establish Asa's criminality and prove that Asa saw his own life as one without a future, the defense mounted by the legal team protecting the police had to establish a series of logical steps that would lead to a justifiable situation where as many as ten or more officers entered a residence without a warrant, tracked someone they were not looking for and did not know into an attic crawl space, and opened fire.[90] Both Asa and his friend had permission to be living at the apartment from the current tenant on the lease and were working to fix the apartment's interior. While the fact that the tenant was facing eviction was brought up repeatedly at the trial, the current tenant still possessed the key and was in ownership of the unit at the time of the shooting. The web of criminality extended by the city's lawyers did not extend to the questionable practices of Park-merced landlords.

The Courtroom as a Site of Direct Action

In the case of Asa, the span of time between the act of state violence and the trial spanned over eight years. By the time the family arrived at the court with their investigation and their dignity, much had already been exhausted and lost. Reclaiming the space of the trial as a site of direct action and knowledge production becomes a way for a community to confront a state that attempts to define and control a "time" of justice, while simultaneously positioning itself as the sole or primary arbiter of justice.

One of these was the space of the trial itself, which exposed a myriad of strategies in the state's attempts to justify the killing and shield the police department. Because the trial occurred within a larger texture of struggle, the context was created to ensure that the trial was reclaimed as a space the community could use. By circulating the state's stories, lies, and strategies out from the courtroom and across a community of struggle that included many other families, Asa's family and those connected to the case converted the trial into a space of knowledge production and direct action of critical importance to larger community safety struggles.[91]

Theorizing temporary autonomous zones of knowledge production and the multiple systems of information that circulate in a community of struggle reveals an insurgent community, one constantly engaged in acts of self-organization against criminalization and militarization.[92] Such theorization makes observable an emergent collective effort to understand, reveal, contest, and escape the numerous counterinsurgency strategies that exist as forces within a more expansive strategy of pacification and social control in the service of capital.[93]

In the case of the killing of Asa Sullivan, the trial became a site of direct action both inside and outside the official judicial territory of the courtroom itself. The People's Investigation with the family at the center and the presence of community collectively discovered the different levels of state investigation, which in turn revealed the changing story of the state. The community efforts exposed layers of criminalization; this made observable an epistemology of criminalization as a process in place across other police killings. Furthermore, the space outside the courtroom and the relationships that traversed the trial emerged as a site of autonomous support and networking from the site of the social factory. Several community members who had learned of the trial through Mesha and through its ongoing resonance across other moments in a larger Bay Area struggle showed up and brought healthy food so that those present—always Kat and where possible, other family and community members—would have something sustaining on the breaks between the long brutal hours of the trial. The food was spread out in the marble halls of the Oakland courthouse. Asa's mother no longer lived in the city and had to travel from Washington state to attend the trial. Attending a month-long trial in a city away from home requires tremendous resources, and often the families that are targeted by the state are those already disenfranchised by capital. Drawing on the knowledges, practices, and resistances from within the social factory, an infrastructure was activated and expanded to surround and support the family. In the conversations outside and beyond the space of the trial among those who knew Asa while he lived and those who knew him through the political fight waged to reclaim him, new relations were established and details and analyses were collaboratively advanced.

Following the trial, community members converged in the space of UniTierra Califas's Social Factory Ateneo, together with Asa's mother by phone and other mothers who had lost children to violence.[94] These were collective moments that affirmed care for each other's presence and projects and ongoing work. These small moments contributed to a circulation of struggle across diverse issues—anti-prisons, disability rights, community gardens, gentrification struggles, and BART occupations. The struggle of the family, the love of Asa, and the efforts to build new relations to fight and live outside the state were archived and shared, through the *ateneo* summaries and in local newspapers, co-written by some of those at the trial together with Mesha.

In another brilliant effort, a counter-narrative was reclaimed through a series of courtroom drawings printed in the *San Francisco Bay View* newspaper; portraits of the expert witnesses appeared in sketches done by Nomy Lamm that seemed to erode both their credibility and power, while the family appeared with a humble grace in these same portraits, including one of Asa remembered and one of Kat on the stand, testifying to how she cared for him, recalling their happy times against the lies of the state. A song was written for Asa by Lisa Ganser and Nomy Lamm, "Stars Out," and performed by Ganser to launch the formal phase of the People's Investigation, along with a collective effort to raise funds for the transcripts necessary for the appeal. Through these moments of protracted "fierce care," the struggle wove those who had come together into enduring struggles and new struggles.

Counterinsurgency Tactics and the Social Factory

The murderous and brash attack on Asa exposes a confluence of counterinsurgency tactics when read through the category of the social factory. Beyond bellicose armaments, elements of everyday policing emerge as a critical component of counterinsurgency. Sergeant McCray testified that when she entered the residence and saw a man cuffed on a bed, he called out "Tracy." Officer McCray explained that she also knew his first name; in what she described in the vernacular, they knew each other from the 7–11 down the street through a relationship of "smoke and joke." When queried, she explained that the phrase was used to describe conversations that occurred in the space of the parking lot or inside the convenience store that had led over time to mutual recognition, exchanges on a first-name basis, and some degree of shared history in a given neighborhood between police and civilians.[95]

From the perspective of the state, these moments of police engagement with civilians are considered part of a central counterinsurgency strategy as officers on patrol engage members of the community in small conversations while they take note of patterns of activity across a community. What the trial revealed in this moment was a strategy that puts forward the illusion of a web of relations across a community that include friendly police officers there to "serve and protect." In fact, it reflects no actual community bonds of mutual protection, listening, or understanding. In other words, if these relationships are being built over time with the community and the call that the officers respond to is a "well-being check" where no crime has been committed and there is no one who has been "injured," and they are arriving in their capacity as "community caretakers," how is it that the situation escalated quickly to deadly force? The fact that both officer and resident exchanged names upon entering confirms that the man in the room was in fact recognized as a member of that community, including by the police who had just pushed open a door to enter his space without a warrant.

Many elements of counterinsurgency are designed to disrupt the ways that marginalized or targeted families and communities have organized themselves to manage their own collective safety and survival—concatenated spaces of "home," negotiated modes of transportation and movement, creative ways to earn a wage around the required appointments of probation, extended connections across family members to share and support each other. Processes of criminalization work in tandem with these strategies and in turn can serve to erase, rewrite, and make illegible a family and community's experience of itself as resilient and caring.

The trial exposed the confluence of counterinsurgency tactics targeting the social factory in a particular moment. The moment when the police respond to a well-being check by entering the premises without a warrant and securing the building quickly, floor by floor, is a militarized response, one where care for a community has been militarized. It reveals a successful attack on the social factory waged through the strategy of neighborhood watch and an extended community policing approach. The moment of the shooting makes observable counterinsurgency as a larger strategy of militarized policing and also reveals new forms of policing at the intersection of racial hierarchies and property. Who has a reasonable expectation of privacy? And what intersection of property and racialized social value does the killing of Asa reveal and uphold?

After nearly a month of testimony and a few days of deliberation, the jury's final verdict did not acknowledge any wrongdoing on the part of the police department. The jury's decision sanctioned an act of state violence and by extension, ratified the city's defense: Asa, the jury unanimously affirmed through their decision, had no reasonable expectation of privacy and had desired a violent death at the hands of the state; he had actively pursued this strategy to end his life by committing "suicide by cop." The jury, and the space of the trial itself, further solidified the nascent term "suicide by cop" in juridical discourse, sanctioning further state violence in the discursive space of the law.

The decision ensured that Asa's family, including his young son, received no financial compensation from the city and county of San Francisco, and that neither the officers nor the department held any responsibility for the decisions and actions that took a life.[96] And while the family and legal team attempted to appeal the decision, the cost of the court transcripts on which a successful appeal of the case depended exceeded $10,000. The family and community did not have time to raise the funds by the deadline for filing an appeal. In response, a People's Investigation was launched, as a commitment to exposing the state and to imagining forms of justice collectively that refuse to be contained by the courts.

In September 2014, as witness testimony was being heard in the month-long federal civil suit for the SFPD killing of Asa, a press conference occurred in the plaza below the courtroom outside the Ronald V. Dellums Federal Building in Oakland to launch the U.S. Department of Justice's national Violence Reduction Network, a strategic plan introduced by Attorney General Eric Holder to provide local departments in selected cities with "greater access to federal resources." The federal anti-violence program prepared to allocate an astounding $124 million nationwide to its Community Oriented Policing Services (COPS) program, including $1.8 million to hire an additional fifteen officers for street patrol in Oakland. Part of a concentrated crime-fighting strategy, the plan highlighted increased use of technology, specialized regional training, "smart policing," and "evidence-based policing strategies." It also committed funds to improving prosecution strategies locally and at the federal level. As Holder inaugurated the latest national anti-violence project on the East Coast, California Congresswoman Barbara Lee announced that as part of this project and despite declining crime rates over the past decade, the grant money would directly bolster the size and presence of local police departments as part of a larger commitment from Lee to "invest in community programs."[97]

Against this ever-increasing police presence, what emerged from the struggle for justice for Asa was a collective will of refusal and defiance over many years and across multiple actors against the lies the state attempted to impose on a family and community. From the first vigils and actions in the streets to the spaces of care and direct action that were constructed within the space of the court as both against and outside the state, Asa's family exposed an intricate web of counterinsurgency, including sites of liberal counterinsurgency, repudiating the "justice" offered by the state and instead fully claiming a fierce care as a collective and shared commitment of community safety.

Part 3

CHAPTER 7

Justice Campaigns

The Morning of the Stockton Picnic

In Stockton in late April 2014, families and community members arrived at a local park for a barbecue. There, they unfurled banners with photographs of their children, killed by various law enforcement agents often acting in collaboration with federal, local, and county agencies; or targeted by other forms of state-manufactured violence; or incarcerated with sentences as long as their lives, often based on questionable policing practices that were upheld and advanced by the courts. Large banners were stretched taut between trees, sturdy pieces of paper tacked onto other trees with photos, including a portrait scripted *Long Live Champ*. One life was commemorated on a deconstructed cardboard box propped on a park bench with a person's name in graffiti calligraphy. Tables were washed down, and people arrived with cakes and salads, coolers of soda and beer. A barbecue had been started earlier in the morning, and people moved through the line of smoke where food was already cooking on the grill. Music played from a large portable speaker propped next to a canopy erected that morning for shade.

A minivan arrived from Oakland and people unloaded boxes containing thousands of glossy postcards bearing photographs of several young men. The postcards highlighted a life taken, often including details about the police weapon used in the killing; the various agencies involved; and when known and available, the names and photographs of the officers present and responsible for the killing. The postcards counted the number of shots fired into each body, or the number and location of police dog bites that had mauled a body before a shooting. These were the descriptions written by families about the bodies of their children, their loved ones. In some cases the family's assessment, including details from when they were finally able to see their child at the morgue, stood in contradiction to the police or coroner's report, the discrepancy alone opening up the chasm between state narratives and community knowledge as counter-narrative. Sometimes two lives were remembered side by side on the same postcard, exposing parallels between killings that may have been separated across time, or simply and starkly functioning to connect a department's acts of violence, a refusal to forget.

As families face the criminalization that occurs through the proliferation of state misinformation and disinformation following a police killing, their first moves are often ones to confront or resist the strategies that attempt to cast their child as "threatening" in the justifying discourse of the state. Nationwide, an outraged public with the family at the center frequently demands a response that advances a counter-narrative, reclaiming an innocence or a sense of promise, witnessed through the repeated assertions at rallies and in grassroots statements and independent media that a loved one was unarmed, or had never had a criminal record, or was enrolled in college or held a full-time job, or was a father or mother. These become critical details to circulate, and served to contest police representations of the incident itself and to refute technologies of criminalization that invariably appear across dominant media sources, most often circulated by police departments themselves following a killing.

However, communities also organize effectively to circumnavigate the strategies put forward by the state and the media that attempt to divide the community around a binary of innocent/thug or unfortunate victim/deserving victim, and so on, and instead claim all victims in community spaces. There is a refusal to accept that the escape from social death demands an exceptional status to win inclusion "back into the fold" of the lives, and the losses of life, that "count." Such a bid for inclusion via the construction of an innocent or undeserving subject may be necessary and have meaning in the construction of a counter-narrative, for example, in the instance of a trial. Yet it is one that communities both advance strategically and also abandon, recognizing that this imperative to differentiate a good subject through a differential process of subjectification in death marks the forces at play that create a certain desire for families to ensure that their loved one is, even in death, "counted among the living."[1] The Stockton barbecue reflected this moment where a community mobilized in a collective refutation of social death and indeed, the biopolitical imperative, hoisting the responsibility of violence back onto the state. It was a moment of fierce care, as the community refused to let someone stand alone when targeted by the state, and refused simultaneously to allow others to be isolated through violence and alienated through criminalization.

Some postcards, instead of highlighting victims, were almost entirely organized around reprinted photographs of law enforcement officers involved in specific killings, captioned with short professional biographical information on each officer. In one case, the postcard included a photograph of the local medical examiner. Through their own research processes, communities had exposed the ways this office, too, was complicit in reproducing and justifying the state's narrative of the necessity or justifications of its violence.

Framing the space of the barbecue were names chalked onto the sidewalk of those targeted by the state, losses remembered collectively, in bright colors. There were buttons with photographs of loved ones handed out among those gathered at the barbecue, updated on a weekly basis to include the most recent killings from across the Bay Area and also across the United States.[2] Some at the barbecue wore T-shirts screened with the faces of the loved ones they had lost, many scripted with *Rest in Peace* or *Rest in Power* followed by the dates spanning the person's life, or the address where the killing occurred, often an intersection of streets that marked the specific spot in the city where the person had been gunned down. This made visible how many cities and towns were present in the space, but also which neighborhoods and intersections were represented. All of this formed a map.

As a site, the barbecue itself was a space of research and a system of information similar to a grassroots think tank. In this way, it stood against organizations like the RAND Corporation or the Cato Institute that produce and circulate hegemonic discourses of security and criminalization, directing criminality and violence back into the communities themselves.

Reflected in multiple systems of information through the banners and signs, postcards and T-shirts, buttons and sidewalk chalkings, the park in Stockton hosted the justice campaigns: Justice for James Earl Rivera Jr., for Donnie Rae Haynes, for Alexander Fontau Mahan, Mario Romero, Alan Blueford, Raheim Brown, Kerry Baxter, Jr., Kayla Moore, Alex Nieto, Oscar Grant. While the majority of the artifacts reflected a commemoration of lives taken by law enforcement or targeted by the carceral state, some remembered lives lost to state-manufactured violence—young people whose lives were taken on city streets, in parks, on the porches of their own homes by stray or purposeful bullets, and other sites of violence. As articles, artifacts, and archive, these systems of information represented focused strands of consistent and dedicated direct action. They also formed an alternate media that circulates in the community itself and often appears embedded in the mainstream media.

The justice campaigns are spaces of convivial research and insurgent learning where grassroots investigations are honed and explored and communities are in control of their own knowledge production; here research and strategy are circulated among the community. Information is tracked about different incidents that have been released by various state agencies and the investigations conducted through various departments—coroner's reports, police reports, morgue photos, CAD reports, and other forms of state documentation. Through the collective investigations, gaps are assessed and calls formulated for pieces of information that remain missing or which remain unaccounted for. Incidents are narrated and demands issued: "Stop the Cover-Ups!" "Release the Dash Cam Videos!" Many called for an independent Department of Justice or FBI investigation into the corruption and brutality that the community knows plagues the police departments.

The campaigns, as investigations, deliberately convene "spaces of encounter" that function as "temporary autonomous zones of knowledge production," or TAZKPs, where the community shares, compares, and filters information that they have about the incident. As TAZKPs, they are always linked to other spaces. As justice campaigns and community-based investigations, they make visible those stories of the violence that communities continue to face. They also reveal information about specific officers, often a history of criminal or violent behavior that the community is able to surface and which is largely sealed from public access. This is a significant aspect of the campaigns, because even in the rare event that a state killing makes it to trial, there is no guarantee that an officer's past history will be revealed as part of a public state archive, as this information is often restricted in court proceedings. As the courts are increasingly understood to shield the police from accountability in myriad ways, the community investigations are critical to a sense of grassroots justice that is directly linked to community safety. The community remembers.[3]

Additionally, stories are swapped while getting to the barbecue, preparing for the barbecue, and during the barbecue—for some, during the two-hour car pools leaving from Oscar Grant Plaza in Oakland to Liberty Park or Eden Park in Stockton, or once there, while washing down tables, or as food is prepared for serving, or errands are run in the morning to fetch this or that, as rides are organized to find restrooms at fast food restaurants close to the park because the local park's public restrooms remain locked for security reasons, despite repeated requests from the families to the city weeks in advance for access.

During an errand run at the April Stockton barbecue, one woman spoke about a home raid her family had just experienced under the justification of a routine probation check on her partner's minor son. The conviction was not a felony, yet she described how a few days earlier as part of this routine check, her house was surrounded by police cars with numerous armed officers entering her house, and then every room was "cleared" in a room-by-room military-style operation. Her family was made to stand together surrounded by police in the center of the living room while her stepson's room was searched. In addition to anger and even a measure of fear each time their home was raided, she spoke of the embarrassment and shame of this regularly occurring situation in front of her neighbors.

The Stockton barbecue in April 2014 emerged from a collective struggle that spanned the Bay Area, with the families of those targeted at the center. The space marked a growing insurgency following the killing of James Earl Rivera Jr. on July 22, 2010, a day before what would have been his seventeenth birthday. James Rivera Jr., according to several witnesses, had been stalked early in the morning of July 22 by Stockton police officers and then shot more than thirty-eight times by police officers Eric Azarvand and Gregory Dunn, and San Joaquin County Sheriff John Nesbitt as part of an operation involving as many as twelve agents, including police, sheriff's deputies, probation officers, and others coordinated through a multi-agency auto theft task force known as Delta RATT (Regional Auto Theft Team). This task force was initiated in 1998 and was comprised of officers from the police departments of Stockton, Lodi, and Manteca, as well as the California Highway Patrol and the San Joaquin County Sheriff's Department; Delta RATT also includes members from the San Joaquin County Probation Department and the San Joaquin County district attorney.

Following the state killing of her son James Rivera Jr. in 2010, Dionne Smith-Downs, together with her partner Carey, their children, and a militant community around them notably undergirded by the care and efforts of local organizer Aaron Paradiso, mobilized around a number of justice struggles in Stockton, continuously led marches that blocked freeways, shut down the Stockton courthouse, stopped traffic, and both confronted and evaded police at various intersections and features across the urban geography of Stockton.[4] These struggles continued to make visible a range of policing practices, including the high number of deaths, particularly police shootings, across San Joaquin County and in Stockton that have involved Delta RATT officers and operations.[5]

While many movement spaces have been more readily accustomed to challenging police murders with the shouts and slogans of the organized Left, there is also a hesitancy across much of the Left to speak out when it comes to responding to forms of state-manufactured violence that are not directly traceable to law enforcement. In Stockton, families came together through a shared commitment to militant forms of care that refused to exclude families whose children were not killed directly by the state. This was also a recognition of the contours laid by the state. In many counties throughout California, the state stràtegically divides families whose children's deaths were not explicitly authored by the state, for example homicide victims, from those whose children were killed by police. As one technology of this division, families whose loved ones were killed by police do not receive any form of compensation or counseling, with the message being that the killing of their child by police confirms that their child was criminal and the family is undeserving of attention or compensation from the state.

In refusing to exile certain community members, the justice struggles advanced a collective and communal care, one that was not separate from their confrontations with the state and its responsibility for the production of violence. They shared resources, supported each other's direct actions, attended press conferences, and in many cases, organized around other issues impacting the family and networked across families and geography in sustained moments of self-organized activity—setting up fundraisers for medical expenses for other children or funeral costs as family elders passed, showing up at court dates, and managing information on each other's behalf in relation to a larger extended community to keep families safe and surviving.

With the common experience in many of these collaborations across families being the loss of a loved one to violence, these convergences across families provoked a complex analysis of violence, particularly as families struggled to represent through *testimonio* the complexity of the ways that they were targeted by the state over an extended period and frequently across multiple family relations. Among tables piled high with summer foods and bright paper goods arranged in lines in preparation for the community feed, people pulled chairs into a semicircle on the grass or leaned under the edge of a small canopy and listened as different mothers and others from the community spoke.

Here, they retold the stories of how their children were killed. For some, this was a story they had told many times and repeated with rage. For others, it was so recent they struggled in their narration, receiving support from others who stood with them in the circle while they pressed forward with the story. Some of the cases had endured for many years. Those close to the cases shared updates and new information that had emerged, almost always produced through their own investigative efforts. Fathers and other family members spoke too. In the circle, the stories shared reflected a range of issues facing the community. People spoke about evictions and the forced distances between families, as many of those present had already been pushed out of Oakland over the years by forces of dispossession and gentrification, with many relocating to Stockton where housing is cheaper. Others were on the verge of being pushed out of Oakland, and others were commuting from Stockton to Oakland or San Francisco to work, while still others had moved back to Oakland and were commuting to Stockton to work. These are not easy commutes; the distance between Stockton and the Bay is roughly eighty miles, and traffic during peak commute times can easily extend this trip to two or more hours one way.

While families from across the greater Bay Area traveled to the picnic in Stockton, families and organizers from Stockton regularly travel to direct action spaces and community gatherings in Oakland and San José and have participated in rallies and marches following prominent incidents of state violence, including the killing of Trayvon Martin and Michael Brown in the summer of 2014. This circulation across periphery zones and urban centers has provided a sustained engagement between communities of struggle based in Stockton and others in the Bay Area.[6]

Stockton as a Periphery Zone

In a 2013 op-ed in *Viewpoint Magazine*, Inderbir Singh Grewal reflects on the circulation of struggle and family bonds across the Bay Area: "It is not just that many working-class communities in the suburbs and cities are locked in the same struggles. One of their struggles is precisely that urban residents are being evicted from their communities and suburban residents are losing economic security. And this has been reflected in resistance."[7] Grewal notes the social antagonisms that are negotiated in relation to capital, and says that "as more low-income and working-class people move into the suburbs, their struggles are bridging the gap to the bigger cities."⁸ The complex relations of community and family across geographies reflect and negotiate a Bay Area organized through economic enclaves.

Yet in what Verónica Gago and Sandro Mezzadra (drawing on the work of Saskia Sassen) characterize as a "conquering of new territories" through the expansion of the extractive operation of financialization, Stockton was also targeted by the orchestrated financial crisis of 2007–08 where through subprime predatory loans and other mechanisms, banks and mortgage companies targeted Black, Latinx, and Indigenous communities and single mothers.⁹ Gago and Mezzadra argue that subprime loans "have as their objective the incorporation of the vital economy of poor or impoverished populations," and that is part of the logic of the extractive operation of financialization to demarcate expulsion and inclusion.¹⁰ Joanne Barker's work on the experiences of Indigenous people across the United States in the subprime crisis of 2008, including predatory loans, notes that these impacts were minimalized and largely invisibilized in the national discourse of the subprime crisis, and argues for a "broader view of debt and the subprime" that includes ongoing dispossession that targets Indigenous people across the United States.¹¹

Located in San Joaquin County in California's Central Valley, with a population of roughly 320,000 people (though the greater metropolitan area of Stockton is over double that at roughly 690,000), Stockton is the eleventh largest city in California. For the majority of 2007, Stockton topped Detroit in the number of home foreclosures. Stockton regularly ranks high on the *Forbes* list of America's most dangerous cities, and from year to year it exchanges places with Oakland as the city with the highest violent crime rates in California, a status arrived at through an analysis of the FBI's Uniform Crime Reports. According to a report from 2008, despite a $500 million downtown revitalization project, growth in Stockton "was based on the booming housing market, which was spurred in large part by relocating Bay Area residents looking for a home they could afford"; Stockton boasted higher wages and a lower cost of living.¹²

But this was only true for certain sectors. Following the "dot-com" crash in the early 2000s, Stockton's population expanded by 17 percent. By 2001, 80 percent of home buyers were coming from the Bay Area, priced out of Oakland and San Francisco. By 2006, the price of a home had tripled in San Joaquin County to an average of $385,000. Yet, average families couldn't afford 95 percent of the homes on the market. And by 2007, one out of twenty-seven homes was foreclosed in Stockton, a 256 percent increase from 2006. After the housing crash, many families defaulted on mortgages, sending some renters back into the city.[13]

Forms of survival in Stockton are visibly linked to the social wage, with many retail stores in the decimated downtown advertising that furniture, food, and household goods can be purchased through plans that align with the fund disbursement schedules of social welfare programs, extracting value through an operation of finance and expansion of debt similar to the forms of social extraction analyzed by Gago and Mezzadra.[14] When in 2008 Vallejo, a city of 117,000 people and roughly about equidistant from both Stockton and San Francisco, declared bankruptcy, the California state legislature passed a law requiring greater austerity cuts before other cities could file for bankruptcy. In response, the city of Stockton cut $90 million in workers' wages, appropriated another $20 million from workers, and then cut health care for retired city workers during mediation. In June 2012 Stockton filed for bankruptcy, the largest municipality ever to file in the state.

In the community barbecue speak-out, people shared stories of trying to survive by piecing together meager strands of social welfare—unemployment checks, disability checks, and food stamps. These checks rarely added up to a monthly income that was even close to sustainable, and the funding remained precarious, easily and suddenly revoked by state bureaucracies whether justified or not, and involving a continuous and complex navigation of state bureaucracies and forms of state control, monitoring, and surveillance that consistently accompanies even the most truncated forms of the social wage.[15] People shared updates on current labor battles in Stockton, police and other attacks on houseless people throughout the city, and the struggle for safe, healthy food for families to eat. For many members of the community, survival was based on a balance of some sort of minimal state subsidy and some form of underground economy that brought them into proximity with other violences while simultaneously increasing their vulnerability to the violence of the state in myriad ways.

Confrontations with the Police

As the circle at the April barbecue continued throughout the early afternoon, those gathered alternated between cooking and setting up for the meal, as well as speaking and sitting and listening. The numbers shifted between 100 and 200 people throughout the morning and early afternoon, including many young children and many women and older people. Several folks navigated the rooted and grassy park in wheelchairs.

And then the barbecue was attacked by police. Adjacent to the food preparation, a march had been planned from the park to the police station with the banners and signs from the justice campaigns. As several children, many of whom were brothers and sisters of those who had been killed, assembled at one corner of the park holding a banner, the doors to several parked police vans that had been stationed discreetly on a side street adjacent to the park suddenly swung open and Stockton police streamed out in full riot gear. Approximately thirty officers poured into the streets in military formation, running shoulder to shoulder in two columns and descended on the park in a mass of hardware and a spectacular display of force. They established a perimeter, surrounding the corner of the park in a right angle that flanked both sides of the public space. Shoulder to shoulder with riot windshield screens down over their faces, they refused to let anyone leave the park.

Young children began crying and screaming. Family members scooped them up and moved to the interior of the park. Others stood behind the children glaring at the lines of police. A few attempted to leave the park in small numbers to get to parked cars, unsure of what orders had been given on that day as a policing strategy, and distrustful of how the police were prepared to respond.

Each time more than a handful of people attempted to leave the park, the police formation shifted to contain them. Refusing this enclosure and the fear it was meant to elicit, a group was able to push into the street and continue part of the march. Immediately, the street was sealed off by the police and the group was beaten with clubs back onto the sidewalk and into the park. A line of jabbing police officers refused to let anyone leave under penalty of more beatings and arrest. For those from Stockton, to continue to attempt to reach the police station and challenge the police exposed them to a visibility that could likely lead to increased harassment—or even death—after the protection offered by the visibility of the community gathering dissipated once folks returned home across the greater Bay Area. For those not from Stockton, the threat of multiple court dates, sometimes taking up to a year to resolve, in a peripheral city two hours from the Bay Area center, was also daunting.

At that point, those inside the park began to experiment, realizing that there were not enough police to surround the entire park; as the crowd shifted inside the park the police were forced to move and establish a new perimeter to contain them. It was cool inside the park, under the shade of the trees. In the street, where the police stood in formation in full gear, it was under direct sun and hot. Quickly realizing this dynamic Dionne Smith-Downs, who faced the same police every day that had killed her son, collected her other young children around her and began to walk the perimeter inside the park and study the police. Picking up the pace inside the park and watching the officers shift to hold the perimeter, Dionne began shouting repeatedly, "Walk them pigs around the park!" and the collective inside the park moved rapidly and continuously along the edges in a tight group with the officers attempting to follow until the police on the outside collapsed, hunched over and gasping for air.

Under this guard, the barbecue resumed, surrounded for several more hours by sweating police, until the evening when everyone finally trickled home. Those residing in Stockton were well aware of the violent reprisals that the department was prepared to exact following these victories. They had other children they knew would have to encounter these same officers as they moved about their neighborhoods and the streets of Stockton. Others left for the two-hour drive back to Oakland and San Francisco, affirming that they would come back, or see folks soon in the Bay, in a shared commitment to maintain the connections between the struggles. But the day marked a critical collective refusal to give up communal space.

The barbecues organized by mothers are strategic spaces of insurgency and encounter where new possibilities are circulated and generated in the struggle to demilitarize and decriminalize community life. The complex systems of information exchanged are critical to understanding and also regenerating the community; these sites mark a critical prefigurative moment in community-based justice that refuses the enclosure offered by the courts and the prison industrial complex.[16]

Several of those gathered and quarantined at the Stockton barbecue, including some of the mothers, were present the following weekend to engage UniTierra Califas's Democracy *ateneo* in San José and to reflect together on the struggles circulating across the Bay Area through networks of families. We celebrated the "living theory" emerging from Stockton and drawing on the work of H.L.T. Quan, who noted that "as mothers take a prominent position in the struggles against militarization across the Bay Area, we can understand 'gender as an infrastructure of resistance . . . [one that] provides the beginning of a vocabulary for the under-analyzed feminist politics of articulation.'"[17] Living theory, like all theory, exposes what we are up against as a proposition to change these conditions, but as living theory, it refuses to impose a future.[18] Here, the barbecues are theorized as spaces of rich collective learning and sites of living theory as well as spaces of assembly, where the articulation of a feminist politics is "based on listening as much as speaking."[19]

In assessing Stockton in its position as the front line of resistance to counterinsurgency, and at the same time where spaces of assembly are being convened against the onslaught of tremendous state and state-manufactured violence, the moment of collective ethnography produced through the networked spaces of the barbecue and the *ateneo* offers the following reflection: "Rather than pleading with the state, making demands of the state, or organizing around media awareness and 'consciousness raising' that the masses simply must respond to, communities organized around their own learning and assembly are engaging the prefigurative. In these spaces, systems of information form a critical component to community convivial research projects and investigations. Convivial research can be seen as a research praxis that constitutes the desired change."[20]

Families and communities in Stockton continue to expose the forces of repression and forms of differential policing. During one protest against police violence, when police arrived with an armored vehicle, those gathered, under the command of Dionne Smith-Downs, made the deliberate decision to take the march into the wealthy white zones of the city on the outskirts of the university district, thus forcing the military vehicle, usually reserved to patrol Black and Brown communities, directly into the neighborhoods where such policing presence was uncommon.[21] These diverse spaces where repression is confronted and resisted provide arenas where the people can read their own power.

A Net of Counterinsurgency and the Carceral State: Terrorizing and Reorganizing the Community

Adjacent to these moments of spectacular policing are the everyday intrusions on the social factory. When a call is placed to the police regarding a violent crime in Black and Brown communities, the state responds with a full repertoire of officers, investigators, crime scene analysts, and paramedics, often from both the fire department and eventually from a hospital, as an ambulance is deployed that may or may not be allowed to cross the crime scene to assist a victim in a timely way. Witnesses are isolated and interviewed by homicide investigators or their contact information is taken for future follow-up.

Any situation of violence in a community generates significant paperwork on the part of the state. This itself is an orchestrated effort of pacification. As an event, it provokes a number of police incident reports, witness statements, search warrants, ballistics reports, hospital reports, coroner's reports, a death certificate, hearing notices, subpoenas, court documents including transcripts of depositions and testimonies, and later, appeals and so on.[22] Each incident leads to a series of queries led by the homicide investigator assigned to the case. These queries initiate further interrogations, provoke search warrants, and direct officers to conduct searches of homes and cars, and the homes and cars of relatives, friends, neighbors, and intimate partners that may be current or date back several years.

In this process, it is common for prior felony convictions to be exposed and old warrants to surface, together with previous infractions and in some cases firearms and drugs. The interrogations and searches make visible to the state a web of familial relations and at the same time make intelligible vectors connecting families and neighbors and a myriad of relations and bonds in a complex series of protections through which a community is organized for its own survival against the unrelenting onslaught of the state—its laws that determine what is considered a crime and what is considered illegal; its courts that determine sentencing and inscribe restrictions on relations and space; its acts of extreme violence, deadly and sadistic; its prisons, colonial schools, juvenile halls, detention and deportation centers; its largely unavailable hospitals and its mental institutions; its services that protect children by removing them from homes; its community centers that dispense pills after perfunctory or no counseling; and so on.

The searches of homes by the state in turn produce various confiscations that may or may not bear a connection to the incident that initially sent the investigators and officers into the home. Cell phones may be confiscated, as well as computers from homes where a suspect may never have lived. In many cases, their contents are later erased and then returned. Community members report that welfare checks and other checks from various state agencies that families depend on for survival have been taken from their envelopes from piles of mail by police and not returned, leaving families without vital month-to-month resources.[23]

An incident of violence exposes a network of relations, intimacies, and a community's meticulously developed strategies organized around its own safety. It also lays bare impossible decisions around care. The state archives contain police reports, witness statements, depositions, and court testimonies that reflect heartbreaking decisions made by family members when, for example, in a search, a gun is dragged from under a bed in a home, often only loosely connected to those labeled suspects. If the search of a home produces a gun and someone in the home is on felony probation and restricted from the proximity of firearms under threat of returning to prison, what story emerges about the presence of the gun? If a mother is incarcerated or institutionalized, and the conditions of guardianship of her child by another family member are contingent on no one in the home having a police record, what decisions must be made when answering to the state to explain something illegal found in the home?

In these moments, a family must decide who will face the force of the state following a raid or a search. Under threat of false information that impacts their entire family and their own position in relation to the juridical system, families are confronted with situations where they must collectively decide to whom to attribute a weapon or any other illegal possession that may have been turned up. This includes calculations about each family member or neighbor's position vis-à-vis the carceral state and whether they are under threat of the loss of their children, among numerous other potential losses. Undergirded by draconian sentencing laws and forms of incarceration and surveillance that will quite possibly sever family and community bonds forever, families are forced to choose between, for example, identifying a gun as something that belongs to a son who may be on felony parole, or attributing it to a son-in-law, who may be the father of two young children, or a mother or grandmother claiming it as her own.

In the first instance, if the gun is attributed to the son who has a previous felony, the son may return to jail for what could be a severe sentence for the parole violation. This could then also easily lead to any number of situations once inside the jail that could result in a range of terrible outcomes; for example, any number of random factors could lead to solitary confinement, which could last for months, years, or decades.

In the second instance, if the gun is attributed to the son-in-law who may not have a previous felony and may have a clean record with no strikes, or it is claimed by the family, this may avoid catalyzing the parole violation of another family member. Yet, it may turn out when the gun is registered with the police department that the serial numbers on the gun match those on a gun reported as stolen that was used in the commission of a violent crime, possibly a homicide. If, for example, the son-in-law is then charged in relation to the crime for which the gun was purportedly involved, for the family and the community to fight the case takes up tremendous resources, both financial and in terms of time (days off work to appear before the court, child care costs, transportation costs, legal fees, etc.). This process alone can cause a primary earner to lose their job, further destabilizing the entire family. If the son-in-law is convicted, he faces incarceration and the children are left without a father. If the mother of the children has been arrested, institutionalized, or is not present to take care of the children, the family must fight for the responsibility of guardianship to maintain the children so they are not lost to the state.

This begins another long process—if one of the grandparents has a past history of convictions, it is likely that the children will not be able to stay in the house of the grandparents. If there are other relatives, for example an aunt who is employed and willing and able to take the children, but she is unmarried, anyone who occasionally or regularly stays at the house—lovers, partners, friends, another teenager under the care of the aunt—must be willing to submit to a background check by the state as well to determine if there is a history of convictions. This may eventually exclude the aunt from taking the children, while offering up another point of state intervention and surveillance beyond the immediate family.

In the case of relatives who do not have prior convictions and are in relationships that the state recognizes as stable (i.e., married) and also have children of their own, there must be enough rooms in the household in order to ensure that the children are separated as demarcated by the state in their sleeping arrangements in relation to the genders and ages of the other children already living in the home. For example, in some cases, there are restrictions imposed by the state that a young male child cannot share a bed or even a room with a female teenage child, and vice versa.

So for a relative to take the children they must have adequate space—extra rooms and beds—in other words, property of a certain size and spatial configuration to accommodate privacy in relation to state classifications of gender in order for the state to recognize the home as "safe." It may be that based on these restrictions, these relatives are only eligible to take one child, and the children must be split up across families or worse yet, one may stay and the other must be given up to the state. It may be that in order to avoid this, the grandparents, whose original house was searched, have to choose whether to give up one or both children to the state in order to keep them together. Or they may petition for the guardianship of both children.

However, if one of the grandparents also has a prior conviction, it may be that the only way to keep the two children together and under the care of the family involves the grandparents moving into separate residences, so as to isolate the family member with no convictions away from those that have convictions. And then, in this new residence, there must be adequate space. And so on.

And even though many of these interventions require warrants, they are frequently done without a warrant or they are made possible through a policy of "no knock raids." Any violation of a family's right to privacy would have to be fought through the courts—costly, time-consuming, and difficult to challenge, given the respectability of police officers in the eyes of the court.[24]

At the moment when a raid produces a gun, the scope of the consequences that a family must navigate before the state is intricate across relations, histories, and geographies. The protections and carefully reasoned care that are required in this moment are often not readily understood as care. How are these stories heard, for example, when they are on display as messy and raw before an all-white jury in the absence of a larger analysis of racialization and the presence of a punitive, carceral state—one that includes the invasive mandate of Child Protective Services that many believe is unquestionably for the good of the child? Additionally, the extreme consequences can pit diverse individual and collective survival strategies, as well as family members and extended communities, against each other. In low-intensity war, the bonds of community are targeted—the very bonds that would protect and nurture both resistance and autonomy, and the bonds that are critical to a community's ability to regenerate itself and maintain itself as intergenerational. Here autonomy is as basic as the space for a community to maintain the right to raise its children.

In many instances, state records reveal the fortresses a community has erected against the state. If a key tenet of a successful counterinsurgency is based on getting to know the population and understanding its relations, communities recognize that it is very difficult to police a population that refuses to speak. State documents reflect a series of stances taken, including in many cases an unwavering testimony before the state that a person who was clearly present on a scene neither heard nor saw anything related to the incident. These positions are often steadfastly maintained against the onslaught of a state-manufactured "snitch culture," as people refuse to bend or speak against family and community—defying court subpoenas against partners, family, and community, declining to bear witness to what might have been seen or refusing to be conclusive about anything about which they are being interrogated. Many children refuse to give their names, and refuse to provide accurate information about their family networks, to officers or even outsiders.

Thus, when gunshots reverberate across a disenfranchised community, they reverberate throughout the social factory. In their wake, state agents enter homes and schools. It is not uncommon to hear stories where police officers remove children and young people from classes and hold them illegally in the backs of squad cars for hours without notifying anyone of the child's whereabouts, interrogating them with no adults present and often threatening them as well. They confiscate cell phones which may have compromising information on them or, at the very least, which generally serve as a map to a field of relations among youth. Officers have been known to illegally detain the partner of a suspect, for example, a partner who is also a mother, caretaker, or legal guardian of a child or multiple children. In some cases as a result of this illegal detention, she may be out of contact with her very young children. There are stories of people perceived to be related to a suspect being handcuffed and interrogated in squad cars or at department precincts for anywhere from 2 to 12 hours.

In addition to the many dangers associated with these illegal detentions, a number of other problems can result. A person may miss work without having time to give notice, or they may miss a job interview. If Child Protective Services has an appointment or reason to visit the house during this time and finds no one home but the children, this opens up a new line of invasion by the state.

In instances where a case is brought to trial, past histories are brought to bear on the incident in an attempt to narrate a criminal subject capable of committing the current charge. Many cases involve people from the same community that the state has opposed to each other as defendant and plaintiff or as co-defendants in the same incident. One example of the state producing plaintiffs and dependents can be seen in domestic violence legislation which mandates that calls placed in cases of domestic violence must be prosecuted through the courts. In many cases, the legal strategy on the part of both lawyers is marked by an attempt to demonstrate that each lawyer's client is innocent, and to do so, each must prove that the other client is the more dangerous of the two. In the case of a violent crime, each lawyer's efforts are often concentrated on demonstrating that their client acted in self-defense and in fear for their life, and an entire landscape of violence and community relations is called forth into the courtroom, pitting community members and often families against each other. The testimonies in court mark the prodding of the state—for example, to retell stories of violence sometimes decades old involving community members who have lived together for generations. The state, in turn, archives these statements.

The space of the court is constructed to support and weave complex processes of criminalization. It documents and archives the relations and networks across a community. The documentation, explanation, and elaboration that take place through the juridical process give shape to the criminalization and pathologization practices that articulate racial and gender regimes and geographies of war. Their documentation becomes embedded in a media apparatus that then constructs specific subjects. In the mandate of the court and the orchestrated duel between legal teams, those asked to testify become "gang-bangers" or multiple felons, aggravated assaulters, sex offenders or traffickers, and so on—dangerous criminal subjects responsible for the violence flaring up across urban streets. The entire police force—with its technologies of surveillance and repression, its necessary violence and packaged falsehoods—is continuously rebuilt around the gunshots, armed robberies, drug exchanges, and sex economies that emerge in the courts in any given year, framed by particular acts of legislation, much of which is authored and lobbied by private companies that continue to profit from the prison industrial complex.

And this violence destroys families—both the families of victims and the families of those convicted. As cases wind their way through the courts, many children, young and older, lose parents to incarceration as a result of increasingly punitive sentencing laws. Homes are split and histories and lessons that would have been passed on are truncated as parents, siblings, and grandparents are locked up. Care and wisdoms are lost. Once incarcerated, many people lose the ability to connect physically with their family; connections are severed as those convicted are placed in institutions in remote areas of the state, and often moved multiple times to different correctional institutions. The population is reorganized through a carceral logic of geography.

It is not unusual for a family to spend several hundred to a thousand dollars to traverse the state to try to visit a loved one for a few hours. Because of the remote location of prisons across California and the size of the state, public transportation is often not an option for the totality of the journey. So even after a long train ride, for example, families must pay hundreds of dollars to secure a taxi or rideshare from an urban center to a more rural prison, and often the trip is so long that the family must spend the night before starting the return voyage home. For many families, the cost of visiting an incarcerated loved one is so prohibitively expensive that they are unable to visit more than once a year or every few years, and sometimes after traveling they are denied visiting privileges at all, for any number of reasons. A prison yard may be on lockdown and no one can accept visits, or a person may have been disciplined for something—including an unfounded allegation by a guard or by another incarcerated person; for example, one seeking privileges or who may be motivated by the wish to be closer to or see their own family. While an allegation may later turn out to be false, it nonetheless can function to restrict a prisoner from seeing their visiting family. In some cases, one member of the family may be allowed to visit, but another, sometimes a child, may not be cleared once they arrive. In other cases, a visit that may cost a family upwards of a thousand dollars may only be allowed to take place across a glass wall.[25]

Each conviction offers an observable moment where the criminal justice system is exposed as a racializing apparatus.[26] Those institutions which form its primary pillars—policing, courts, prisons and detention centers—are not merely built on racist views and racist practices that can then be examined through a focus on structural racism, though certainly this is the case. From community patrol practices and police investigations, to court orders and trials, to incarceration and parole and probation restrictions, the institutions of the carceral state are not only sites where racism is embedded: as institutions they manufacture race at the same time that they manufacture violence. Drawing on Manuel Callahan's work on the U.S.–Mexico border that situates the border as a *dispositif* in the service of W. E. B. Du Bois's "democratic despotism," the various moments of community-based investigation that occur in multiple sites, from sidewalks to parks to autonomous learning spaces, interrogate criminalization as a sustained racial strategy productive of multiple subjectivities and supported by the criminal justice apparatus.[27]

The struggles of mothers and families have emerged from these injustices and restrictions as much as from moments of extreme violence.

In many cases, family members have found each other through losses that they have explicitly linked to the state. In these struggles, certain refusals are sharpened and explored. In a movement that often remains focused on police killings as the most salient moment of state violence, connections across families as they grapple with a spectrum of state violence provides a context for a honed analysis to emerge about counterinsurgency warfare articulated across the relations and bonds of community. These become struggles to find meaning about how the state and capital are functioning in a particular moment and geography. These then merge with larger community struggles. In many cases, this is also a struggle to advance a counter-narrative, to build a collective analysis, to co-generate a strategy. Tracing the struggles of these families and the reverberations produced through moments of violence has proved critical in situating the social factory as a category and a site of struggle and involves an interrogation of the state manifested locally.

The Barbecue Migrates as a Shared Convivial Tool

Dionne Smith-Downs learned the strategy of the community barbecue from Occupy Oakland, transformed it according to her own family and community history of gathering and sharing food, and simultaneously worked with Aaron Paradiso to sharpen it into a new kind of militancy. As a convivial tool, the barbecue became something that various families and regions picked up and modified in the service of their community struggles. The barbecues migrated from Oakland and San Francisco to Stockton, where they maintained a kind of permanent position, and where they could be activated at any time in response to any number of urgent issues: from new developments in court cases to new moments of violence, or in response to any number of tactics of decomposition that threatened to silence local struggles.

The barbecues also migrated to San José, including on a Saturday afternoon on February 21, 2015, when Laurie Valdez hosted a memorial barbecue for the one-year anniversary of the shooting death of her partner, Antonio Guzman Lopez, by the San José State University police. Antonio was shot in the back while carrying a drywall saw on his way home from work. Families from across the greater Bay Area came to the barbecue—from Half Moon Bay, Oakland, Stockton, San José, San Francisco, and Vallejo. Some arrived at the barbecue after spending the morning at a direct action organized through the Anti-Police Terror

Project in Oakland to shut down the Home Depot store in Emeryville, where a few weeks earlier on February 3, Yuvette Henderson had been fatally shot in the street by Emeryville police after a security guard for Home Depot reportedly called the police to alert them that he suspected Yuvette might have shoplifted from the store.

Like Stockton, the park in San José was arranged with justice banners, drawings and photos of loved ones, a *piñata* for the children, face painting, and generous helpings of food spread across the tables in the warm spring air. At least one family was encountering other families in the justice struggle for the first time. Others had been supporting each other for years. Several families shared that their calls for support for a loved one experiencing crisis had instead resulted in a deadly shooting by law enforcement when they arrived at the family's home.[28]

The gathering reflected both the expanding network of interconnected families, and their use of community spaces outside the state to celebrate, grieve, support each other, and share vital and often interrelated information gleaned from their ongoing investigative efforts and occasional updates from lawyers. Drawing on Gustavo Esteva's "living hammock," the barbecue created a living theory around "expandable points of connected support" that families rely on to "weave together shared struggles and collective experiences of grief and resilience."[29] The word "hammock" also suggests that a community once networked can hold space. As families crisscross hundreds of miles to be together, "they are constructing a mesh formed of care and forms of justice outside the state, a mesh prepared to catch new families who are targeted."[30] The barbecues are always anniversaries of violence and are difficult for those who must host them, and difficult as well for those for whom the anniversary recalls their own family anniversaries. Stories are swapped and new plans discussed as the community reflects itself back to itself in its strength and dignity.[31]

CHAPTER 8

Spaces of Encounter

In spring 2012 the People's Community Medics appeared across the Bay Area, providing a series of free first-aid skill shares focused on best practices for responding to seizures, bleeding traumas, and gunshot wounds. Speaking before crowds gathered in high school auditoriums, recreation centers, on street corners, and on makeshift platforms in parks and parking lots, the People's Community Medics physically acted out life-saving techniques while narrating incidents of violence. The trainings proceeded much like *guerrilla* street theater—a dash of bright blood-like paint was cast onto a living volunteer while the two women who form the base of the Community Medic team, both from Oakland, explained how when responding to someone who has been shot, it is critical to cover both the bullet's entry and exit wounds to stop the bleeding. They then demonstrated how to swap people when fatigue sets in so that direct pressure applied to an open wound can be maintained for over thirty minutes at a time, often relying on common items often found in a pocketbook or backpack. They reminded those gathered, often standing, of the "golden hour," explaining that if the bleeding can be stopped and a person can be delivered to a hospital within the first hour after they've been shot, there's a strong chance they can live. Those gathered interjected with questions or quietly communicated with each other during the performance, exchanging nods and murmurs of recognition and collective loss. Often when a skill share was over, the crowd remained with more questions that then turned into stories that revealed shared experiences of violence across communities.

The spaces convened through the trainings of the People's Community Medics are one of several spaces organized around fierce care and insurgent knowledge production that emerged from within communities across the Bay Area as assertions of dignity in response to specific police shootings and community violence. They mark spaces

197

of autonomy animated by shared learning and collective care and mark mobilizations to confront an ongoing low-intensity war aimed at social reproduction, particularly targeting Black, Brown, and Indigenous communities.

This chapter will explore a series of four interrelated projects that unfolded in response to specific moments of state and state-manufactured violence occurring within an already mobilized community committed to challenging militarization and advancing community regeneration as part of a larger community safety effort underway across the Bay Area. These projects were the People's Community Medics, a grassroots, life-saving skill share project launched in Oakland in 2011; the Love Balm Project, a series of theatrical performances and workshops based on mothers' *testimonios* for their children murdered across Oakland, San Francisco, and San José; the Bayview Community Feed, a monthly convergence and food giveaway organized by the mother of Kenneth Harding and the community around her; and Stockton's Mobile Response Team, a community initiative organized around practices of care started by two mothers, Dionne Smith-Downs and Denise Friday, who lost sons to Stockton police.

All of the projects highlighted here are autonomous projects organized with Black women, in most cases mothers, at the center. They stand as testimony that there has always been a strong presence across the United States of Black women's autonomous organizations and projects, though Chinyere Oparah examines how too often historically these efforts have not been archived. This parallels the invisibilization of violence that targets women of color and in particular Black, Brown, and Indigenous women, as well as trans women and trans people in general, as many feminist, and especially women of color and queer collectives, scholars, and community efforts have continued to make visible.[1]

As moments of self-organized activity, each of the projects reflects a complex confrontation with the immediate, corporal violences of the state; and as spaces of encounter, they also point to the importance and power of collective knowledge production emerging from community struggles as key sites of rupture in a global colonial "epistemicide," a concept generated by Boaventura de Sousa Santos, to link forms of epistemological dominance to forms of genocide.[2] The projects explored here make use of various convivial tools including performances, skill shares, community speak-outs, relational *testimonios*, collective remembering, and convivial research approaches to reclaim and construct communal spaces and "reweave the social fabric" of community.[3] Together, in the words of Juan Herrera, they constitute an "archive of organized practices of community care."[4]

Incidents in a Low-Intensity War

In June 2011, two and half years after the execution of Oscar Grant, the Oakland Fire Department (OFD) paramedic and whistleblower Sheehan Gillis filed a suit against the OFD for alleged mistreatment of Grant after he was shot in the back, with the bullet exiting through his chest while he was lying on the Fruitvale BART Station platform. Gillis pointed out that Grant was allowed to bleed out because OFD responders covered the entry wound but not the exit wound. Gills also alleges that the OFD destroyed evidence related to the incident and that Grant's death evidences "system-wide discrimination against people of color" at the hands of the OFD.[5] The other young men detained on the platform with Grant, his comrades, contribute to the formation of a counterknowledge that was vital to the community in this moment. They attest to BART Officer Mehserle's statement directed at Grant after shooting him in the back, and as the young man's friends begged BART police to call an ambulance: "Fuck that. I'm not calling any ambulance."[6] Grant was later pronounced dead at Highland Hospital in Oakland.

When James Earl Rivera Jr. was shot forty-eight times while pinned behind the steering wheel of a minivan he was driving, no one, including his mother, was allowed near his body as he lay dying. She was not allowed to ride in the ambulance, and police and a sheriff deputy barred her from seeing him in the hospital. The first time she was allowed to touch James after the shooting was several days later in the funeral home.

In San Francisco when Kenneth Harding, Jr. fell to the street in the plaza at 3rd and Palou with a bullet wound in his neck, police officers established a cordon, securing the area around Harding's body as a crime scene. As Harding lay on the plaza, SFPD officers refused to allow any permeation of their imposed security boundary by neighbors and others passing by on the street who had gathered in a ring around the dying young man, who from time to time tried to raise himself from the sidewalk. Many observers repeatedly tried to provide water, pleading and demanding to be allowed to offer some sort of care or solace.

For twenty-eight minutes of visible agony in the blaring July sunlight of the plaza, no one from the community was allowed near the young man, the police refused to perform any life-saving measures, and no medical help arrived to assist Harding.[7] Harding Jr. died on the afternoon of July 16, 2011, after being removed from a public bus by San Francisco police and detained on the street in Bayview-Hunters Point for failing to provide proof of payment for a $2 transit fare. Notably one of the last remaining largely Black neighborhoods in San Francisco, Bayview-Hunters Point is the only neighborhood in the city where fare inspections are carried out by armed police; in other areas of the city, unarmed MUNI officers are responsible for this task.[8]

As Colby Friday lay bleeding on the sidewalk a short distance from his home on the afternoon on August 12, 2014, after being shot in the back by the Stockton police officer David Wells while walking to the store, no one was allowed near his body. In an incident that was first narrated as Colby going after a gun, then as Colby going to pick up a dropped cell phone, and finally as a case of mistaken identity on the part of the police, the Stockton Police Department struggled to advance a credible narrative as to why Colby had been shot in the back at midday. He bled to death on the sidewalk of a Stockton suburban development in the middle of the afternoon.

To different degrees and across different but connected communities of East Oakland, Bayview-Hunters Point, and Stockton, each of these violent events provoked immediate and enduring direct actions and prolonged, extended acts of insurgency that spread across the greater Bay Area. People's rage and demands for justice took over streets and plazas through protests, rallies, vigils, blocked intersections, and other gatherings. In a battle sustained over time that included organized demands at city hall, mobilizations at churches, campus panels, and numerous gatherings, community members and local groups organized protests that shut down freeways and city hall in Stockton; a complete shutdown of the Port of Oakland; and MUNI shutdowns in San Francisco.

In the cases of both Grant and Harding, community recordings of the incidents were circulated widely and globally, exposing millions of people to instances of extrajudicial killing accompanied by deliberate forms of securitized abandonment, a strategy well known across Black and Brown communities as "bleeding out." The familiar and widely witnessed practice of "letting bleed out" exposes a startling reality. These can be seen as pedagogical moments, situated within Rita Segato's pedagogy of cruelty in the new phase of apocalyptic capitalism, with its technologies of disposability and extractivism.⁹ How else but to respond, then, but with the refusal embodied in "fierce care," a refusal which is no less than the refusal of the subjects towards which this pedagogy is directed?

Out of the rebellions that raged across Oakland, Stockton, and San Francisco in response to these and other killings, a new imagination of insurgency arose. Working from within the terrain of a racialized and militarized landscape, a diversity of projects responded to the shootings as evidence of the urgent need to understand and confront the many violences aimed at communities racialized through and marginalized by capital. Many of these projects were deliberate in not only reclaiming space, but in their reproduction of space where communities of struggle could generate critical cartographies, engage questions, and imagine alternatives collectively.¹⁰ They also provided a path for a collective desire across communities to strengthen and create spaces of autonomy currently advanced as part of a larger community safety effort underway across the Bay Area. While this chapter focuses on a particular configuration of projects linked to these deaths, the responses across the Bay Area were varied and vast, demonstrating profound refusals, support for struggles for change across society and forms of governance, commitments to collective care and healing, and a range of other desires and dreams.

Each of the community safety projects that emerged in response to these killings can be read as a space of convivial research and insurgent learning and also as a convivial tool, producing a site for knowledge to not only be shared but co-generated, opening up new possibilities for political life. The claims they advance are complex efforts of a resistant occupation, to "embrace [occupation] as a process and strategy." In this way, the "occupation" of space is also in many ways a call to assembly.¹¹

The People's Community Medics

As a grassroots first-responder initiative that emerged in response to people being left to "bleed out" across the Bay Area, the People's Community Medics regularly host trainings in basic emergency first aid, providing free basic emergency first-aid kits to participants. Through the trainings, they convene community speak-outs addressing violence and care. The medics also deploy via cell phone in their own well-worn vehicles in response to emergency calls across Oakland. In some cases, they arrive well before the ambulances and are frequently restricted from providing further care when the police arrive. It has become increasingly common across the Bay Area for police to establish a perimeter around a body and identify the space as a crime scene and force the community, especially care workers, out of the space.

The women who formed the project and continue into the present as its main medics originally belonged to the Oscar Grant Committee, one of many autonomous projects to arise out of the mobilization following the killing of Grant. They have spent a good portion of their years in close proximity to the many textures and struggles of Oakland and the Bay Area.[12] The medics' presence and practice at the intersection of violent, racialized policing practices and their prominence in Oakland's Occupy movement drew attention to an important political intersection between struggles against police violence and mobilizations that were more closely aligned with anarchist commitments and which drew on the legacy of the alter-globalization movement.[13] By the spring of 2012, Oakland's Occupy movement had fanned out into neighborhood parks across Oakland, offering free community barbecues and skill shares where the medics presented their trainings, along with families speaking about the violent deaths of their loved ones and Know Your Rights trainings from local cop-watching groups.

In their own political genealogy, the medics locate their emergence as a response to the execution of Grant and everyday policing practices, along with the absence of emergency medical response units directed at Black and Brown communities across Oakland. Working under the motto "each one, teach one," the medics credit trainings made possible by friends trained as health care workers, as well as the presence of well-organized street medics who formed a critical component of the Occupy movement. These care workers and medics were active in the everyday functioning of the Oakland commune's camp and in the street battles between police and protestors, which were filled with tear gas, rubber bullets, sound cannons, flash bang grenades, and physical interactions with brutal law enforcement agencies. The medics also travel with supplies to mitigate the impact of chemicals used by police, to counter the effects of tear gas and pepper spray.

The Love Balm Project

The Love Balm Project was a series of performances and spaces unfolding through the *testimonios* of mothers and grandmothers who had lost loved ones to state and state-manufactured violence.[14] A project of remembering and mourning as well as a celebration of life, the Love Balm was catalyzed by the killing of Oscar Grant and conceived by Arielle Julia Brown of Oakland, who shares an entwined family history with the victim. Not long afterwards, it expanded to encompass community losses to police and street violence across the Bay Area. Initially, it focused on the stories of loss of six Bay Area women and their children: Bonnie Johnson, the grandmother of Oscar Grant; Anita Wills, mother of Kerry Baxter, Sr., incarcerated since April 2001 at 30 years old and serving a 66-year sentence as a result of questionable policing practices and juridical failures, and grandmother of Kerry Baxter, Jr., fatally shot at 19 years old in a still unresolved homicide in Oakland on January 16, 2011; Ayanna Davis, mother of 25-year-old Khatari Gant, killed on the street in Oakland on August 4, 2007; Brenda Grisham, mother of 17-year-old Christopher La Vell Jones, shot and killed on the family's front porch in Oakland on December 31, 2010; Denika Chatman, mother of 19-year-old Kenneth Harding Jr.; and Yasmin Flores, mother of 27-year-old Daniel Booker, shot and killed outside a nightclub in San José on December 19, 2009. The lives that were remembered by the mothers and grandmothers belonged to Black and Latino men, from 17 to 27 years old.

The early stage of the project was based on its director, Arielle Julia Brown, listening and documenting stories of mothers and grandmothers about their lost children. These narratives were then formed into monologues that were read out loud by each of the women during a performance at the EastSide Arts Alliance, a community center in East Oakland. In the next phase of the Love Balm Project, the mothers' stories were carefully woven together into a theater piece, *Love Balm for My SpiritChild*, performed in community theaters across the East Bay over the fall and winter of 2012–13. As the play began, a basket was passed through the crowd filled with photocopied images of the young men who had been killed. Those present to watch the play were invited to consider the many images and could also take them home. In the theater performances, local actors, many of them active in community safety struggles, revolved on the stage speaking words from the mothers' original monologues that had been rewoven, putting the stories into a kind of conversation or dialogue. At the end, the actors and director facilitated a community conversation that included many of the family members who were present in the audience whose loss, reflections, and struggles formed the play.

The *Love Balm* play was then disaggregated into a series of site-specific performances known collectively as *Our Hallowed Ground*. Over the summer of 2013, each woman's *testimonio* was performed by a local actor speaking at the site where the violence occurred in the words of the mother whose child had been killed there. The performances, like the lives and losses they represented, spanned the Bay Area from Oakland to San Francisco to San José. There was no monetary exchange for those who assembled as the "audience." Some of the performances took place several times over the course of the day, so the act of witnessing was not necessarily restricted to a particular time. At every site, the families were present, often with many children and layers of extended family. They were invited to speak or stay silent, each having worked with the director and the actors and community members as the project had unfolded over time.

For the following summer, the play was then recomposed again as *Love Balm for My SpiritChild* for a ten-day run from July 11 through 20, 2014, at the Brava Theater in San Francisco's Mission District. Evenings were organized to include a discussion following each performance with those in attendance. This exchange was facilitated by families represented in the play. The dialogue also wove in more recent justice struggles engaging other families and community members present in the theater who saw reflected in the performance similar experiences of violence. Thus, they were presented with a space where these stories could be shared.

The Love Balm Project also extended beyond the performances to include the Love Balm Institute, which held *testimonio* workshops across the Bay Area and Los Angeles. Relying on popular education strategies and making use of open spaces of *testimonio*, the Love Balm Institute facilitated dialogues on violence across communities and created space to explore focused conversations, including the role of art and the artist in social movements and struggles, and strategies for engaging justice and peace-building.

The Community Feed at Kenny's Corner

The Community Feed at Kenny's Corner was started on February 19, 2012, by Kenneth Harding's mother, Denika Chatman, and community supporters in Bayview-Hunters Point. It was strategically situated in the cordoned-off area of 3rd and Oakdale where Kenneth Harding Jr. was left to bleed out. Every third Sunday for over a year, community members and supporters gathered to set up tables, make healthy sandwiches for bag lunches, and assemble grocery bags of food to hand out from 10 A.M. to 2 P.M. to people in the Bayview-Hunters Point community, distributing as many as 150 bags of food each month. They also hosted a coat drive, providing free coats, shoes, and other clothing to people who came by the Community Feed. The project was deliberate in its two aims: "to give back to the community and to reclaim the space from murdering SFPD."[15] Similar to Oscar Grant Plaza, part of this project has involved a community renaming of what was formerly Wendell Plaza to Kenny's Plaza. The Community Feed acknowledged roots in a community feed initiated by the local collective Black Star Line Incorporated in August 2011 in commemoration of Black August and less than a month after the death of Harding.[16]

The space of the plaza is also the space where Denika Chatman's *testimonio* was performed as part of the site-specific performances of Love Balm's *Our Hallowed Ground* series in the summer of 2013. At a gathering of families celebrating life in honor of their children killed by police in 2015, Denika Chatman said to those gathered, "as long as my son's blood is on those streets, that's where I'll be."[17]

Stockton's Mobile Response Team

When Colby Friday was killed by Stockton police, his mother, Denise Friday, received a call while at work in Hayward. She recalls being stuck in traffic trying to leave the Bay Area in late afternoon and could not get to where Colby lay dying until well after his body had been removed from the street and pronounced dead in the hospital. Dionne Smith-Downs, whose own son, James Earl Rivera Jr., had been killed by law enforcement in Stockton six years earlier, went to the spot where Colby had been shot while walking to the store in the afternoon. She refused to leave for two weeks until Colby Friday's body was buried. Dionne states of her own action that she wanted the community to know that people care, that they cannot just be gunned down. Her actions refused, from the first moment, the forces of criminalization she knew would be produced to attack Colby immediately following the shooting.

During the occupation, other members of the community would also come by, among them Dionne's thirteen living children, and replenish water supplies and food, and join her in her occupation of the territory where Colby's life was taken. Denise drove up regularly from Hayward to sit at the spot where Colby was killed. She questioned neighbors and others who passed by, inquiring whether they knew anything about the killing. She learned, among other things, that the cell phones of those present and in the surrounding apartment complex had been confiscated by police, several people had moved away out of fear of the police, and most of Colby's friends had also left town, though the police maintain, in what was their third released version of events, that the killing of Colby was a situation of "mistaken identity."

It was from these crossed vectors that Stockton's Mobile Response Team, made up of Dionne Smith-Downs and Denise Friday, emerged. The Mobile Response Team is organized to confront state violence and establish networks of care across their communities by convening community spaces to bring families together from across the state, including spaces of *testimonio*, barbecues, and other gatherings. In the summer of 2016, they initiated a community food program to provide free lunches one day a week during the lull in the school lunch program that occurs when school is out. They extended their project to share lunches with houseless people across Stockton, and have provided first responder supplies, including water, following a residential fire and during heat waves in the Central Valley. While both women are critical nodes of support in their own extended families and have few resources, all of the actions are organized through their own means and donations. They also regularly travel across the state on their own resources to connect with other families isolated from more prominent struggles due to remote locations.[18]

Occupation and Reclaiming Space

The projects that arose out of direct police shootings emerged within a territory defined by the logic, codes, and practices of a state organized around neoliberal security and mark an active engagement, assessment, and confrontation against this organization. They navigate a complex geography, enacted in a specific relationship to the spatial grids of the metropolis, with its racialized demarcations and multiple internal boundaries and borders.[19] Each of these resistances confronts capital's imposition on the architectural forms and flows of the city, calling attention to its circuits, transfer points, spaces, and hierarchies of violence.[20]

Connecting the occupation of space with the "sexual uprising of Stonewall," Maria Serrano and Silvia López of La Eskalera Karakola, in Madrid, lay claim to urban space through an assertion of collective presence, "because we are part of these territories we daily struggle to construct them and reorganize them . . . legitimate re-appropriation of our own living space, of our bodies, our boroughs, our world." Serrano and López begin from the understanding that space is never neutral but "an accumulation of history and an incarnation of power." Urban space, they argue, "forms us and transforms us; we are molded by the spaces through which we move, which structure our daily life, which determine whom we encounter and in what terms." In theorizing occupations, they engage feminist debates at the intersection of public/private, the political, visibility, and urban space. This is an effort to make explicit a unity, a non-differentiation, between "the public" and "the personal," insisting that it is in this complex environment that politics is done. Like many feminist struggles, it is a matter of making visible the invisible, of denaturalizing what passes for natural, of destabilizing divisions between public and private. A reclaiming and reorganization of public space can pose questions about the hidden economy of domestic work (alongside discourses of love and devotion) that conceals both exploitation and sexual violence.[21] The efforts of mothers to reclaim public space and circulate details of intimate attacks on their families expose a crisis of social reproduction, one buttressed by criminalization and organized as war. Similarly, these efforts of remembering refuse a strict and definitive line between the living and the dead. "The difference between the living and the dead [is] the beginning binary," Sharon Patricia Holland asserts, a difference that is "the model for creating other dichotomous systems such as black and white or straight and queer."[22]

For Serrano and López, this making visible through occupations—claiming and creating space—is a collective act of citizenship not sanctioned by the abstraction of the nation-state, but by vernacular living in new territories of collective organization. They write: "creating our own spaces is a matter of insisting that citizenship is a daily practice collectively built through the active and conscientious habitation of space."[23] For Katherine McKittrick, the production of space is imbricated in power relations and violent processes of racialization, including discourses that "despatialize" a sense of space. McKittrick emphasizes that "geography can be remade through struggle." And similar to Serrano and Lopez, who emphasize movement and daily life, for

McKittrick, "social practices create landscapes and contribute to how we organize, build, and imagine our surroundings."[24] There are possibilities that things can be unmade, and remade differently.[25]

In her work theorizing community relations to space in Los Angeles, Gaye Therese Johnson theorizes "spatial entitlement" as a way of occupying, inhabiting, and transforming physical places," and asserting new forms of "social citizenship." Johnson argues that through space, communities create new collectives based on "the knowledge that meaningful space is essential for the survival of communities, but also for the discursive practices encoding the stories that define and redefine who people are, where they fit into the world, and what they envision for the future."[26] Johnson's work draws attention to the critical role of reclaiming space. This can be understood as a way of inscribing vernacular life onto urban spaces, in refutation of the securitized zones that banish certain forms of life.

The projects organized by women to reclaim space in the wake of police killings advance a collective belonging and community regeneration concurrently. They recoup spaces of intense violence that include state executions, state-manufactured violence appearing as random criminality and unsafety, and barbaric moments of the refusal of life—in most cases witnessed by the community whose lives traverse that space. Several of the projects have been enacted over stretches of concrete still stained with blood or shattered by bullets. They are, drawing on Juan Herrera, part of a cartographic process in the production of space as collective memory. The actions that animate these spaces occupy a similar space as vigils; they reclaim space as a public act of remembering, mourning, and celebration of life—a moment of insurgent knowledge that is a collective refusal against forgetting through a living memorialization that has the power to overwrite the space with care and unity.[27]

These spaces have the power to produce, even if momentarily, a collective subject centered around both shared loss and refusal as well as a reclaiming. Thus, they function as collective sites for remembering and continuing to mingle the dead with the living, allowing families to maintain connections to those that have passed, even extending this network across the geography of a city.

Yet, these sites are not constructed primarily as urban cemeteries, nor do they represent a "cult of the dead."[28] Foucault theorizes the role of the cemetery in modern bourgeois life, noting that "in correlation with the individualization of death and the bourgeois appropriation of the cemetery, there arises an obsession with death as an 'illness.'" Foucault's theorization of the movement of cemeteries to urban peripheries overlaps with, rather than contradicts, other reasonings that highlight the role of rising real estate prices in an expanding metropolis. The result, in modern bourgeois life, which is to say white life, is the same: death is banished from the city. This "banishment of death," which at the same time offers a promise of an always present future, offers an important point of juxtaposition against the daily violences and murder that are inscribed by the state into the everyday urban geographies of Black and Brown communities.[29]

These spaces function as a refusal to let the violence go unmarked and without response in a securitized urban environment, exposing, in the case of the People's Community Medics, those who voluntarily provide life-saving medical attention and are restricted from doing so by police. The commitments to return to the location of violence makes visible new forms of securitized space or abandonment critical to the biopolitical regime, one governed according to an organizational hierarchy of "make live and let die." These moments of "occupation" as care and resistance place similar moments side by side to expose critical observations and questions, as this collective ethnography, advanced in relation to these and other related projects, seeks to do.

We ask, what continuity can be read from a moment of militarized or securitized abandonment where police surround a dying person and refuse to let others enter the space and provide care, or the moment when a SWAT team surrounds a vigil where a person was killed that day, or a month or a year before, where the whole family is on the inside of the perimeter, in a space of mourning? What continuities exist when police surround a family barbecue and refuse to let people leave the park except in configurations smaller than two or three people? When police raid a home and force all the members of the household to stand in the middle of a common family room?

These efforts carve out another kind of space, one where information vital to the defense, survival, and reproduction of the community can circulate. This is a prefigurative space. It is also a convivial space of care and collective investigation, where the spontaneous conversation and inquiry, the trainings and refusals to leave, become simultaneously occupation and invitation. It is space for a range of "witnesses" to come forward and for the story of the violence to live in opposition to the state's statements validating the presence of police and the criminalized subject categorized as a sufficient "threat." As occupations, these moments challenge a foundational myth of the police's role to "serve and protect." Rather, the space becomes an invitation for a different story to be told, a narrative that contests state hegemony and contributes to the elaboration of a community's counter-narrative.

An Emergent Conviviality

In his analysis of the Occupy movement in San José, Manuel Callahan identifies among the successes of Occupy its ability to "facilitate politically potent moments of conviviality," and poses the question, "how to disrupt dominant forces and still maintain convivial reconstruction?"[30] At stake, he argues, "is the challenge of moving beyond the initial 'spontaneity' to constructing a space for co-generation of intercultural knowledges and strategies capable of embracing or inventing alternatives to capital and the state."[31]

In opening his analysis of "heterotopias," Foucault reminds us that "space itself has a history in Western experience" and further, that spaces exist as relational, where each site "is defined by relations of proximity between points or elements" which can be described as series, trees, or grids." Foucault's heterotopia "is capable of juxtaposing in a single real place several spaces, several sites that are in themselves incompatible. Relying on the visualization of the theater, he theorizes that "it is that the theater brings onto the rectangle of the stage, one after the other, a whole series of places that are foreign to one another."[32] His theorization of heterotopias ("linked to the accumulation of time") and heterochronies allows for an understanding of a complex layering of space, events, and time as a political moment of encounter.[33] Here, the "encounter" does not necessarily privilege a subject or isolate a subject from a context.[34] In the theater production of *Love Balm*, as actors representing different stories circle and respond to one another on stage, the "space of encounter" is not limited to the mothers encountering each other. Stories of police killings coexist with stories of community violence, as well as oppositions and the construction of alternatives across an expansive geography of violence extending from San José to Oakland and beyond. State violence and state-manufactured violence are placed in proximity to provoke new connections for thinking through and against the militarization of community space and counterinsurgency warfare aimed at the community's own reproduction. Killings otherwise separated by many years exist adjacent in "an accumulation of time" through the stories recounted contemporaneously in the voices of the mothers. Among the significant achievements of the *Love Balm* project has been this cohabitation in a shared space of stories of young people lost to police violence next to stories of young people lost to state-manufactured or "subaltern violence."

As *Love Balm* is disaggregated back out into the site-specific performances on the streets, including sharing space with Kenny's Community Feed in Bayview-Hunters Point as overlapping projects marking a site of violence, each specific site remains interconnected and layered with the other sites, providing a living map where entwined violences advance possibilities for a shared analysis of the complexity of counterinsurgency and pacification, providing a circuit for resistances and knowledges to travel across communities.

Circulating and Archiving Systems of Information

Police violence and policing practices reveal an array of social antagonisms. For CCRA, "any situation of social antagonism necessarily produces competing systems of information, or formal and informal interventions, that archive knowledge."[35] The performances of *Love Balm for My SpiritChild* in theaters and its corollary, *Our Hallowed Ground*, on the streets reiterated a series of statements retrieved from conversations between Arielle Julia Brown as a playwright and the mothers who had lost children to violence. In each reenactment, statements were also circulated as forms of subjugated, situated, and strategic knowledges within the context of the performance. On stage, the actors voice statements that speak to what has been lost and where the injustices lie, statements that advance details and give shape to a collective, oppositional knowledge. Several women circle each other on a sparsely designed set, sharing profound reflections and insights. Each woman recalls the past of her child, their growing and their living over time. These stories deny state tactics that are contingent on criminalizing and in the end erasing those it targets to maintain its own legitimacy. The details situate each young person within a web of relations—a family, a community, a workplace—and within a trajectory of life that includes a past where they were loved and cared for and with a future that was theirs to be shared with others and was stolen. They reveal these as elements that the state seeks to overwrite. In the functioning of the state, the past is only called forth when its details can be deployed to establish those targeted as criminal, violent, a threat or a menace, and not wanting or deserving of their own future. These collective acts of remembering woven through performance hold brilliant possibilities and can do many things. In addition to reclaiming a life taken, they can, for example, reveal patterns through which those speaking "in dialogue" with those gathered can detect and expose the strategies of an unfolding counterinsurgency.

One woman says of her murdered child, "he was my life's work."[36] Her statement speaks to her incredible loss and her work of care and reproduction from within the social factory that the state has attempted to erase. Increasingly, reproductive justice issues are focusing on the extreme violence targeting the children of Black, Brown, and Indigenous women, as feminist collectives organized around care, well-being, and survival establish a continuity of attack, situating the violence targeting those children as attacks on the communities whose young people are no longer safe.[37] This statement from the mother whose child has been taken from her advances an understanding of violence that is linked to capital—not only to the police as an instrument of brute and deadly force. Women's struggles against racial violence and against the violent targeting of family and community reveal capital's violent intrusions into the spaces and rhythms of reproductive life. The violence of murdering someone's child, whatever the age of that child, is also the violence of stealing what a woman and community have labored, for years, to produce—not as commodity, but as human life.

Another woman advanced a statement that exposes a counterinsurgency strategy deployed by the state against many families targeted by violence, noting, "we still haven't received the coroner's report."[38] Thus, the state disseminates its narrative of the violence, but refuses to reveal the report and vital information that might offer the family either a more concrete understanding of what violence their child endured or a document to counter with details from their own investigations, or both.

The knowledges given space to circulate—situated, poetic, strategic, oppositional, subaltern—contribute to larger, more complex systems of information vital to community efforts to fight back, to assess strategies, to compare previously isolated experiences of violent loss and to move forward with new tools at the community's disposal.

For Arielle Julia Brown, the process of creating the Love Balm Project was intimately linked to forms of community-based justice emerging from situations of violence, learned from a women's collective in Rwanda that adopted children orphaned as a result of the Rwandan genocide, a moment of extreme state-manufactured violence. In "traditions of counter-memorial" as practices of justice, communities came forward over many years to bear witness together in assemblies convened as spaces of relational *testimonio*, as community members shared what they saw, what they participated in, what role they played, and what they endured in relation to collective violence.[39] In relational *testimonio*, conversations emerge as co-generated, from a space of shared dialogue. Here, justice processes are about healing, but also about sharing information that exposes the role of the state in producing violences among communities.[40] Like the assemblies in Rwanda, the extended Love Balm Project becomes both a process of healing and autonomous justice; it serves as a convivial tool for regenerating community.

Similarly, the People's Community Medics' emphasis on the "golden hour" can be seen as a response that both advances care and promotes community defense as it calls attention to a specific strategy of low-intensity war, that of systematic, strategic abandonment, deployed across multiple shootings and orchestrated through several agencies. This abandonment can also be seen as a way of isolating the criminal/insurgent/deviant from the population, moving them "beyond the care" of the community while affirming the state's role in protecting and maintaining the security of the community, key tenets of counterinsurgency warfare. The medics' work makes vivid the state's committed refusal to save a wounded and immobilized person under the guise of a "threat" or a "suspect."

Yet, the work of the medics is not aimed at reforming the sanctioned medical institutions in Oakland or dismantling or even replacing the institutions of the state. Rather, their work functions as an observable at the same time that it exists as a prefigurative practice. As a tool, it serves as both a skill share and a community speak-out. Information is exchanged in a shared space of community in a context of rage and care, creating a critical potential component in the proliferation of neighborhood assemblies. Similarly, Kenny's Community Feed and Stockton's Mobile Response Team can also be understood in terms of what each exposes about a crisis of care and its imbrication with low-intensity war. Both emerge from and mark a spot where a young person's life was denied them because the life-saving care they needed was restricted. As a site of food distribution, the space of the Community Feed also poses an interrogation of privatization and in particular the crises made manifest through the externalization of the home.[41] Every third Sunday, the community continues to come together there, to share food and information critical to their own survival and resilience. As other families across the Bay are confronted with forms of state violence and the murder of their loved ones, the small collective organized at Kenny's Corner continues to provide connections and support from their entrenched position in the Bayview neighborhood.

From Stockton, both Dionne Smith-Downs and Denise Friday, like other families, continuously face unimaginable interruptions by the state, yet they continue to share what scant resources they have in collective acts of absolute refusal of what the state and capital attempt to impose on them as mothers and on their communities. They reach out when they hear of new losses, to create a space for families and to generously share hard-earned strategies and information in the hope that it might alleviate some of the burden of others. They initiate investigations and convene spaces of assembly.

In his analysis of the Oaxaca Commune (2006), Gustavo Esteva writes, "the reorganization or creation of assemblies at the grassroots continues at its own pace, looking for more solid ground."[42] These projects, too, continue at their own pace within a network of related projects, opening space for new possibilities of community formation to emerge. These efforts reflect a commitment to community safety in opposition to security and as an assertion of autonomy across the greater San Francisco Bay.

A Note on Methodology
Convivial Research, Collective Ethnography, Insurgent Learning

Various regimes of representation function to organize hierarchies of difference along a vertical axis that produces a myriad of subjects and populations, and includes the production of disposability. At the same time, liberal democracy claims legitimacy organized through forms of representation where many are increasingly condensed into one, similarly progressing along a verticality of political decision-making from the local to the state. This both reflects and reproduces the violences of the Western episteme. From here, this book argues that efforts to engage in horizontalism exceed a process of decision-making, often fetishized as the central feature of the assembly as a site of grassroots power. Rather, horizontalism is a prefigurative practice that engages a commitment to new forms of knowledge production, social organization, relationality, and ways of being. In the words of the Zapatistas, "first, we must learn how to learn."

As part of a global decolonial process, across struggles and spaces of movement, the politics of knowledge production and a range of practices and commitments that engage this politics have taken on new urgency and vibrancy. From the Zapatistas with their emphasis on spaces of encounter and "learning to learn," to the *picateros* of Argentina and the barricades of the Oaxaca Commune; to the communes of the Rojava Revolution; and the "movements of the squares" in Greece, Egypt, and Spain; from the Occupy movement, to a range of struggles in particular locales, there emerges a collective recognition of the possibilities in horizontal processes organized around shared listening, learning, and research as critical to social transformation and racial, feminist, and decolonized justice initiatives. Knowledge production is linked to new democratic possibilities. The rupture with the state is a rupture with the old forms of thought.[1]

Following the proliferation of mobilizations in the wake of the police killing of Oscar Grant in 2009, communities of struggle across the greater Bay Area have also become more deliberate in engaging in spaces of "reflection and action," investing in forms of "convivial research" and "insurgent learning" as critical components of a community safety that begins to organize itself outside the state and against the discourses of neoliberal security. This is an emerging praxis across an emergent network of often ephemeral spaces, "places of dislocation and epistemological invention."[2] Unique socialities, alternative sociabilities, and radically new subjectivities can appear in this carved-out space, where listening and learning are bound to a refusal of the illusions of the old thought—and the refusal to recognize a singular, objective reality or truth is likewise a questioning and dismantling of the domain where the forces that marshal such truths operate.[3]

This refusal is also a claim to dignity.[4] In this refusal, and through the intersubjective processes alive in the streets, the sidewalk vigils, the community barbecues, and the *taquerias*, a collective subject (always emergent) takes shape.[5] This emergent collective subject is not organized through a shared consciousness and is not organized as a mass social movement. It is not synonymous with the amorphous "community." Nor is it a collective identity. It is not organized around belonging, but "acts on a shared desire" and "requires a rebel pedagogy."[6] A collective subject is produced through horizontal, democratic processes and coheres as an agent of social transformation and emancipation.

It is in this context that "insurgent learning" reflects an orientation based on collective, horizontal forms of knowledge production, where a community claims its own learning process outside of the discipline of the Western episteme and outside routinized, bureaucratized, commodified forms of education. Insurgent learning refuses theory "as a privileged position from which to see things" and which is "almost always constructed from the dominant social position."[7] Rather, insurgent learning carries within itself a commitment to "living theory," a recognition that communities of struggle are always and already circulating and producing new knowledges, provoking new questions, and collectively developing new strategies and tactics as central to their struggles to resist the relations that racial patriarchal capitalism attempts to impose through violence, criminalization, discipline, control, enclosure, containment, and subjectification. This commitment to "living theory" is simultaneously a refusal to impose a fixed, predetermined future. Insurgent learning is critical to a convivial research approach.[8]

A convivial research approach is at the base of this project and is central to an ongoing approach to struggle. Developed by Manuel Callahan and further elaborated through the work of the Center for Convivial Research and Autonomy, convivial research is organized through a strategy of knowledge production that engages a series of open spaces of research and learning that are also spaces of direct action. Convivial research overlaps and intersects with other prominent research approaches that emphasize and aim to bring out social transformation, including militant research, participatory action research, and feminist epistemological approaches and decolonial methodologies; and it shares many of the same commitments, reappropriating and refashioning a number of tactics and practices familiar to these approaches but also placing a greater emphasis on the situated tools that emerge out of specific moments of struggle.

As a strategy of grassroots research and horizontal learning in the service of community struggles, a convivial research approach is based on four central commitments: (1) it refuses to objectify communities of struggle; (2) it takes seriously the obligation to include the community at every step of the process, from formulating research questions to engaging spaces of direct action; (3) it is committed to the co-generation of knowledge and claims shared processes of knowledge production, while at the same time making this process transparent, accessible, and accountable through the co-generation of specific tools; and (4) it reflects an agreement to organize ourselves as a community around horizontal prefigurative spaces of reflection, action, and decision-making.[9]

Based on these four commitments, convivial research advances two central features. First, drawing on the work of Ivan Illich, convivial research highlights the formation of convivial tools as a critical component of the research process. A convivial tool in this sense is one collectively developed to regenerate the community. Second, convivial research is organized around the possibility of a collective subject; it aims to facilitate the emergence, even if sometimes ephemerally, of a collective subject as central to the research process, and in its emphasis on convivial tools, it aims to produce over time a more profound sense of a collective subject as a critical aspect of regenerating and reproducing the community.[10]

A Convivial Research Approach to Collective Ethnography

This book marks an attempt at collective ethnography as a convivial research approach; it advances a series of claims about the role of research, learning, and archiving in relation to a community of struggle. By "collective ethnography," I hope to highlight three central areas here that are imbricated with a commitment to struggles for autonomy. First, collective ethnography reflects both the research process and the research product; it is not only the work that is produced (where the document can be understood as "a collective ethnography"); rather, the research strategy itself is at every moment collective (transparent, based on agreements, containing moments of reflection and assessment, and so on), and greater emphasis is placed on the collective process itself. The process is not in service of an anticipated final product, but rather is a strategy towards a nascent assembly, towards "relearning the arts of assembly." Second, collective ethnography refuses to represent; it is wary of all attempts to represent the problems or the issues facing a community, and declines to represent, interpret, or narrate the various individual actors who participate in the unfolding research process.

Callahan writes: "The future in the present is animated by learning and inquiry where participants can discover in a shared space how to re-learn the habits of assembly, reclaim processes of collective decision-making, and collaborate to find new ways to regenerate community through dignity, obligation, reciprocity, stewardship, and care."[11] Critical to this is also a refusal to situate a researcher (as subject) in relation to a field of issues or actors (as objects) that the researcher then attempts to engage within a more or less ethical framework, more or less care, more or less objectivity, more or less capacity to listen, and to identify silences, to "do justice" and so on.[12]

While all processes of selection and arrangement contain an interpretative gesture which this work acknowledges, at the same time, this book marks a committed attempt to not impose a particular reading by instead exposing the cultural tools that impose or direct a particular interpretation of events, situations, and unfoldings. Thus, thirdly, collective ethnography marks an attempt as a research process for a community to organize itself through co-research and to have the statements, documents, articles, artifacts, actions, and so on that a community produces about itself serve as the text and archive through which a community in struggle can recognize and reflect on itself and its shared refusals and desires in order to manage the terms of its self-determined survival.

In this last effort, collective ethnography is committed to the possibility, always nascent, of an emergent collective subject—in this case, a collective subject that is self-organized around its own safety as a community, and self-determined to make decisions in the service of its own social reproduction.

Collective Ethnography as Process and Product

As both the document produced and the process of its production, collective ethnography is a way of documenting how what we know comes into being, and a way of creating conditions to continue learning and engaging as a shared process. The collective ethnography here emerges from a series of spaces where "one must participate in knowing" and through deliberate practices of sharing stories, documenting, summarizing, archiving, and retelling the struggles of a community so that a community continuously recognizes itself in the retelling.[13]

As a practice and a process, collective ethnography serves to elucidate the ways that knowledge is produced, shared, and remembered collectively. Collective ethnography, like living theory, refuses to impose a predetermined narrative, allowing for a shared narrative and related conceptual and direct action tools to emerge collectively. The very co-production of the tools, narrative and otherwise, when made explicit can be pedagogical as well as the basis for self-organization.

An important aspect of this is reimagining how we understand political actors and political processes, and the value that we place on fostering and listening to epistemologies from below—ways of knowing that reflect and give shape to ways of being; storytelling that is heuristic, relational, communal, ancestral, and pedagogical, as well as images and language that emerge from within communities of struggle. As a practice and process, collective ethnography reflects a commitment to a shared listening; it simultaneously reflects the archive of statements that can be assembled when an organized community emphasizes this commitment.

As part of this collective ethnography, spaces were regularly convened across networks of women already engaged in movement spaces and theorizing forms of liberation and justice, relying on *testimonios* to weave elements of storytelling, oral history, and diverse moments of witnessing and local knowledges, as well as contributing to a collective memory and history.[14] As families gather to hear and share *testimonio*, they not only resist forces of erasure, they also share reflections that are critical to each other's struggles. In many cases, the knowledges that emerge also draw attention to a heuristic that has been similarly disqualified—it is not only the "knowing" but the ways of knowing that are devalued and then discarded. Collective questions are generated.

UniTierra Califas has elaborated on a distinction posed by the Latina Feminist Group between *testimonio* and "relational *testimonio*" where the latter refers to collective, co-generated processes of knowledge production in which stories are shared and collaboratively produced as people retell memories, experiences, reflections, and insights in the space of conversation. Both *testimonio* and relational *testimonio* are critical to community-based investigations as well as the health and strength of a community. UniTierra Califas situates relational *testimonio* within a convivial research approach, weaving together the work of the Latina Feminist Group with Jorge Gonzalez's *cibercultur@* theorizations on knowledge production, as well as marking the central role of shared research as critical to advancing our struggles, as in the work of Costa Vargas's elaboration of activist scholarship[15]

In these moments, a networked community safety project is unearthed and advances. Beginning roughly in 2011, this project has been theorized as an autonomous horizontal research and learning initiative, collaboratively working across groups to uncover and connect a collective reflection and action project on "community safety" across the Bay Area. In these spaces, the stories and knowledge that emerge are determined by how "'we structure the ways we come together and tell our stories' . . . [a] precept [that] resonates with a fundamental approach . . . drawn from cybercultur@ and the work of Jorge Gonzalez and the Laboratorio de Investigación y Desarrollo en Comunicación Compleja (LabCOMplex), namely, 'the way we organize ourselves to produce knowledge determines the knowledge we produce.'"[16]

These "spaces of encounter" that create conditions for *testimonio*, relational *testimonio*, and other forms of disqualified, subjugated, and insurrectionary knowledge production to surface and circulate are critical to the shared efforts of families and communities to confront the violences they face.[17] They contribute to a collective "system of information" upon which a community of struggle relies in order to reflect on what they know, what they must do, and what their hopes are. This echoes a strategic outline advanced by C.L.R. James (drawing on Immanuel Kant): "what do we know, what must we do, what do we hope for?" that serves as a basis for a series of facilitation practices and direct action strategies advanced by CCRA and UniTierra Califas in many community and popular learning spaces.[18] Systems of information both draw on and expand the situated and local knowledges that communities deploy strategically to respond to a number of violences and injustices.[19]

The circulation of subversive, disqualified, insurrectionary, and vernacular knowledges remains a critical component of struggles against police, carceral, and settler-colonial violence in the Bay Area. These knowledges work in opposition against state discourses and weave a variegated fabric that contests dominant historical narratives, including those advanced by the state and "official" history, and narrated through discourses that privilege neoliberal security over community safety, discourses that manufacture the criminalization and pathologization on which racial patriarchal capital rests. This approach takes seriously the experiences of women and communities of color as sites of knowledge production in deliberately convening spaces that make possible the emergence over time of a collective ethnography. These ways of telling and the spaces convened collectively *through the telling* make possible the erosion of those truths on which a white, patriarchal, commodity-intensive social order depends. New relations and alternative subjectivities emerge in relation to the circulation of subversive, insurgent knowledges.

Collective Ethnography as Refusal to Represent

The crisis of representation within the discipline of anthropology provoked by Indigenous, anticolonial, queer, and feminist struggles reflects a recognition of the historical role of ethnography and anthropological methods in advancing the colonial project, the development project, and the occupation project, materially and as epistemic violence. This crisis of representation is not only one of hindsight, and locked in the past; it is also focused on present regimes, including regimes of representation at the heart of human rights discourse, or for example as "human terrain analysis" advanced with the support of anthropologists working with the U.S. military in Afghanistan and beyond.[20] These regimes are manifested in the discursive framing of problems for intervention, policy questions, and solutions. In short, the act of representing through the subject-object framework marks an ethnographic project in the service of intervention and war—whether it is a war from above, or a war on the poor or on Brown women in militarized target zones. Collective ethnography, sometimes more or less successfully, marks a refusal to map populations for this service, a refusal to represent populations as deficient, as a "problem." It is anti-development, anti-modernity, and anti-security.[21]

In its refusal to represent, collective ethnography bears within itself the memory of ethnography's complicity with an ongoing colonial project—and with that project's regimes of representation, its ossification of the subject-object binary relation (which is always a relation of hierarchy), its strategies of accumulation, forms of governance, and policies and practices of enclosure both social and material.[22] Historically, these processes proved critical in establishing the conditions of possibility for an ongoing colonial violence.[23]

In this refusal, collective ethnography recalls the historical role of colonial anthropologists in their study of the relations and habits of kinship structures, tribes, villages, and geographies in order to make legible and intervene in the service of colonial occupation and expropriation.[24] The colonial ethnographic project served an imperative of intelligence-gathering put in the service of settler-colonial and other colonial policing projects: to dispossess and eradicate people; to incite and exacerbate divisions between local groups; to buttress occupations and advance the tactics of modern warfare; to map and reorganize populations in an emergent elaboration of counterinsurgency warfare; and to study and enter the realm of power relations in the service of colonial domination.[25] After all, the Bureaux Arabes of French-occupied Algeria were as much a project of militarized ethnography as of administration; they coordinated information on local populations in the service of colonial rule.[26]

The decolonial scholarship advanced by Indigenous scholars, often women, as well as work emerging from Black and Brown communities in the United States, has been central to exposing the forms and strategies of knowledge production that continue to produce the Western episteme, to promote universal truths, suture knowledge and power, and (re)make violence possible.[27] Recent methodological advances in participatory action and militant research underscore the importance of putting the community at the center of our study, examining the exploitative nature of many research methodologies, and emphasizing the importance of cooperative, collaborative research as a way of addressing objectifying methodologies.[28] Similarly, convivial research marks a commitment to a collective process, not an ethical or epistemological position that reproduces and coheres a Western subject.[29] The emphasis on convivial research that refuses to objectify communities of struggle is best understood not as being limited to a particular self-reflexive ethical commitment or interrogation to which the researcher holds herself and positions herself ethically; rather, it is a commitment to a collective process through which new knowledges, new convivial tools, new relations, and community obligations emerge.

A convivial approach focused on interconnected sites of organized self-activity, theorized as "temporary autonomous zones of knowledge production" (TAZKP), and anticapitalist, prefigurative praxis stand as an intervention against more traditional left-wing politics and orthodox Marxisms that continue to dominate much current literature and circumscribe the realm of the "political" according to Western epistemological frames that privilege specific class subjects and revolutionary programs.[30] A convivial research approach aligns with Black feminist scholars who continue to theorize how Black women's historical experience as slaves and domestic workers exposes many traditional Marxist categories (including the bifurcation of public/private) as untenable or unviable for an analysis, demonstrating how the categories themselves have contributed to an illegibility of the insurgencies, resistances, and refusals of Black women historically and in the present. When Saidiya Hartman poses the question, drawing on Fred Moten, "where does the *impossible domestic* fit in to the general strike?" this question travels through a multiplicity of unwaged and precarious positions. It reverberates in the realm of social reproduction and the spaces of caring labor and across feminist and Indigenous struggles that are expanding the field of the political by highlighting, for example in the work of Precarias a la deriva, precarious workers participating in solidarity with workers' strikes in the streets of Spain, or Indigenous struggles confronting extractivism across the Americas. Exceeding a demand or desire for inclusion or recognition, the question razes the illusory border between public and private, and heralds the insurgencies.[31]

These questions and theorizations forge new possibilities for thinking through capital as a relation that exceeds the wage relation, the factory, the discipline of full employment, and so on. Rather than replacing the revolutionary subject of an earlier period, this work has sought to invigorate and extend the realm of the political and understandings of revolutionary subjects and change agents and indeed, class itself, while working collaboratively across workers' struggles to research, confront, and disengage from capital.

Raúl Zibechi's dispersion of power poses an intervention that situates the role of the community and neighborhood councils as long-term, rooted anti-state projects that offer ways to theorize resistance beyond the summit-hopping of the 1990s and more traditional readings and practices of resistance that have historically been dominated by orthodox Marxism. This is echoed in Raquel Gutiérrez's "politics in the feminine," which recognizes "the more or less 'masculine-dominant' set of codes that have been associated with revolutionary politics for decades."[32]

In other recent scholarship, the street retains a privileged status as the primary space of revolutionary possibility, continuously reinscribed as the site where social antagonisms are most glaringly exposed and social change occurs, even if scholars do not identify this with specific modes of production or leftist programs. This has been true of ethnographic studies and scholarship on social movements coming out of the academy, which, while often advancing a more anarchist position vis-à-vis the state, nonetheless often center the presence and experience of the activist scholar in relation to public space so as to articulate theories of rebellion and insurgency—the deep roots and networks of which, across multiple communities and connections and relations of care, are often less visible and less accessible given that they lie outside the discursive framework through which social change is "read."[33]

Of course, there is movement in the street, and the struggles organized around care and social reproduction are there too—but the street is always connected to other spaces of rebellion and regeneration, as collective experiences that challenge and refuse capital. The barricades of Oaxaca—or the barricades, occupations, and strikes anywhere—are sustained through strong bonds and elaborate systems of social reproduction.[34]

The autonomous project underway across the Bay Area to advance community safety is organized around "spaces of encounter" and moments of convergence where knowledge is shared across groups and generated in specific contexts of struggle. Thus, while this work is closely aligned with several local social justice organizations, the collective ethnography is based primarily on a series of gatherings, workshops, trainings, performances, and conversations across the greater Bay Area as spaces where different positions of the community convene around shared issues, including community safety.[35]

An effort to refuse representation and collectively engage in an ethnographic process participates in a decolonial imaginary. Rather than simply celebrating a multi-vocal or multi-perspectival account, a collective ethnography emerging from a multi-sited narrative imposes a fracture on singular authority and hierarchical ways of knowing that serve a dominant epistemology, and often condone and justify violence and exclusion.[36] A collective ethnography recognizes the presence and celebrates the possibility of multiple epistemologies, including vernacular knowledges.[37] This book marks a deliberate refusal to "represent" or "portray" and instead relies on the knowledges that emerge from these spaces—the documents, texts, narratives, social facts, and community truths—to create a shared history of the community.

Collective Ethnography and the Emergent Collective Subject

In claiming a collective ethnography, this book recognizes the potential—subversive and regenerative—in the practice of engaging in spaces of action and reflection together, theorized as temporary autonomous zones of knowledge production—interconnected, networked spaces where disqualified, subversive, and insurgent knowledges are shared, formed, circulated, and accumulated.[38] These spaces of encounter serve to co-generate information, arrive at a shared analysis, collectively narrate a community's own struggles, and support a series of interconnected strategic actions. It is in these spaces that the cultural tools of ethnography, narrative, tropes, metaphor, and so on are exposed and examined, to either be discarded or reclaimed in a shared narrative with agreed-upon cultural tools. This is the case, for example, with "security" versus "safety." These spaces form one of the central sites of elaboration and exploration for the process and production of a collective ethnography. Building on the temporary autonomous zones of anarchist praxis as spaces that exist ephemerally outside of the state and are set against the permanence of institutions, this modification places the co-generation of knowledge at the center of these spaces as a convivial praxis.[39]

This is a commitment to TAZKP as insurrectionary moments. Similar to Foucault's "insurrection of subjugated knowledges," these are insurrections that both challenge the dominant epistemology and the displacements that it effects by exposing certain silences and at the same time "reactivat[ing] local knowledges" and memories.[40] This is also a commitment to engage the commons, including various knowledge commons.[41] These commons support the ongoing formation of a community of struggle as a collective subject, aware of itself and the possibilities it contains for harboring and generating different worlds. This process itself is one of de-subjectification and decolonization.[42]

By focusing on community safety as an autonomous initiative underway in a number of interconnected spaces and palpable in ongoing diverse direct actions, as a collective ethnography, this book does not claim a particular reading so much as to provide a way of seeing, theorizing, and mobilizing, in short, a way of engaging, that can support a more complete disengagement from capital, stimulating the possibilities for new ways of being together in the present.

Relying on a convivial research approach which takes as its premise that communities are already self-active and organized around their own safety, learning, and regeneration, this collective ethnography emerges from a community of struggle, in particular women organized around issues of social reproduction both in the home and in the larger spaces of community; these women are already constituted to some degree as a collective subject actively engaging the conditions of their own existence, namely, the struggle against, within, and beyond capital.[43] The details and knowledges circulate through various texts and forms—as reports and maps, press releases and grassroots fact sheets, songs and storytelling, images and fragments, poems and chants, "artifacts" and things, movements and gestures, warnings and whispers—to build a rich archive of collectively produced knowledge relevant to a community's survival.

Convivial Tools as a Research Strategy

Throughout, this book relies on a number of research tools, many of them borrowed, appropriated, or refashioned from research and action collectives that are critical to how, as an organized community, we reflect on struggles in the Bay Area. Theorized as "convivial tools" following the work of Manuel Callahan, these are tools generated and implemented to regenerate community.[44] These projects and this book both engage and reflect a variety of strategies and approaches: community investigations organized around "fierce care," drawing on the Combahee River Collective; the moving inquiry "drifts" of Precarias a la deriva, a women's collective in Madrid, and the reimagined stationary drifts of Maria Isabel Casas-Cortes and Sebastian Cobarrubias; spaces of relational *testimonio* or shared storytelling, drawing on practices theorized by the

Latina Feminist Group; collective mapping projects similar to those facilitated by Iconoclasistas; community timelines inspired by the work of grassroots activist groups like Project South; collective constructions of observables advanced by Jorge Gonzalez and the LabCOMplex and *cibercultur@*; the *ateneo* spaces of UniTierra Califas; and Arielle Julia Brown and participatory street theater, as well as oral history interviews with mothers and their families who have lost children to police violence and whose efforts have been critical to advancing struggles over decades in the Bay Area.[45]

One such research tool was the Social Factory Ateneo, an autonomous space of convivial research and insurgent learning that was launched as a project of UniTierra Califas in May 2014 in the Fruitvale neighborhood of Oakland by members of the Center for Convivial Research and Autonomy and in conversation and conjunction with local mothers impacted by low-intensity war and forms of carceral violence. It was deliberately organized in response to the growing numbers of police killings occurring in the same communities already targeted in various ways by the prison industrial complex. Our commitment to come together and establish the Social Factory Ateneo stemmed from a shared and ongoing participation over several years in spaces of struggle with mothers and families at the center where we collectively recognized the need to understand what we perceived as a new level of police violence directed at particular communities. The *ateneo* emerged as part of a series of networked learning spaces associated with an autonomous learning effort, UniTierra Califas, that brought together several community safety projects with women at the center, including a number of spaces organized over the fall and spring of 2013–14, as well as collaborative skill shares, community clinics, policing timeline workshops, and grassroots investigations.[46] As a space of encounter, the *ateneo* was imagined within a larger effort aimed at proliferating and building spaces to "relearn the habits of assembly" in order to collectively promote and eventually claim neighborhood assemblies where the community could determine its own needs and imagine its own future collectively and autonomously.[47]

The Social Factory Ateneo was conceived as a space in which to collaboratively generate a collective ethnography; from the beginning, it was convened as a space that deliberately and through collective processes would facilitate connections across multiple spaces, and would archive and advance struggle as a collective process. The spaces and projects that traversed the space, from people's investigations to other community safety and regeneration projects, contributed to a "circulation of struggle" weaving together direct actions and grassroots initiatives from across the Bay.[48] We initiated the space and remained committed to it as part of a larger strategy to "reweave the social fabric," bringing together care work, justice struggles, community defense projects, and community investigations, with families targeted by state violence at the project's center.[49] From its inception, the Social Factory Ateneo explicitly drew on the work of Silvia Federici, Mariarosa Dalla Costa and Selma James, Leopoldina Fortunati, and others in positioning women at the center of an analysis of capitalist social relations, as well as Precarias a la deriva's efforts to imagine a "politics of care" in response to the privatization of care and the externalization of the home, which we further elaborated in our own context through the *ateneos* to include the militarization of care, and as "fierce care."

Similarly, drawing upon a long history of anticolonial struggles, including French-occupied Algeria and British-occupied Northern Ireland, we rely on the tool and strategy of the "safe house," where the *ateneo* and collective ethnography are organized as space and practice, and where knowledges are co-produced and circulated in a way that seek to protect the community and those speaking from forms of identification and further intrusion by the state. Often, the "safe house" is cultivated and defended by mothers and women.

As struggles in the present increasingly emphasize the politics of knowledge production, autonomous spaces of research and learning are emerging as critical to how we engage and advance these struggles. This work of collective ethnography highlights a number of convivial tools as a strategy of community regeneration, put to use for expanding spaces of prefigurative politics and imagining new ways of being together and new relations, outside of capital and the violences marshaled in its service.

NOTES

Introduction

1. This was part of the larger Love Balm Project created by Arielle Julia Brown working closely with families and community groups, and which will be explored more fully in chapter 8, "Spaces of Encounter."

2. For the purposes of this study, "the greater San Francisco Bay Area" or "the Bay Area" refers generally to the South Bay, Peninsula, North Bay (San Francisco), and the East Bay. The Greater Bay Area also encompasses other outlier zones, explored here as peripheries in relation to the more central urban zones of San José, San Francisco, and Oakland. These include Stockton, Vallejo, Santa Rosa, Salinas, Fresno, and other surrounding areas. Not only defined by the computer industry and digital culture associated with big tech companies, the Silicon Valley as treated throughout this text is a geopolitical designation that extends from Livermore to Santa Barbara and, in addition to the digital economy, includes the research, government, and business collaborations that form the military industrial complex and the biotech industry. In this instance, the San Francisco Bay Area with its periphery zones is read in relation to Silicon Valley as an economic enclave notable for its desirable geography and lifestyle as well as a critical center of cognitive capitalism that shapes both the violences and cycles of struggle that unfold here.

3. UniTierra Califas and Acción Zapatista have been engaged in community safety struggles as part of an effort to advance an urban Zapatismo across California since 2003. 50.50 Crew was a youth collective based in San José that was committed to community safety efforts by working with youth to confront the militarization of schools.

4. On "habits of assembly," see Manuel Callahan, "Conviviality Rooted in Struggle: Learning from the Zapatistas," in *What Makes an Assembly? Stories, Experiments, and Inquiries*, ed. Anne Davidian and Laurent Jeanpierre (London: Evens Foundation and Sternberg Press, 2023); and Manuel Callahan, "The Politics of Autonomous Spaces of Learning," HKW Instituting, November 2021, https://newalphabetschool.hkw.de/the-politics-of-autonomous-spaces-of-learning/. On Zapatismo as a "politics

of refusal, space, and listening" see Manuel Callahan, "Zapatismo Beyond Chiapas," in *Globalize Liberation: How to Uproot the System and Build a Better World*, ed. David Solnit (San Francisco: City Lights, 2004), 217–28: 217; on urban Zapatismo as "forms of action that are expressive not instrumental" and the reconstruction of the bonds of community, see John Holloway, "Zapatismo Urbano," *Humboldt Journal of Social Relations* 29, no. 1 (2005), 168–78: 177. Urban Zapatismo will be further elaborated throughout this introduction and subsequent chapters.

5. For an elaboration of TAZKP, see Manuel Callahan, "Insurgent Learning and Convivial Research: Universidad de la Tierra *Califas*," ArtsEverywhere, January 26, 2017, https://artseverywhere.ca/2017/01/26/insurgent-learning-convivial-research-universidad-de-la-tierra-califas/; and Callahan, "In Defense of Conviviality and the Collective Subject." *Polis*, no. 33 (2012). See also Hakim Bey, *T.A.Z.: The Temporary Autonomous Zone, Ontological Anarchy, Poetic Terrorism* (New York: Autonomedia, 1991), 98–101.

6. Denise Friday Hall, in conversation with the author, October 2016.

7. The Center for Convivial Research and Autonomy (CCRA) is a transterritorial research collective based in San José and the San Francisco Bay Area, with extended networks across Mexico.

8. There has been a great deal of literature on accumulation and the nature of capitalist expropriation. See, for example, Jodi A. Byrd, Alyosha Goldstein, Jodi Melamed, and Chandan Reddy, "Predatory Value: Economies of Dispossession and Disturbed Relationalities," *Social Text* 36, no. 2: 135 (June 2018): 1–18; Robert Nichols, *Theft Is Property! Dispossession and Critical Theory* (Durham, NC: Duke University Press, 2020); and David Harvey, *The New Imperialism* (Oxford: Oxford University Press, 2005).

9. On informalized war, see Rita Laura Segato, "Patriarchy from Margin to Center: Discipline, Territoriality, and Cruelty in the Apocalyptic Phase of Capital," *South Atlantic Quarterly* 115, no. 3 (July 2016). On racial regimes, see Cedric J. Robinson, *Forgeries of Memory and Meaning: Blacks and the Regimes of Race in American Theater and Film before World War II* (Chapel Hill: University of North Carolina Press, 2007).

10. Ana Esther Ceceña, "On the Complex Relation between Knowledges and Emancipations," *South Atlantic Quarterly* (Winter 2012): 111–32, 121.

11. Michel Foucault's discussion of "insurgent knowledges" has been instrumental to the work of numerous scholars who (along with Foucault) I draw on throughout this work; see Michel Foucault, *Society Must Be Defended: Lectures at the Collège de France, 1975–1976*, ed. Mauro

Bertani and Alessandro Fontana, trans. David Macey (New York: Picador, 2003). The concept of "open spaces of encounter" or "spaces of encounter" is advanced in relation to an urban Zapatismo by Manuel Callahan. See Callahan, "Why Not Share a Dream? Zapatismo as Political and Cultural Practice," special issue, *Humboldt Journal of Social Relations* 29, no. 1 (2005): 12.

12. On situated knowledges, see Donna Haraway, "Situated Knowledges: The Science Question of Partial Perspective," *Feminist Studies* 14, no. 3 (Autumn 1988): 575–99. On situated knowledges and their diverse genealogies as critical to a feminist methodology, see Verónica Gago, *Feminist International: How to Change Everything*, trans. Liz Mason-Deese (New York: Verso, 2020); and Susana Draper, "Strike as Process: Building the Poetics of a New Feminism," *South Atlantic Quarterly* 117, no. 3 (2018): 682–91.

13. Joy James, "Political Trauma," in *The Bloomsbury Handbook of 21st-Century Feminist Theory*, ed. Robin Truth Goodman (New York: Bloomsbury Academic, 2021), 345. See also James, "The Womb of the Western Theory: Trauma, Time Theft, and the Captive Maternal," in *Challenging the Punitive Society*, ed. Perry Zurn and Andrew Dilts, Carceral Notebooks, vol. 12, 2016 (Columbia University), 253–96.

14. Ivan Illich, *Gender* (New York: Marion Boyers, 1983).

15. There is much room for excess in these terms throughout, and I am grateful for theorists (including Laura Briggs) who advance a position in writing that encompasses these complexities. See Laura Briggs, *How All Politics Became Reproductive Politics: From Welfare Reform to Foreclosure to Trump* (Oakland: University of California Press, 2018).

16. Cedric J. Robinson, *Black Marxism: The Making of the Black Radical Tradition* (Chapel Hill: University of North Carolina Press, 2021), 26. I would like to thank an anonymous reviewer for drawing my attention to this passage in Robinson's work.

17. Ruth Wilson Gilmore, "Abolition Geography and the Problem of Innocence," in *Futures of Black Radicalism*, ed. Gaye Teresa Johnson and Alex Lubin (New York: Verso, 2017), 240.

18. Subcomandante Insurgente Marcos, *Notes on Wars*, trans. El Kilombo (Central Valleys, Mexico: El Rebozo, 2014), 6, 10, 14.

19. Mark Neocleous, *War Power, Police Power* (Edinburgh: Edinburgh University Press, 2014), 5.

20. Mark Neocleous, "Air Power as Police Power," in *War, Police, and Assemblages of Intervention*, ed. Jan Bachmann, Colleen Bell, and Caroline Holmqvist (New York: Routledge, 2014), 173–75, 169.

21. On "politics as war," see Foucault, *Society Must Be Defended*. On pacification, see Neocleous, *War Power*, esp. chap. 1; and Mark Neocleous, "War as Peace, Peace as Pacification," *Radical Philosophy* 159 (January/February 2010): 8–17. See also Center for Research on Criminal Justice, *The Iron Fist and the Velvet Glove: An Analysis of the U.S. Police* (New York: Pluto, 1977); Stuart Schrader, "To Secure the Global Great Society: Participation in Pacification," *Humanity: An International Journal of Human Rights, Humanitarianism and Development* 7, no. 2 (2016): 225–53; Stuart Schrader, *Badges without Borders: How Global Counterinsurgency Transformed American Policing* (Oakland: University of California Press, 2019); Brendan McQuade, "A Critical View of Counterinsurgency: World Relational State (De)formation," *Younsei Journal of International Studies* 4, no. 1 (2012): 67–90; Kristian Williams, William Munger, and Lara Messersmith-Glavin, eds., *Life during Wartime: Resisting Counterinsurgency* (Oakland: AK, 2013); and Kristian Williams, "The Other Side of the COIN: Counterinsurgency and Community Policing," *Interface* 3, no. 1 (May 2011): 81–117, 84.

22. This book is indebted to Laleh Khalili's work mapping the most comprehensive genealogy of counterinsurgency as an ongoing praxis shaping pacification in the present, as well as Joy James's work, in particular *Warfare in the American Homeland*, for excavating pacification practices historically to mark the convergence of war powers and police powers in a U.S. context. Similarly, Ather Zia's writing on women's resistance in Kashimir relies on ethnography to establish a profound map of counterinsurgency in the present. Laleh Khalili, *Time in the Shadows: Confinement in Counterinsurgencies* (Stanford, CA: Stanford University Press, 2012); Joy James, *Warfare in the American Homeland: Policing and Prison in a Penal Democracy* (Durham, NC: Duke University Press, 2007); Joy James, *States of Confinement: Policing, Detentions, and Prisons* (New York: St. Martin's Press, 2000); Ather Zia, *Resisting Disappearance: Military Occupation and Women's Activism in Kashmir* (Seattle: University of Washington Press, 2019).

23. On the idea of war as domesticated, see Manuel Callahan, "Democratic Despotism: War and the Production of Ideological Surplus Value," unpublished manuscript, 2021; and Manuel Callahan, "Zapatista Civic Pedagogy in a Time of War," in *When the Roots Start Moving: To Navigate Backwards, Resonating with Zapatismo*, ed. Alessandra Pomarico and Nikolay Oleynikov (Berlin: Archive Books and Lecce: Free Home University, 2021).

24. The term "war:police assemblages" is advanced by Bachmann et al. and is especially useful for understanding overall shifts in policing

and securitization at a local and global level; see Bachmann, Bell, and Holmqvist, *War, Police, and Assemblages of Intervention*.

25. On the concept of "war-police," see Neocleous, "Air Power," 167; and Neocleous, *War Power*. On Foucault's "social relations as a model of war," see Neocleous, "Air Power," 173. On necropolitics, see Achille Mbembe, "Necropolitics," trans. Libby Meintjes, *Public Culture* 15, no. 1 (2003): 11–40.

26. Neocleous, "Air Power," 173–75.

27. Neocleous, *War Power*. See also George S. Rigakos, *Security/Capital: A General Theory of Pacification* (Edinburgh: Edinburgh University Press, 2016). On disability, race, and police violence, see Leroy F. Moore Jr., Tiny aka Lisa Gray-Garcia, and Emmitt H. Thrower, "Black & Blue: Policing Disability & Poverty beyond Occupy," in *Occupying Disability: Critical Approaches to Community, Justice, and Decolonizing Disability*, ed. Pamela Block, Devva Kasnitz, Akemi Nishida, and Nick Pollard (New York: Springer, 2015), 295–318.

28. Neocleous, *War Power*; Mark Maguire, Catarina Frois, and Nils Zurawski, eds., *The Anthropology of Security: Perspectives from the Frontline of Policing, Counter-Terrorism and Border Control* (London: Pluto, 2014); Derek S. Denman, "The Logistics of Police Power: Armored Vehicles, Colonial Boomerangs, and Strategies of Circulation," *Environment and Planning D: Society and Space* 38, no. 6 (2020): 1138–56.

29. Stefano Bloch and Dugan Meyer, "Implicit Revanchism: Gang Injunctions and the Security Politics of White Liberalism," *Environment and Planning D: Society and Space* 37, no. 6 (2019): 1100–1118, 1102.

30. Toynbee Prize Foundation and Timothy Nunan, "Policing the 'Slums of the World': A Conversation about Exporting American Police Expertise with Stuart Schrader," November 24, 2016, Toynbee Prize Foundation, para. 40, https://toynbeeprize.org/posts/stuart-schrader/. See also Schrader, *Badges without Borders*; and Frederick Turner and Bryanna Fox, *Police Militarization: Policy Changes and Stakeholders' Opinions in the United States* (New York: Springer, 2018).

31. Numerous scholars have developed this analysis on mutual contamination. See, for example, Mark Neocleous, "The Police of Civilization: The War on Terror as Civilizing Offensive," *International Political Sociology* 5, no. 2 (June 2011): 144–59; Christian Parenti, *Lockdown America: Police and Prisons in the Age of Crisis* (New York: Verso, 1999); Bernard E. Harcourt, *The Counterrevolution: How Our Government Went to War Against Its Own Citizens* (New York: Basic Books, 2018); Peter Kraska and Victor E. Kappeler, "Militarizing American Police: The Rise and Normalization of

Paramilitary Units," *Social Problems* 44, no. 1 (February 1997): 1–18; Alex Vitale, *The End of Policing* (New York: Verso, 2018); Micol Seigel, *Violence Work: State Power and the Limits of Police* (Durham, NC: Duke University Press, 2018); Thomas Rid, "The Nineteenth-Century Origins of Counterinsurgency Doctrine," *Journal of Strategic Studies* 33, no. 5 (2010): 727–58; and Alfred W. McCoy, *Policing America's Empire: The United States, the Philippines, and the Rise of the Surveillance State* (Madison: University of Wisconsin Press, 2009).

32. On the RAND conference, see Stephen T. Hosmer and S. O. Crane, *Counterinsurgency: A Symposium, April 16–20, 1962* (Santa Monica, CA: Rand Corporation, 2006). See also James, *Warfare in the American Homeland*, especially Dhoruba bin Wahad, "The War Within: A Prison Interview," 76–97, on police training and Vietnam. See also Kristian Williams, *Our Enemies in Blue: Police and Power in America* (Oakland, CA: AK, 2015); Vitale, *End of Policing*; Schrader, *Badges without Borders*; and Nikhil Pal Singh, *Race and America's Long War* (Berkeley: University of California Press, 2019).

33. On Bratton, see Bernard E. Harcourt, *Illusion of Order: The False Promise of Broken Windows Policing* (Cambridge, MA: Harvard University Press, 2005); Parenti, *Lockdown America*; Rachel Herzing, "No Bratton-Style Policing in Oakland: Unraveling the Fraying Edges of Zero Tolerance," *San Francisco Bay View*, January 22, 2013, http://sfbayview.com/2013/no-bratton-style-policing-in-oakland-unraveling-the-fraying-edges-of-zero-tolerance; and Jordan T. Camp and Christina Heatherton, eds., *Policing the Planet: Why the Policing Crisis Led to Black Lives Matter* (New York: Verso, 2016). See also Micol Seigel, "William Bratton in the Other L.A.," in *Without Fear . . . Claiming Safe Communities without Sacrificing Ourselves*, ed. Southern California Library (Los Angeles: Southern California Library), 54–62.

34. Ronald J. Ostrow, "Casual Drug Users Should Be Shot, Gates Says," *Los Angeles Times*, September 6, 1990, A1. On Gates, see Mike Davis, *City of Quartz: Excavating the Future of Los Angeles* (New York: Vintage, 1992); Max Felker-Kantor, *Policing Los Angeles: Race, Resistance, and the Rise of the LAPD* (Chapel Hill: University of North Carolina Press, 2018); and João H. Costa Vargas, *Catching Hell in the City of Angels: Life and Meanings of Blackness in South Central Los Angeles* (Minneapolis: University of Minnesota Press, 2006). See also James, *Warfare in the American Homeland*. On counterinsurgency and knowledge production, see Roberto J. González, *American Counterinsurgency: Human Science and the Human Terrain* (Chicago: Prickly Paradigm, 2009).

35. Extensive research has been done to elaborate the role of the Office of Public Safety and its impact on policing in the United States. See Schrader, *Badges without Borders*; and Seigel, *Violence Work*. On Burge, see Julilly Kohler-Hausmann, "Militarizing the Police: Officer Jon Burge's Torture and Repression in the 'Urban Jungle,'" in *Challenging the Prison-Industrial Complex: Activism, Arts, and Educational Alternatives*, ed. Stephen Hartnett (Urbana: University of Illinois Press, 2010), 43–71; Marissa Faustini and Sharyln Grace, "Jon Burge and Chicago Police Torture" (pamphlet), Historical Moments of Police Violence, vol. 8 (Chicago: Black and Blue, 2013). On Dan Mitrione, see Brett Wilkins, "Teaching Torture: The Death and Legacy of Dan Mitrione," CounterPunch, August 13, 2020, https://www.counterpunch.org/2020/08/13/teaching-torture-the-death-and-legacy-of-dan-mitrione/.

36. See, for example, Barry J. Ryan, "A Mediterranean Police Assemblage," in Bachmann et al., *War, Police and Assemblages*, 147–63, 155. See also Norman Friedman, *Network-Centric Warfare: How Navies Learned to Fight Smarter through Three World Wars* (Annapolis, MD: Naval Institute Press, 2009). For a genealogy of air power and its relation to populations and space in colonial warfare, including surveillance, see Neocleous, "Air Power." A similar assemblage can be observed as well in federal agencies in relation to the border; see Jennifer G. Correra and James M. Thomas, "From the Border to the Core: A Thickening Military-Police Assemblage," *Critical Sociology* 45, no. 7-8 (2019): 1133–47. See also Caren Kaplan and Andrea Miller, "Drones as 'Atmospheric Policing': From U.S. Border Enforcement to the LAPD," *Public Culture* 31, no. 3 (2019): 419–45; Nicholas Mirzoeff's work on "neovisuality" and the representation and control of space, in *The Right to Look: A Counterhistory of Visuality* (Durham, NC: Duke University Press, 2011; and Mirzoeff, "War Is Culture: Global Counterinsurgency, Visuality, and the Petraeus Doctrine," *PMLA* 124, no. 5 (2009): 1737–46.

37. See, for example, Casey Delehanty, Jack Mewhirter, Ryan Welch, and Jason Wilks, "Militarization and Police Violence: The Case of the 1033 Program," *Research and Politics* 4, no. 2 (June 14, 2017).

38. See Segato, "Patriarchy from Margin to Center," esp. 623.

39. "Authorized crime" is a concept advanced by Carlos Spector to make visible the orchestrated complicity between the Mexican state and forms of violence, including narco violence, that are generally situated as outside the state, and which occur with U.S. collusion and consent. See Marcela Arteaga, dir., *The Guardian of Memory* (*El guardián de la memoria*), Gefilte Films (Mexico), 2019.

40. See, for example, Alexandra Natapoff, *Snitching: Criminal Informants and the Erosion of American Justice* (New York: NYU Press, 2011).

41. On the LAPD Ramparts Division violence, see *Ovando v. City of Los Angeles*, No. CV99–11835-GAF(AJWx) 92 F.Supp.2d 1011 (2000) (U.S. District Court, C.D. California, March 28, 2000.) See also Felker-Kantor, *Policing Los Angeles*. On the Oakland Riders, see *Allen v. City of Oakland*, PN-CA-0010, C00–4599 TEH (JL), Northern District of CA (U.S.), 12/17/2000. See also Ali Winston and Darwin BondGraham, *The Riders Come Out at Night: Brutality, Corruption, and Cover-up in Oakland* (New York: Atria Books, 2023).

42. For a narrative of overlapping moments of state-manufactured violences, see Pamela Thompson, "Growing Up in Compton: A Woman's Story," *San Francisco Bay View*, January 28, 2016.

43. Anita Wills, UniTierra Califas/CCRA Social Factory Ateneo, Oakland, 2014 (author's notes). See also Anita Wills, "The Killing of Kerry Baxter Jr.," Redwood Curtain Copwatch, July 15, 2011, https://www.redwoodcurtaincopwatch.net/node/850.

44. On industrial tools versus convivial tools, see Ivan Illich, *Tools for Conviviality* (New York: Marion Boyers, 2001).

45. This includes both state-sanctioned death and social death. See Ruth Wilson Gilmore, "Fatal Couplings of Power and Difference: Notes on Racism and Geography," *The Professional Geographer* 54, no. 1 (February 2002): 15–24, 16; and Lisa Marie Cacho, *Social Death: Racialized Rightlessness and the Criminalization of the Unprotected* (New York: New York Press, 2012).

46. Christopher Lowen Agee, *The Streets of San Francisco: Policing and the Creation of a Cosmopolitan Liberal Politics, 1950–1972* (Chicago: University of Chicago Press, 2014), 74.

47. Obscenity policing in San Francisco is also discussed in Agee, *Streets of San Francisco*, 111. See also Eric A. Stanley and Nat Smith, *Captive Genders: Trans Embodiment and the Prison Industrial Complex* (Oakland: AK, 2015). On LGBT communities and demands for law-and-order policing, see Christina B. Hanhardt, *Safe Space: Gay Neighborhood History and the Politics of Violence* (Durham, NC: Duke University Press, 2013).

48. Agee, *Streets of San Francisco*, 146.

49. See Verónica Gago and Sandro Mezzadra, "A Critique of the Extractive Operations of Capital: Toward an Expanded Concept of Extractivism," trans. Liz Mason-Deese, *Rethinking Marxism* 29, no. 4 (2017): 574–91.

50. See Donna Murch, "Crack in Los Angeles: Crisis, Militarization, and Black Response to the Late Twentieth-Century War on Drugs," *Journal of*

American History 102, no. 1 (June 2015): 162–73. On sustained chaos as a coordinated political and military strategy, see Nicholas Mirzoeff, "Global Counterinsurgency and the Crisis of Visuality," in Mirzoeff, *The Right to Look*, 277–309.

51. See Gary Webb, *Dark Alliance: The CIA, the Contras, and the Crack Cocaine Explosion* (New York: Seven Stories, 1998); Daniel Finn, "What We Really Know About the CIA and Crack," *Jacobin*, November 12, 2021, https://jacobin.com/2021/11/what-we-really-know-about-the-cia-and-crack; Michelle Alexander, *The New Jim Crow: Mass Incarceration in the Age of Colorblindness* (New York: New Press, 2010); Deborah Chasman and Joshua Cohen, "Racist Logic: Race, Markets Sex," *Boston Review*, June 4, 2019, and particularly, Donna Murch, "How Race Made the Opioid Crisis," 7–22.

52. See Davis, *City of Quartz*; and Ruth Wilson Gilmore, *Golden Gulag: Prisons, Surplus, Crisis, and Opposition in Globalizing California* (Berkeley: University of California Press, 2007). The word "gang" occurs in quotes here not out of a denial that there are forms of street organizing that continue to impact communities, often in violent ways, but to draw attention to the fact that "gangs" as understood in the present are state-produced, both discursively and materially. On the emergence of the L.A. Crips, see Stanley Tookie Williams, *Blue Rage, Black Redemption: A Memoir* (New York: Simon and Schuster, 2007). See also Victor Rios, *Punished: Policing the Lives of Black and Latino Boys* (New York: NYU Press, 2011).

53. Murch, "Crack in Los Angeles"; Davis, *City of Quartz*.

54. See Timothy J. Dunn, *The Militarization of the U.S.–Mexico Border, 1978–1992: Low-Intensity Conflict Doctrine Comes Home* (Austin: University of Texas Press, 1996).

55. I owe this point to conversations emerging from UniTierra Califas and Acción Zapatista, and also drawing on the work of Mike Davis, "Realities of the Rebellion," *Against the Current*, no. 39 (July/August 1992): 14–18.

56. See Radley Balko, *Overkill: The Rise of Paramilitary Police Raids in America* (Washington, DC: Cato Institute, 2006); and Kraska and Kappeler, "Militarizing American Police."

57. For an example of revenue accumulation through policing that explains the conflict in Ferguson, see Jodi Rios, "Racial States of Municipal Governance: Policing Bodies and Space for Revenue in North St. Louis County, Missouri," *Law & Inequality* 37, no. 2 (2019): 235–308.

58. Thompson, "Growing Up in Compton."

59. See, for example, Center for Research on Criminal Justice, *Iron Fist*; K. Williams, *Our Enemies in Blue*; Vitale, *End of Policing*; Singh, *Race and*

America's Long War; Ana Muñiz, *Police, Power, and the Production of Racial Boundaries* (New Brunswick, NJ: Rutgers University Press, 2015); Angela J. Davis, ed., *Policing the Black Man: Arrest, Prosecution, and Imprisonment* (New York: Vintage, 2018); Khalil Gibran Muhammad, *The Condemnation of Blackness: Race, Crime, and the Making of Modern Urban America* (Cambridge, MA: Harvard University Press, 2019); and João H. Costa Vargas, "Activist Scholarship Limits and Possibilities in Times of Black Genocide," in *Engaging Contradictions: Theory, Politics, and Methods of Activist Scholarship*, ed. Charles R. Hale (Berkeley: University of California Press, 2008), 164–82. On the role of violence in the ongoing production of racial capitalism, see Chris Chen, "The Limit Point of Capitalist Equality: Notes towards an Abolitionist Anti-Racism," in *End Notes 3: Gender, Race, Class and Other Misfortunes*, ed. Jasper Bernes (September 2013), 202–23. See also Robinson, *Black Marxism*; and W. E. B. Du Bois, "The African Roots of War," www.webdubois.org/dbAfricanRWar.html.

60. See Manuel Callahan, "Crisis and Permanent War on the U.S.-Mexico Borderlands," unpublished manuscript, June 17, 2014.

61. Ranajit Guha, "The Prose of Counter-Insurgency," in *Selected Subaltern Studies*, ed. Ranajit Guha and Gayatri Chakravorty Spivak (New York: Oxford University Press, 1988), 45–86. See also Manuel Callahan, "Mexican Border Troubles: Social War, Settler Colonialism and the Production of Frontier Discourses, 1848–1880" (PhD diss., University of Texas at Austin, 2003). On "crime," see Muhammad, *Condemnation of Blackness*; and Jonathan Simon, *Governing through Crime: How the War on Crime Transformed American Democracy and Created a Culture of Fear* (New York: Oxford University Press, 2007).

62. See Callahan, "Insurgent Learning"; and Callahan, "In Defense of Conviviality."

63. On "bad debt," Stefano Harney and Fred Moten write, "It is not credit that we seek, nor even debt, but bad debt—which is to say real debt, the debt that cannot be repaid, the debt at a distance, the debt without creditor, the black debt, the queer debt, the criminal debt." "Bad debt" offers a way a marking those relations that are always outside the capitalist logic of credit and debt; we can relate to each other through "bad debt" as a way of making explicit a break with capital and to engage a refusal, which is a refusal to be an instrument of capital, and to participate in its logic. Stefano Harney and Fred Moten, *The Undercommons: Fugitive Planning and Black Study* (Brooklyn, NY: Autonomedia, 2013): 61.

64. Critical to facilitating this conversation was Pablo Obando (FrayBa) and Tony Nelson (MSN). These connections were likewise amplified by a

series of MSN tours organized with Stuart Schussler, and including Edith López Ovalle of HIJOS on collective memory against imprisonment, assassinations, and disappearances across Mexico.

65. See Manuel Callahan, "Rebel Dignity," *Kalfou* 3, no. 2 (2016): 259–77.

66. See Manuel Callahan, "Repairing the Community: UT Califas and Convivial Tools of the Commons," *Ephemera: Theory & Politics in Organization* 19, no. 2 (2019): 369–87.

67. See, for example, Women's Group of the Indigenous Governing Council and National Indigenous Congress, "Mexican Women of the National Indigenous Congress Stand with Black Lives Matter," Voices in Movement, June 22, 2020, https://voicesinmovement.org/national-indigenous-congress-black-lives-matter/.

68. Ceceña, "On the Complex Relation," 111.

69. On "within, against, and beyond the state," see John Holloway, *Crack Capitalism* (London: Pluto, 2010).

70. Ceceña, "On the Complex Relation," 119.

71. Manuel Callahan, "UT Califas Theses Clinic Summary, 5-3-14" (summary), message to UniTierra discussion list, May 28, 2014.

72. On Mario Tronti's theorization of the social factory, see, for example, Harry Cleaver, "The Inversion of Class Perspective in Marxian Theory: From Valorisation to Self-Valorisation," in *Open Marxism, Volume 2: Theory and Practice*, ed. Werner Bonefeld, Richard Gunn, and Kosmas Psychopedis (London: Pluto, 1992), 115. For a history, see Louise Toupin, *Wages for Housework: A History of an International Feminist Movement, 1972–77* (Vancouver: University of British Columbia Press, 2018); Silvia Federici, *Revolution at Point Zero: Housework, Reproduction, and Feminist Struggle* (Oakland: PM, 2012); Mariarosa Dalla Costa, "Introduction to the Archive of Feminist Struggle for Wages for Housework," Viewpoint Magazine, October 31, 2015; Mariarosa Dalla Costa, "The Door to the Garden: Feminism and Operaismo," paper delivered at a seminar on Operaismo in Rome, Italy, June, 2002, https://libcom.org/library/the-door-to-the-garden-feminism-and-operaismo-mariarosa-dalla-costa; Leopoldina Fortunati, "Learning Struggle: My Story between Workerism and Feminism," Viewpoint Magazine, September 15, 2013; and Anna Curcio, "Marxist Feminism of Rupture," Viewpoint Magazine, January 4, 2020.

73. Critical feminist texts include Mariarosa Dalla Costa and Selma James. *The Power of Women and the Subversion of the Community* (London: Falling Wall, 1975); Federici, *Revolution at Point Zero*; Leopoldina Fortunati, *The Arcane of Reproduction: Housework, Prostitution, Labor, and*

Capital (Brooklyn, NY: Autonomedia, 1996); Mariarosa Dalla Costa, *Family, Welfare, and the State: From Progressivism to the New Deal* (Brooklyn, NY: Common Notions, 2015); and Giovanna Franca Dalla Costa, *The Work of Love: Unpaid Housework, Poverty & Sexual Violence at the Dawn of the 21st Century* (Brooklyn, NY: Autonomedia, 2008). Further theorization on the wage as an instrument of invisibilization was subsequently developed by the Zerowork Collective; see "Introduction to Zerowork I," in *Midnight Oil: Work, Energy, War 1973–1992*, ed. Midnight Notes Collective (New York: Autonomedia, 1992), 109–14. See also Maria Mies, *Patriarchy and Accumulation on a World Scale: Women in the International Division of Labour* (Atlantic Highlands, NJ: Zed, 1999).

74. Social reproduction as a category of analysis, including as social reproduction theory, continues to be elaborated across a range of Marxist-feminist orientations in the current moment, notably Nancy Fraser, *Fortunes of Feminism: From State-Managed Capitalism to Neoliberal Crisis* (New York: Verso, 2020); and Tithi Battacharya, ed., *Social Reproduction Theory: Remapping Class, Recentering Oppression* (New York: Pluto, 2017).

75. See Convivial Research and Insurgent Learning, "Social Factory," http://ccra.mitotedigital.org/ateneo/social_factory.

76. See Gago and Mezzadra, "Critique of the Extractive Operations of Capital."

77. See Rios, "Racial States of Municipal Governance."

78. Marina Vishmidt, "Permanent Reproductive Crisis: An Interview with Silvia Federici," Metamute, March 7, 2013, http://www.metamute.org/editorial/articles/permanent-reproductive-crisis-interview-silvia-federici.

79. For W. E. B. Du Bois's notion of "democratic despotism," including its relationship to the "white working-class bargain," I draw on Manuel Callahan's use of Du Bois's "African Roots of War" to develop a theory of race in relation to capital and violence in the present. On the "bargain," see Callahan, "In Defense of Conviviality." See also David R. Roediger, *The Wages of Whiteness: Race and the Making of the American Working Class* (New York: Verso, 2007).

80. See George Lipsitz, *Possessive Investment in Whiteness: How White People Profit from Identity Politics* (Philadelphia: Temple University Press, 2006).

81. Angela Y. Davis, *Women, Race, and Class* (New York: Vintage, 1981), 235–36.

82. On the imperative to "clear, hold, build" and "destroy, build, secure," see Tyler Wall, Parastou Saberhi, and Will Jackson, eds., *Destroy, Build, Secure: Readings on Pacification* (Ottawa, ON: Red Quill Books, 2017).

83. Fred Moten, "Uplift and Criminality," in *Next to the Color Line: Gender, Sexuality, and W. E. B. Du Bois*, ed. Susan Gillman and Alys Eve Weinbaum (Minneapolis: University of Minnesota Press, 2007), 330. On the criminalization and pathologization of rebellion, insurgent life, and autonomy, see Saidiya Hartman, *Wayward Lives, Beautiful Experiments: Intimate Histories of Riotous Black Girls, Troublesome Women, and Queer Radicals* (New York: W. W. Norton, 2019).

84. See Denise Ferreira da Silva, "Unpayable Debt: Reading Scenes of Value against the Arrow of Time," in *The Documenta 14 Reader*, ed. Quinn Latimer and Adam Szymczyk (Munich: Prestel, 2017), 81–112. See also Paula Chakravarty and Denise Ferreira da Silva, eds., *Race, Empire, and the Crisis of the Subprime* (Baltimore, MD: Johns Hopkins University Press, 2013); and Katherine McKittrick and Clyde Woods, eds., *Black Geographies and the Politics of Place* (Toronto: Between the Lines, 2007).

85. Silvia Federici, *Re-Enchanting the World: Feminism and the Politics of the Commons* (Oakland, CA: PM, 2019).

86. On reproductive justice as a right to raise and care for children in safe and healthy environments, see Loretta J. Ross and Rickie Solinger, *Reproductive Justice: An Introduction* (Oakland: University of California Press, 2017). On "fierce care," see Manuel Callahan and Annie Paradise, "Fierce Care: Politics of Care in the Zapatista Conjuncture," *Transversal.at* (blog) and *Oekologien der Sorge* (in German), http://transversal.at/blog/Fierce-Care.

87. Segato, "Patriarchy from Margin to Center."

88. On "inventions" and "reinventions," see Katherine McKittrick, "Rebellion/Invention/Groove," *Small Axe* 49 (March 2016): 79–91.

Chapter 1

1. Mesha Monge-Irizarry, oral history interview, April 2015.

2. A. C. Thompson, "SFBG: The Tragedy of Idriss Stelley," *San Francisco Bay Guardian* repost on IndyBay, January 25, 2002, https://www.indybay.org/newsitems/2002/01/25/1144241.php.

3. Mesha Monge-Irizarry, oral history interview, April 2015.

4. See Willie Ratcliff, "They Butchered My Child!" San Francisco Bay Area Independent Media Center (IndyBay), June 20, 2001, https://www.indybay.org/newsitems/2001/06/25/1013811.php.

5. Ratcliff, "They Butchered My Child!"

6. Policewatch, "Idriss Stelley's Mom Files Civil Claim," San Francisco Bay Area Independent Media Center (IndyBay), September 4, 2001, https://www.indybay.org/newsitems/2001/09/04/1036671.php.

7. Mesha Monge-Irizarry, oral history interview, April 2015.

8. In this section I draw on Isabell Lorey, *State of Insecurity: Government of the Precarious*, trans. Aileen Derieg (New York: Verso, 2015), as a work that also explores critical connections between the crisis of care, securitization, and biopolitics; as well as the research methodology of Precarias a la deriva. See "A Very Careful Strike—Four Hypotheses," *The Commoner*, no. 11 (2006): 33–45; and "Adrift through the Circuits of Feminized Precarious Work," *Feminist Review*, no. 77 (August 2004): 157–61.

9. For an analysis of the roots of this problem, see Elizabeth Hinton, *From the War on Poverty to the War on Crime: The Making of Mass Incarceration in America* (Cambridge, MA: Harvard University Press, 2017); and Julilly Kohler-Hausmann, *Getting Tough: Welfare and Imprisonment in 1970s America* (Princeton, NJ: Princeton University Press, 2019).

10. The concept of the "militarization of care" is explored more fully in chapter 4.

11. On dependency as the creation of "needs," see Ivan Illich, *Toward a History of Needs* (Berkeley, CA: Heyday Books, 1977). Angela Mitropoulos reminds us that the Keynesian welfare state was built on settler-colonial accumulation; see Mitropoulos, "From Precarity to Risk Management and Beyond," ecipcp.net, 2011, http://eipcp.net/transversal/0811/mitropoulos/en.

12. Precarias a la deriva, "A Very Careful Strike."

13. KPFA Morning Mix, "Police Violence in San Francisco: Mesha Irizarry on the New KPFA Morning Show," January 5, 2011, San Francisco Bay Area Independent Media Center (IndyBay), https://www.indybay.org/newsitems/2011/01/05/18668378.php.

14. Carol Harvey, "SFPD Facing People in Crisis: No Gun, No Taser! Talk 'Em Down," *San Francisco Bay View*, September 29, 2012; Justin Berton, "Gascón Faulted for Ending Training of Officers," SFGate, January 8, 2011.

15. See Berton, "Gascón Faulted," para. 15.

16. See, for example, Alissa Greenberg, "U.S. Police Killed Someone in Mental or Emotional Crisis Every 36 Hours This Year, Report Says," *Time*, July 1, 2015.

17. The Bay Citizen, "Reporters Play Police," YouTube, posted January 6, 2011, https://www.counterpunch.org/2020/08/13/teaching-torture-the-death-and-legacy-of-dan-mitrione/.

18. This is evidenced, for example, in the comments section of the segment posted online. See The Bay Citizen, "Reporters Play Police."

19. Segato, "Patriarchy from Margin to Center," 623; Segato's theorization on pedagogy here is valuable as a concept and as a tool, though in

conversation with CCRA, we shift away from the language of "pedagogy" (in order to retain the liberatory potential around shared learning) and instead rely on a notion of discipline or training, or dressage.

20. Segato, "Patriarchy from Margin to Center," 623.

21. Lorey, *State of Insecurity*, 42.

22. Maribel Casas-Cortez, "A Genealogy of Precarity: A Toolbox for Rearticulating Fragmented Social Realities in and out of the Workplace," *Rethinking Marxism* 26, no. 2 (April 2014): 209; Camille Barbagello and Nicholas Bueret, "Starting from the Social Wage," *The Commoner* (October 2012): 159–84. See also Kohler-Hausmann, *Getting Tough*.

23. Segato, "Patriarchy from Margin to Center," 622.

24. Precarias a la deriva, "Adrift through the Circuits," 157–58; Lorey, *State of Insecurity*, 92.

25. Craig Dalton and Liz Mason-Deese, "Counter (Mapping) Actions: Mapping as Militant Research," *ACME: An International Journal for Critical Geographies*, vol. 11 (2012): 439–66, 447;. See also the work of the Counter Cartographies Collective at UNC Chapel Hill, including Maria Isabel Casas-Cortes and Sebastian Cobarrubias, "Drifting through the Knowledge Machine," in *Constituent Imagination/Militant Investigations*, ed. Stevphen Shukaitis and David Graeber (Oakland, CA: AK, 2007), 112–26.

26. Callahan, "Repairing the Community."

27. The quote is from Oficina de Derechos Sociales; see Javier Toret and Nicolás Sguiglia, "Cartography and War Machines: Challenges and Experiences around Militant Research in Southern Europe," trans. Maribel Casas-Cortés and Sebastian Cobarrubias, Notas Rojas Collective, Chapel Hill, http://transform.eipcp.net/transversal/0406/ tsg/en.

28. Gilmore, "Fatal Couplings," 16.

29. Mesha Monge-Irizarry, oral history interview, April 2015.

30. See Manuel Callahan, "UT Theses Clinic, Saturday, May 3, 2014" (announcement), message to UniTierra discussion list, April 26, 2014. On *testimonios*, see Latina Feminist Group, "Introduction: *Papelitos Guardados*: Theorizing *Latinidades* through *Testimonio*," in *Telling to Live: Latina Feminist Testimonios* (Durham, NC: Duke University Press, 2001), 1–24.

31. A convivial research strategy that emphasizes autonomous learning spaces, the co-production of knowledge, and collective ethnography not only seeks to draw attention to the way we produce knowledge. It is also advanced as a "safe house" strategy, a site that protects the community and those speaking from identification and further intrusion from the state. Multiple stories of police stalkings emerged from these spaces, and those

who documented them remain anonymous here; this is true throughout this work.

32. These details and analysis emerged further in conversation with a member of the investigative team of a subcommittee of the Oscar Grant Committee in the space of UniTierra Califas's Social Factory Ateneo, convened in Oakland from May 2014 to May 2015, and other spaces convened by UniTierra Califas during this time. See also Anita Wills and Cynthia Morse, "Unnamed Young Black Man Killed by Oakland Police," *San Francisco Bay View*, October 6, 2011.

33. UniTierra Califas' Social Factory Ateneo, May 2014–May 2015.

34. See, for example, Henry K. Lee, "Oscar Grant's Friend Is Shot, Killed," *San Francisco Chronicle*, July 16, 2011.

35. Direct action casework draws on the work of the Ontario Coalition Against Poverty. See Jeff Shantz, "Fighting to Win: The Ontario Coalition Against Poverty," *Capital and Class* (2002): 464–71.

36. See Convivial Research and Insurgent Learning, "Social Factory Ateneo 12-27-14," http://cril.mitotedigital.org/announcement_12-27-14.

37. Avery F. Gordon, "Methodologies of Imprisonment," *PMLA* 123, no. 3 (May 2008): 651–57, 652.

38. Foucault, *Society Must Be Defended*, specifically lecture "7 January 1976," 7–8.

39. See, for example, Michel Foucault, "Nietzsche, Genealogy, History," trans. Donald F. Bouchard and Sherry Simon, in *Language, Counter-Memory, Practice*, ed. Donald F. Bouchard (Ithaca, NY: Cornell University Press, 1993), 139–64; Foucault, *Society Must Be Defended*; Foucault, "Questions of Method," trans. Robert Hurley, in *Power: Essential Works of Foucault 1954–1984*, vol. 3, ed. James D. Faubion and Paul Rabinow (series ed.) (New York: New Press, 2000), 223–38.

40. See also, for example, Boaventura de Sousa Santos, *Epistemologies of the South: Justice against Epistemicide* (Boulder, CO: Paradigm, 2014).

41. See Sara C. Motta, "Decolonising Critique: From Prophetic Negation to Prefigurative Affirmation," in *Social Sciences for an Other Politics: Women Theorizing without Parachutes*, ed. Ana Cecilia Dinerstein (London: Palgrave Macmillan, 2016), 33–48, 35.

42. Idriss Stelley Foundation, "Enough Is Enough! Justice 4 Asa Sullivan Candlelight Vigil," San Francisco Bay Area Independent Media Center (IndyBay), June 18, 2006, https://www.indybay.org/newsitems/2006/06/18/18281245.php?show_comments=1, para. 2.

43. See Ram Narayan Kumar, Amrik Singh, Ashok Agrwaal, and Jaskaran Kaur, *Reduced to Ashes: The Insurgency and Human Rights in Punjab: Final*

Report, Volume One (1) (Kathmandu: South Asia Forum for Human Rights, 2003). See also Idriss Stelley Foundation, "Enough Is Enough!"

44. Alex Breitler, "SJ Pathologist to Resign," Recordnet, November 28, 2017, https://www.recordnet.com/news/20171128/sj-pathologist-to-resign-says-sheriff-moore-interfered-in-investigations.

45. See CCRA, "Stockton Timeline of Officer-Involved Killings," 1997–2007, 2008–2018, https://ggg.vostan.net/ccra/#758.

46. Silvia Federici, "Forward: The Common Is Us: Principles of Health Autonomy," in *For Health Autonomy: Horizons of Care beyond Austerity: Reflections from Greece*, ed. CareNotes Collective (Brooklyn, NY: Common Notions, 2020), xvii, xv.

47. See, for example, Idriss Stelley Foundation, "I Live Here, Please Don't Kill Me: Justice 4 Asa Sullivan," which highlights each of these areas, San Francisco Bay Area Independent Media Center (IndyBay), June 11, 2006, https://www.indybay.org/newsitems/2006/06/11/18280096.php.

48. This is the community safety project theorized and advanced by Uni-Tierra Califas.

49. Foucault, quoted in Andrew W. Neal, "Goodbye War on Terror? Foucault and Butler on Discourses of Law, War, and Exceptionalism," in *Foucault on Politics, Security, and War*, ed. Michael Dillon and Andrew W. Neal (New York: Palgrave Macmillan, 2011), 43–64.

50. Convivial Research and Insurgent Learning, "Analytical Frameworks," http://ccra.mitotedigital.org/convivialres/analytical-frameworks, para. 3.

51. For conversations on the vernacular and valorization, I draw on Callahan, "Repairing the Community"; and Cleaver, "Inversion of Class Perspective."

52. Convivial Research and Insurgent Learning, "Analytical Frameworks," para. 3.

53. Gustavo Esteva, "Regenerating People's Space," *Alternatives* 12, no. 1 (January 1998): 125–52.

54. Contrary to a political community of protection, Precarias a la deriva therefore develops the common notion of a "care community"; Lorey, *State of Insecurity*, 94.

Chapter 2

1. Cleaver, "Inversion of Class Perspective," 129.

2. Vyjayanthi Rao, "Embracing Urbanism: The City as Archive," *New Literary History* 40 (2009): 371–83.

3. On blockade as the central strategy of the current conjuncture to obstruct the flow of capital, see the Invisible Committee, *To Our Friends* (South Pasadena, CA: Semiotext(e), 2015). See also Jason E. Smith, "Since the End of the Movement of the Squares: The Return of the Invisible Committee," *The Brooklyn Rail*, June 15, 2015.

4. Bachmann et al., *War, Police and Assemblages*.

5. There are several key moments when the docks have been shut down in support of and to advance the alter-globalization movement (e.g., since 1994 or 1999). For a history of the ILWU and its militant past, see Charles P. Larrowe, *Harry Bridges: The Rise and Fall of Radical Labor in the U.S.* (Westport, CT: Lawrence Hill, 1972); and David Wellman, *The Union Makes Us Strong: Radical Unionism on the San Francisco Waterfront* (New York: Cambridge University Press, 1997). See also Jeremy Brecher, *Strike!* (Oakland, CA: PM, 2020).

6. On TAZKP, see Callahan, "In Defense of Conviviality"; "Insurgent Learning"; and "Rebel Dignity."

7. On the commons and the politics of the commons, see, for example, Federici, *Revolution at Point Zero*, especially "Feminism and the Politics of the Common in an Era of Primitive Accumulation," 138–48. On "institutions of the commons," see Gigi Roggero, *The Production of Living Knowledge: The Crisis of the University and Transformation of Labor in Europe and North America* (Philadelphia: Temple University Press, 2011). On "spaces of encounter," see Callahan, "In Defense of Conviviality."

8. Many militant researchers and collectives have offered a powerful analysis of the collective resistance of the witnesses trapped on the BART trains. See Bring the Ruckus, "Do the Right Thing: New Start for Abolitionism in Oakland," in *Raider Nation, Vol. 1: From the January Rebellions to Lovelle Mixon and Beyond* (Oakland, CA: Raider Nation Collective, 2010); George Ciccariello-Maher, "From Oscar Grant to Occupy: The Long Arc of Rebellion in Oakland," in *We Are Many: Critical Reflections on Movement Strategy from Occupation to Liberation*, ed. Kate Khatib, Margaret Killjoy, and Mike McGuire (Oakland, CA: AK, 2012), 39–45; and Anonymous, "Unfinished Acts: January Rebellions," Oakland, California, 2009, https://unfinishedacts.noblogs.org/, among others.

9. See Anonymous, "Unfinished Acts." Much critically important and formative analysis and writing came out of these insurgencies, including through pamphlets and articles widely circulated at the time. Among them are Anonymous, "Unfinished Acts"; Raider Nation Collective, *Raider Nation, Vol. 1*; Ciccariello-Mayer, "From Oscar Grant to Occupy"; Kali Akuno, "An Open Letter to the Justice for Oscar Grant Movement:

Suggestions on Next Steps, Strategy and Unity Building," *Navigating the Storm* (blog) (June 15, 2010), https://navigatingthestorm.blogspot.com/2010/07/open-letter-to-justice-for-oscar-grant.html; Advance the Struggle, "Justice for Oscar Grant: A Lost Opportunity?" pamphlet, 2009; and Bring the Ruckus, "Bring the Ruckus Responds to Advance the Struggle on the Oscar Grant Rebellion," San Francisco Bay Area Independent Media Center (IndyBay), July 29, 2009, https://www.indybay.org/newsitems/2009/07/29/18613005.php. Details and analysis of the incident also circulated widely through publications outside of Oakland; see, for example, from a pamphlet series out of Chicago, Olivia Perlow and Lakeesha J. Harris, "The Police Execution of Oscar Grant" (pamphlet), Project NIA and the Chicago PIC Teaching Collective, vol. 5.

10. Ciccariello-Mayer, "From Oscar Grant to Occupy"; see also Anonymous, "Unfinished Acts."

11. See Winston and BondGraham, *Riders Come Out*.

12. I am grateful to conversations with Roxanne Dunbar-Ortiz on this history. Other departments across the Bay Area (and beyond) are governed by similar racial perspectives. See, for example, Peter Santina, "Jim Crow in San Francisco," *San Francisco Bay View*, March 24, 2015, which provides evidence not only of virulent racism, but of outright support for white power. See also Winston and BondGraham, *Riders Come Out*, esp. 100–120.

13. A number of sources document and further analyze and explain the role of the NPIC in containing the rebellion at different stages. See, for example, K. Williams, "Other Side"; Raider Nation Collective, "Introduction," in *Raider Nation, Vol. 1*; Advance the Struggle, "Lost Opportunity?"; and Bring the Ruckus, "Bring the Ruckus Responds."

14. The role of nonprofits in a broader counterinsurgency strategy of the state is examined in K. Williams, "Other Side"; see also Raider Nation Collective, "Introduction."

15. Sylvia Wynter in McKittrick, "Rebellion/Invention/Groove," 86.

16. See Barnor Hesse and Juliet Hooker, "On Black Political Thought inside Global Black Protest," *South Atlantic Quarterly* 116, no. 3 (July 2017): 443–56; Barbara Ransby, *Making All Black Lives Matter: Reimagining Freedom in the Twenty-First Century* (Berkeley: University of California Press, 2018); and Minkah Makalani, "Black Lives Matter and the Limits of Formal Black Politics," *South Atlantic Quarterly* 116, no. 3 (July 2017): 529–52.

17. On "black rage," see Hesse and Hooker, "Black Political Thought"; and Makalani, "Black Lives Matter."

18. See Anonymous, "Unfinished Acts."
19. See Smith, "Movement of the Squares," para. 16.
20. On the "routine stop," see Makalani, "Black Lives Matter."
21. For a discussion of police actions and reasonable responses to violence in relation to *Tennessee v. Garner*, see Makalani, "Black Lives Matter."
22. See, for example, the analysis of the Raider Nation Collective, "The Ambivalent Silences of the Left: Lovelle Mixon, Police, and the Politics of Race/Rape," in *Raider Nation, Vol. 1*.
23. Raider Nation Collective, "Ambivalent Silences," 35.
24. This sentiment surfaced in an interview with J. R. Valrey, who in reference to the Mixon case states, "The saying among low-income Black people in the streets of East Oakland, and in the Bay area, is 'How does it feel when the rabbit has the gun?'" Diane Bukowski, "Reporter Faces Felony Charges for Covering Oscar Grant Rebellion," Final Call, September 4, 2009, para. 7. The Black Panthers were among early theorists to name the conditions of occupation in Oakland, and specifically in relation to uneven development, as a colonial occupation; see Robert O. Self, *American Babylon: Race and the Struggle for Postwar Oakland* (Princeton, NJ: Princeton University Press, 2003). See also Raider Nation Collective, "Ambivalent Silences," 34; and Stokely Carmichael (Kwame Ture) and Charles V. Hamilton's analysis in *Black Power*, discussed in Makalani, "Black Lives Matter."
25. For a discussion of the police as an occupying army repressing and producing colonial subjects and citizens, see Makalani, "Black Lives Matter."
26. See Sam Stoker, dir., *The Ghosts of March 21st* (Tijuana, Mexico: CRONISTAS/Digital Media Collective, and Oakland, CA: We Copwatch, 2014).
27. Sandra Gonzales, "Cop Killer Was Depressed about Heading Back to Prison, Family Says," *Mercury News*, March 22, 2009.
28. Michel Foucault, "On Popular Justice: A Discussion with Maoists," in *Power/Knowledge: Selected Interviews and Other Writings 1972–1977*, trans. Colin Gordon, Leo Marshall, John Mepham, and Kate Soper, ed. Colin Gordon (New York: Pantheon Books, 1980), 1–36, 22.
29. See, for example, Robert F. Williams, *Negroes with Guns* (Detroit, MI: Wayne State University Press, 1999).
30. By the spring of 2015, the community claimed a hard-won and significant victory in successfully pushing the injunctions out of Oakland. See the Stop the Injunctions Coalition, "Our Oakland, Our Solutions" in Williams et al., *Life during Wartime*.

31. Matthew Edwards, "Insurrection, Oakland Style: A History," Viewpoint Magazine, October 30, 2011, 11; Fredric Jameson, "Spatial Equivalents in the World System," in *Postmodernism, or the Cultural Logic of Late Capitalism* (Durham, NC: Duke University Press, 1991), 97–130, 137.

32. See Cacho, *Social Death*. See also Edwards, "Insurrection, Oakland Style."

33. Hardin, quoted in Maria Mies and Veronika Benholdt-Thomsen, "Defending, Reclaiming and Reinventing the Commons," *Canadian Journal of Development Studies* 22, no. 4 (2001): para. 67.

34. Richard J. F. Day, *Gramsci Is Dead: Anarchist Currents in the Newest Social Movements* (New York: Pluto, 2005), 13. Day refers to these practices as affinity-based practices (18).

35. See Henry A. Giroux, "Reading Hurricane Katrina: Race, Class, and the Biopolitics of Disposability," *College Literature* 33, no. 3 (Summer 2006); and Cacho, *Social Death*.

36. According to Malaika Kambon, "all jurors had ties to law enforcement through friendship, past service, or relatives"; Malaika Kambon, "Centuries of Rage: The Murder of Oscar Grant III," *San Francisco Bay View*, February 25, 2015, para. 9.

37. See Michel Foucault, "The Mesh of Power," trans. Christopher Chitty, Viewpoint Magazine, September 12, 2012; and Raquel Gutiérrez Aguilar, *Rhythms of the Pachakuti: Indigenous Uprising and State Power in Bolivia* (Durham, NC: Duke University Press, 2014), esp. 59.

38. These questions and the development of new strategies are being read against Thomas Nail's analysis of Zapatista organizing as retreating from and refusing the traditional forms of revolution, namely the capture of the state, the political representation of the party, the centrality of the proletariat, and the leadership of the vanguard. These points were made central in a Democracy Ateneo in the fall of 2013 in thinking through struggles and urban Zapatismo in the present. See Thomas Nail, *Returning to Revolution: Deleuze, Guattari, and Zapatismo* (Edinburgh: Edinburgh University Press, 2012). See also Convivial Research and Insurgent Learning, "Democracy Ateneo Announcement 11-16-13," http://cril.mitotedigital.org/announcement_11-16-13.

39. "Kettling" is a form of entrapment of a crowd, in this case relying on features of urban geography to funnel and then encircle a group of people. In many cases, law enforcement proceed to arrest whoever is trapped in the center, thus removing people from the streets.

40. Marina Sitrin and Dario Azzelini, *They Can't Represent Us! Reinventing Democracy from Greece to Occupy* (New York: Verso, 2014).

41. See, for example, Gustavo Esteva, "The Oaxaca Commune and Mexico's Coming Insurrection," *Antipode* 42, no. 4 (2010): 978–93; Marianne Maeckelbergh, "Experiments in Democracy and Diversity within the Occupy Movement(s)," Kosmos, Spring/Summer 2013; and Marina Sitrin, "Horizontalism and the Occupy Movements," *Dissent* (Spring 2012).

42. On San Francisco, see, for example, Sitrin and Azzellini, *They Can't Represent Us!*; on San José, see Callahan, "In Defense of Conviviality." See also Rebecca Solnit, "Forward: Miracles and Obstacles," in Nathan Schneider, *Thank You, Anarchy: Notes from the Occupy Apocalypse* (Berkeley: University of California Press, 2013).

43. On desire and struggle, see Claire Fontaine, ""Human Strike within the Field of Libidinal Economy," in *Human Strike Has Already Begun and Other Writings* (Lüneburg: Mute and Post-Media Lab, 2013), 35–52; Gilles Deleuze, "Desire and Pleasure," trans. Melissa McMahon with a foreword by Francois Ewald, 1997, http://www.artdes.monash.edu.au/globe/delfou.html. Mapping this struggle follows a genealogical approach as theorized by Foucault, but with struggles for autonomy as the category of analysis for the genealogy. In situating struggles for autonomy as a category of analysis for the genealogy, see Nick Dyer-Witheford, *Cyber-Marx: Cycles and Circuits of Struggle in High Technology Capitalism* (Chicago: University of Illinois Press, 1994); as well as Roggero, *Production of Living Knowledge*.

44. On Occupy and encampment, see Marianne Maeckelbergh, "Occupy the US: Musings on Horizontal Decision Making and Bureaucracy," STIR, Spring 2012; and Maeckelbergh, "Experiments in Democracy."

45. See Sitrin and Azzellini, *They Can't Represent Us!*

46. See Sitrin, "Horizontalism and the Occupy Movements."

47. For a narrative on some of the challenges and interventions of these struggles by Indigenous activists, see Joanne Barker, "Territory as Analytic: The Dispossession of Lenapehoking and the Subprime Crisis," *Social Text* 36, no. 2: 135 (2018).

48. See Barker, "Territory as Analytic"; and Chakravarty and Ferreira da Silva, eds., *Race, Empire, and the Crisis of the Subprime*.

49. See, for example, Sitrin and Azzellini, *They Can't Represent Us!*; and Mike King, *When Riot Cops Are Not Enough: The Policing and Repression of Occupy Oakland* (New Brunswick, NJ: Rutgers University Press, 2017).

50. For reflections on the port shutdown and other actions that unfolded within Occupy Oakland, see Mike King and Emily Brissette, "Kindling for the Spark: Eros and Emergent Consciousness in Occupy Oakland," in *Spontaneous Combustion: The Eros Effect and Global Revolution*, ed. Jason Del Gandio and AK Thompson (Albany: SUNY Press, 2017), 171–89.

51. Emily Brissette, "Beyond Tear Gas and Torched Dumpsters: Rethinking Violence at Occupy Oakland," *Humanity & Society* 42, no. 2 (2018): 221–44.

52. Ali Winston, "OPD Used Violent Cops Against Occupy," *East Bay Express*, December 21, 2011. Much has been written, including in real time during the waves of police attacks, on the repression and ongoing resistance of the Oakland Commune and more broadly, Occupy Oakland; see, for example, King, *When Riot Cops Are Not Enough*. See also Winston and BondGraham, *Riders Come Out*.

53. On re-territorialization as a strategy for the rupture opened by movements "from Greece to Occupy," see Sitrin and Azzellini, *They Can't Represent Us!*

54. Against the Hired Guns gathering in downtown Oakland, March 2012.

55. Colectivo Situaciones, "On the Researcher Militant," trans. Sebastian Touza, Variant, September 2003, https://variant.org.uk/strickdistro/KINN_CoR/Co-r_PDFs/Reading-6-Nov-2012-Colectivo-Situaciones-2003.pdf.

56. John D. Márquez and Junaid Rana, "Black Radical Possibility and the Decolonial International," *South Atlantic Quarterly* 116, no. 3 (2017): 505–28, 511, 508.

57. On "societies in movement," see Raúl Zibechi, *Territories in Resistance: A Cartography of Latin American Social Movements*, trans. Ramor Ryan (Edinburgh: AK, 2012).

58. Heidi Rimke, "Security: Resistance," in *Anti-Security*, ed. Mark Neocleous and George Rigakos (Ottawa: Red Quill Books, 2011), 191–215, 192.

59. Jameson, "Spatial Equivalents," 137.

60. See Day, *Gramsci Is Dead*, 18.

61. Many collectives, authors, and projects—from both the Left and the Right—have claimed the phrase a "new kind of politics." Here I draw on the formulation advanced by the Zapatistas over many years, as well as the work of Colectivo Situaciones, including through the spaces of relational *testimonio* convened with Mesa de Escrache in Colectivo Situaciones, *Genocide in the Neighborhood* (see, for example, p. 43), trans. Brian Whitener, Daniel Borzutzky, and Fernanda Fuentes (Oakland, CA: Chainlinks, 2009).

62. Esteva, "Regenerating People's Space," 136; Harry Cleaver, "On Self-Valorization in Mariarosa Dalla Costa's 'Women and the Subversion of the Community,'" 1970, https://caringlabor.wordpress.com/2011/01/16/harry-cleaver-on-self-valorization-in-mariarosa-dalla-costa's-women-and-the-subversion-of-the-community/.

63. This reflects a discussion from UniTierra Califas's Ateneo; see Convivial Research and Insurgent Learning, "Democracy Ateneo Summary 10-19-13," para. 4.

64. This multiplicity of perspectives is reflected in Barbara Ransby, *Making All Black Lives Matter*.

65. These three strands were mapped out by CCRA with mothers from Stockton who advance "Black Lives Matter 2.0" as praxis to both engage and critique the more liberal elements of more dominant, mainstream groups organizing under the rubric of Black Lives Matter.

66. On missed opportunities, see Advance the Struggle, "Justice for Oscar Grant"; on lost momentum, see Edwards, "Insurrection, Oakland Style," 11.

67. See Ciccarello-Maher, "From Oscar Grant to Occupy"; and King and Brissette, "Kindling for the Spark."

68. For strategic concepts, see Callahan, "Rebel Dignity."

69. Callahan and Paradise, "Fierce Care"; on the claiming of a "we" that resists the heuristic of individual time/space but instead lays claim to a collective subject, see Sitrin and Azzelini, *They Can't Represent Us!*; on the always emergent collective subject, see Callahan, "In Defense of Conviviality."

Chapter 3

1. Once known as "the Industrial City," South San Francisco or "South City" has a population of less than 70,000 people. It is situated on the San Francisco Peninsula, south of San Francisco and north of San Francisco International Airport, and is serviced by BART and CalTrain. During World War II, like much of the Bay Area's western coastline, South City was a site of shipbuilding, and it was also historically home to meatpacking plants, warehouses, and factories, making it a working-class city. Following widespread de-industrialization and given its proximity to UC Berkeley, UC San Francisco, and Stanford, South City has reemerged as the "birthplace of biotechnology" and is home to over forty biotech companies, including Amgen and Genentech, two of the largest biotech firms in the world. Property values (and population) have risen steadily in pace with the growth of Silicon Valley, and while South City still maintains much of its industrial zoning, condominiums, office parks, residential housing, and high-rise hotels have been significant sites of development in the shift from the "Industrial City" to a biotech enclave. The population is now predominately Asian and Latinx, making up more than 70 percent combined,

with an additional 20 percent white. City of South San Francisco, *Our City* (blog), https://www.ssf.net/our-city.

2. See Terri Kay, "Derrick Gaines, Killed by Police at 15," *Workers World*, October 10, 2013, http://www.workers.org/articles/2013/10/10/derrick-gaines-killed-police-15/, para. 3; and Alex Darocy, "Family Files $10 Million Wrongful Death Suit," San Francisco Bay Area Independent Media Center (IndyBay), November 3, 2012, https://www.indybay.org/newsitems/2012/11/03/18725038.php.

3. Simon Springer's work on anarchist geography situates reclaiming the commons as an act of mutual aid, asserting that "property is a relation of domination." See Simon Springer, *The Anarchist Roots of Geography: Towards Spatial Emancipation* (Minneapolis: University of Minnesota Press, 2016), 10.

4. Clayton Plake and Siddharth Patel, "Derrick Gaines: They Treated Him like a Statistic: Interview with Rachel Guido-Red and Dolores Piper," *Socialist Worker*, August 21, 2012.

5. Darocy, "Family Files $10 Million Wrongful Death Suit." Cabillo transferred to the San Francisco Police Department after the shooting of Derrick Gaines. He continued his violent legacy with the SFPD. See Julian Mark, "SFPD Shooting Victim Files Suit vs. City of San Francisco," Mission Local, May 13, 2109.

6. Plake and Patel, "Derrick Gaines"; Clayton Plake, "Injustice Duly Served," *Socialist Worker*, September 13, 2012.

7. Plake and Patel, "Derrick Gaines."

8. See Damien M. Sojoyner, *First Strike: Educational Enclosures in Black Los Angeles* (Minneapolis: University of Minnesota Press, 2016).

9. Guha, "Prose of Counter-Insurgency"; Callahan, "Crisis and Permanent War."

10. See South San Francisco Police Department, "South San Francisco Police Department Community Outreach and Staffing Increases," http://www.ssf.net/home/showdocument?id=718.

11. See Dwayne A. Mack and Felicia W. Mack, "Policing with Impunity: Racialized Policing in the 21st Century," in *Law Enforcement in the Age of Black Lives Matter: Policing Black and Brown Bodies*, ed. Sandra E. Weissinger and Dwayne A. Mack (Lanham, MD: Lexington Books, 2017), 13–36, 24.

12. Officer Cabillo is also that: a "bad apple" cop. See Mack, "SFPD Shooting Victim."

13. Victoria Colliver, "No Fault Found in Police Shooting of Teen," SFGate, August 29, 2012.

14. On the relation between terror and policing, see Chen, "Limit Point of Capitalist Equality."

15. Roger Trinquier, an early French architect of counterinsurgency, advocated sheer force and raw brutality as critical to the exercise of counterinsurgent warfare. See Khalili, *Time in the Shadows*; Harcourt, *Counterrevolution*; and Jasbir K. Puar, *Terrorist Assemblages: Homonationalism in Queer Times* (Durham, NC: Duke University Press, 2017). See also Roger Trinquier, *Modern Warfare: A French View of Counterinsurgency* (Westport, CT: Praeger Security International, 2006).

16. On pacification, see Neocleous, *War Power*. For a discussion of security in relation to an increasing militarization of space, see Davis, *City of Quartz*. See also "militarization of space" in Toret and Sguiglia, "Cartography and War Machines."

17. Dolores Piper, CCRA People's Investigation workshop, San Francisco, December 2015, author's notes.

18. Gutiérrez Aguilar, *Rhythms of the Pachakuti*, xxi.

19. See Alex S. Vitale and Brian Jordan Jefferson, "The Emergence of Command and Control Policing," in *Policing the Planet: Why the Policing Crisis Led to Black Lives Matter*, ed. Jordan T. Camp and Christina Heatherton (New York: Verso, 2016). See also Wall et al., *Destroy, Build, Secure*, on community policing as counterinsurgency and pacification.

20. Herzing, "No Bratton-Style Policing," para. 6. See also Harcourt, *Illusion of Order*; INCITE! Women of Color Against Violence, "Quality of Life Policing" (pamphlet), http://www.incitenational.org/sites/default/files/incite_files/resource_docs/3316_toolkitrev-qualitylife.pdf.

21. See Parenti, *Lockdown America*, 82.

22. See Andrea R. Nagy and Joel Podolny, "William Bratton and the NYPD: Crime Control through Middle Management Reform," Yale case 07–015 rev., February 12, 2008, Yale School of Management; and Parenti, *Lockdown America*, 73. On the Law Enforcement Assistance Administration, see Parenti, *Lockdown America*; Hinton, *War on Poverty*; and Simon, *Governing through Crime*.

23. On Bratton and the Boston Transit Police, and their resemblance to military operations, see Parenti, *Lockdown America*. On the militarization of police, see also Kraska and Kepplar, "American Police"; and Radley Balko, *The Rise of the Warrior Cop: The Militarization of America's Police Forces* (New York: Public Affairs, 2017).

24. On punitive population management, see, for example, Mack and Mack, "Policing with Impunity."

25. On trainings and exchanges under Bratton, see Seigel, "William Bratton in the Other L.A." See also Jordan T. Camp and Christina Heatherton, "Broken Windows, Surveillance, and the New Urban Counterinsurgency: Interview with Hamid Khan," 151–55, 154; and Ruth Wilson Gilmore and Craig Gilmore, "Beyond Bratton," 173–99, both in *Policing the Planet: Why the Policing Crisis Led to Black Lives Matter*, ed. Jordan T. Camp and Christina Heatherton (New York: Verso, 2016). On consultancies, see, Seigel, *Violence Work*; Schrader, "Global Great Society" and *Badges*; and Harcourt, *Counterrevolution*.

26. On Bratton and zero-tolerance policing, see Vitale and Jefferson, "Emergence of Command and Control," 164; Nagy and Podolny, "Bratton and the NYPD"; and Harcourt, *Illusion*.

27. Vitale, *End of Policing*, 158. See also Rajiv Shah and Brendan McQuade, "Surveillance, Security, and Intelligence-Led Policing in Chicago," in *Neoliberal Chicago*, ed. Larry Bennett, Roberta, Garner, and Euan Hague (University of Illinois Press, 2016), 243–59.

28. Khalili, *Time in the Shadows*, 201, italics mine.

29. On intelligence-gathering in a colonial context, see Khalili, *Time in the Shadows*; Rid, "Nineteenth Century Origins"; Thomas Rid, "Razzia: A Turning Point in Modern Strategy," *Terrorism and Political Violence* 21 (2009): 617–35, esp. 626; and Talal Asad, ed., *Anthropology and the Colonial Encounter* (New York: Humanity Books, 1995), in particular, Abdel Ghaffar M. Ahmed, "Some Remarks from the Third World on Anthropology and Colonialism: The Sudan," 259–70.

30. This is the archictecture of counterinsurgency that governs and terrorizes Indian-occupied Kashmir in the present.

31. See Moten, "Uplift and Criminality," 332. As legacy, these restrictions form the basis, for example, of the Indian-administered counterinsurgency in occupied Kashmir in the present, based on a British colonial model of population control and pacification.

32. Wall et al., *Destroy, Build, Secure*, 6.

33. On the Bureaux Arabes, see Khalili, *Time in the Shadows*; and Rid, "Nineteenth Century Origins."

34. On COINTELPRO, see Ward Churchill and Jim Vander Wall, *Agents of Repression: The FBI's Secret Wars against the Black Panther Party and the American Indian Movement* (Boston: South End, 2001); Churchill and Wall, *The COINTELPRO Papers: Documents from the FBI's Secret Wars against Dissent in the United States* (Boston: South End, 2001); Andres Alegria, Prentis Hemphill, Anita Johnson, and Claude Marks, producers,

Cointelpro 101, documentary/video, 56 mins. (San Francisco: Freedom Archives, 2016); and David Cunningham, *There's Something Happening Here: The New Left, the Klan, and FBI Counterintelligence* (Berkeley: University of California Press, 2004). On "social network analysis," see K. Williams, "Other Side of the COIN," 87. Recently, Roberto J. González has also done work exposing the human terrain system; see González, "Human Terrain: Past, Present, Future Applications," *Anthropology Today* 24, no. 1 (February 2008); González, *American Counterinsurgency*; and González, "The Rise and Fall of the Human Terrain System," CounterPunch, June 29, 2015. Also, the American Anthropological Association (AAA) issued a statement specifically against the human terrain system in 2007, "AAA Opposes U.S. Military's Human Terrain System Project," 2007, http://www.aaanet.org/issues/AAA-Opposes-Human-Terrain-System-Project.cfm. On crime mapping, see Brian Jordan Jefferson, "Digitize and Punish: Computerized Crime Mapping and Racialized Carceral Power in Chicago," *Environment and Planning D: Society and Space* 35, no. 5 (October 2017): 775–96. On the emerging centrality of information-gathering in counterinsurgent warfare, see Mizroeff, *The Right to Look*.

35. See González, "Rise and Fall of the Human Terrain System." See also the Network of Concerned Anthropologists, *The Counter-Counterinsurgency Manual* (Chicago: Prickly Paradigm, 2009).

36. Marcos, *Notes on Wars*, 14.

37. See Peter K. Manning, *The Technology of Policing: Crime Mapping, Information Technology, and the Rationality of Crime Control* (New York: New York University Press, 2008).

38. Wall et al., *Destroy, Build, Secure*, 6.

39. See Segato, "Patriarchy from Margin to Center," 622.

40. On the rise of predictive policing, see Andrew Guthrie Ferguson, *The Rise of Big Data Policing: Surveillance, Race, and the Future of Law Enforcement* (New York: New York University Press, 2017).

41. On fusion centers, see Brendan McQuade, *Pacifying the Homeland: Intelligence Fusion and Mass Supervision* (Berkeley: University of California Press, 2019).

42. See INCITE! "Quality of Life Policing," 17.

43. INCITE! "Quality of Life Policing." Bernard Harcourt draws on Foucault to situate "an order maintenance approach to criminal justice" and the creation of subjects as a strategy visible in juvenile prisons in France in 1840; see Harcourt, *Illusion of Order*, 160.

44. Vitale, *End of Policing*, 158.

45. Vitale, *End of Policing*, 158.

46. On the composition of the CRTs, see, for example, Ali Winston, "Deadly Secrets: How California Law Shields Oakland Police Violence," Colorlines, August 17, 2011.

47. Parenti, *Lockdown America*, 114–19.

48. Parenti, *Lockdown America*; Balko, *Overkill*; Kraska and Kappeler, "Militarizing American Police."

49. Kay, "Derrick Gaines," para. 6.

50. *ABC 7 News*, "Gang Violence a Continuing Problem in SSF," May 4, 2012, https://abc7news.com/archive/8649480/.

51. City of South San Francisco, "Neighborhood Response Team," http://www.ssf.net/departments/police/divisions/operations.

52. See South San Francisco Police Department, "Community Outreach and Staffing Increases."

53. Alex Vitale draws attention to this point in *End of Policing*.

54. *ABC 7 News*, "Gang Violence."

55. See Drew Himmelstein, "Poll: Keep the Neighborhood Response Team?" Patch News, March 22, 2012, https://patch.com/california/southsanfrancisco/poll-keep-the-neighborhood-response-team.

56. *ABC 7 News*, "Gang Violence."

57. *ABC News*, "Gang Violence."

58. See Neocleous, *War Power*, 14. See also Foucault's "plague-stricken town" which he cites as a "panoptic establishment," in *Discipline and Punish: The Birth of the Prison*, trans. A. M. Sheridan Smith (New York: Vintage, 1995), 205.

59. Herzing, "No Bratton-Style Policing," para. 7, para. 28. On "*quadrillage* and *ratissage*," see Khalili, *Time in the Shadows*.

60. For a discussion of neoliberal security and territory, see, for example, Callahan, "Permanent War"; and Rimke, "Security: Resistance." For a discussion of space as a category of analysis in relation to power and violence, see Michel Foucault, *Security, Territory, Population: Lectures at the Collège de France, 1977–1978*, trans. Graham Burchell, ed. Michel Senellart, François Ewald, and Alessandro Fontana (Hampshire, UK: Palgrave Macmillan, 2007); see also Edward W. Soja, *Postmetropolis: Critical Studies of Cities and Regions* (Hoboken, NJ: Wiley-Blackwell, 2000). On social control and urban space, see Katherine Beckett and Steve Herbert, *Banished: The New Social Control in Urban America* (New York: Oxford University Press, 2011). On property as space, see Self, *American Babylon*. On race and the production and reproduction of space, see Katherine McKittrick, *Demonic Grounds: Black Women and the Cartographies of Struggle* (Minneapolis: University of Minnesota Press, 2006); and McKittrick and Woods,

Black Geographies. See also Rashad Shabazz, *Spatializing Blackness: Architectures of Confinement and Black Masculinity in Chicago* (Champaign: University of Illinois Press, 2015).

61. See Marcos, *Notes on Wars*, 14. See also Mirzoeff's discussion of the "commander's view" in *The Right to Look*.

62. Maribel Casas-Cortes, "Politics of Disobedience: Ensuring Freedom of Movements in a B/ordered World," *Spheres* 4 (2017): 1–6, 4.

63. See James Joseph Scheurich, "Policy Archaeology: A New Policy Studies Methodology," *Education Policy* 9, no. 4 (1994): 297–316; and Stefano Harney and Fred Moten, "Planning and Policy," in *The Undercommons: Fugitive Planning and Black Study* (Brooklyn, NY: Autonomedia, 2013), 73–83. On necropolitical racial regimes, see Mirzoeff, *The Right to Look*.

64. This territory and control of populations is always in relation to borders and thus, capital, racial hierarchies, and "differential laboring subjects" and "differential inclusion" through a "multiplication of labor." See Callahan, "Permanent War," 4. For "differential inclusion" and "differential laboring subjects" produced through the border, see Sandro Mezzadra and Brett Neilson, *Border as Method, or the Multiplication of Labor* (Durham, NC: Duke University Press, 2013). Yen Le Espiritu also advances this category of "differential inclusion" in *Home Bound: Filipino American Lives across Cultures, Communities, and Countries* (Berkeley: University of California Press, 2003), 47. Also, recalling Foucault, the securitization of space occurs at the intersection of multiple forms and operations of power—sovereign and disciplinary; repressive and productive; biopolitical and necropolitical. For more on necropolitical power and necropolitics, see Mbembe, "Necropolitics." See also Giroux, "Reading Hurricane Katrina." A notable study on the militarization of space is Mike Davis's *City of Quartz*, in particular, "Fortress LA," 221–63.

65. On uneven development in the greater Bay Area, see Self, *American Babylon*. See also Arturo Escobar, *Encountering Development: The Making and Unmaking of the Third World* (Princeton, NJ: Princeton University Press, 2011).

66. Muñiz, *Police, Power*. See also Bloch and Meyer, "Implicit Revanchism."

67. Sandro Mezzadra and Brett Neilson, "Borderscapes of Differential Inclusion: Subjectivity and Struggles on the Threshold of Justice's Excess," in *The Borders of Justice*, ed. Etienne Balibar, Sandro Mezzadra, and Ranabir Samaddar (Philadelphia: Temple University Press, 2012), 181–203. On citizenship and uneven development, see H.L.T. Quan, *Growth Against Democracy: Savage Developmentalism in the Modern World* (Lanham, MD: Lexington Books, 2012).

68. EZLN, "Truth and Justice Will Never, Ever Come from Above," *Chiapas Support Committee: Compañero Manuel* (blog), August 20, 2015, https://compamanuel.wordpress.com/2015/08/20/ezln-truth-and-justicewill-never-ever-come-from-above/, para. 25. This statement was part of a larger statement on truth, justice, and impunity issued by the EZLN following the murder of Compañero Galeano (the Zapatista José Luis Solís López) by paramilitary forces working in collusion with the Mexican state on May 2, 2014, in La Realidad. See Marta Molina, "After an Assassination, the World Stands in Solidarity with the Zapatistas," Truthout, May 20, 2014.

69. George S. Rigakos makes this point about Israel's relationship with Palestine; see Rigakos, *Security/Capital*.

70. Draper, "Strike as Process," 686.

71. Liz Mason-Deese, "Translator's Foreword," in Verónica Gago, *Feminist International: How to Change Everything*, trans. Liz Mason-Deese (New York: Verso, 2020), vii.

72. Annie Paradise and Manuel Callahan, "Vigil as Convivial Tool and Convivial Praxis," *Ecoversities* (blog), June 19, 2022, https://ecoversities.org/vigil-as-convivial-tool-and-convivial-praxis/.

73. McKittrick and Woods, *Black Geographies*; McKittrick, *Demonic Grounds*, 4. On questions of mapping, geography, and reconquering, see M. Jacqui Alexander and Chandra Talpade Mohanty, "Cartographies of Knowledge and Power: Transnational Feminism as Radical Praxis," in *Critical Transnational Feminist Praxis*, ed. Amanda Lock Swarr and Richa Nagar (Albany: State University of New York Press, 2010), 23–45.

74. *Escrache* as a convivial tool is elaborated in the next chapter of this work, "Kayla Moore." See also Colectivo Situaciones, *Genocide in the Neighborhood*.

75. Marcos, "Notes on Wars"; Neocleous, "Air Power."

76. See Segato, "Patriarchy from Margin to Center." See also Silvia Federici, Susanna Draper, and Liz Mason Deese, eds., *Feminicide and Global Accumulation: Frontline Struggles to Resist the Violence of Patriarchy and Capitalism* (Brooklyn, NY: Common Notions, 2021); and Silvia Federici, *Witches, Witch-Hunting and Women* (Oakland, CA: PM, 2018).

77. This is in reference to a project of Indymedia Estrecho focused on the Gibraltar Strait; see Toret and Sguiglia, "Cartography and War Machines." On re-subjectivization as a critical component of struggles in the present, see Claire Fontaine, *Human Strike and the Art of Creating Freedom*, trans. Robert Hurley (South Pasadena, CA: Semiotext(e), 2020).

78. Toret and Sguiglia, "Cartography and War Machines."

79. Marta Malo, "Common Notions, Part I: Workers-Inquiry, Co-Research, Consciousness-Raising," trans. Maribel Casas-Cortés and Sebastian Cobarrubias/Notas Rojas Collective, February 2006, https://transversal.at/transversal/0406/malo-de-molina/en.

80. On "study," see Harney and Moten, *The Undercommons*.

81. On the militarization of space, see Davis, *City of Quartz*; and Toret and Sguiglia, "Cartography and War Machines." On the concept of "the war entering the city," see Stephen Graham, *Cities Under Siege; The New Military Urbanism* (New York: Verso, 2011).

82. On convivial tools as essential elements of convivial research and insurgent learning in the context of community regeneration, see Callahan, "Repairing the Community"; and Callahan, "In Defense of Conviviality."

83. On re-signification and also an "inventory of knowledges," see Toret and Sguiglia, "Cartography and War Machines."

84. Segato, "Patriarchy from Margin to Center," 617. See also Silvia Rivera Cusicanqui, *Ch'ixinakax utxiwa: On Practices and Discourses of Decolonization*, trans. Molly Geidel (Medford, MA: Polity, 2020).

85. Maria Serrano and Silvia López, "Positions, Situations, Short-Circuits," paper presented at "Gender and Power in the New Europe," the 5th European Feminist Research Conference, Lund University, Sweden, August 20–24, 2003, p. 3, http://www.atria.nl/epublications/2003/gender_and_power/5thfeminist/paper_305__303.pdf.

86. Saidiya Hartman, "The Anarchy of Colored Girls Assembled in a Riotous Manner," *South Atlantic Quarterly* 117, no. 3 (July 2018): 476.

87. Draper, "Strike as Process," 682–83.

88. On the growth of policing and the rise of the automobile, and the racialized questions that this produced around legal understandings of public and private, see Sarah A. Seo, "How Cars Transformed Policing," *Boston Review*, June 3, 2019.

89. Neocleous, *War Power*, 144.

90. Denise Ferreira da Silva, "Towards a Critique of the Socio-logos of Justice: The Analytics of Raciality and the Production of Universality," *Social Identities* 7, no. 3: 421–54.

91. On democratic despotism and capital as war, see Callahan, "Zapatista Civic Pedagogy."

92. See Simone Browne, *Dark Matters: On the Surveillance of Blackness* (Durham, NC: Duke University Press, 2015).

93. Fred Moten, "Do Black Lives Matter? Robin D.G. Kelley and Fred Moten in Conversation," public talk hosted by Critical Resistance, December 13, 2014, https://vimeo.com/116111740.

94. Hartman, *Wayward Lives*, 6. See also Terrion L. Williamson, *Scandalize My Name: Black Feminist Practice and the Making of Black Social Life* (New York: Fordham University Press, 2016).

95. See Jennifer C. Nash, "The Political Life of Black Motherhood," *Feminist Studies*, vol. 44 (2018): 699–712; Segato, "Patriarchy from Margin to Center"; and Browne, *Dark Matters*.

Chapter 4

1. Kayla Moore identified as a woman and as Kayla among her friends and in her everyday life. According to Kayla's family, given that Kayla had grown up as a child named Xavier, in many cases, she still chose to remain as Xavier among her family, as this too remained an identity that she recognized. Throughout this book, I refer to Kayla using the female pronoun and the name she chose for herself as an adult, Kayla Moore. This understanding draws from a relational *testimonio* space convened by the author with Kayla's father Arthur, stepmother Elysse, and sister Maria on April 18, 2015, in Berkeley, California.

2. City of Berkeley Mental Health Division, "Hours of Operation," para. 1, http://www.ci.berkeley.ca.us/Health_Human_Services/Mental_Health/Mobile_Crisis_Team_(MCT).aspx; People's Investigation, "In-Custody Death of Kayla Moore" (report), Berkeley Copwatch, October 2010.

3. Details from the incident are culled from the People's Investigation into the in-custody death of Kayla Moore, which drew on documents from the police investigation, among them the Police Incident Report from the night of the incident, the Case Narrative, Police Report Supplementals from officers involved in the incident, narrative statements from individuals involved or present at the incident, the Case Report Summary, the Report Narrative, the Alameda County Sheriff's Office Coroner's Bureau Report, and transcribed interviews between BPD Sergeant Hong and the officers involved in the incident. Berkeley Police Department, "Police Report, Case Narrative, and Police Report Supplemental" (report), February 12, 13, 2013. The People's Investigation was a collective community-based research effort begun in February 2013 and extending over a year. See People's Investigation, "In-Custody Death," 5.

4. Andy Nguyen, "Man Dies after Being Taken into Police Custody," *Daily Californian*, February 14, 2013, http://www.dailycal.org/2013/02/14/man-dies-after-being-taken-into-police-custody/.

5. Nguyen, "Man Dies," para. 4.

6. The taxonomy of officer involvement was a graph designed by Andrea Prichett of Berkeley Copwatch comprised of, on one axis, the officers involved, and on the other axis, the progression of their actions after arriving on the scene. As more documents became available, the graph was collectively expanded in group sessions as part of the investigation. These tools become increasingly important, since often agents of the state are the only witnesses to the violence they enact, and grassroots investigations must work to elucidate and expose contradictions and inconsistencies.

7. By the time the pamphlet was reproduced in the journal *Radical America*, the number was up to eight; it would climb to twelve that same year. See Combahee River Collective, "Why Did They Die? A Document of Black Feminism," *Radical America* 13, no. 6 (November-December 1979): 41–50. See also Laura Smith, "When Feminism Ignored the Needs of Black Women, a Mighty Force Was Born," Timeline, February 20, 2018, https://timeline.com/feminism-ignored-black-women-44ee502a3c6. For a historical review of this pamphlet in the context of a broader national movement, see Emily L. Thuma, *All Our Trials: Prisons, Policing, and the Feminist Fight to End Violence* (Chicago: University of Illinois Press, 2019).

8. On the dismantling of the welfare state, see Toupin, *Wages for Housework*, esp. 233. See also Silvia Federici, "From Commoning to Debt: Financialization, Microcredit, and the Changing Architecture of Capital Accumulation," *South Atlantic Quarterly* 113, no. 2 (2014): 231–44; Federici, *Revolution at Point Zero*; and Precarias a la deriva, "Very Careful Strike."

9. Author's conversation with Manuel Callahan, August 31, 2013.

10. People's Investigation, "In-Custody Death."

11. A collective analysis was generated through the many direct action spaces of the People's Investigation, as well as through Uni Tierra Califas's *ateneos* in San Francisco, Oakland, and San José from 2013 to the present.

12. On surveillance and gender, see Toby Beauchamp, *Going Stealth: Transgender Politics and U.S. Surveillance Practices* (Durham, NC: Duke University Press, 2019).

13. See Brenna Bhandar, "Organized State Abandonment: The Meaning of Grenfell," *Sociological Review*, December 3, 2018, https://thesociologicalreview.org/magazine/october-2022/verticality/organised-state-abandonment/.

14. See Stanley and Smith, *Captive Genders*; and Dean Spade, *Normal Life: Administrative Violence, Critical Trans Politics, and the Limits of Law* (Durham, NC: Duke University Press, 2015).

15. Andrea J. Ritchie, *Invisible No More: Police Violence against Black Women and Women of Color* (Boston: Beacon, 2017); Moore Jr. et al., "Black & Blue."

16. Press conference, October 16, 2013, Berkeley, author's notes. See Maria Moore, "Copwatch to Release Findings of People's Investigation, Demand That Police Review Commission Hold Special Hearing into the Death of Kayla Moore" (press conference), Veterans Memorial Building, Berkeley, October 16, 2013.

17. Gilmore, *Golden Gulag*; Spade, *Normal Life*; Beauchamp, *Going Stealth*; Stanley and Smith, *Captive Genders*.

18. On dispossession, disposability, and settler colonialism, see Lorenzo Veracini, "Containment, Elimination, Settler Colonialism," *Arena* no. 51/52 (2018). See also Raúl Zibechi, drawing on Ramón Grosfoguel and Franz Fanon, on "zones of non-being," in Zibechi, "The Red-Hot Currency in Fanon," trans. Chiapas Support Committee, *Chiapas Support Committee: Compañero Manuel* (blog), September 4, 2015, https://chiapas-support.org/2015/09/19/zibechi-red-hot-interest-in-fanon/. On anti-Blackness, see Adam Bledsoe and Willie Jamaal Wright, "The Anti-Blackness of Global Capital," *Environment and Planning D: Society and Space* 37, no. 1 (2019): 8–26. Lorenzo Veracini elaborated these ideas more fully in conversation in the space of UniTierra's Fierce Care Ateneo in Oakland on March 25, 2017.

19. See David T. Mitchell, *The Biopolitics of Disability: Neoliberalism, Ablenationalism, and Peripheral Embodiment* (Ann Arbor: University of Michigan Press, 2015).

20. Spade, *Normal Life*.

21. Beauchamp, *Going Stealth*.

22. See, for example, Emilie Raguso, "Man Dies after Struggle with Berkeley Police," Berkeleyside, February 13, 2013; Lance Knobel, "Coroner, Police Deliver Reports on Xavier Moore Death," Berkeleyside, May 3, 2013.

23. Quan, *Growth Against Democracy*, 1–23.

24. Raúl Zibechi, "'Extractivism Creates a Society without Subjects': Raúl Zibechi on Latin American Social Movements," trans. Seth Kershner, Upside Down World, July 30, 2015, http://upsidedownworld.org/archives/international/extractivism-creates-a-society-without-subjects-raul-zibechi-on-latin-american-social-movements/. See also Zibechi, *Territories in Resistance*.

25. Silvia Federici, lecture at California Institute of Integral Studies, Fall 2012. Esteva also frequently references the "urban marginal" in various

articles and editorials. Harry Cleaver draws on both Esteva and Illich to theorize specific subjects who resist normalization as an aspect of vernacular subsistence and self-valorization; see Cleaver, "Inversion of Class Perspective," 123–25. See also Raúl Zibechi, "Subterranean Echoes: Resistance and Politics 'desde el Sótano,'" *Socialism and Democracy* 19, no. 3 (March 5, 2011).

26. On the Fourth World War, see Subcomandante Insurgente Marcos, "The Fourth World War," trans. irlandesa, In Motion Magazine, November 11, 2001, http://www.inmotionmagazine.com/auto/fourth.html.

27. Cleaver, "Inversion of Class Perspective," 124, italics mine.

28. Convivial Research and Insurgent Learning, "Democracy Ateneo Announcement 11-16-13."

29. Colectivo Situaciones, *Genocide in the Neighborhood*, 44. See also People's Investigation, "In-Custody Death," 21.

30. Colectivo Situaciones, *Genocide in the Neighborhood*, 45.

31. Colectivo Situaciones, *Genocide in the Neighborhood*, 44.

32. Colectivo Situaciones, *Genocide in the Neighborhood*, 102.

33. On within, against, and beyond the state; see Holloway, *Crack Capitalism*.

34. Colectivo Situaciones, *Genocide in the Neighborhood*, 105. The sites of collaborative knowledge production convened through UniTierra Califas and CCRA offered space for collective theorization on resistance, autonomy, and movement-building in relation to community safety throughout the process of the People's Investigation.

35. Byrd et al., "Predatory Value," 9

36. See Mitchell, *Biopolitics of Disability*.

37. Spade, *Normal Life*; Beauchamp, *Going Stealth*.

38. See Nail, *Returning to Revolution*; and Day, *Gramsci Is Dead*.

39. Here I draw on the work of Gustavo Esteva and Madhu Suri Prakash, *Grassroots Post-Modernism: Remaking the Soil of Cultures* (London: Zed Books, 1998), to think about what it means to have our struggles engage those practices that "get the state out" of our most intimate moments, both individual and in our relations.

40. On the role of militant research in relation to resistance and movement-building, see Colectivo Situaciones, *19 & 20: Notes for a New Social Protagonism* (Brooklyn, NY: Autonomedia, 2011); and Colectivo Situaciones, "Something More on Research Militancy: Footnotes on Procedures and (In)Decisions," in *Constituent Imagination/Militant Investigations*, ed., Stevphen Shukaitis and David Graeber (Oakland, CA: AK, 2007), 73–93. See also Jeffrey S. Juris and Alexander Khasnabish, eds.,

Insurgent Encounters: Transnational Activism, Ethnography, and the Political (Durham, NC: Duke University Press, 2013).

41. Khalili, *Time in the Shadows*.
42. People's Investigation, "In-Custody Death," 20.
43. In response to ongoing police killings, including those resulting from police responses to people in mental crisis, a number of projects have emerged in recent years across the Bay Area aimed at reducing calls to the police and imagining community alternatives. These include the Oakland Power Projects, a project of Critical Resistance launched in 2015; POOR Magazine's "How Not to Call the Police Ever" workshops, first launched in 2016; and other efforts, including more recent efforts by Oakland's Anti-Police Terror Project aimed at minimizing contact between community and police.
44. Emotional CPR is advanced by the National Coalition for Mental Health Recovery (NCMHR) and is "an educational program designed to teach people to assist others through an emotional crisis by three simple steps: connecting, empowering, and revitalizing." See National Coalition for Mental Health Recovery, "What Is Emotional CPR?" https://www.ncmhr.org/emotional-cpr.htm. The People's Investigation highlights eCPR advocate and NCMHR member Lauren Spiro's description of eCPR as "a tool of peacemaking." People's Investigation, "In-Custody Death," 30.
45. See Mark Neocleous, "War on Waste: Law, Original Accumulation and the Violence of Capital," *Science & Society* 75, no. 4 (October 2011): 506–28.
46. Colectio Situaciones, *Genocide in the Neighborhood*, 48; Precarias a la deriva, "Very Careful Strike."
47. Spade, *Normal Life*.
48. Lorenzo Veracini, "Containment, Elimination, Endogeneity: Settler Colonialism in the Global Present," *Rethinking Marxism* 31, no. 1 (2019): 118–40.
49. Byrd et al., "Predatory Value," 2.
50. Barker, "Territory as Analytic," 29.
51. Barker, "Territory as Analytic," 34, 24.
52. Barker, "Territory as Analytic," 34.
53. On the juridical impossibility for some people to be law-abiding, see Cacho, *Social Death*.
54. Bruno Latour, Naisargi N. Dave, Mary L. Gray, Cymene Howe, Tom Boellstorff, Rudolf Gaudio, Martin F. Manalansan IV, and David Valentine, "A Question from Bruno Latour," *Society for Cultural Anthropology* (blog), July 21, 2015, https://culanth.org/fieldsights/a-question-from-bruno-latour.

55. See California Coalition for Women Prisoners, "Shout Their Names: A Town Hall," http://womenprisoners.org/2016/07/shout-their-names-a-town-hall/.

56. See Victoria Law, "#MeToo Behind Bars: When the Sexual Assaulter Holds the Keys to Your Cell," Truthout, March 18, 2018.

57. Ritchie's book *Invisible No More* marks a commitment to this project on a national level.

58. EZLN, "Truth and Justice," para. 30–37.

Chapter 5

1. George Ciccariello-Maher, "We Must Disband the Police: Body Cameras Aren't Enough—Only Radical Change Will Stop Cops Who Kill," Salon, April 24, 2015, para. 17, https://www.salon.com/2015/04/24/we_must_disband_the_police_body_cameras_arent_enough_only_radical_change_will_stop_cops_who_kill/; ACLU Northern California, "Frequently Asked Questions about Copley Press and SB 1019" (blog post), https://www.aclunc.org/blog/frequently-asked-questions-about-copley-press-and-sb-1019, para. 1; Ciccariello-Maher, "We Must Disband the Police."

2. See Liam Dillon, "California's Landmark Police Transparency Law Takes Effect after Court Denies Police Union Effort to Block It," *Los Angeles Times*, January 2, 2019.

3. David Galula, *Counterinsurgency Warfare: Theory and Practice* (Westport, CT: Praeger Security International, 2006), ix.

4. Galula, *Counterinsurgency Warfare*; David Galula, *Pacification in Algeria, 1956–1958* (Santa Monica, CA: Rand Corporation, 2006); Khalili, *Time in the Shadows*.

5. My use of the terms "misinformation" and "disinformation" specifically calls attention to strategies of low-intensity war, as framed through the work of Dunn, *Militarization of the U.S.–Mexico Border*; and Callahan, "Mexican Border Troubles."

6. The complete policies are outlined in San Francisco Police Department, "Investigation of Officer Involved Shootings and Discharges," General Orders, 1–7, September 21, 2005, http://www.sf-police.org/modules/ShowDocument.aspx?documentid=14739.

7. On inconsistencies in the Nieto autopsy report, see Justice for Alex Nieto, "Drawing and Analysis of Autopsy Report" (blog post), http://justice4alexnieto.org/?s=autopsy.

8. See Van Jones, "Lessons from a Killing: Changing News Coverage of Police Brutality in San Francisco," *FAIR: Fairness and Accuracy in Reporting*, originally published in *Extra!* 11, no. 3 (May/June 1998): para 5.

9. On "excited delirium" as an emergent syndrome and evidence of the role of the dominant media in promoting the syndrome, see Maria Alicia Gaura, "Clues to Police Custody Deaths / New Syndrome Identified as Combination of Risk Factors," SFGate, April 8, 1996.

10. See Ruth Wilson Gilmore, "Globalisation and U.S. Prison Growth: From Military Keynesianism to Post-Keynesian Militarism," *Race and Class* 40, no. 2–3 (March 1999): 171–88, 178; and Callahan, "In Defense of Conviviality," 6.

11. A community's construction of tools is used here in the sense of Ivan Illich's convivial tools, and is theorized through a larger convivial research approach highlighting the collective generation of new tools in the service of community struggles. See Callahan, "Repairing the Community."

12. See Jorge González, "The Willingness to Weave: Cultural Analysis, Cultural Fronts, and Networks of the Future," *Media Development* 44, no. 1 (1997): 30–36; Jorge González, "Cultural Fronts: Towards a Dialogical Understanding of Contemporary Cultures," in *Culture in the Communication Age*, ed. James Lull (London: Routledge, 2001), 106–31; Francisco J. Varela, "Whence Perceptual Meaning?: A Cartography of Current Ideas," in *Understanding Origins: Contemporary Views on the Origins of Life, Mind, and Society*, ed. Francisco Varela and Jean-Pierre DuPuy (Dordrecht: Kluwer Academic, 1992), 235–63. See also Convivial Research and Insurgent Learning, "Constructing Observables," http://ccra.mitotedigital.org/convivialres/observables.

13. Self-valorization, or valorization outside the state and capital, remains central to a community's struggles for regeneration and justice. See Cleaver, "Inversion of Class Perspective"; and Esteva, "Regenerating People's Space."

14. The ICMMC event took place at Humanist Hall in Oakland on Friday, November 14, 2014.

15. "Bleeding out" refers to the way that people die due to extreme blood loss. The term usually implies intentional negligence, or it marks, for example, the absence of (ordinarily available) life-saving services in disenfranchised communities.

16. On relational *testimonio*, see Manuel Callahan, "UT Califas Theses Clinic Announcement, 11-2-13," message to UniTierra discussion list, October 24, 2013, para. 2. For further elaboration on UniTierra's approach

and use of relational *testimonio*, see also Callahan, "UT Theses Clinic, Saturday, May 3, 2014"; and Callahan, "UT Califas Theses Clinic Summary, 5-3-14."

17. This statement was made by Cynthia Mitchell. See Cacho, *Social Death*.

18. See Self, *American Babylon*; and Mezzadra and Neilson, "Borderscapes of Differential Inclusion," 190.

19. See Haraway, "Situated Knowledges."

20. Foucault, *Society Must Be Defended*, 7, 10. See also Gordon, "Methodologies of Imprisonment," 7.

21. Michael Dillon and Andrew W. Neal, eds., *Foucault on Politics, Security, and War* (New York: Palgrave Macmillan, 2011), 5.

22. I draw here on the work of CCRA in formulating intersecting violences.

23. Community presence at recent trials has shaped a growing collective analysis on state impunity, including the trial for the Eureka killing of Peter Stewart in 2011 and the trial for Asa Sullivan in fall 2014. I am also grateful for the statements of Adriana Camarena of J4AN at the December rally, where she spoke to these issues. This information is also made explicit in the updates from the rally, as well as the flyer handed out that day. See also the Justice for Alex Nieto (J4AN) website. See, in particular, J4AN, "Call to Community Action: We Want Names! Wed. 12/3/2014, Federal Courthouse, 8–10am" (blog post), November 26, 2014, http://justice4alexnieto.org/2014/11/26/call-to-community-action-we-want-names/; and also "Court Update (Wed. 11/19/2014): City Refuses to Name 4 Shooters, 8–10 Officers Present at Shooting, and 20 Officers Responding to Homicide Scene" (blog post), http://justice4alexnieto.org/2014/11/19/court-update-wed-11192014-city-refuses-to-name-officers/.

24. In addition to shared community knowledge, see Police State USA, "Police Shoot Special Needs Girl," June 13, 2014; http://www.policestateusa.com/2014/yanira-serrano-garcia/.

25. Mesha Monge-Irizarry, oral history interview, April 2015.

26. Many of the drawings at the time were done by the local artist Oree Originol, in a consistent and recognizable style.

27. Cadine Williams, public statement, J4AN rally, December 3, 2014.

28. See Erin Ivie, "Pacifica Man Shot by Police Hours after Release of New Officer-Involved Shooting Protocol," *Mercury News*, March 20, 2014.

29. See Robert Salonga, "Coroner: Man Killed by San José State Cops Was Shot Twice in the Back," *Mercury News*, February 27, 2014.

Chapter 6

1. Kahlil Sullivan, "In That Attic I Saw My Brother's Blood Covering the Floor and Walls . . . ," *San Francisco Bay View*, June 10, 2009, https://sfbayview.com/2009/06/in-that-attic-i-saw-my-brothers-blood-covering-the-floor-and-walls/.

2. Sullivan, "In That Attic."

3. Sullivan, "In That Attic," para. 10.

4. Sullivan, "In That Attic." The SFPD chief at the time of the killing of Asa was Heather Fong. The presence of an eyeglass case was disputed at the trial by the family's lawyer, and at least one officer on scene who was the first to check Asa's body confirmed that he did not recall the presence of an eyeglass case. Yet, the eyeglass case as a stand-in for a gun that catalyzed the police shooting featured prominently in the trial, a point to which I will return later in the chapter. Author's trial notes, *Kathleen Espinosa v. the City and County of San Francisco*. The trial ran from September 3, 2014 (jury selection) to October 6, 2014 (closing arguments) at the Ronald V. Dellums Federal Courthouse, Oakland.

5. Sullivan, "In That Attic" (includes Kathleen Espinosa, 'A Mother's Response'), paras. 25, 32, 33.

6. Sullivan, "In That Attic," para. 30.

7. Jaxon Van Derbeken, "Family of Man Killed by Police Files Lawsuit," SFGate, August 3, 2006, https://www.sfgate.com/bayarea/article/SAN-FRANCISCO-Family-of-man-killed-by-police-2491787.php.

8. Kathleen Espinoza, conversation with the author, October 2014.

9. Guha, "Prose of Counter-Insurgency." On a prose "fully and decidedly constructed," see Callahan, "Crisis and Permanent War."

10. Author's trial notes, September–October 2014.

11. This is documented in the "Event History Detail" of the SFPD Computer-Aided Dispatch (CAD) reports from June 6, 2006. Author's trial notes, September 22, 2014. See also Jeffrey S. White, "Appeal from the United States District Court for the Northern District of California," argued and submitted on October 5, 2009, San Francisco, California, filed March 9, 2010, http://cdn.ca9.uscourts.gov/datastore/opinions/2010/03/09/08-16853.pdf.

12. At the trial, the defense focused significant attention on a T-shirt that was found inside with dried blood on it, arguing that the officers progressed through the house to determine if someone was hurt and in need of care.

13. Author's trial notes, including from the testimony of Officer Yukio Oshida, September 24, 28, and 29, 2014.

14. Author's trial notes, September 24, 28, and 29, 2014.

15. Author's trial notes, including from the testimony of Officer Darren Choy, September 22, 2014.

16. Author's trial notes, September–October 2014, including the testimony of Tracy McCray on September 22, 2014.

17. Bernadette Harakati, "Tributes to Asa Sullivan 1980–2006," Gone Too Soon (online memorial site), September 10, 2008, http://www.gonetoosoon.org/memorials/asa-sullivan-1980-2006.

18. People's Investigation for Asa Sullivan, "We Remember Asa," San Francisco Bay Area Independent Media Center (IndyBay), June 6, 2018, https://www.indybay.org/newsitems/2018/06/06/18815542.php.

19. Also referred to as Kathleen Ecklund.

20. See Wyatt Buchanan, "Indecision on Filing Charges in Fatal Shooting," *Justice for Cammerin Boyd* (blog), https://cammerinboyd1stlove.blogspot.com/.

21. See Justice for Cammerin Boyd, "Press Release: 1 Year Anniversary Community Rally and March," San Francisco Bay Area Independent Media Center (IndyBay), May 5, 2005, https://www.indybay.org/newsitems/2005/05/02/17357081.php.

22. Nick Devito, "Officers Exonerated in Suicide-by-Cop Case," Courthouse News Service, August 11, 2009; Buchanan, "Indecision on Filing Charges."

23. See George L. Kelling, "Community Policing Rightly Understood," *Manhattan Institute City Journal* (Winter 2019). See also James N. Speros (Lt.), "Community Policing and Problem Solving: Transition and Survey, 1994," San Francisco Police Department memo, January 6, 1995.

24. Victor E. Kappeler and Larry K. Gaines, *Community Policing: A Contemporary Perspective*, 6th ed. (Waltham, MA: Elsevier, 2011), 11, 7.

25. INCITE! "Quality of Life," 17.

26. Vitale, *End of Policing*.

27. San Francisco Police Department, "San Francisco Community Policing: A Report on Current Efforts," San Francisco Police Department/San Francisco Mayor's Office, November 2006, 13–14.

28. San Francisco Police Department, "San Francisco Community Policing," 13–14.

29. Galula, *Pacification in Algeria*, 71.

30. Patrik Jonsson, "After Atlanta Raid Tragedy, New Scrutiny of Police Tactics," *Science Monitor*, November 29, 2006, https://www.csmonitor.com/2006/1129/p03s03-ussc.html. On the rise of SWAT, see Balko, *Overkill*; Kraska and Kappeler, "Militarizing American Police."

31. Jaxon Van Derbeken, "Police Raid Zeroes in on Drug Turf War: 19 Arrested in Sweep of Western Addition," SFGate, September 16, 1999, https://www.sfgate.com/crime/article/Police-Raid-Zeroes-In-On-Drug-Turf-War-19-2909050.php.

32. Chris Roberts, "SFPD 'Shaken' by Federal Indictments Against Officers," *San Francisco Examiner*, February 27, 2014.

33. On mapping and the struggle for the control and support of the population, see Galula, *Pacification in Algeria*. For an extended discussion of pacification, see Neocleous, *War Power*, esp. chap 1.

34. For a historical analysis of garden living, property values, whiteness, and the rise of Bay Area suburbs and urban housing complexes, see Self, *American Babylon*.

35. Marion Merriouns, "Why Destroy Parkmerced?" *San Francisco Bay View*, March 9, 2001, https://sfbayview.com/2011/03/why-destroy-parkmerced/.

36. Dean Preston, "Time to Pull the Plug on Parkmerced Project," BeyondChron, February 3, 2011, https://beyondchron.org/time-to-pull-the-plug-on-parkmerced-project/.

37. Brayton Purcell, "SF Rent Control Board Rules That Villas Parkmerced's 'Bonus Bucks' Rebate Coupon Scheme Violates Rent Control, as Tenants' Class Action Suit Contends," "SF Rent Control Violations" (blog post), October 17, 2006, http://www.braytonlaw.com/blog/2006/10/sf-rent-control-violations.shtml.

38. Preston, "Time to Pull the Plug."

39. Merriouns, "Why Destroy Parkmerced?" para. 5.

40. Coalition to Save Parkmerced, "S.F. Planning Commission Approves Demolition of Parkmerced Townhomes and Eviction of Over 1,500 Families," *San Francisco Bay View*, March 9, 2011, para. 3, https://sfbayview.com/2011/03/why-destroy-parkmerced/.

41. San Francisco has a long history of entrenched resistance to displacement and dispossession. See, for example, James Tracy, *Dispatches Against Displacement: Field Notes from San Francisco's Housing Wars* (Oakland: AK, 2014).

42. On "economies of dispossession," see Byrd et al., "Predatory Value."

43. For an analysis of the drawing and deployment of gang injunctions in relation to property, value, and demographic shifts, see Muñiz, *Police, Power*.

44. On gentrification in San Francisco theorized in relation to ethnic cleansing, see Don Santina, "Ethnic Cleansing in San Francisco,"

CounterPunch, September 29–October 1, 2007, https://www.counterpunch.org/2007/09/29/ethnic-cleansing-in-san-francisco/; and Merriouns, "Why Destroy Parkmerced?" See also Ali Winston, "Are San Francisco's Gang Injunctions Working?" *KALW News*, January 20, 2011. For a historical analysis of how demands for "safe space" by LGBT communities articulated with urban development policies, privatization, and policing and the impact of those demands and mobilizations on Black and Brown communities, see Hanhardt, *Safe Space*.

45. On gang injunctions as buffer zones deployed to manage property values and population, see Muñiz, *Police, Power*.

46. In San Francisco, the police station and the coroner's office are in the same building.

47. Sangh's testimony, read out during the trial. Author's trial notes, September 30, 2014.

48. Sullivan, "In That Attic," para. 13.

49. Sullivan, "In That Attic," para. 13.

50. Author's trial notes from the testimony of Officer Cleary, September 30, 2014.

51. Van Derbeken, "Family of Man," para. 21.

52. Josh Voorhees, "The Problem with 'Suicide by Cop,'" Slate, August 27, 2014, https://slate.com/news-and-politics/2014/08/suicide-by-cop-the-dangerous-term-that-stops-us-from-asking-hard-questions-about-police-shootings.html.

53. Voorhees, "Problem with 'Suicide by Cop.'"

54. Ariela J. Gross, *What Blood Won't Tell: A History of Race on Trial in America* (Cambridge, MA: Harvard University Press, 2008).

55. Author's trial notes from testimony of Officer Cleary, September 30, 2014.

56. Van Derbeken, "Family of Man," para. 14.

57. Author's trial notes from Officer Cleary's testimony, September 30, 2014.

58. Author's trial notes, including the witness testimony and cross-examination of Tracy McCray and Darren Choy, both on September 22, 2014.

59. Sergeant Choy, who was on the scene, stated during his trial testimony that he did not intervene. Author's trial notes, September 22, 2014.

60. In addition to Mesha, these included, in various spaces and actions, the families of SFPD killings of Mark Garcia (April 6, 1996); Cammerin Boyd (May 5, 2004); Oliver "Big O" Leftiti (June 24, 2007); and Gus Rugley (June 29, 2004). There were also merged actions with families

targeted by the South San Francisco police, including Julia Ayala (October 2, 2005); and by the Oakland police, including Luke Grinage and Rafael Grinage, son and father killed on December 15, 1993; Julio Paredes (July 4, 2005); Andrew Moppin-Buckskin (December 31, 2007); "Jody" Mac Woodfox (July 25, 2008); "Acorn" Leonard Peters, killed by the Mendocino County Sheriff Department on the Pond Valley Reservation in northern California (April 14, 1995); and of Anita Gay, killed by the Berkeley police (March 7, 2008). See, for example, Idriss Stelley Foundation, "'I Live Here, Please Don't Kill Me' Justice 4 Asa Sullivan," *San Francisco Bay Area Independent Media Center (IndyBay)*, June 11, 2006, https://www.indybay.org/newsitems/2006/06/11/18280096.php; Joanna Letz, "Two Thousand Stolen Lives, We Refuse to Close Our Eyes," POOR Magazine, May 7, 2007; Revolution, "February 6 March of Stolen Lives Braves Massive Police Intimidation," undated, likely February 2009, https://revcom.us/a/156/slideshow/pages/Family%20Members_jpg.htm.

61. Cacho, *Social Death*, 4.

62. Guha, "Prose of Counter-Insurgency."

63. Callahan, *Mexican Border Troubles*, 9, 8. On state investigations and the production of racial subjectivities, see also Gross, *What Blood Won't Tell*.

64. Sullivan, "In That Attic," para. 17.

65. Khalili, *Time in the Shadows*, 4.

66. Harcourt, *Counterrevolution*, 213.

67. San Francisco Police Department, "Chief's Office: Risk Management Office, Management Control Division," http://sf-police.org/index.aspx?page=3133, para. 3.

68. "The MCD unit coordinates with the OCC [Office of Citizen Complaints], the EEO[Equal Employment Opportunity] section, and other investigative agencies." San Francisco Police Department, "Chief's Office: Risk Management Office," para. 3.

69. Author's trial notes from testimony of Officer McCray, September 22, 2014.

70. Author's trial notes, September 22, 2014.

71. On the courtroom and juridical process of the trial as a site of knowledge production, see Gross, *What Blood Won't Tell*.

72. Convivial Research and Insurgent Learning, "Social Factory Ateneo 10-25-14," http://ccra.mitotedigital.org/announcement_10-25-14, para. 10.

73. See Isaac D. Balbus, *The Dialectics of Legal Repression: Black Rebels before the American Criminal Courts* (New York City: Russell Sage Foundation, 1974).

74. Cacho, *Social Death*, 4.
75. Cacho, *Social Death*, 4.
76. Cacho, *Social Death*, 4
77. Cacho, *Social Death*, 8.
78. Author's notes from trial, September 28, 2014.
79. Author's trial notes, including the cross-examination of the expert witness Alexander Jason by the plaintiff's legal team, September 28, 2014.
80. Author's trial notes, including from the testimony of Dr. Kris Mohandie, from September 30, 2014.
81. Author's trial notes. Keram also provided depositions and trial testimony in other cases designated as "suicide by cop," including in the trial for Cammerin Boyd. In short, Keram and Mohandie were paid to produce assessments that legitimized police violence.
82. U.S. Department of the Army, *U.S. Army and Marine Corps Counterinsurgency Field Manual: FM 3–24* (Washington, DC: Department of the Army, 2006), 35.
83. Harcourt, *Counterrevolution*, 230.
84. See Illich, *History of Needs*.
85. Author's trial notes from the defense's closing arguments, October 6, 2014.
86. Author's trial notes, October 6, 2014.
87. Author's trial notes, October 6, 2014.
88. Khalili, *Time in the Shadows*, 3. See also Gutiérrez Aguilar, "Rhythms: Brief Reflections," 59.
89. Author's trial notes, September–October 2014.
90. The instructions to the jury were structured around a "burden of proof" that disadvantaged the plaintiffs, an issue which the lawyers attempted to address in the appeal. Author's conversation with plaintiff's legal team and family, March 2015.
91. UniTierra Califas's Social Factory Ateneo announcement for October provides an analysis of the courtroom as a site of direct action and as a space of knowledge production connected to other spaces outside the courtroom. See Convivial Research and Insurgent Learning, "Social Factory Ateneo 10-25-14." The *ateneo* space for October also took up this conversation among families and people who had been in attendance at the trial and others participating in the space. See also Gross, *What Blood Won't Tell*; and Dan Berger, *Captive Nation: Black Prison Organizing in the Civil Rights Era* (Chapel Hill: University of North Carolina Press, 2016), esp. chapter 5.
92. Callahan, "Insurgent Learning."

93. See also Neocleous, "Police Power."

94. As discussed earlier in this work, the *ateneos* of UniTierra Califas are conceived as "open critical space[s] of encounter committed to facilitating insurgent learning and convivial research." The Social Factory Ateneo was convened to explore "'the community' as a principal site of struggle, with women as key agents undermining capital's efforts to impose capitalist social relations, as well as generating new forms of reproducing the community that are dignified and autonomous." It convened monthly in Oakland from May 2014 to May 2015. See Convivial Research and Insurgent Learning, "Ateneo"; and "Social Factory," http://ccra.mitotedigital.org/ateneo; http://ccra.mitotedigital.org/ateneo/social_factory.

95. Author's notes from trial testimony of Officer McCray, September 22, 2014. On counterinsurgency tactics, see K. Williams, "Other Side of the COIN." On the "community as a site of intervention" in counterinsurgency strategy, see Schrader, "To Secure the Global Great Society." See also Khalili, *Time in the Shadows*; and Galula, *Counterinsurgency Warfare*.

96. *Kathleen Espinosa v. the City and County of San Francisco*. The trial ran from September 3, 2014 (jury selection) to October 6, 2014 (closing arguments) at the Ronald V. Dellums Federal Courthouse, Oakland.

97. Convivial Research and Insurgent Learning, "Social Factory Ateneo 10-25-14," para. 2. UniTierra Califas's Social Factory Ateneo announcement for October marks this intersection, charting the confluence of numerous court cases as families respond to police violence across the Bay.

Chapter 7

1. Michel Foucault, "Right of Death and Power over Life," trans. Robert Hurley, in *History of Sexuality* (New York: Vintage Books, 1990), 133–59.

2. Among the sidewalk chalkers was Lisa Ganser, who would often weave together names from local and national justice struggles. The buttons were designed and distributed by George Russell of Oakland.

3. Although this figure is informal, in conversation with a local lawyer whose office handles hundreds of police cases from across the Bay Area, the lawyer estimated that fewer than 10 percent of cases involving police make it to trial. The lawyer asked to remain anonymous. While the past history of a person targeted by the police or charged with a crime is readily allowed into court proceedings as relevant to a case, it is almost never the case that reciprocally, the past history of an officer is allowed into the court record or proceedings. This is true even if the officer has a past history of convictions for lying under oath or falsifying documents. It is also the

case that an officer who has been fired from a department may testify in court as an officer, without it being revealed that the officer is no longer employed by the department. Author's notes from conversation with a lawyer who represents clients in civil and criminal suits involving the police, April 2015.

4. See, for example, "Hundreds Protest Outside Stockton Police Station," *KCRA News*, April 11, 2012, https://www.kcra.com/article/hundreds-protest-outside-stockton-police-station/6395909.

5. See Center for Convivial Research and Autonomy, "Justice for James Rivera, Jr." (tri-fold pamphlet), 2018, http://ggg.vostan.net/ccra/assets/attachments/Rivera_trifold2018.pdf.

6. Convivial Research and Insurgent Learning, "Democracy Ateneo Announcement 4-19-14," http://cril.mitotedigital.org/announcement_4-19-14.

7. Inderbir Singh Grewal, "Class War Is Not Contained by Municipal Codes," in "Dear Comrades," *Viewpoint Magazine: Worker's Inquiry*, ed. Ben Mabie, no. 3 (September 30, 2013), https://viewpointmag.com/2013/08/19/dearcomrades/, para. 4.

8. Grewal, "Civil War Is Not Contained."

9. See Briggs, *How All Politics Became Reproductive Politics*, 18. For an analysis of subprime mortgages, predatory lending, and race that situates neoliberal modes of power in a broader context of colonial expropriation, dispossession, and the production of racial subjects, see Chakravarty and Ferreira da Silva, eds., *Race, Empire, and the Crisis of the Subprime*.

10. Gago and Mezzadra, "Critique of the Extractive Operations of Capital."

11. Barker, "Territory as Analytic," 31, 33. On Indigenous dispossession as ongoing and the basis of all dispossession in the U.S. present framed by settler-colonial rationality, see Jodi. A. Byrd, "Variations under Domestication: Indigeneity and the Subject of Dispossession," *Social Text* 36, no. 2: 135 (2018): 123–41.

12. Scott Johnson, "City of a Thousand Foreclosures," CounterPunch, March 7, 2008, https://socialistworker.org/2008/03/07/Stockton-foreclosures.

13. All figures taken from Johnson, "City of a Thousand Foreclosures."

14. See Gago and Mezzadra, "Critique of the Extractive Operations of Capital," 578.

15. Kevin Kearny, "Pensions and Health Care Slashed for City Workers," World Socialist Web Site, December 12, 2012, http://www.wsws.org/en/articles/2012/12/12/stoc-d12.html.

16. Callahan, "In Defense of Conviviality." See also Convivial Research and Insurgent Learning, "Social Factory Ateneo 10-25-14."

17. See Convivial Research and Insurgent Learning, "Democracy Ateneo Announcement 4-19-14," para. 5. The quote from Quan originally occurs in H.L.T Quan, "Geniuses of Resistance: Feminist Consciousness and the Black Radical Tradition," special issue, "Cedric Robinson and the Philosophy of Black Resistance," *Race & Class* 47, no. 2 (2005): 39–53.

18. On "living theory," see Convivial Research and Insurgent Learning, "Analytical Frameworks," para. 3; and Callahan, "Rebel Dignity."

19. Convivial Research and Insurgent Learning, "Democracy Ateneo Announcement 4-19-14," para. 5.

20. Convivial Research and Insurgent Learning, "Democracy Ateneo Announcement 4-19-14."

21. This story emerged in a space of collective storytelling with Dionne Smith-Downs and other Stockton groups and members of the ICMMC and AZ during spring 2015.

22. Guha, "Prose of Counter-Insurgency."

23. Many of these details come from the collective space of research convened through the Social Factory Ateneo spanning from May 2014 to May 2015. For a description, listing of announcements, and summaries, see Convivial Research and Insurgent Learning, "Social Factory," http://ccra.mitotedigital.org/ateneo/social_factory.

24. This information draws on multiple networked spaces where systems of information circulate, and in particular in the ongoing space of the Social Factory Ateneo, as well as in my conversations over more than a decade of research with mothers, grandmothers, aunts, and sisters in various spaces as they struggle with tremendous resilience and ingenuity to find ways to hold their families together against the intricate web of pacification. Details have been modified and made general to obscure details that may point to a specific incident or family.

25. These stories emerge from many conversations with families over the years, including through work with the California Coalition for Women Prisoners from 2010 to 2021.

26. Arielle Gross's work examines this process through the courtroom trial; Gross, *What Blood Won't Tell.*

27. On apparatus and *dispositif*, see Michel Foucault, "The Confession of the Flesh," trans. Colin Gordon, Leo Marshall, John Mepham, and Kate Soper, in *Power/Knowledge: Selected Interviews and Other Writings 1972–1977*, ed. Colin Gordon (New York: Pantheon Books, 1980), 194–228. On the border as *dispositif*, including his use of Du Bois's concept of

democratic despotism, see Callahan, "Crisis and Permanent War." See also Du Bois, "African Roots of War."

28. The details here were part of a public community speak-out, and also circulated in newly updated postcards as part of the ongoing multiple systems of information that form the critical backbone of the justice campaigns.

29. On "living hammock," see Esteva, "Regenerating People's Space," 34. All other quotes here are taken from Convivial Research and Insurgent Learning, "Social Factory Ateneo 2-28-15," http://cril.mitotedigital.org/announcement_2-28-15, para. 4.

30. Convivial Research and Insurgent Learning, "Social Factory Ateneo 2-28-15."

31. Convivial Research and Insurgent Learning, "Social Factory Ateneo 2-28-15."

Chapter 8

1. See Julia Sudbury (Chinyere Oparah), *Other Kinds of Dreams: Black Women's Organizations and the Politics of Transformation* (New York: Routledge, 2005), 9–12. Scholars have continued to produce scholarship that excavates resistance and resilience against this erasure both in the present as state and state-manufactured violence, and as a consequence and strategy of ongoing settler colonialism, particularly targeting Indigenous women. See Susan Sleeper-Smith, Jeffrey Ostler, and Joshua L. Reid, eds., *Violence and Indigenous Communities: Confronting the Past and Engaging the Present* (Evanston, IL: Northwestern University Press, 2021); Rosa-Linda Fregoso and Cynthia Bejarano, *Terrorizing Women: Feminicide in the Americas* (Durham, NC: Duke University Press, 2010); Federici et al., *Feminicide and Global Accumulation*; Silvia Federici, *Caliban and the Witch: Women, the Body, and Primitive Accumulation* (Brooklyn, NY: Autonomedia, 2004); Maria Pia Lopez, *Not One Less: Mourning, Disobedience, and Desire*, trans. Frances Riddle (Medford, MA: Polity, 2020); Beth E. Richie, *Arrested Justice: Black Women, Violence, and America's Prison Nation* (New York: NYU Press, 2012); Hartman, *Wayward Lives*; and also Saidiya Hartman, "The Plot of Her Undoing," in *Notes on Feminisms* (Feminist Art Coalition, 2019); and Saidiya Hartman, "Venus in Two Acts," *Small Axe* 26 (June 2008): 1–14.

2. Boaventura de Sousa Santos, ed., *Another Knowledge Is Possible: Beyond Northern Epistemologies* (New York: Verso, 2008), xix. See also de Sousa Santos, *Epistemologies of the South*; and Callahan, "In Defense of Conviviality," 13.

3. This is a concept to which Esteva returns throughout much of his writing, including in "Regenerating People's Space"; and Esteva and Prakash, *Grassroots Post-Modernism*. On convivial tools, see Callahan, "Repairing the Community."

4. Juan Herrera, "Spatializing Chicano Power: Cartographic Memory and Community Practices of Care," *Social Justice* 42, no. 3-4 (2015): 48.

5. Phil Horne, "Paramedic Whistleblower Alleges Oscar Grant Cover-Up, System-Wide Racism," *San Francisco Bay View*, June 23, 2011, para. 10, https://sfbayview.com/2011/06/paramedic-whistleblower-alleges-oscar-grant-cover-up-system-wide-racism/; and Phil Horne, "Kenneth Harding, Raheim Brown, Oscar Grant: Can You Believe the Police?" *San Francisco Bay View*, July 31, 2011, https://sfbayview.com/2011/07/kenneth-harding-raheim-brown-oscar-grant-can-you-believe-the-police/. An extensive interview produced by the Labor Video Project, "Oscar Grant Murder Cover-up, Privatization & Case of OFD EMT IFPTE Local 21 Trainer Sean Gillis," https://www.youtube.com/watch?v=QFCppga0cdQ, offers a thorough analysis of the situation.

6. Occupy Patriarchy Barbecue, Rainbow Park, April 14, 2012; recording by filmmaker Caitlin Manning. See Manning, dir., "Oakland Occupy Patriarchy Barbecue and Speakout 2012," film recording from Occupy Patriarchy Barbecue, Rainbow Park, April 14, 2012, https://youtu.be/LN5sHErn04A.

7. See Kenneth Harding Jr. Foundation, "Two Years since SFPD Murdered Kenneth Harding: Muni Shutdown July 16, 2013," *San Francisco Bay View*, July 2, 2013, https://sfbayview.com/2013/07/two-years-since-sfpd-murdered-kenneth-harding-muni-shutdown-july-16–2013/.

8. MUNI or SF MUNI stands for the San Francisco Municipal Railway and is the public transit system serving the city and county of San Francisco. See Horne, "Can You Believe?"

9. Segato, "Patriarchy from Margin to Center."

10. Callahan, "In Defense of Conviviality."

11. Callahan, "In Defense of Conviviality," 5.

12. The project was founded by Sharena Diamond Thomas and Lesley Phillips.

13. Sitrin and Azzellini, *They Can't Represent Us!* See also Daniel Burton-Rose, Eddie Yuen, and George Katsiaficas, eds., *Confronting Capitalism: Dispatches from a Global Movement* (Brooklyn, NY: Soft Skull, 2004).

14. On *testimonios*, see Latina Feminist Group, "Introduction: *Papelitos Guardados*."

15. See Kenneth Harding Jr. Foundation, "Celebrating Our First Year of Continual Community Service!" *Kenny's Foundation* (blog), February 17, 2013, http://kennysfoundation.blogspot.com, para. 1.

16. Kenneth Harding Jr. Foundation, "Celebrating Our First Year," para. 5. See also Denika Chatman, "Kenneth Harding Jr.: Three Years after SFPD Murdered My Son, Just Demonizing, No Justice," *San Francisco Bay View*, July 16, 2014, https://sfbayview.com/2014/07/kenneth-harding-jr-three-years-after-sfpd-murdered-my-son-just-demonizing-no-justice/.

17. Denika Chatman speaking at Celebration of Life, commemorating the birthday of O'Shaine Evans and others, San Francisco, July 18, 2015. Author's notes.

18. See Center for Convivial Research and Autonomy, "Stockton's Mobile Response Team," San Francisco Bay Area Independent Media Center (IndyBay), August 8, 2017, https://www.indybay.org/newsitems/2017/08/08/18801318.php; Callahan and Paradise, "Fierce Care."

19. On police mapping, see Manning, *Technology of Policing*.

20. See Precarias a la deriva, "Adrift through the Circuits."

21. Serrano and López, "Positions, Situations," 2–3.

22. Sharon Patricia Holland, *Raising the Dead: Readings of Death and (Black) Subjectivity* (Durham, NC: Duke University Press, 2000), 4.

23. Serrano and López, "Positions, Situations," 2–3.

24. McKittrick, *Demonic Grounds*.

25. Serrano and Lopez's reclaiming of citizenship can be read around recent work on differential inclusion. It also echoes Renato Rosaldo's notion of cultural citizenship. See Rosaldo, "Cultural Citizenship, Inequality, and Multiculturalism," in *Latino Cultural Citizenship: Claiming Identity, Space, and Rights*, ed. William V. Flores and Rina Benmayor (Boston: Beacon, 1997), 27–38.

26. Gaye Theresa Johnson, *Spaces of Conflict, Sounds of Solidarity: Music, Race, and Spatial Entitlement in Los Angeles* (Berkeley: University of California Press, 2013), x, xxii, 1.

27. Herrera, "Spatializing Chicano Power."

28. See Michel Foucault, "Of Other Spaces: Utopias and Heterotopias," *Architecture, Mouvement, Continuité*, no. 5 (October 1984): 46–49; trans. Jay Miskowiec in *Diacritics* 16, no. 1 (Spring 1986): 22–27: 6, http://web.mit.edu/allanmc/www/foucault1.pdf.

29. Foucault, "Of Other Spaces."

30. Callahan, "In Defense of Conviviality," 5.

31. Callahan, "In Defense of Conviviality," 5.

32. Foucault, "Of Other Spaces."

33. Foucault, "Of Other Spaces."

34. One is reminded of similar displacements effected by Deleuze with his theorization that "the event" is the one speaking. Gilles Deleuze, *Nietzsche and Philosophy*, trans. Hugh Tomlinson (New York: Columbia University Press, 1993).

35. Convivial Research and Insurgent Learning, "Systems of Information," http://cril.mitotedigital.org/convivialres/system-information, para. 1.

36. Arielle Julia Brown, dir., *Love Balm for my SpiritChild*, play performed at Brava Theater Center, San Francisco, California, on July 11, 2014.

37. This was the primary focus of the Social Factory Ateneo in East Oakland in 2014–15, which coincided with a number of grassroots justice struggles and autonomous feminist collectives, including actions of the International Women's Strike and families advancing the project of "caring not killing," drawing connections between care work, gendered labor, and violence. See also Ross and Solinger, *Reproductive Justice*.

38. Brown, *Love Balm*.

39. See Callahan, "UT Califas Theses Clinic Summary, 5-3-14," para. 3. This connection between *testimonio*, relational *testimonio*, storytelling, and knowledge production was the focus of UniTierra's Theses Clinic in May 2014. See also Manuel Callahan, "Relational *Testimonio taller* w/ Quad Productions," message to UniTierra discussion list, June 4, 2014.

40. Author's oral history interview with Arielle Julia Brown, April 7, 2014. See also Convivial Research and Insurgent Learning, "Social Factory Ateneo 7-26-14," http://ccra.mitotedigital.org/announcement_7-26-14. I am grateful here for a series of spaces in May–July 2014 where this conversation emerged and that included Arielle Julia Brown and Anita Wills of the Love Balm Project, H.L.T. Quan and Crystal Griffith of Quad Films, and participants in UT Califas's Democracy and Social Factory Ateneos and Theses Clinic, as well as the *tertulia* convened on May 29 at La Estrellita in Oakland with comrades from the Transgender, Gender Variant, and Intersex Justice Project, Communities United Against Violence, the California Coalition of Women Prisoners, and Acción Zapatista South Bay.

41. See Precarias a la deriva, "Very Careful Strike."

42. Esteva, "Oaxaca Commune," 991.

A Note on Methodology

1. Callahan, "Insurgent Learning and Convivial Research"; Colectivo Situaciones, *19 &20*; Team Colors Collective, *Uses of a Whirlwind:*

Movement, Movements, and Contemporary Radical Currents in the United States (Oakland, CA: AK, 2010); de Sousa Santos, *Epistemologies of the South*; Juris and Khasnabish, *Insurgent Encounters*; Ana Cecilia Dinerstein, ed., *Social Sciences for an Other Politics: Women Theorizing without Parachutes* (London: Palgrave Macmillan, 2016); Gutiérrez Aguilar, *Rhythms of the Pachakuti*; Gutiérrez, "Rhythms: Brief Reflections"; Ana Esther Ceceña, "The Subversion of Historical Knowledge of the Struggle: Zapatistas in the 21st Century," *Antipode* 36, no. 3 (June 2004): 361–70.

2. See Ceceña, "Complex Relation," 117.

3. See Ceceña, "Complex Relation." See also Dinerstein, *Social Sciences for an Other Politics*, especially Raquel Gutiérrez Aguilar, Lucia Linsalata, and Nina Lorena Navarro Trujillo, "Producing the Common and Reproducing Life: Keys towards Rethinking *the Political*," 79–92; Ana Cecilia Dinerstein, "The Radical Subject and Its Critical Theory: An Introduction," 1–17; Emily Brissette, "The Prefigurative Is Political: On Politics beyond 'The State,'" 109–20; and Motta, "Decolonising Critique." The project of dismantling and contesting dominant narratives as a way to not only mark a proliferation of resistances across time, but also as a project of resistance in and of itself, is also the work undertaken by Cedric Robinson in *Black Marxism*.

4. On dignity, see John Holloway, "Dignity's Revolt" (pamphlet), San José, Zapatista Autonomy Project, 2011. Callahan links claims to dignity directly to knowledge production as a critical site of an alternative social relation. Callahan, "Rebel Dignity."

5. On the always emergent collective subject, see Callahan, "In Defense of Conviviality"; Holloway, "Dignity's Revolt"; and Ceceña, "Subversion."

6. Callahan, "In Defense of Conviviality"; see also Gutiérrez Aguilar et al., "Producing the Common."

7. Gutiérrez Aguilar, "Rhythms: Brief Reflections," 52.

8. Convivial Research and Insurgent Learning, "Insurgent Learning," http://cril.mitotedigital.org/insurgentlearning.

9. The Convivial Research and Insurgent Learning *taller*, a web-based infrastructure, offers an elaboration on the approach and its commitments and possibilities for decolonial praxis and collective regeneration.

10. See Illich, *Tools for Conviviality*. See also Callahan, "Repairing the Community."

11. See Callahan, "Repairing the Community."

12. On the desire to "do justice" as a desire to impose a will or a truth, see Colectivo Situaciones, "On the Researcher Militant."

13. McKittrick, "Rebellion/Invention/Groove," 88. On ethnographic research as process, see Mariana Mora, *Kuxlejal Politics: Indigenous*

Autonomy, Race, and Decolonizing Research in Zapatista Communities (Austin: University of Texas Press, 2017).

14. See Latina Feminist Group, *Telling to Live*; and Theresa Barnett and Chon A. Noriega, *Oral History and Communities of Color* (Los Angeles: UCLA Chicano Studies Research Center Press, 2013).

15. Costa Vargas, "Activist Scholarship Limits"; Charles Hale, ed., *Engaging Contradictions: Theory, Politics, and Methods of Activist Scholarship* (Berkeley: University of California Press, 2008). See also Callahan, "UT Califas Theses Clinic Announcement, 11-2-13"; "UT Theses Clinic, Saturday, May 3, 2014"; and "UT Califas Theses Clinic Summary, 5-3-14." This theorization has been elaborated collectively as part of ongoing collective ethnography produced in numerous shared, horizontal research spaces and is reflected in the Theses Clinic as well as the Democracy and the Social Factory *ateneo* summaries between 2011 and 2015.

16. Callahan, "UT Califas Theses Clinic Summary, 5-3-14," para. 3. This connection between *testimonio*, relational *testimonio*, storytelling, and knowledge production was the focus of UniTierra's Thesis Clinic in May 2014.

17. Here, I specifically reference Foucault's "knowledges," from *Society Must Be Defended*, 1–22.

18. C.L.R. James, "Black Power," in *The C.L.R. James Reader*, ed. Anna Grimshaw (Oxford: Blackwell, 1992): 362–74: 372.

19. See Convivial Research and Insurgent Learning, "Questions," para. 2. Accessed July 13, 2015. http://cril.mitotedigital.org/questions.

20. González, "'Human Terrain."

21. Scheurich, "Policy Archaeology"; Colectivo Situaciones, *19 & 20*; Harney and Moten, *Undercommons*; Wolfgang Sachs, ed., *The Development Dictionary: A Guide to Knowledge as Power* (New York: Zed Books, 2010), esp. Ivan Illich, "Needs," 95–110, and Gustavo Esteva, "Development," 1–23, in *The Development Dictionary: A Guide to Knowledge as Power*, ed. Wolfgang Sachs (New York: Zed Books, 2010); and Escobar, *Encountering Development*. On anti-security, see Mark Neocleous and George S. Rigakos, eds., *Anti-Security* (Ottawa: Red Quill Books, 2011), including Rimke's "Security: Resistance."

22. On subject-object, for example, see Motta, "Decolonising Critique." On accumulation and dispossession, see, for example, Nichols, *Theft Is Property!*; Byrd et al., "Predatory Value"; Byrd, "Variations under Domestication"; and Barker, "Territory as Analytic." See also Mora, *Kuxlejal Politics*.

23. See Asad, *Colonial Encounter*; and Edward Said, *Orientalism* (New York: Vintage, 1979).

24. T. E. Lawrence, "Twenty-Seven Articles," The Free Library, November 1, 2007, https://www.thefreelibrary.com/The+27+articles+of+T.E.+Lawrence.-a0174747656.

25. Network of Concerned Anthropologists, *Counter-Counterinsurgency Manual*.

26. Khalili, *Time in the Shadows*; Rid, "Nineteenth-Century Origins"; Asad, *Colonial Encounter*, see especially Ahmed, "Some Remarks."

27. See, for example, Linda Tuhiwai-Smith, *Decolonizing Methodologies: Research and Indigenous Peoples* (London: Zed Books, 2002).

28. See especially Hale, *Engaging Contradictions*; and Juris and Khasnabish, *Insurgent Encounters*. See also Kim Tallbear, "Standing with and Speaking as Faith: A Feminist-Indigenous Approach to Inquiry," *Journal of Research Practice* 10, no. 2 (2014): article N17. On co-research and militant research strategies, see Colectivo Situaciones, *19 & 20*: and Roggero, *Living Knowledge*.

29. A seminal text of feminist ethnography remains Kamala Visweswaran's *Fictions of Feminist Ethnography* (Minneapolis: University of Minnesota Press, 1994). See also Ruth Behar and Deborah E. Gordon, eds., *Women Writing Culture* (Berkeley: University of California Press, 1996).

30. On TAZKP, see Callahan, "In Defense of Conviviality"; "Convivial Research and Insurgent Learning"; and "Rebel Dignity."

31. Saidiya Hartman, "Belly of the World: A Note on Black Women's Labors," *Souls* 18, no. 1 (January–March 2016): 166–73, 171. See also Precarias a la deriva, "A Very Careful Strike"; Lorey, *State of Insecurity*; and Fontaine, "Human Strike."

32. Raúl Zibechi, *Dispersing Power: Social Movements as Anti-State Forces*, trans. Ramor Ryan (Edinburgh: AK, 2010); Gutiérrez Aguilar, *Rhythms of the Pachakuti*, 63. See also Molina, "Common Notions."

33. Throughout, references to "the academy" refer to the Western university and college system as an institution, including the traditions that this institution upholds, and the scholarship that is produced through, and continues to preserve, the institution. On the everyday networks that sustain insurgency, see, for example, Ceceña, "On the Complex Relation"; and Ceceña, "Subversion of Historical Knowledge."

34. See Diana Denham, *Teaching Rebellion: Stories from the Grassroots Mobilization in Oaxaca* (Oakland, CA: PM, 2008).

35. Other ethnographic works rooted in collective documentation that I draw on here include Gloria Muñoz Ramírez's history of the Zapatista struggle, *The Fire and the Word: A History of the Zapatista Movement*, trans. Laura Carlsen with Alejandro Reyes Arias (San Francisco: City Lights

Books, 2008), as well as a range of grassroots efforts to document a collective experience of struggle, among them Colectivo Situaciones, *Genocide in the Neighborhood*. Among notable ethnographies focused on women's struggles for justice in response to contexts of state violence directed at them, their families, and their communities, including through enforced disappearances, torture, and other tactics of low-intensity war, see Marguerite Guzman Bouvard, *Revolutionizing Motherhood: The Mothers of the Plaza de Mayo* (New York: Rowman and Littlefield, 2002); Irina Carlota Silber, *Everyday Revolutionaries: Gender, Violence, and Disillusionment in Postwar El Salvador* (New Brunswick, NJ: Rutgers University Press, 2010); Begoña Aretxaga, *Shattering Silence: Women, Nationalism, and Political Subjectivity in Northern Ireland* (Princeton, NJ: Princeton University Press, 1997); and Zia, *Resisting Disappearance*. I also draw on Alan Eladio Gómez's work, including his historical ethnographic work, on feminist insurgencies, the Black Radical tradition, and genealogy as insurgent methodology. See Gómez, "*Puente de Crystal* (Crystal Bridge): Magdalena Mora and Multiple Feminist Insurgencies," *African Identities* 11, no. 2 (2013): 159–84.

36. Motta, "Decolonising Critique"; de Sousa Santos, *Epistemologies of the South*.

37. Callahan, "Repairing the Community."

38. On TAZKP, see Callahan, "In Defense of Conviviality"; "Insurgent Learning"; and "Rebel Dignity"; and Foucault, *Society Must Be Defended*, 7, 10.

39. Callahan, "Insurgent Learning"; and "In Defense of Conviviality."

40. Foucault, *Society Must Be Defended*, 10.

41. Roggero, *Production of Living Knowledge*; Gutiérrez Aguilar et al., "Producing the Common"; Federici, *Re-Enchanting the World*.

42. A number of scholars are advancing questions and possibilities in the current conjuncture at the intersection of knowledge production, social emancipation, autonomy, and new forms of collective ways of being and life in common. To highlight some exciting recent work, see, for example, on the prefigurative and collective life, Brissette, "The Prefigurative Is Political"; Gutiérrez Aguilar, "Rhythms: Brief Reflections"; and Dinerstein, "Radical Subject."

43. John Holloway, *Change the World without Taking Power: The Meaning of Revolution Today* (New York: Pluto, 2005); Marina Sitrin, "Against and Beyond the State: An Interview with John Holloway," *Upping the Anti*, no. 4 (October 26, 2009), https://uppingtheanti.org/journal/article/04-against-and-beyond-the-state. See also Brissette, "The Prefigurative Is Political."

44. See, for example, Callahan, "Repairing the Community."

45. Combahee River Collective, "Why Did They Die?"; Precarias a la deriva, "Very Careful Strike"; Casas-Cortes and Cobarrubias, "Drifting through the Knowledge Machine"; Latina Feminist Group, "Introduction: *Papelitos Gurdados*"; Iconoclasistas, https://www.iconoclasistas.net/. On Project South timelines, see https://projectsouth.org/education/timelines/. On CCRA timelines, see "Community Action Timelines," http://ccra-tech.art/#747. On González and cibercultur@, see, for example, "'Cibercultura' y Cibercultur@," Flow, April 20, 2007. On UniTierra Califas's *ateneos*, see Universidad de la Tierra Califas, http://cril.mitotedigital.org/ateneo and https://ggg.vostan.net/ccra/#18.

46. Among these were the Democracy Ateneo, in place in the South Bay continuously from 2011 to 2018, as well as several prominent events in San José in the year leading up to the launch of the Social Factory Ateneo.

47. On "relearning the habits of assembly," see Callahan, "Repairing the Community" and "Conviviality Rooted in Struggle." On assembly, see Marianne Maeckelbergh, "Horizontal Democracy Now: From Alterglobalization to Occupation," *Interface* 4, no. 1 (May 2012): 207–34; Maeckelbergh, "Occupy the U.S."; Marina Sitrin, *Everyday Revolutions: Horizontalism and Autonomy in Argentina* (New York: Zed Books, 2012); and Davidian and Jeanpierre, eds., *What Makes an Assembly?* See also Esteva, "Oaxaca Commune," for a discussion of neighborhood assemblies and the Popular Assembly of the Peoples of Oaxaca; and Gago, *Feminist International*.

48. On the circulation of struggle, see Harry Cleaver, "The Zapatistas and the International Circulation of Struggle: Lessons Suggested and Problems Raised," paper originally prepared for the Globalization from Below conference at Duke University, Durham, NC, February 1998, http://la.utexas.edu/users/hcleaver/lessons.html.

49. See Convivial Research and Insurgent Learning, "Social Factory Ateneo: Announcements," http://ccra.mitotedigital.org/ateneo/social_factory.

INDEX

abandonment: inclusion and, 22; militarized, 209; securitized, 200–201, 209; strategic, 213
ABC, 89
"ablenationalism," 114
abolitionist movement, 62, 64, 120. *See also* prison and jail abolitionist movements
Acción Zapatista (AZ), 1, 70, 229n3. *See also* Zapatistas
accompanying, 48
accountability, 39, 116, 133
accumulation, 13, 17
acknowledgments, 134
action, 217
"acute excited delirium," 132
"administrative violence," 121
affordable housing, 109, 110–11, 152–53
Africa, 83
Against Hired Guns, 67–68
Agee, Christopher Lowen, 13, 14
agencies, cooperation across, 130–31
air power, 6, 95
air surveillance, 9
Alameda County, 42; courts in, 62; district attorney, 52
Algeria, 83, 91, 222, 228
alienation, 177
Alvis, Michelle, 135, 143, 145, 147, 148, 150, 159
American Civil Liberties Union, 127
Americans with Disabilities Act, 123
analysis, shared, 3
anarchists, 54, 70
Andaya, Marc, 132
Anglo settlers, 161
anthropology: colonialism and, 221–22; discipline of, 221–22

anti-apartheid movement, 50
anti-Black racism, 110
anti-carceral struggle, 62
anticolonial struggles, 70, 228
anti-fascist movement, 50
anti-gang laws, 91
anti-imperialism rallies, 50
anti-occupation solidarity movements, 50
Anti-Police Terror Project, 194–95, 265n43
anti-security politics, 51
anti-state projects, 224
"anti-tumult ordinances," 83
antiwar rallies, 50
apartheid, 23
"apocalyptic capitalism," 33, 200–201
architecture, 70–71
archiving, 218; archive of organized practices of community care, 198–99; collective archiving, 37; community archives, 39
Argentina, 4, 25, 63, 68, 114, 215; Dirty War in, 113
armed/unarmed, debates around, 58
AROC (Arab Resource Organizing Center), 61
arrests, for minor infractions, 14
assembly, 51, 72, 200, 201, 206; Occupy movement and, 64–65; "relearning arts of," 218; relearning habits of, 227; rules of, 83; spaces of, 117; at Stockton picnic, 181–86
association, rules of, 83
ateneo spaces, 113, 169, 185, 186, 226–28, 249n38, 262n11, 274n91, 275n94, 277n24
ATF, 151
"authorized crime," 11, 235n39

287

autonomist theorists, 111
autonomy, 20, 24, 26, 39, 65, 68, 72; assertion of, 24–25, 214; autonomous elements, 70; autonomous justice, 95; autonomous organizations, 198–99; autonomous projects, 224; autonomous struggles, 70; autonomous subjects, 111; interruption of, 32; spaces of, 201; struggle for, 3, 18, 20–21, 134, 218
autopsies, independent, 131–32
autopsy reports, 41, 132, 139, 155, 158; access to independent, 44; families and, 43–44
Ayestes, Yvett, 123
Ayotzinapa, Guerrero, Mexico, 69–70
Azavand, Eric, 135, 179

"bad debt," 18, 238n63
ballistics reports, 187
Baltimore, Maryland, 69, 135; insurgency in, 9
Barker, Joanne, 121–22, 182
BART (Bay Area Rapid Transit), 51, 53
BART (Bay Area Rapid Transit) police, 1, 51, 53, 135, 199
Baton Rouge, Louisiana, 69
battle zones, 49
Baumgartner, Margaret, 126
Baxter, Kerry Jr., 12, 135, 177, 203
Baxter, Kerry Sr., 12, 135
Bay Area Police Watch, 31
Bayview Community Feed, 198
Bayview neighborhood, 153; Bayview-Hunters Point, 153, 199–200, 204–5, 211, 213–14; Bayview public plaza, 135
Bellingham, Washington, 50
Bellusa, John, 135
belonging, 61, 157
Benholdt-Thomsen, Veronika, 61
Berkeley, California, 1, 42, 103, 107, 123; City Hall, 117; civilian review board, 116; police shootings in, 25–26
Berkeley City Council, 116–17
Berkeley Copwatch, 105–6, 262n6
Berkeley Mobile Crisis Team, 104, 107

Berkeley Police Department (BPD), 1, 104, 106, 112, 116, 123, 135, 262n6
Berkeley Police Review Commission (PRC), 117–19, 120
Bernal Heights Park, 125, 142
Bhatt, Barhin, 67, 135
biopolitics: biopolitical order, 35; biopolitical regimes, 151–52, 154; biopolitical technology, 108
biopower, 85, 92, 110
birthday party, 103
Black communities, 7, 8–9, 10, 98, 100, 153; crack cocaine in, 14–15; subprime lending crisis and, 182; targeting of, 22, 101; "uplift" and, 23–24; war against social reproduction and, 198
Black feminism, 24, 223
Black geographies, 95
Black life, 4
Black Lives Matter, 55, 71, 72
Black men, police violence and, 52
Blackness, 110
Black Panther Party, 50
Black people, killed by police, 52, 109–10
Black Power Movement, 50, 70, 163
"Black rage," 55
Black Star Line Incorporated, 205
Black women, 198; murders of, 106–7; projects organized by, 198–99; violence targeting, 123–24
Blank Panthers, 248n24
"bleeding out," 200–201, 204–5, 267n15
Blockade, as strategy of obstruction, 72
Blueford, Alan, 1, 135, 177
body, as site of knowledge production and value production, 40–44
body camera footage, 129
Boggs, Grace Lee, 61
Booker, Daniel, 1–2, 203
borders: "border regimes," 92; border security, 15; proliferation of, 137
Boston Transit Police, 82
Boyd, Cammerin, 56–57, 149, 157
Bratton, William, 8, 9, 25, 81–82, 84, 85, 88, 149

Bratton-style policing, 81–82, 84, 86, 87, 91, 149, 150
Brava Theater, 204
Brazil, 63, 69
Breed, Charles, 149
Breyer, Charles, 123
Brissette, Emily, 66
"broken-windows" policing, 84, 101
"broken windows" theory, 149
Brown, Arielle Julia, 1, 203, 211, 212–13, 227, 229n1
Brown, Gwendolyn, 104, 135
Brown, Michael, 9, 43, 58, 69, 134, 181
Brown, Raheim, 1, 67, 135, 177
Brown communities, 7, 8–9, 10, 98, 100, 153; crack cocaine in, 14–15; targeting of, 101; war against social reproduction and, 198
Brown life, 4
Brown people, killed by police, 109
Brown Power Movement, 50, 70
Brown women, 198; violence targeting, 123–24
brutality, 11
bullets, 2
Bureaux Arabes, 83, 222
Burge, Jon, 9
Byrd, Jodi A., 114, 121

Cabillo, Joshua, 77–78, 80, 88, 96, 134–35
Cacho, Lisa Marie, 60, 136, 160, 163
CAD reports, 178
California, 19; as carceral state, 64; division of families by, 180; incarceration rates in, 62; legislation in, 90; Police Officers' Bill of Rights, 127; prisons in, 193; Proposition 21, 90; Proposition 184, 90; SB 1421, Peace Officers: Release of Records, 127, 128; state legislature, 183; Supreme Court, 127; "Three Strikes" law, 90. *See also specific locations*
California Coalition for Women Prisoners, 123
California Department of Correction and Rehabilitation, 123

California Highway Patrol (CHP), 149, 179
California Institute for Women (CIW), suicide crisis at, 123
California Supreme Court, 127
Callahan, Manuel, 107–8, 152, 161, 193, 210, 217, 218, 226
"call to struggle," 121
Camarena, Adriana, 268n23
Cameron, Don Stewart, 164
capital: blocking circulation as strategy of obstruction and, 50, 72; resistance to, 49; the state and, 133
capitalism, 5–6, 13, 17, 22, 24, 34, 100, 124, 133–34, 168, 228; "apocalyptic capitalism," 24, 200–201; disengagement from, 223, 226; neoliberal, 5–6; racial differences and, 5; refusal of, 224; trans subjects and, 110. *See also* racial patriarchal capitalism
"captive maternals," 4–5
caracoles, 20
carceral regimes, 15, 17, 62, 124, 188, 193; carceral violence, 227; counterinsurgency and, 186–94; expanding, 3; targeting by, 177
Cardoza, Benjamin, 119, 135
Cardoza, John, 119
care, 24, 29–48, 111, 117, 188, 190, 192, 208, 209–10, 212–13, 218, 224; acts of, 160; archive of organized practices of community care, 198–99; "care communities," 47; collective, 180; communal, 180; crisis of, 22, 25, 31–40, 35, 107; disallowed, 199–200; externalization of, 32, 120; fierce care, 24–25, 29–48, 51, 73, 107, 122, 124, 140, 169, 172, 176–77, 201, 226, 228; militant forms of, 180; militarization of, 31–32, 107–8, 113, 228; "politics of," 65; politics of, 26, 228; politics of representation, recognition, and inclusion," 60, 108; professionalization of, 120; relations of, 140–41; securitized,

care (*continued*)
107–8; spaces of, 172. See also care work; fierce care
care work, 24, 65, 73, 107, 223
cartography, 83; critical cartographies, 201; operative maps, 93–97. See also counter-cartographies
Casas-Cortes, Maribel, 92, 226
Cato Institute, 177
Ceceña, Ana Esther, 4, 21
cell phones, confiscation of, 36, 52, 187–88, 191
cemeteries, movement to urban peripheries, 208–9
Center for Convivial Research and Autonomy (CCRA), 3, 4, 19–20, 42–43, 47, 106, 211, 217, 221, 227
Central America, 20. See also specific countries
Central California Women's Facility in Chowchilla, 16, 123
ceremonial gatherings, 125
Chang, Errol, 142
chaos, 14
Chatman, Denika, 203, 204–5
chattel slavery, 16
Chiapas, Mexico, 4, 18–20, 50, 63, 69
Chiapas Solidarity Network, 70
Chicago, Illinois, 69
Chicago Police Department, 9
Chicano Movement, 50
Chicanx community, 70
Chief Medical Examiner's (CME) Office, 41–43, 131–32. See also autopsy reports
Child Protective Services, 166, 190, 191
children: loss of, 1, 3, 29, 142, 169, 175–76, 177, 198, 202–4, 211; refusal to provide information, 191; removal and placement of, 188–90, 191
chisme, 43
chokeholds, 2
Chopper City gang, 153
Choy, Darren, 145
CIA, 9
cibercultur@ theory, 220, 227
Ciccariello-Maher, George, 55, 127

citizenship, 161–62; collective acts of, 207; racial contestation and, 157; racial production and, 157; "social citizenship," 208
class struggle, 49; war as, 6–7
clearing a building, police strategies for, 164
Cleary, Thomas, 156, 158
Cleaver, Harry, 111, 263–64n25
climate justice, 50
Clinton, William J., 87; Violent Crime Control and Law Enforcement Act in 1994, 87, 90
CNI's Women's Encuentro in Veracruz, 20
Coalition for a Safe Berkeley, 106
Cobarrubias, Sebastian, 226
"Coffee Not Cops" action, 126
COINTELPRO, 83–84
co-learning, space of, 51
Colectivo Situaciones, 4, 20, 68, 115
collective analysis, 60–61, 68, 70, 72, 81, 194
collective archiving, 37
collective ethnography, 3, 4–5, 22, 186, 226–28; emergent collective subject and, 225–26; as refusal to represent, 221–25
collective imagination, of community safety, 2–3
collective investigation, 36, 80–81, 209–10
collective learning, 68, 70
collective life, fight for, 4
collective mapping, 227
collective memory, 97, 198, 208, 219–20
collective refusal, 158
"collective security," 85
collective strategies, 67
collective subject: communities of struggle as, 225–26; emergent, 60–61, 71, 216, 217, 219, 225–26
collective violence, 37–38
colonial desire, production of, 83
colonialism, 4, 6, 8, 83, 121, 221; anthropology and, 221–22; global colonial "epistemicide," 198; "prose of counterinsurgency" and

colonialist knowledge, 160–61; security and, 8; settler colonialism, 6, 65, 83, 121, 222
colonial knowledge, 83
colonial occupation, 83
colonial subjectivities, production of, 83
Combahee River Collective, 4, 94, 121, 226; "6 Black Women: Why Did They Die?," 106–7
command-and-control mode, 32
command-and-control policing, 82
commensurability, systems of, 114–15
commons: engagement of, 225–26; institution of, 51; institutions of, 107; privatization of, 61; reclaiming of, 51
communities: of struggle, 225–26. See also specific communities
Communities United Against Violence, 106
community archives, 39
community-based justice projects, 123–24
community bonds, severing of, 188, 190
community clinics, 227
community cohesion, 14
community/communities, 24; as collective subjects, 225–26; destabilization of, 91, 187–89; devaluation of, 133; inclusion of, 217; rebuilding, 138–39; regeneration of, 46–47, 72, 217; reorganization of, 186–94; reproduction of, 217; self-determination and, 46–47; self-organization of, 218; targeting of, 137; terrorizing, 186–94; war against, 4
community councils, 224
community engagement, 82
Community Feed at Kenny's Corner, 204–5, 211, 213–14
community food programs, 206. See also specific programs
community formation, 214
community investigations, 38–40
community knowledge, 38, 80, 176

community meetings, 88–89
Community Oriented Policing Services (COPS), 87, 172
community partnerships, 12–13
community patrol practices, 193
community policing, 7, 81, 87–88, 99, 100, 101; counterinsurgency warfare and, 81–84; models of, 84; neoliberal securitization and, 91; paramilitarization and, 82; in San Francisco, California, 148–52; as war on youth and social factory, 81–89
community regeneration, 20, 25, 36, 73
community relations, space and, 208
community resilience, 107
community safety, 3–4, 11, 14, 18–21, 26, 51, 61, 73, 107, 138, 216, 220, 224; as autonomous initiative, 226; collective imagination of, 2–3; as convivial tool, 19–20, 21; fierce care and, 24–25; networked, 220; as praxis, 21; as response to racial patriarchal capitalism, 18–19; vs. security, 133–34; struggle for, 3, 26
community self-defense, 14, 51, 59–60, 63, 73, 138–39, 190–91, 213
community timelines, 227
commuting, 154–55, 181
Compstat, 8, 84–85
Compton, California, 16
constructing observables, methodology of, 133–34
containment, 14, 216; spaces of, 154
contestation, 69
control, 83, 216
conviviality, emergent, 210–11
convivial research, 4, 25, 26, 106, 107, 178, 186, 198, 201, 215–28, 243–44n31, 275n94. See also people's investigations
convivial space, 209–10
convivial tools, 35–36, 97, 198–99, 201, 217, 267n11; new imaginaries of justice and, 111–17; produced by Occupy Oakland, 66; as research strategy, 226–28; shared, 194–95; sharing, 72–73

Copley Press v. the City of San Diego, 127
"cops on the street," 87, 90
cop-watching, 38
coroner's office, 155; police departments and, 41–43. *See also* Chief Medical Examiner's (CME) Office
coroner's report, 103, 106, 112, 117, 158, 178, 187. *See also* autopsy reports
corruption, 11, 13, 178
counter-cartographies, 26, 77–102. *See also* remapping
counterinsurgencies, liberal, 90, 161–63, 167
counterinsurgency, 83, 137, 150–51, 156, 184–86, 232n22; carceral state and, 186–94; counterinsurgency doctrine, 128; counterinsurgency practices, 152; counterinsurgency strategies, 39; counterinsurgency tactics, 82, 170–72; liberal, 116, 167; net of, 186–94; "prose of," 17, 79, 146, 152, 160–61; web of, 172. *See also* counterinsurgency warfare
counterinsurgency warfare, 5–9, 25–26, 34, 51, 92, 98, 102, 128–29, 134, 146, 148; braiding of, 3; community policing and, 81–84; policing as, 17; "prose of counterinsurgency," 161; recent shift in, 95–96; spaces of encounter and, 210–13
counterknowledges, 4
counter-mapping. *See* counter-cartographies
counter-narratives, 38–41, 79–81, 144–46, 160, 169, 181, 194, 221; media and, 176–77; of police violence, 46; spaces of encounter and, 211–12
court bias, 163
court documents, 187
courts, 160, 191–94; racial hierarchies and, 163; reclaiming of courtroom, 168; social control and, 163; space of, 168, 192
court trials, showing up at, 180

CPR, 105, 117; denial of, 77–78, 80
crack cocaine, 14–15
CRASH units, LAPD and, 11–12
Crawford, John, 58
Crenshaw, Kitt, 151
crime: "authorized crime," 11, 235n39; crime control, 61; crime mapping, 84; "crime reduction teams" (CRTs), 87–88; epistemology of, 17; interrogation of, 60; racialized understandings of, 137
criminality, discursive regime of, 93
criminalization, 39, 133, 146, 154–55, 160, 180, 191–92, 205, 207, 209, 213, 216, 221; in aftermath of police killings, 2–4, 10, 21–23, 26, 56–57, 59, 61, 84, 87, 94, 96, 100, 107, 160, 162–63, 166–68; autopsy reports and, 41; community policing and, 148, 150–51; discursive, 136–37; epistemology of, 168; failure of, 52–53; hegemonic discourses of, 177; media and, 176; processes of, 170–71; as racial strategy, 193; refusal of, 21; self-organization against, 168; technologies of, 176
criminal justice system, racialization and, 193–94
crisis calls, police responses to, 107–8
critical methodologies, knowledge production and, 41–42
Critical Resistance, 60, 82; Peers Envisioning and Engaging Recovery Services, 106
cruelty, pedagogy of, 33, 200–201
CS tear gas, 8
curfew restrictions, 14, 83

Daily Californian, 105
Dakota Access Pipeline protests, 9
Dalla Costa, Mariarosa, 228
Da Silva, Denise Ferreira, 24
databases, 84, 86
data gathering, 84–85
Dave, Naisargi N., 122
Davis, Angela, 23, 61
Davis, Ayanna, 203
Day, Richard J. F., 71

DEA, 151
death, banishment of, 209
death certificates, 187
debt, 121–22, 182. See also "bad debt"
decision-making, 217
decolonization, 25, 65, 69, 122, 215, 226; decolonial imaginary, 224–25; decolonial methodologies, 217, 222–23; decolonized justice initiatives, 215; global, 215
de-escalation strategies, 32
defense, 51. See self-defense; community self-defense
"defund the police" movement, 17
de-industrialization, 14
Delta RATT (Regional Auto Theft Team), 179, 180
demilitarization, 17, 120
democracy: liberal, 215; radical, 65; representative, 65
"democratic despotism," 23, 193
demolitions, 152, 153
desire, fear and, 22
de-subjectification, 226
detentions: detention centers, 193–94; illegal, 191
development and redevelopment projects, 13
deviance, 13, 14
difference, hierarchies of, 215
"differential citizenship," 93
"differential inclusion," 24, 258n64
differential policing, 99, 186
differentiation, 5, 59
dignity, claim to, 216, 218
direct action, 46, 103–24, 125, 131, 133, 136–37, 178, 180, 194–95, 226; courtroom as site of, 168–69; "direct action casework," 39; direct action tools, 219; spaces of, 119–20, 172
disability activists, 114
discipline, 37, 92, 216
disempowerment, 115
disenfranchisement, 111
disinformation, 12, 96, 125–42, 176, 266n5
displacement, 50, 95–96, 137, 154, 166

disposability, 3, 121, 154; manufacturing of, 17; production of, 215; settler-colonial logic of, 110; technology of, 201
dispositifs, 6–7, 17, 35, 50, 80, 85, 111, 132, 163, 167, 193
dispossession, 3, 17, 65, 95–96, 121–22, 124, 137, 153, 154, 181
disqualified secrets, 73
dissent, 50
District Attorney's Offices, 52, 130, 131
division, 54; countering, 176–77
dockworkers, 63
documentation, 73, 84, 115, 160, 178, 192, 203, 219
dog attacks, 2
Domenici, Marisol, 51
domestic violence legislation, 191–92
"dot-com" crash, 182–83
Draper, Susanna, 94, 98
drift(s), 35, 37, 72, 226
"drug turf war," 151
Du Bois, W. E. B., 23, 59, 193
due process, 101
Dunn, Gregory, 135, 179

Earth Day, 50
EastSide Arts Alliance, 61, 203
Ecklund, Karen, 149
economies, illegal, 2, 15
Eddy Rock gang, 153
Egypt, 215
Ejército Zapatista Liberación Nacional (EZLN), 20, 124, 259n68. See also Acción Zapatista (AZ); Zapatistas
emancipation, 216; knowledges and, 21
emergency first-aid, 201–2
emergency measures, 83
emergent collective subject, 60–61, 71, 216, 217, 219, 225–26; collective ethnography and, 225–26
emergent conviviality, 210–11
Emeryville police, 195
"emotional CPR" (eCPR), 117, 265n44
empathy, lack of, 33
empire, 121
encampments, 72, 73

enclosure, 3, 32, 37, 61, 91–93, 124, 129, 148, 184, 216; race and, 161; resistance to, 46
encounter: political moment of, 210–11; space of, 50–51, 62–63, 71, 80, 95, 102, 112, 115, 123, 178, 210, 220–21, 224, 225
entrapment, 156
epistemology: genocide and, 198–99; interrogation of, 65. See also knowledge(s); Western episteme
equity, 122
erasures, 3, 67, 94, 105, 121, 123–24, 136–37, 160; fight against, 4; inclusion and, 122; resisting, 220
escalation, 30–31, 106
escraches, 25, 95, 113–15, 116
Espinosa, Kathleen (Kat), 135, 143–45, 154, 166, 169
Esteva, Gustavo, 47, 111, 195, 214, 263–64n25, 264n39
ethnographic process, participation in, 224–25
ethnography, 3–4, 215–28; collective, 3, 4–5, 22, 186; ethnographic studies, 224
Evans, Angela, 141
Evans, O'Shaine, 134, 141
evictions, 13, 152–53, 181
exclusion, 92, 122, 148; inclusion and, 114–15
experts, 169; in defense of the police, 164–68; as "self-justifying," 165
exploitation, 13, 24
expropriation, 3, 17
expulsion, 14, 92
extermination, settler-colonial logic of, 121
"externalization of the home," 32
extractivism, 13, 17, 61, 201, 223
extrajudicial killings, 200–201. See also police violence

false information, threat of, 188
families, 24, 40–41, 58–59, 81, 101–2, 117, 119, 123–24, 130, 136, 175–76; autopsy reports and, 43–44; barbecues organized by, 175–95, 206, 209; body camera footage and, 129; Chief Medical Examiner's (CME) Office and, 42; compensation of, 180; counseling of, 180; destabilization of, 91, 187–90; devaluation of, 133; disruption of, 44–45; division of, 180; financial hardship and, 44–46; funeral homes and, 42; incarceration and, 192–93; interrogation of, 155, 157, 166; investigations and, 143–44; isolation of, 29, 136; mobilization of, 137; narratives of, 181; networks of, 140, 180, 195; severing of family bonds, 188–90, 192, 193–94; at Stockton picnic, 175–86; struggle for justice and truth, 44–46, 131, 193–94; targeted by state violence, 134–38; *testimonios* by, 136; traumatization of, 129; vigils and, 95. See also *specific family members*
fascism, 55
FBI, 151, 178; Uniform Crime Reports, 182
fear/desire, biopolitical, 22, 34
Federici, Silvia, 46, 111, 228
feminicide, 20, 140
feminism, 22, 23, 24, 34–35, 94, 223; Black feminism, 24, 223; feminist collectives, 198; feminist epistemological approaches, 217; feminist inquiry, 35; feminist justice initiatives, 215; feminist strike, 94
Ferguson, Missouri, 43, 134, 135, 141; insurgency of 2014, 9, 22, 58, 69
fierce care, 51, 73, 107, 122, 124, 140, 158, 169, 172, 176–77, 226, 228; definition of, 24–25; Monge-Irizarry and, 29–48; refusals and, 201; ungovernability and, 120–21; vigils as, 94
50.50 Crew, 1, 106, 229n3
Fillmore District, 153
finance, 152, 154
financial crisis of 2007–08, 121–22, 182–83
financial hardship, families and, 44–46

financialization, extractive operation of, 182
first responders, 201–2
518 Valencia, 61
Flores, Yasmin, 1–2, 203
Floyd, George, 9, 135
Fong, Heather, 130–31, 269n4
Forbes, 182
force, increasing visibility of, 17
force policy, 120
foreclosures, 65
Forensic Pathology Department, San Francisco, California, 131–32
Fortunati, Leopoldina, 228
Foucault, Michel, 6–7, 40, 59, 108, 208–9; on cemeteries, 208–9; on "heterotopias," 210; on "insurrection of subjugated knowledges," 225–26
Fourteenth and Broadway: legacy of, 72; as space of dissent and possibility, 49–73; as space of encounter, 71; as TAZKP, 51
Fourth World War, 3, 5–10, 11, 15, 18, 23–24, 69, 111
France, 83, 91, 222, 228
Frank Ogawa Plaza, 64
Fray Bartolomé de Las Casas (Frayba) Center for Human Rights in Chiapas, 18–20
freedom, 114
Freedom Archives, 61
Fresno, California, Violent Crime Suppression Unit, 88
Friday, Colby, 3, 200, 205–6, 214
Friday, Denise, 198, 205–6
Fruitvale neighborhood, 227
Fruitvale Station, 51, 199
"fugitive public," 18
fundraisers, 180
funeral homes, families and, 42
funerals, funds for, 46

Gago, Verónica, 14, 182, 183
Gaia Building, 103, 105, 107–12, 118
Gaines, Derrick, 25–26, 77–81, 86–87, 89, 91, 93, 95–96, 98–100, 102, 134–35
Gaines, Larry, 149

Galbreath, Summer, 30
Galeano, Comrade, 69
Gallieni, Joseph, 83
Galula, David, 128, 150
gang activity, 84, 90, 153, 192; gang-banger nexus, 78–80; gang violence, 85, 87, 88, 89, 90–91, 92, 101; "gang" wars, 15, 16
gang injunctions, 60, 92–93, 137, 153
gang response strategy, South San Francisco Police Department (SSFPD), 78–79
Ganser, Lisa, 275n2
Gant, Khatari, 203
Garbayo, Joseph, 30, 134
Garcia, Anton, 140
Garcia, Victor, 66
Gardner, Tim, 135
Garner, Eric, 58, 69, 134
Gascon, George, 130
gated communities, 92
Gates, Daryl K., 8
gay and lesbian population, in San Francisco, California, 13
Gaza, 69
Gehry, Frank, 70–71
Gelhaus, Erick, 135
gender, 5; gender regimes, 25; history of, 97–98; reorganization of, 108
gendered hierarchies, 13
gendered violence, 106–7
gender-nonconforming identity, 5, 111
gender sensitivity trainings, 120
general strike, 64, 65
General Strike of 1946, 50
genocide, epistemological dominance and, 198–99
gentrification, 181
geography: carceral logic of, 192; "remade through struggle," 207; of San Francisco Bay Area, 51
ghettoization, 14
Gill, Danny, 89
Gillis, Sheehan, 199
Gilmore, Ruth Wilson, 5, 35, 107
Giuliani, Rudolph, 81
Global South, 63, 98
Goff, David, 134
"golden hour," 197, 213

Goldstein, Alyosha, 114, 121
González, Jorge, 133–34, 220, 227
Gonzalez, Patrick, 56, 66
good subject/bad subject dichotomy, 57
Goodwill Industries, 166
Gordon, Avery F., 40
governance, biopolitical regimes of, 39
Grant, Oscar, 1, 9, 25, 49–73, 177; criminalization of, 59; daughter of, 53; justice for, 61; police shooting of, 49–55, 56, 60, 135, 199, 200–203, 216. See also Oscar Grant rebellions
Graves, Shaylene, 123
Gray, Freddie, 9, 135
Greece, 215
Grewal, Inderbir Singh, 181–82
"grey" policing tactics, 11
Grisham, Brenda, 203
Gross, Ariela J., 157
guard abuse and violence, 123
Guerrero, Mexico, students missing from, 69–70
guerrillas, 5
guerrilla street theater, 197
Guha, Ranahit, 146, 160–61; "prose of counterinsurgency," 17
Guido-Red, Rachel, 78
gun violence, 2
Gutiérrez Aguilar, Raquel, 81, 224
Guzman Lopez, Antonio, 194

"habits of assembly," 2
Half Moon Bay, 139, 140, 194
Hall, Denise Friday, 3
Harakati, Bernadette, 148
harassment policing, 2, 14, 82, 83, 92, 99–100, 101
Haraway, Donna, 137–38
Harcourt, Bernard, 162, 165
Hardin, Garret, 61
Harding, Kenneth, Jr., 135, 198, 199–201, 204–5
Harney, Stefano, 238n63
Harrington, Michael, 149
Harris, Kamala, 130, 149
Hartman, Saidiya, 98, 101, 223
Hastings, Richard, 135
Haynes, Donnie Rae, 177

healing, justice processes and, 213
hearing notices, 187
Helmsley, Leona, 152
Henderson, Yuvette, 195
Herrera, Dennis, 153
Herrera, Juan, 199, 208
Herzing, Rachel, 82
heterochronies, 210
heteronormativity, 5, 13, 14
heterotopias, 210
hierarchy, rejection of, 65
Highland Hospital, 199
HIJOS, 113–14, 115, 120
history, 219–20
Holder, Eric, 172
The Holdout/Qilombo, 61
Holland, Sharon Patricia, 207
Home Depot, 195
home(s), 24, 101–2; attack on, 98; externalization of, 120, 213; raids of, 2, 16, 108, 131, 137, 148, 151, 170, 171, 179, 187–88; searches of, 187–88
horizontalism, 215, 217; horizontal learning, 217; horizontal research and learning initiative, autonomous, 220; Occupy movement and, 65
hospital reports, 187
"hot spot policing," 87–88
households, war against, 4
housing. See affordable housing
housing crisis, 65
housing vouchers, gerrymandered allocation of, 13
Humanist Hall, 134, 136, 137–38
human rights discourse, 221
humiliation, 14, 53
Hunters Point neighborhood, San Francisco, California, 14
Hurricane Katrina, 24, 61

I am Oscar Grant, 55
Iconoclasistas, 227
identification, 36
Idriss Stelley Foundation, 31, 41, 106
Idriss Stelley v. City & County and SFPD, 31
illegal aliens, 160

INDEX

Illich, Ivan, 5, 165, 217, 263–64n25, 267n11
immigrants, undocumented, 140, 160
Immigration and Customs Enforcement Agency (ICE), 36
impunity, 63, 106, 128; pedagogy of, 33
incarceration, 175; families and, 192–93; incarceration rates, 62; threat of, 188–89. *See also* carceral regimes
incident reports, 187
INCITE! Women of Color Against Violence, 86
inclusion, 14, 122, 176–77; abandonment and, 22; exclusion and, 114–15; inclusionist methodologies, 121–22
in-custody deaths, 149; counter-narratives of, 35
India, 160–61; extrajudicial killings and enforced disappearances of Sikhs in, 41–42
Indigenous activists, 65
Indigenous Americans, 17
Indigenous autonomy, 20
Indigenous communities, 4, 7, 8–9, 10, 98, 100, 121; struggles of, 223; subprime lending crisis and, 182; war against social reproduction and, 198
Indigenous genocide, 16
Indigenous land: dispossession of, 65, 121–22; Indigenous land struggles, 50
Indigenous National Congress (CNI), 20
Indigenous people, 161; killed by police, 109; violence targeting, 123–24
Indigenous women, 198; violence targeting, 123–24
informalization, of war, 10, 11
information: accumulation of, 82; call for disclosure of, 133; control of, 132; exchange of, 39; networks of, 159. *See also* information-gathering; information systems
information-gathering, 83, 95–96, 99–100, 139

information systems, 138, 177–78, 211–14; circulating and archiving, 211–14; collective, 220–21; subversive, 73
innocence, reclaiming of, 176
instability, 22, 35
insubordination, 119–20
insurgencies, 10, 25, 179, 200–201; insurgent communities, 5, 64; TAZKPs as, 225–26
insurgent communities, 168
insurgent knowledges, 4, 29–48, 73, 121, 138, 208, 221, 225
insurgent learning, 25, 178, 201, 215–28, 275n94
intelligence-gathering, 82, 84, 92, 131, 222
interagency cooperation, 130–31
Inter Council for Mothers of Murdered Children (ICMMC), 134–38, 142
International Longshore and Warehouse Union (ILWU), 50
International Women's Strike, 94, 98
interrogation, 59, 86, 99, 155, 157, 187, 191; of families, 155, 157, 166; spaces of, 134
intervention, 14
intimidation, 38
invasion, 99, 100, 108, 131, 137, 148, 151–52, 170, 171, 179, 187–88
investigations, 30–31, 34–41, 85–86, 129–30; collective, 143–45, 178, 209–10; community-based, 178, 193; families and, 143–44, 158; grassroots, 37, 38–39, 95, 105–6, 107, 116, 120, 131, 227; internal, 148, 158, 159, 161, 162; internal affairs investigations, 130; official, 119 (*see also* coroner's report; police reports); police investigations, 193. *See also* people's investigations
invisibilization, 67, 106. *See also* erasures
involuntary psychiatric hold, 104; in-custody deaths after, 105, 106
Iran-Contra deal, 14–15
isolation, 177, 213
Israel, 69

"Jail All Killer Cops" slogan, 62
James, C.L.R., 220–21
James, Joy, 4–5
James, Selma, 228
Jameson, Fredric, 70–71
January rebellions, 51–55, 57
Jaramillo, Hernan, 1
Jason, Alexander, 164–65
Jefferson, Brian Jordan, 82
Johnson, Bonnie, 203
Johnson, Cephus, 52
Johnson, Gaye Therese, 208
Johnson, Lyndon, 82
Johnson, Wanda, 52
Jones, Chrisopher La Vell, 203
Joseph, Dustin B., 135
Joyner, Ersie III, 66
juridical process, 37, 161–63, 191–92, 213. *See also* courts; criminal justice system
juridical spaces, 85–86. *See also* courts
justice, 51, 124, 161–62; community-based, 212–13; demand for, 200; financial hardship and, 44–45; grassroots, 123–24; new imaginaries of, 111–17, 121; questioning and renegotiation of, 51; reclaiming of, 62, 138; repudiation of, 172; state-organized, 63, 138–39; struggle for, 25–26, 44–46, 120–21, 136, 139, 140–41, 145–46, 168, 193–94. *See also escraches*; juridical process; justice campaigns
justice campaigns, 26, 175–95
Justice for Alan Blueford, 106
Justice for Alex Nieto (J4AN), 69, 125, 133, 137–38, 139–40, 268n23

K-9 unit dog attacks, 2
Kant, Immanuel, 220
Kappeler, Victor, 149
Kastmiler, Nikos, 135
Keesor, John, 135, 143, 145, 147, 148, 150, 159
Kelling, George L., 149
Keram, Emily A., 165
"kettling," 249n39

Khalili, Laleh, 83, 90, 161–62, 167, 232n22
King, Rodney, 15
Kipp, Jacob, 83–84
Knock Out Posse gang, 153
knowing, gendered ways of, 40
knowledge commons, 225–26
knowledge production, 4, 20–21, 35, 46–49, 69, 73, 83, 92, 95–96, 134, 138–39, 156, 178, 243–44n31; body as site of, 40–44; collaborative, 141; collective, 198–99; courtroom as site of, 162, 168; critical methodologies and, 41–42; "disqualified" or "buried" knowledges, 40; horizontal forms of, 216–17; insurrectionary, 40, 220–21 (*see also* insurgent knowledges); interrogation of, 65; methodology and, 219–22; new forms of, 215; policing as site of, 84; politics of representation, recognition, and inclusion, 215; reorganization of, 70; shared processes of, 217; sites of, 114–15; space as site of, 72; "subjugated knowledges," 40. *See also* temporary autonomous zone of knowledge production (TAZKP)
knowledge(s), 211; circulation of, 46, 212, 220–21; community, 38, 80, 176; "disqualified" or "buried," 47; emancipation and, 21; exposure of, 134; insurgent (*see* insurgent knowledges); local, 219–20; oppositional, 67; sharing of, 132; situated, 137–38, 140–41; strategic, 3, 39–40; subjugated, 139, 225–26. *See also* knowledge production
Know Your Rights trainings, 38

Laboratorio de Investigación y Desarrollo en Comunicación Compleja (LabCOMplex), 220, 227
labor movement, 50
La Eskalera Karakola, 207
Lamm, Nomy, 169
Lara, Sarah, 123

Latina Feminist Group, 220, 227
Latin America, 2, 9, 20. *See also specific locations*
Latinx communities, 70, 182
"law and order," discourses of, 13
law-and-order policing, 84
Law Enforcement Assistance Administration (LEAA), 82
learning, 218; collective space of, 108; horizontal, 217; insurgent learning, 178, 201, 216–17; "learning to learn," 215; shared, 20, 215. *See also* insurgent learning
Lee, Barbara, 172
Lefiti, Oliver "Big O," 149
Leung, Eric, 145
liberal democracy, 215
liberalism, confrontation with, 62
life: celebration of, 208; devaluation of, 133, 136–37; spaces of, 90–93; value of, 163
life-saving techniques, 197
life without parole (LWOP) sentencing, 90
listening, 218; shared, 215, 219
"living hammock" support network, 44–48, 195
"living theory," 47, 112, 185–86, 216–17
Lodi Police Department, 179
London, England, 69
Long Beach, California, 50
longshoremen's union, ILWU Local 10, 63
"looters," 60, 61
Lopez, Andy, 58
Lopez, Anthony, 135
Lopez, Matt, 135
López, Silvia, 98, 207–8
Lopez Guzman, Antonio, 142
Lorey, Isabell, 34
Los Angeles, California, 16, 50; rebellions in, 61; trial of Mehserle moved to, 61
Los Angeles Police Department, 8–9; CRASH units, 11–12; Ramparts Division, 11–12
Los Angeles Rebellion, 15
loss, shared, 208

Lotta Femminista (Feminist Struggle), 22
Louima, Abner, 82
Louisville, Kentucky, 9, 135
Love Balm for My SpiritChild, 203–4, 210–11
Love Balm Institute, 204
Love Balm Project, 198, 202–4, 205, 212–13, 229n1
loved ones, loss of, 1–2 (*see also* children)
low-intensity war, 199–201, 213, 227, 266n5
Luera, Ana Maria, 1
Lugones, Maria, 40
lynching, 101

Madrid, Spain, 4, 34–35, 207, 226
Mahan, Alexander Fontau, 177
Manteca police department, 179
mapping, 84, 92
marches, 65, 123, 125, 135, 136, 179
Marcos, Subcomandante, 5–6, 84, 95
Márquez, John D., 69
Martin, Trayvon, 181
Marxism, 223, 224
Mason-Deese, Liz, 94
Masso, Miguel, 135
Mathias, Brian, 135
McCray, Tracy, 145, 162, 170
McKittrick, Katherine, 95, 207–8
Measure Y, 87–88
media, 39, 52, 56, 61, 89, 95, 167, 176, 192; alternative, 178; body camera footage and, 129; challenging, 160; corporate, 54; counter-narratives and, 176–77; criminalization and, 176; families and, 158; mainstream, 137, 178; minimization by, 41; police departments and, 56; rebellions and, 54–55; "second death" in, 145. *See also* social media
Meehan, Michael, 118
Mehserle, Johannes, 51, 52, 62, 135, 199; trial of, 55, 56, 61, 63
Melamed, Jodi, 114, 121
memorialization, living, 208
memory, 91; collective, 97, 198, 208, 219–20

mental crisis, 142; police responses to, 30–33
mental disabilities, police responses to, 33
mental illness, 103–4, 109–10. *See also* mental crisis
methodology, 4, 26, 215–28
Metreon Theater, 30, 31, 33
Mexicanos, 161
Mexico, 2, 4, 18–20, 63, 64, 69–70
Mexico Solidarity Network, 19
Mezzadra, Sandro, 14, 93, 137, 182, 183
Middle Passage, 17
Mies, Maria, 61
migrants, 111; migrant community, 70; at U.S.–Mexico border, 9. *See also* immigrants, undocumented
militancy, 73
militant research, 54–55, 72, 106, 116, 145, 162, 217
militarization, 17, 25, 107–8, 171, 201, 210–11; of care, 228; challenging, 198; militarized equipment and technology, 9–10; militarized policing, 9–10, 171; self-organization against, 168
Minneapolis, Minnesota, 9, 135
Mirzoeff, Nicholas, 95–96
misidentification, 78–80, 98, 105
misinformation, 12, 96, 136, 176, 266n5
misrecognition, violent effects of, 79–80
Mission District, 125, 153
Mitchell, Cynthia, 135, 145
Mitchell, David T., 114
Mitrione, Dan, 9
Mixon, Lovelle, 25, 55–56, 248n24; attempts to reclaim, 57–59; criminalization of, 56–57, 59; family of, 59; police shooting of, 55–57, 58–59; right to self-defense and, 59–60
Mobile Crisis Unit, 104
mobility: mobility rights, 92; state control of, 80–81
Modern Times Bookstore, 61
Mohandie, Kris, 165
Molina, Marta, 96

Monge-Irizarry, Mesha, 25, 29–31, 32, 35–36, 43, 46–47, 134, 140, 159, 160, 168–69
Moore, Kayla, 1, 25–26, 103–24, 177, 261n1, 261n3; anniversary of her death, 118; birthday party for, 103, 112–13, 115–17, 122; coroner's report, 103, 106, 112, 117; dispossession and, 122; family of, 123; justice for, 117, 122, 123–24; killing of, 103–6, 108–12, 115–20, 135; police reports, 116, 117; vigil for, 118; why she died, 121
Moore, Maria, 119, 123
Moore, Steve, 42–43
morality, 163
Morgado, Paulo, 145, 147
morgue photos, 178
morgues, 42
Moten, Fred, 23–24, 101, 223, 238n63
mothers, 4–5, 207. *See also* children; *specific mothers*
Mothers of the Plaza de Mayo, 113
Motta, Sara C., 40
mourning, 208, 209
Movement for Black Lives, 55
"movements of the squares," 215
Movimento di Lotta Femminile (Women's Struggle Movement), 22
MUNI officers, 200
MUNI shutdowns, 200
mutual aid, 18, 73
mutual aid agreements, 130–31

NAACP, 106
NAFTA, 20
Nagle, John A., 128
Nail, Thomas, 249n38
narrative, shared, 219
National Coalition for Mental Health Recovery (NCMHR), 265n44
negative resistance, 49
Negotiated Settlement Agreement, 53
Negri, Antonio, 49
neighborhood councils, 224
Neighborhood Watch programs, 12–13, 85, 148, 150
Neilson, Brett, 93, 137
Nelson, Jessica, 123

INDEX 301

Neocleous, Mark, 6, 95, 99–100
neoliberalism, 34, 94. See also neoliberal securitization
neoliberal securitization, 31–32, 82, 87, 107–8, 148, 221; community policing and, 91; discourses of, 216
Nesbitt, John, 135, 179
networks, 29–38, 46; creation of, 64; of families, 140, 159–60, 180; "living hammock" support network, 44–48, 195; networked community safety project, 220; of resistances, 35; visibilization of, 187–88
Nevin, Mike, 33
New Orleans, Louisiana, 61
"new social paradigm," 20–21
New York, New York, 150. See also Staten Island
New York City Police Department, 81, 82, 84
Nieto, Alex, 26, 125–42, 177, 268n23; family of, 139, 140, 141–42; killing of, 125, 129, 130, 132–33, 139–40
Nieto, Elvira, 126
Nieto, Refugio, 126
Nisenbaum, Ben, 164–65
Nixon, Richard, 82
non-being, zones of, 111
nonbinary identity, 5
nonprofit industrial complex (NPIC), 47, 52, 54
non-state actors, 11
Norteños gang, 153
Northern Ireland, 228

Oakdale Mob, 153
Oakland, California, 1, 25, 106, 123, 142, 181, 194, 248n24, 248n30; gang injunctions in, 60; Humanist Hall, 134–38; insurgencies in, 25, 200–201; "January rebellions" in, 52; Measure Y, 87–88; Occupy Oakland, 9; Oscar Grant rebellions in, 9; police violence in, 25, 49–73, 198–99, 203; protests in, 50, 60–61, 62–63 (see also specific events); Ronald V. Dellums Federal Building, 171–72. See also specific locations

Oakland docks, Israeli ZIM ship prevented from unloading at, 69
Oakland Fire Department (OFD), 199
Oakland General Assembly, 64
Oakland Police Department, 1, 12, 56, 132, 135; Occupy Oakland and, 66; "Tango Team," 66
Oakland Police Department (OPD), 87–88
Oakland Power Projects, 265n43
Oakland Riders scandal, 12, 53
Oakland Unified School District (OUSD) police, 135
Oakland Unified School District police, 1, 67
Oaxaca, Mexico, 20, 63, 69, 140; barricades of, 224
Oaxaca Commune, 214, 215
obfuscations, 148
"observables," 42
obstruction, 128–29, 132, 133, 139, 158, 161
occupation(s), 65, 108, 209–10; making visible through, 207–8; moving, 72; reclaiming of space and, 201, 206–10; resistant, 201; theorizing, 206–10. See also Occupy movement; specific occupations
Occupy 4 Prisoners, 64
Occupy movement, 71–72, 121–22, 163, 210, 215; assembly and, 64–65; emergence of, 63; encampments of, 64, 65, 73 (see also specific locations); "horizontalism" and, 65; in San Francisco, California, 64; in San José, California, 64; skill shares and, 73. See also Occupy Oakland
Occupy Oakland, 9, 25, 55, 61, 63–66, 70, 121–22, 194, 202; convivial tools produced by, 66; encampments of, 64, 65; Oakland Police Department and, 66; Oscar Grant Plaza and, 64; policing and, 66; repression and, 66; re-territorialization by, 67–68; at Snow Park, 64; at Veterans Camp, 64

Occupy the Justice Department, mock trial held by, 64
officer-involved shootings (OIS), 129–30, 158. *See also* police violence; *specific victims*
Oficina de Derechos Sociales (Center for Social Rights), Seville, Spain, 35
Oparah, Chinyere, 198
operaismo, 22, 23
Operation SafeHome IV, 151
operative maps, 93–97
oppositional knowledges, 67
oral history, 219–20, 227
order-based policing, 100
Orloff, Tom, 52
Oscar Grant Committee, 202
Oscar Grant Plaza, 64, 67, 205
Oscar Grant rebellions, 9, 55, 66, 67, 70, 72
Oshita, Yukio "Chris," 145, 147, 164
Our Hallowed Ground series, 1, 204, 205, 211
outrage, 73
"outsiders," 60

Pacifica, California, 142
Pacifica Police Department, 142
pacification efforts, 8, 17, 54–55, 80–84, 92, 120, 146, 148, 156–57, 168, 187, 211
Palestine, 50, 69–70, 141
pamphlets, 61, 67, 72
Paradiso, Aaron, 179, 194
paramilitarization, 8, 9–10, 82, 87
Parenti, Christian, 82
Paris, France, 69
Parker, Susan, 42–43
Parkmerced, California, 152–55, 167
participatory action research, 217
pathologization, 22, 100, 192, 221
patriarchy, 97–98
pedagogies, 242–43n19; of impunity, 24
Peltier, Leonard, 70
penal law, 59
People's Community Medics, 73, 197–98, 201–2, 209, 213

people's investigations, 37–39, 95, 105–7, 108, 110, 112–13, 115, 117–18, 120–21, 123–24, 168–69, 171
people with disabilities, 114, 149; violence targeting, 123–24
Perez-Angeles, Eriberto, 66
performances, 198, 202–4, 211–12, 227. *See also specific performances*
Philadelphia, 83
picateros, 215
Piper, Dolores, 78–79, 81, 88, 96, 97, 98, 99, 134
Pirone, Tony, 51
police: abolitionist movement against, 64; as "community caretakers," 164, 170; confrontations with, 183–86; demand for privacy and, 139; experts in defense of, 164–68; as first responders, 106; monitoring of, 116; paramilitarization of, 8, 9–10; police contact, 84; police engagement, 170; police intimidation, 36; police investigations, 193; protection of, 133; transparency requirements and, 127; transphobic, 110. *See also* police departments; police officers; police violence; policing
police actions, records of, 127
police departments, 9; coroners and, 41–43; press and, 56. *See also specific departments*
police narratives, 144, 145, 146, 148, 156–59, 160, 162–66, 168; inconsistencies in, 131–32
police officers, 9; identification of, 178; stalking by, 179; training of, 32, 33. *See also specific departments and officers*
Police Officers Association, 37, 127
police patrols, 85–86
police power, 6, 99–100, 127
police presence, 209; ever-increasing, 172; in public schools, 78–79
police reform, 120
police reports, 116, 117, 178, 187
Police Review Commission, 37, 117–19, 120

INDEX

police shootings. *See* police violence; *specific victims*
police stops, 85–86
police terror, acts of, 17
police training, 164
police union representatives, 37
police unions, 37, 127, 128
police violence, 1, 25–26, 55–57, 70, 77, 123, 149–51, 156, 175, 178–80, 210–11, 213, 227; Black Lives Matter movement and, 71; cases involving, 275–76n3; community response to, 67–68; counter-narratives of (*see* counter-narratives); documentation of, 25, 37, 38–39, 115, 116–17; "good" vs. "bad" victims of, 59; investigations of (*see* investigations; people's investigations); reclaiming space in wake of, 208; reconstruction of, 33; re-territorialization after, 72–73; youth of color and, 52. *See also specific victims*
policing, 193–94; Bratton-style policing, 81–82, 84, 86, 87, 91, 149, 150; as counterinsurgency warfare, 17; differential policing, 186; discretionary, 14; escalation of, 3; "evidence-based policing strategies," 172; excessive force and, 14; harassment policing, 2, 14, 82; militarized, 171; new intensity of, 16–17; Occupy Oakland and, 66; order-based policing, 100; as pacification and, 17; production and reproduction of, 85; racist, 53; "smart policing," 172; speak-outs against, 50; spectacular, 66, 184–86, 209; street-level, 15–16; war and, 6–8, 9–10. *See also* community policing
policing power, 3, 95
policing practices, deceptive, 148
policing timeline workshops, 227
political control, 17
politics: of care, 228; new way of doing, 71; "politics as war," 6; "politics in the feminine," 224; "politics of representation, recognition, and inclusion," 71; positive, prefigurative, 49; prefigurative, 51; reimagining, 219. *See also* biopolitical regimes
population management, punitive, 82
populations: management of, 8, 9, 10, 86, 95–96; mapping, 85; reorganization of, 154, 192; territory and, 90–93. *See also* communities
Port of Oakland, 50, 63, 200; shutdown of, 64, 65
postcards, 175–77
power, 68, 85; Foucault's analysis of, 6–7; grassroots, 215; power relations, 71, 207. *See also* biopower
Prakash, Madhu Suri, 264n39
praxis, 73
Precarias a la deriva, 4, 34–35, 110, 120, 223, 226, 228
precarious living, as collective research approach, 35
precariousness, 34–35
precaritization, 34, 94
precarity, 24; neoliberal, 107; state and, 34
predatory behavior, 38
predatory equity, 152
"predictive policing," 92
prefigurative elements, 70
prefigurative encampments, 65
prefigurative politics, 107, 228
prefigurative practice, 213, 215, 223
prefigurative space, 209–10, 217
premature death, 25
press. *See* media
press conferences, 180
Prevention and Public Safety Act (Measure Y), 90
Prichett, Andrea, 262n6
prisons, 2, 193–94; abolitionist movement against, 64, 70; in California, 193; prison hunger strikes, 70; prison industrial complex, 13; schools and, 79; speak-outs against, 50; violence in, 123. *See also* carceral regimes; incarceration

privacy: demand for, 127; expectation of, 171; right to, 190
"private security," 11
private sphere, 97–98, 100, 101–2, 223
privatization, 17, 91, 107–8, 213; professionalization and, 120; of social services, 107
projects, 210–11; autonomous, 198–99, 201. *See also specific projects*
Project South, 227
property, 148; confiscation of, 187–88, 191; property damage, 60–61; racial hierarchies and, 171. *See also* raids
"prose of counterinsurgency," 17, 79, 146, 152, 160–61
protesters, attempts to divide, 54
protests, 38–39, 52, 62–63, 65, 66, 200. *See also* direct action; *specific events*
psychological torture, 156
public meetings, 37
Public Records Act (PRA) requests, 106, 116
public safety, 83. *See also* community safety
public schools, police presence in, 78–79, 88
public space, 97–98, 224; reclaiming of, 72, 206–10; reorganization of, 206–10
public sphere, 97–98, 100, 223
Puerto Rican liberation, 70
Punjab, India, 41–42

Qilombo social center, 70
"*quadrillage* and *ratissage*," 91
"quality of life," 82, 87–88, 151
Quan, H.L.T., 110–11, 185–86
quarantine, 92, 154
queer collectives, 198
queer/crip activists, 114
queer liberation, 50
queerness, 122, 123
questionable entry practices, 151

race, 59; courts and, 163; enclosure and, 161; production of racial differences, 5; property and, 171; racial boundaries, 148; racial hierarchies, 59, 163, 171; reorganization of, 108
racial hierarchies, 59; courts and, 163; property and, 171
racialization, 87, 121, 137, 201, 207; criminal justice system and, 193–94; racialized geographies, 17, 137; racialized harassment, 101; racialized hierarchies, 13; racialized violence, 106–7; racialized wage hierarchies, 148
racial justice initiatives, 215
racial patriarchal capitalism, 5, 16–17, 91, 97, 107, 121; community safety as response to, 18–19; insurgency against, 69; resistance to, 216–17
racial patriarchal capitalist accumulation, 3
racial quarantine, 154
racial regimes, 25, 91, 101–2; apartheid, 23; biopolitical/necropolitical, 34; production of, 5, 61; racial hierarchies, 59, 163, 171. *See also* racial patriarchal capitalism
racism, 23, 193; structural, 60, 163, 193–94. *See also* racial regimes
radical democracy, 65
Radio Autonomía, 70, 106
rage, 31, 44, 52–56, 69, 73, 80, 93, 98, 106, 116, 119, 176, 181, 200, 213
Raheim Brown Free School and Library, 67
raids, 151, 187–88, 209; of home(s), 2, 16, 108, 131, 137, 148, 151, 170, 171, 179, 187–88; multi-agency, 151; "no-knock," 16, 151, 190
rallies, 38–39, 50, 64, 123, 125–26, 129–30, 133, 135, 136, 139–40, 200. *See also specific events*
Rana, Junaid, 69
RAND Corporation, 8, 177
Ratcliff, Mary, 30
Ratcliff, Willie, 30
Razzak, Arshad, 30, 134
rebellions, 50, 60–63, 69, 73; attempts to contain, 53–54; as collective

INDEX

laboratories, 68–69; media and, 54–55; space of, 50 (*see also* direct action)
reciprocity, 218
record-keeping, interference with, 132
Reddy, Chandan, 114, 121
redevelopment, 152–53
redistricting, 13
redlining, 13
Red Power Movement, 50
Redwood Summer, 50
reenactments, 33, 211
reflection, 217
"reflection and action," spaces of, 216
Refugio & Elvira Nieto v. City and County of San Francisco, 125
refusal(s), 39, 49, 50, 71, 91, 93–94, 115, 134, 160, 184, 194, 208, 216; of capitalism, 224; collective ethnography as refusal to represent, 221–25; collective refusal, 158; fierce care and, 201; refusing the state, 117–22
regeneration, sites of, 138
relationality, new forms of, 215
relations, disruption of, 85
relocations, 115
remapping: as convivial tool, 93–97; social factory and, 97–102
remembering: collective, 211–12, 219 (*see also* collective memory)
rents, 152, 153; rent control, 152, 154
representation: crisis of, 221–22; refusal of, 224; regimes of, 215
representative democracy, 64–65
repression, 60; justification of, 111; Occupy Oakland and, 66; strategies of, 34
reproductive justice issues, 212
research, 39, 143–44, 218; body as site of knowledge, 41–42; convivial tools as research strategy, 226–28; grassroots, 217; research methodologies, 41–42; shared, 215, 220; spaces of, 134. See also convivial research
research tools, 226–28. See also convivial tools
resilience, 134

resistances, 25, 47, 49–50, 71, 73, 133, 137, 181, 184–86, 211; to capital, 49; narrating, 17; negative resistance, 49; networks of, 35; theorizing, 224
re-subjectivation, 97
retelling, 2
re-territorialization, 65, 67–68, 72, 97, 99
revolutionary politics, "masculine-dominant," 224
revolutionary subjects, 223
Rice, Tamir, 58
"ride alongs," 89
Rio de Janeiro, Brazil, 69
Rivera, James Jr., 1, 43, 135, 177, 199; killing of, 179–80; police killing of, 205
Rivera Lopez, Oscar, 70
Robinson, Cedric, 5
Rocha, Erika, 123
Rojas, Stacey, 123
Rojava Revolution, 215
Romero, Mario, 1, 135, 137, 145, 177
Ronald V. Dellums Federal Building, 171–72
Ruff, Marlon, 149
Russell, George, 275n2
Rwanda, women's collective in, 212–13
Rwandan genocide, 212–13

"safe house" models, 117, 228, 243–44n31
"safe streets," 87
safety, 107. See also community safety
Safety Awareness for Everyone (SAFE), 150
San Bernardino County Sheriff's Employees' Benefit Association, 127
San Diego, California, 50
San Francisco, California, 1, 25–26, 61, 69, 72, 123, 138, 143–72, 194, 198–200, 252–53n1; City Attorney's Office, 164; Civic Center, 126; community policing in, 148–52; District Attorney's Office, 159; Forensic Pathology Department, 131–32; gay and

San Francisco, California (*continued*)
lesbian population in, 13;
Hunters Point neighborhood, 14;
insurgencies in, 200–201; Mayor's
Office, 150; Mission District,
125, 141, 142, 153, 204; Occupy
movement in, 64; Office of Citizen
Complaints (OCC), 161; protests
in, 31
San Francisco Bay Area, 1, 2–3, 19,
20, 42–43, 229n2; community
safety and, 18; geography of,
51; struggle of working-class
communities in, 181–83. *See also
specific locations*
San Francisco Bay View newspaper, 30,
143, 169
San Francisco County, 42
San Francisco Federal Building, 125,
129, 137–38, 139–40, 141
San Francisco Police Department
(SFPD), 29–48, 125–42, 143–72,
199–200, 205, 269n4; Community
Policing assessment, 150; General
Orders, 129–30; internal affairs
investigations, 130; investigation
of, 30–31, 34–40; Management
Control Division (MCD), 162;
police killings in, 149; Police
Officer Standards and Training
manual, 159; police shootings by,
56–57; Risk Management, 162;
training and, 32, 33
San Francisco State University, 152
San Joaquin County, California, 1, 42–
43, 180, 181–83; district attorney,
179; Sheriff's Departments, 135
San Joaquin County Probation
Department, 179
San Joaquin County Sheriff's
Department, 1, 179
San José, California, 1, 72, 106, 123,
142, 181, 185, 194, 195, 210;
Occupy movement in, 64; police
shootings in, 198; police violence
in, 203
San José Peace and Justice Center, 2
San José State University police
officers, 142, 194

San Mateo County, 80; Sheriff's
Department, 139–40
San Quentin Prison, rally and speak-
out in front of, 64
Santa Rosa, California, 58
Santos, Boaventura de Sousa, 198–99
Santos, Mike, 142
Sassen, Saskia, 182
"savage developmentalism," 110–11
Sawyer, Georgia, 30, 134
schizophrenia. *See* mental illness
schools: prisons and, 79; punitive
school policies, 2
Schrader, Stuart, 8
searches, 131, 187–88. *See also* raids
search warrants, 187
Seattle, Washington, WTO protests
in, 9
"second death," 145
secrecy, 127–29, 139
Section 8 housing, 109, 110–11,
152–53
securitization, 4, 95–96, 100, 107–8;
modes of, 21; neoliberal, 31–32,
148; securitized abandonment,
200–201
security, 3–5, 15, 29–48, 59, 80, 81,
85, 146, 160; colonialism and,
8; vs. community safety, 133–34;
destabilizing and deconstructing,
70; discourses of, 87;
epistemological framework of, 21,
79–80, 92; hegemonic discourses
of, 177; neoliberal emphasis on, 7
Segato, Rita Laura, 10, 24, 33, 34, 95,
97, 200–201, 242–43n19
self-defense, 107; community, 14, 51,
59–60, 63, 73, 138–39, 190–91,
213; right to, 59–60
self-determination, 46–47, 59–60
self-organization, 168, 218, 219
self-valorizations, 71, 134, 138,
267n13
sentencing laws, draconian, 188
Serrano, Maria, 98, 207–8
Serrano-Garcia, Yanira, 139–40, 142
settler colonialism, 6, 65, 83, 121, 222
Sguilia, Nicolás, 96
Sheriff's Departments, 41–43

INDEX 307

Sheriff's Work Alternative Program (SWAP), 166
shipbuilding industries, 153
"shoot to kill" policies, 83
shutdowns, 65
Sikhs, extrajudicial killings and enforced disappearances of, 41–42
silence, 127–29, 139, 143–44
Silicon Valley, 86, 90, 160, 236n2
situated knowledges, 137–38, 140–41
Situationists, 34
skill shares, 38, 73, 198, 213, 227
Smith, Brandon, 135
Smith, Jason E., 55
Smith-Downs, Carey, 179
Smith-Downs, Dionne, 43, 134, 135, 179–80, 185, 186, 194, 198, 205–6, 214
"snitch culture," 191
social antagonism, 161, 211, 224
social bonds: disruption and reconfiguration of, 13; reconstruction of, 2
social control, 13, 17, 163, 168
social death, 136–37, 143–72; collective refutation of, 176–77; imposition through judicial apparatus, 26; state-sanctioned, 13
"social defense process," 19
social emancipation, 81
social extraction, 182, 183
social factory, 22–25, 73, 223; attack on, 91; care work and, 65; counterinsurgency tactics and, 170–72; remapping of, 97–102; resources of, 169; support from, 168–69; war on, 81–89, 98
social justice, 52, 122
social media, 39
social movements, 224
social network analysis, 83–84
social organization, new forms of, 215
social relations, gendered, 40
social reproduction, 16, 24, 26, 32, 35, 65, 98, 100, 120, 219, 223–24, 226; analysis of, 23; crisis of, 22, 207; war against, 3, 198, 210, 212

social services, privatization of, 107
social theory, mainstream bourgeois, 111
social transformation, 215, 216, 217
social value, 163, 171
Sojoyner, Damien, 79
solidarities, 69–70
Sonoma County Sheriff's Department, 135
South Africa, 23, 50
South America, 64
South Central Los Angeles, 16
South San Francisco, 25–26, 252–53n1; district attorney, 93
South San Francisco Police Department (SSFPD), 77, 88, 134–35; Gang Intelligence Unit, 88–89; gang response strategy, 78–79; Neighborhood Response Team (NRT), 88–89, 96
space(s), 83, 94–95, 219–20; collective memory and, 208; community relations and, 208; control of, 9; of encounter, 4, 18, 26, 50–51, 62–63, 71, 80, 95, 102, 112, 115, 123, 178, 197–214, 220–21, 224–25; of life, 90–93; militarization of, 96; occupation of, 201, 206–10; people and, 83; public space, 97–98; reclaiming of, 112, 201, 206–10; as site of quarantine and restriction, 93; state control of, 80–81
Spain, 34–35, 63, 64, 215, 223
"spatial entitlement," 208
speak-outs, 50, 64, 117, 125, 183, 198, 213
spectacular policing, 66, 184–86, 209
Spector, Carlos, 235n39
speculation, 152, 154
stability, instability and, 22
stalking, 38, 179
Standing Rock, 9
state, the, 69; capital and, 133; contestation of, 138; delegitimizing, 121; precarity and, 34; refusal of, 160; refusing, 117–22; rupture with, 215–16
state documentation, 178
state functioning, obstruction of, 72

state-manufactured violence, 1, 10–16, 25, 59, 175, 202–4, 210–13; counter-narratives of, 35; responses on the Left, 180; state-manufactured, 10–16; taxonomy of, 11; three categories of, 11–13
state narratives, 176, 191–92, 212
Staten Island, 69, 134, 135
state violence, 1, 25, 34, 59, 115, 138–39, 202–4, 210–11; confrontations with, 198–99; documentation of, 73, 115, 116–17; justification of, 168; making visible, 71; monitoring of, 73; sanctioning of, 156–59, 171. *See also* police violence; state-manufactured violence
Station 40, 125, 126
statistical analysis, 84
Stelley, Idriss, 1, 25, 29, 32–33, 41, 134
Stephens, Boyd, 132
stewardship, 218
Stewart, Peter, 268n23
Stockton, California, 1, 3, 42–43, 50, 72, 135, 194–95, 198, 214; bankruptcy of, 183; confrontations with police in, 183–86; insurgencies in, 200–201; Mobile Response Team, 198, 205–6, 213; as periphery zone, 181–83; police shootings in, 200; police violence in, 205
Stockton Mobile Response Team, 198, 205–6, 213
Stockton picnic, 175–81; attacked by police, 184–86; march planned for, 184
Stockton Police Department, 179, 198, 200
Stoker, Sam, 58
Stonewall Rebellion, 207
"stop and frisk," 96
Stop the Injunctions Coalition, 60
storytelling, 219, 226–27. *See also* counter-narratives; narrative; *testimonios*
strategic knowledges, 3, 39–40
street, the, 224
street-level policing, 15–16

street suppression, intelligence-gathering and, 82
Street Terrorism Enforcement and Prevention Act (STEP Act) of 1988, 90
street theater, 227
strikes, 50, 64, 65; as action-process, 94; feminist strike, 94; International Women's Strike, 98
structural racism, 60, 163, 193–94
struggles, 49–50, 68–72; connecting, 123–24; for justice, 25–26, 44–46, 120–21, 136, 139, 140–41, 145–46, 168, 193–94; privatization of, 54; sites of struggle, 3
student movements, 50
"subaltern violence," 211
subjectivization, 3, 21, 33, 92, 176–77, 216
subjects. *See* emergent collective subject
subpoenas, 187, 191
subprime lending crisis, 121–22, 182–83
subsistence, war against, 3
subversive knowledges, 221
"sudden in-custody death syndrome," 132
Suhr, Greg, 126, 130
"suicide by cop," 146, 148, 149, 156–59, 165, 171
Sullivan, Asa, 1, 56–57, 135, 143–72, 268n23, 269n4; aftermath of his killing, 155–61; criminalization of, 157–58, 160, 161, 166–67; family of, 143–46, 154–60, 166–69, 171; justice for, 145–46; killing of, 143–48; trial and, 148, 156–58, 161–69; vigil for, 159
Sullivan, Kahlil, 143–45, 155, 156, 158, 161
Sullivan, Sangh, 154, 156, 157, 158, 162, 166
"superpredators," 90–91
supervision, 79
support networks, 46
surveillance, 2, 9, 14, 79, 86, 100, 188
survival, fight for, 4
sustainability, 32, 65

SWAT teams, 16, 32, 56, 77, 82, 88, 91, 95, 97, 99, 142, 151, 209

Taraval Station, 150
taxonomy of officer involvement, 106
Taylor, Breonna, 9, 135
teach-ins, 65
technologies: for control and management of populations, 86; police use of, 172
technologies of, of criminalization, 176
temporary autonomous zone of knowledge production (TAZKP), 3, 18, 51, 112, 114, 168, 178, 223, 225–26
1033 Program, 10
territory, 65; populations and, 90–93; "territory as an analytic," 122. *See also* space(s)
terrorist suspects, 160
testimonios, 1–2, 136–38, 140, 180, 198, 202–6, 213, 219–21, 226–27; "relational *testimonio*," 37–38
"thinking across the Bay," 70–71
Third World Resistance, 50
Thompson, Pamela, 16
"threat perception failure," 79–80
threats, 38
Till, Emmett, 43
Toret, Javier, 96
torture, 9
total war, 102
"tours," 65
town halls, 36
toxicology reports, 41
traffic, blocking, 69, 179, 200
transgender people, 103–4, 105, 109–10, 115, 123, 198
transparency, 129, 133; obstacles to, 127–28, 132, 133, 139; transparency requirements, 127
transphobia, 110
trials, 191–92
Trieu, Mehn, 139–40
Tronti, Mario, 22
truth, 124; state imposition of, 39; struggle for, 141, 145–46
Tsega Center, 106
Tu, Kenneth, 135

24th Street Mission (BART) Station, 126, 142
2 Garces, 146–48, 156–57, 162, 164, 167

"ultra-leftists," 54
undocumented immigrants, 140, 160
ungovernability, 111, 115, 120–21
union movement, 50
Unist'ot'en, 69
unity, 208
Universidad de la Tierra Califas (or UniTierra Califas), 1, 19, 20, 21, 24, 47, 70, 73, 113, 220, 221, 227, 229n3; *ateneo* spaces, 169, 185, 186, 226–28, 249n38, 262n11, 274n91, 275n94, 277n24; Democracy *ateneo*, 185, 186, 249n38; Social Factory Ateneo, 169, 226–28, 274n91, 277n24
University of California, Berkeley, 61, 63, 108–9
University of California, Santa Cruz, 63
"uplift," 23–24
"urban marginal," 111, 263–64n25
urban space, 207, 208; analysis of, 92–93; production of, 93
urban Zapatismo, 2
U.S. Army, 83–84; *Counterinsurgency Field Manual*, 165
U.S. Department of Homeland Security, 125; Office for State and Local Law Enforcement, 130–31
U.S. Department of Justice, 10, 131, 178; Violence Reduction Network, 171–72
U.S. District Court for the Northern District, 123
U.S. government: Office of Public Safety, 9; War on Drugs and, 14–15. *See also specific departments and agencies*
U.S.–Mexico border, 9, 15, 161, 193

Valdez, Laurie, 142, 194–95
Vallejo, California, 1, 183
Vallejo Police Department, 1, 135, 137, 145, 194

Valrey, J. R., 248n24
value production, body as site of, 40–44
Van der Hoek, Frits, 142
Vargas, João H., 220
Veracini, Lorenzo, 121
vernacular life-worlds, 26
verticality, 215
victims, claiming all, 176–77
Vietnam War, 8–9
Viewpoint Magazine, 181–82
vigils, 36–39, 77, 80–81, 93–95, 98–99, 125, 135–36, 159, 172, 200; as action-process, 97; as convivial tool, 94; as fierce care, 94; for Kayla Moore, 118; as a response to rage and grief, 93–94; space of, 36; for Sullivan, Asa, 159
Vignati, Colleen, 150
violence, 1, 2, 3, 5, 10, 61, 94, 146, 216; documentation of, 3; epistemic, 66; escalation and, 30–31; indifference to, 33; invisibilization of, 198; justification of, 111, 132; narratives of, 197; normalization of, 33; state-sanctioned, 25; structural, 66; struggles against, 221; visibilization of, 137; Zapatista analysis of, 5–10. *See also* police violence; state-manufactured violence; state violence
Violence Prevention and Public Safety Act, 87–88
Violent Crime Control and Law Enforcement Act in 1994, 87, 90
visibility, 112, 123–24, 137, 178, 187, 207
Visitacion Valley, 153
visuality, 95
Vitale, Alex, 81–82, 87
vulnerability, 34, 35, 94, 107, 110

waged labor, 148
"wages of whiteness," 23
Wagstaff, Steve, 80
Walsh, Thomas, 30, 134
war, 5; as basis of all relations and institutions of power, 46–47; as class antagonism, 6–7; confronting, 3; domestication of, 125–42; informalization of, 10, 11; new era of warfare, 81–82; policing and, 6–8, 9–10; war power, 6
"war from above," 6, 91–92, 95–96
war of oblivion, 3
"war on crime" program, 82
"war on drugs," 82, 151; U.S. government and, 14–15
"war on gangs," 151
war: police assemblages, 5–10, 17, 50, 81–89
warrants, 16; "no-knock," 190; old, 187; outstanding, 2, 166; search, 2, 16
ways of being, new, 215, 228
ways of seeing, 226. *See also* visuality
weapons, attribution of, 188–89
weight, 110
welfare programs, 183
welfare state, 32; dismantling of, 107
"well-being" checks, 138, 146–48, 170, 171
Wells, David, 3, 200
Wendell Plaza, 205
Western Addition apartment complex, 151, 153
Western episteme: ruptures in, 40; violences of, 215, 222–23
white communities, 100
"white injury," 60
"white man's bargain," 59
whiteness, 23, 148; reproduction of, 59
white supremacism, 23–24, 107
Williams, Aaron, killing of, 132
Williams, Cadine, 134, 141
Willis, Anita, 12, 134, 135, 203
Winston, Ali, 66
wisdoms, 192
witnesses, 36, 51–52, 158–59, 209, 219–20; expert witnesses for the police, 164–68; interview of, 187; isolation of, 187; statements of, 80 (*see also testimonios*)
woman/women, 2, 226; as socially produced category, 5; war against, 3, 4
women of color, 2; women of color collectives, 198
women's movement, 50
women's prisons, 123
Woods, Clyde, 95

workers' struggles, 223
working class, 49
workshops, 38
WTO protests, in Seattle, 9
Wynter, Sylvia, 54

Yellow Power Movement, 50
youth: targeting of, 84; war on, 81–89
youth of color, police violence and, 52

Zapatismo, 2, 20, 48, 229n3
Zapatista Escuelita ("Little School"), 70
Zapatistas, 3, 4, 5–10, 18–20, 70, 71, 93, 215, 249n38, 259n68
Zapatista Women's Encuentro, 20
"zero tolerance," 82, 88, 96, 149
Zibechi, Raúl, 111, 224
Zim ship blockade, 69